HARMONY NOTES

HARMONY NOTES

BOOK 1

JEAN ARCHIBALD and MARIE MORAN

PETER LANG
Oxford • Bern • Berlin • Bruxelles • New York • Wien

Bibliographic information published by Die Deutsche Nationalbibliothek.
Die Deutsche Nationalbibliothek lists this publication in the Deutsche National-bibliografie; detailed bibliographic data is available on the Internet at http://dnb.d-nb.de.

A catalogue record for this book is available from the British Library.

Library of Congress Cataloging-in-Publication Data

Names: Archibald, Jean, 1950- author. | Moran, Marie, 1965- author.
Title: Harmony notes. book 1 / Jean Archibald, Marie Moran.
Description: [1.] | Oxford ; New York : Peter Lang, 2023.
Identifiers: LCCN 2021025136 (print) | LCCN 2021025137 (ebook) | ISBN 9781800795563 (paperback) | ISBN 9781800795570 (ebook) | ISBN 9781800795587 (epub) | ISBN 9781800795594 (mobi)
Subjects: LCSH: Harmony. | Composition (Music)
Classification: LCC MT50 .A707 2023 (print) | LCC MT50 (ebook) | DDC 781.2/4--dc23
LC record available at https://lccn.loc.gov/2021025136
LC ebook record available at https://lccn.loc.gov/2021025137

The ePub and ePDF for this book can be accessed from the Peter Lang website <https://doi.org/10.3726/b18563>; in order to listen to the audio available in the book, please click on the audio icon from the respective files from the website.

Alternate method: You can also download the eDPF from the website, open it in Adobe Reader and listen to the audio by clicking on the icon.

Cover design by Brian Melville for Peter Lang Ltd.

ISBN 978-1-80079-556-3 (print)
ISBN 978-1-80079-557-0 (ePDF)
ISBN 978-1-80079-558-7 (ePub)

Published by Peter Lang Ltd, International Academic Publishers,
Oxford, United Kingdom
oxford@peterlang.com, www.peterlang.com

This publication has been peer reviewed.

TABLE OF CONTENTS

Preface

As a result of numerous requests from music colleagues and friends for a book that would take the mystery and hardship out of learning harmony, we finally succumbed and endeavoured to fill the brief by writing 'Harmony Notes'.

Our first priority was to make it easily understood using uncomplicated language; aiming to fill it with accessible and numerous music examples, encouraging an imaginative and always creative approach within the bounds of common practice vocal harmony. Drawing on the experience of our many years of teaching we saw the need to have the information carefully and incrementally graded, bolstered by numerous exercises to ensure a deep understanding and application of the points under discussion.

We have used tonic solfa as an essential tool encouraging a musical approach and providing a viable means of attaching the sound to the symbol. All the examples are recorded to enable the student to track the sound in parallel with the written score.

Once we progress beyond the initial chapters, we adopt a learning sequence which provides a consistent approach, offering a working method which secures the learning.

1. Where a bass line of progressions is given, the emphasis is placed on crafting a shapely soprano melody with real musical content.
2. Where a soprano line is given, suitable progressions are selected to harmonise the melody.
3. Where soprano and bass lines are given, parts for alto and tenor voices are added to create a full and complete four-part harmonisation.

As the chapters progress and the vocabulary becomes more extensive, demonstrations of musical solutions are offered with extensive explanation providing a working method. However, we have held back from a single prescriptive solution as there is never one definitive answer.

Significant grammatical nuggets are flagged by 'lightbulb' icons. Salient points are highlighted in 'checklist' boxes, while all audio examples are indicated by 'head phone' logos.

To broaden the scope a little beyond four-part vocal harmony we have introduced some short extracts for analysis from piano and string quartet literature. This enables the student to hear, recognise and appreciate learnt progressions in a new context. This occurs at three strategic points throughout the book.

The appendices offer an opportunity for further exercise material in an extended range of keys. By request, these are coupled with a single sample working. However, it must be emphasised that this provides only one of many possible solutions.

We hope that this book provides the student with a secure foundation and thorough understanding of four-part harmony, opening the door to explore the rich tapestry of harmonic language.

Both the audio recordings and audio analysis extracts can be accessed on the Web. Similarly, all exercises are available as downloads for ease of completion and correction.

Acknowledgements

We would like to thank many people and in particular Deborah Kelleher, Director of the Royal Irish Academy of Music whose fulsome support, encouragement and enthusiasm was unwavering throughout the entire life of this project.

Central to the ethos of the project and as a way of elucidating information, the principle of 'sound and symbol' was at the core. This became a reality thanks to the four RIAM undergraduate students; Sarah Keating (soprano), Katie Richardson McCrea (alto), Rory Lynch (tenor), and David Callaghan (bass), who prepared, rehearsed and sang all the vocal musical examples. Their generosity of time and good humour was greatly appreciated.

We are indebted to our loyal and supportive friends namely Bernadette Marmion, Annette Perry and Nuala Moran for their encouragement and numerous suggestions. Their meticulous care and attention to detail was invaluable.

We would like to extend a special thanks to Jonathan Nangle whose patience and expertise knows no limits! The recordings, subsequent edits and cover image would not have been possible without his valued contribution.

Special thanks are due to Réamonn Keary for readily agreeing to play and record some of the piano extracts included for analysis.

Philip Shields, librarian in the RIAM deserves a special mention for his guidance and direction at various stages of the project.

We thank Naxos for permission to use the recorded analysis extracts. A special thanks to Tadhg Kinsella for preparing these extracts for inclusion on the web.

Finally, we would like to thank Dr. Dan Farrelly of Carysfort Press, Dublin and Peter Lang Ltd. (International Academic Publishers), for undertaking this publication.

CHAPTER 1

PRIMARY TRIADS

Taking the notes of a major scale (***d r m f s l t d'***) and building a triad on each note produces the following variety of chords. Each chord consists of a root (highlighted), a 3rd and a 5th.

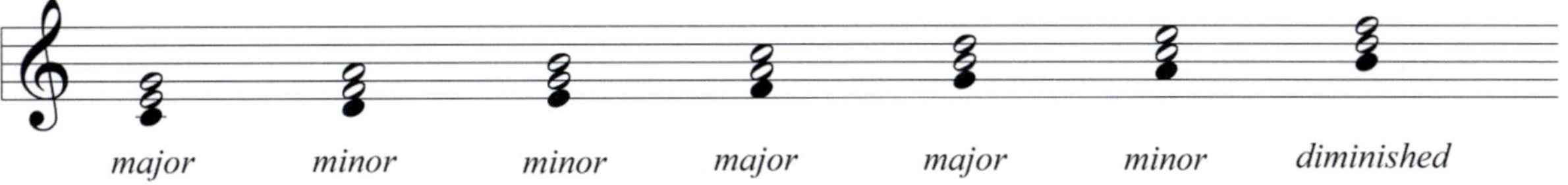

Roman numerals are generally used to label the chords.

Notice that major chords use upper case while minor chords use lower case and diminished chords use lower case and a small circle symbol.

The most important, useful and most commonly used of these triads are those built on the tonic, subdominant and dominant i.e. **I, IV, V.** These are known as the **primary triads**.

Exercise 1.1

Write the primary triads in each of the following major keys.

(a)

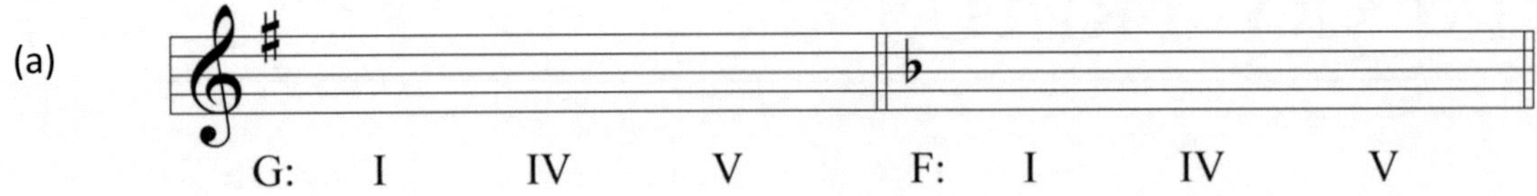

(b)

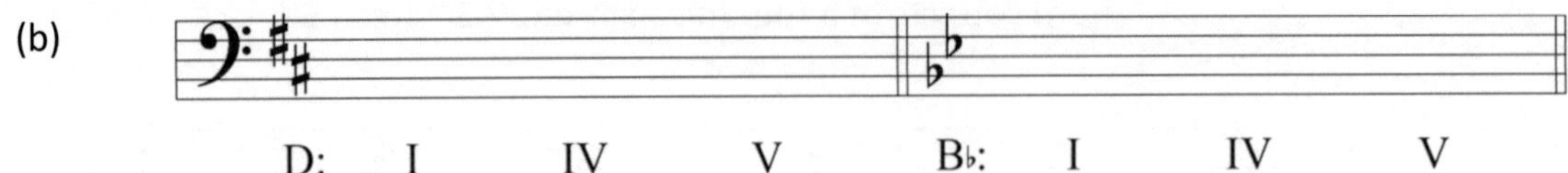

Building triads on the harmonic minor scale (***l t d r m f si l'***) produces a different variety of chords as follows:

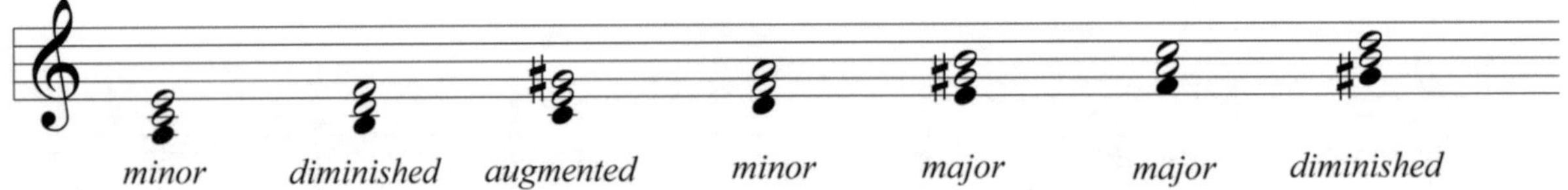

When using roman numerals notice that the augmented triad uses upper case with a small plus symbol attached.

Here are the primary triads in the minor key:

Exercise 1.2

Write the primary triads in each of the following minor keys.

(a)

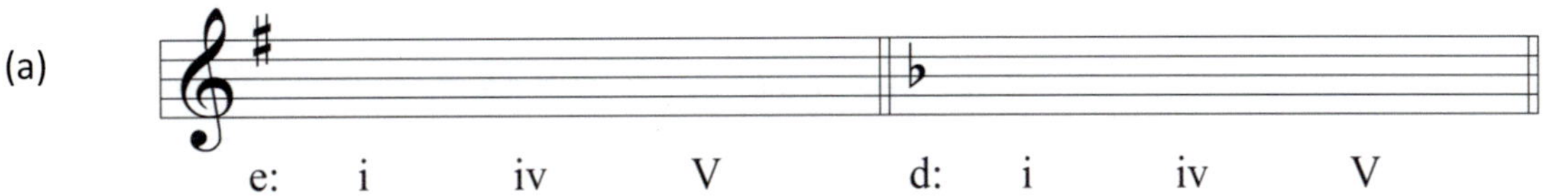

(b)

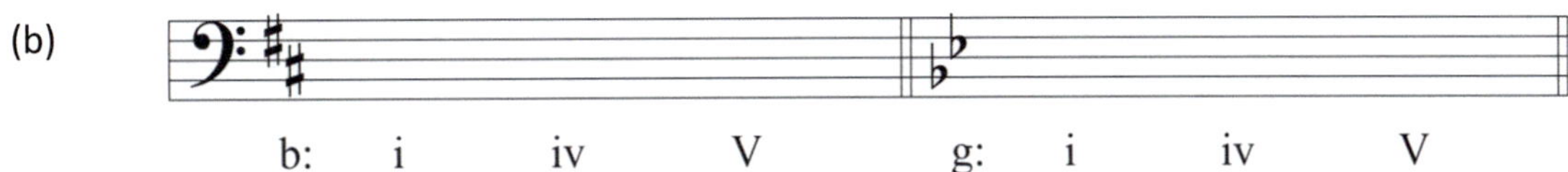

Harmony is found in most types of music that has more than a single melody line, e.g. piano music, orchestral music, guitar music and so on, but perhaps the medium most preferred for the early study of harmony is vocal/choral music. Historically, there is a vast amount of literature from which examples may be drawn and studied.

Audio 1.1

Listen to this well-known Christmas Hymn *'Adeste Fideles'*. It is written below in **short/close score** using two staves.

The four-part texture which you have just listened to consists of soprano, alto, tenor and bass voices (SATB for short). Notice that S and A use the treble stave while T and B use the bass stave.

Here is the first line of the same extract rewritten in **open score**. Notice that each voice has an individual stave, with the tenor using the treble clef and sounding an octave lower.

Range

The normal range of each voice must be considered as shown below.

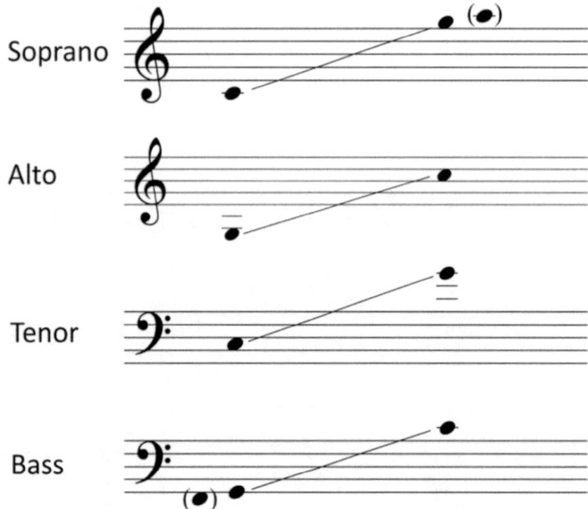

Stems

In general our harmony will be written in **close score**. Notice the direction of the stems; soprano and tenor go upwards, alto and bass go downwards.

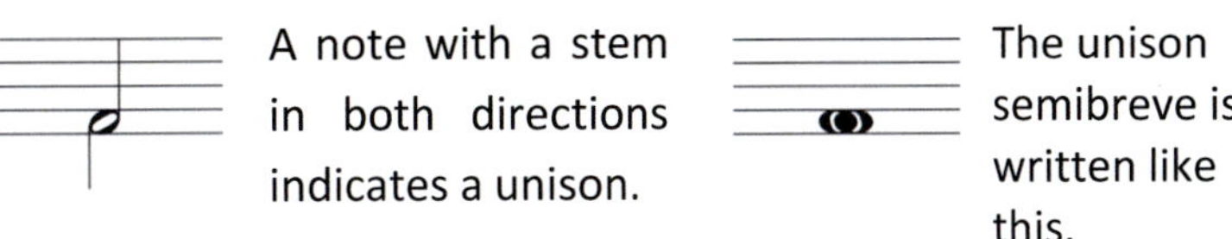

Root position

We will begin by writing chords in root position. This means that the root of the chord will be the lowest sound and therefore must be written in the bass part.

Doubling

To create a four-part chord, one note of the triad must be used twice, i.e. doubled. The best note to double is the root as it produces a well-balanced sound.

You will hear several different arrangements of a C major chord.
The first four examples double the root – sounding 'balanced'. This is recommended.
The next two double the 5th – sounding 'hollow'. This is possible but a weaker choice.
The last one doubles the 3rd – sounding 'thick'. This is normally to be avoided.

Aim for the best balance in sound – always double the root

Spacing

A well-balanced sound also depends on how the voices are vertically spaced. Normally, adjacent voices do not exceed an octave except between the tenor and bass parts, where the distance can be up to an octave and a 5th. It is not unusual for the tenor to use ledger lines.

Here are some possibilities:

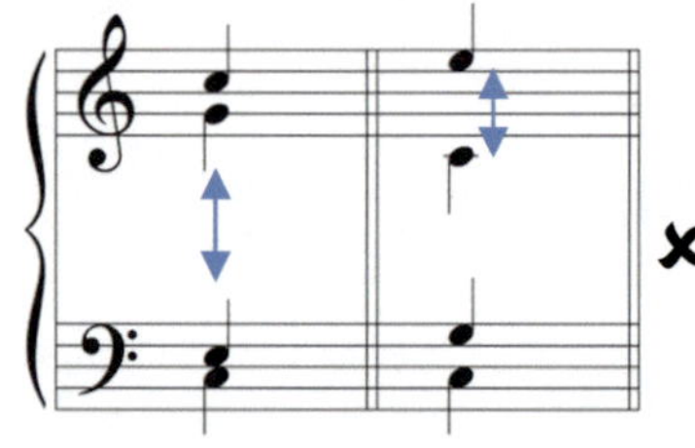

✗

In these examples the incorrect **wide spacing** is highlighted by the arrows.

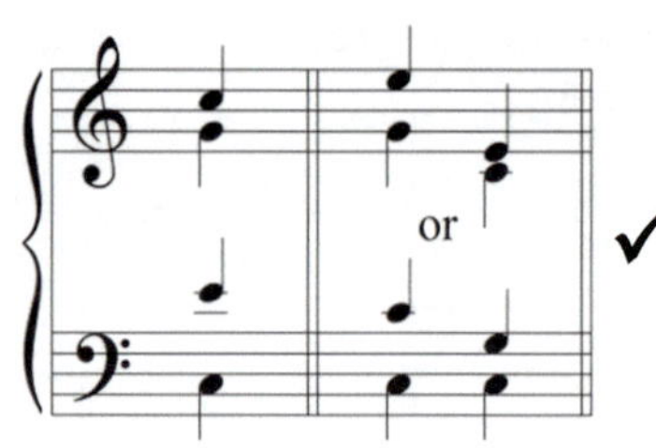

✓

To correct the problem of the **wide spacing** above in the first example, the tenor must be placed high in its range necessitating ledger lines.

In the second example there are two solutions. The alto and tenor must be placed higher **or** the soprano may be moved down an octave.

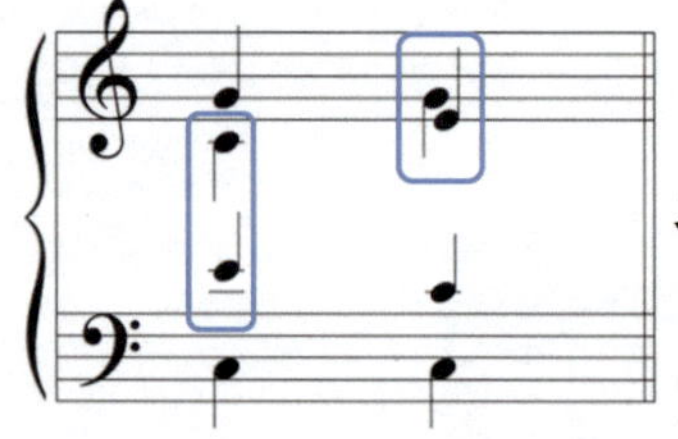

✗

Take care not to **overlap** the voices, as shown in the boxes:

Soprano – highest
Alto – lower
Tenor – lower again
Bass – lowest

Exercise 1.3

Complete each of the following chords for SATB by adding the alto and tenor parts. Take care with range, doubling and spacing.

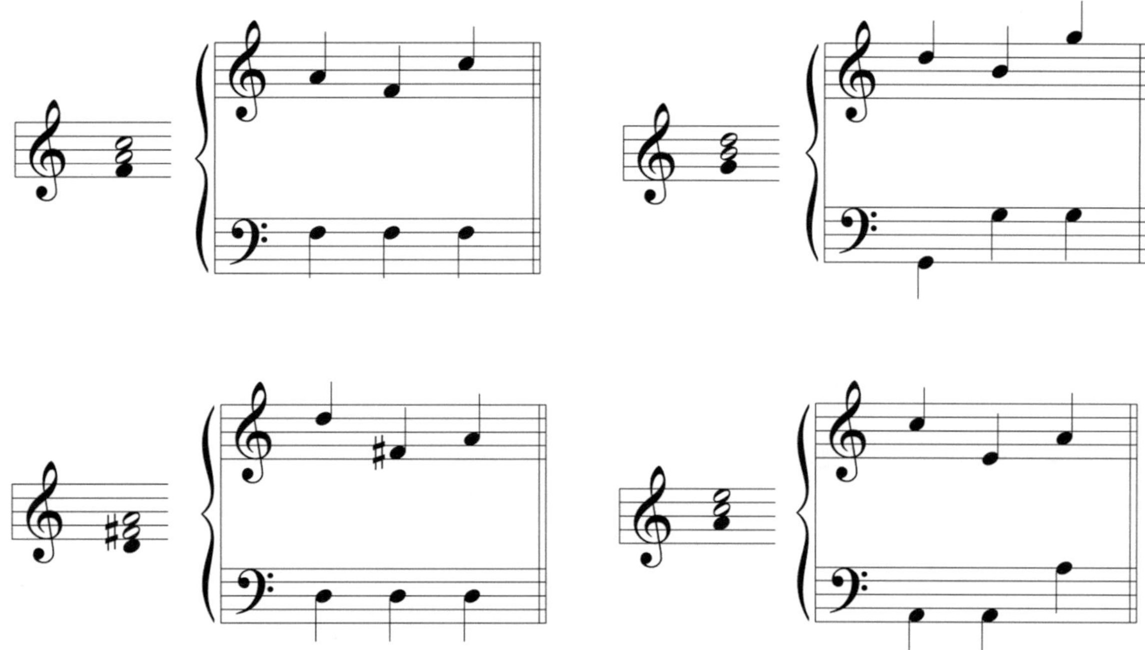

Exercise 1.4

Arrange each of the following triads for SATB by adding soprano, alto and tenor parts. Take care with range, doubling and spacing.

Using the Primary Triads in a Major Key

It is useful to make a 'chord plan', highlighting the root, showing roman numerals and solfa names for each of the triads.

Exercise 1.5

Complete each of the following for SATB by adding alto and tenor parts. The chord plan and roman numerals are included for you.

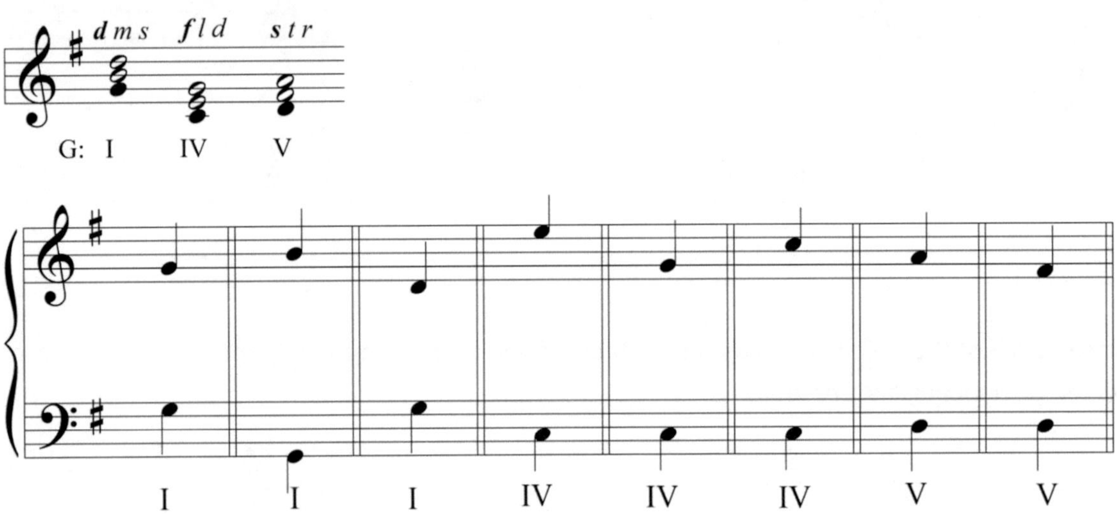

Exercise 1.6

Complete each chord plan. Add the roman numerals and write parts for alto and tenor.

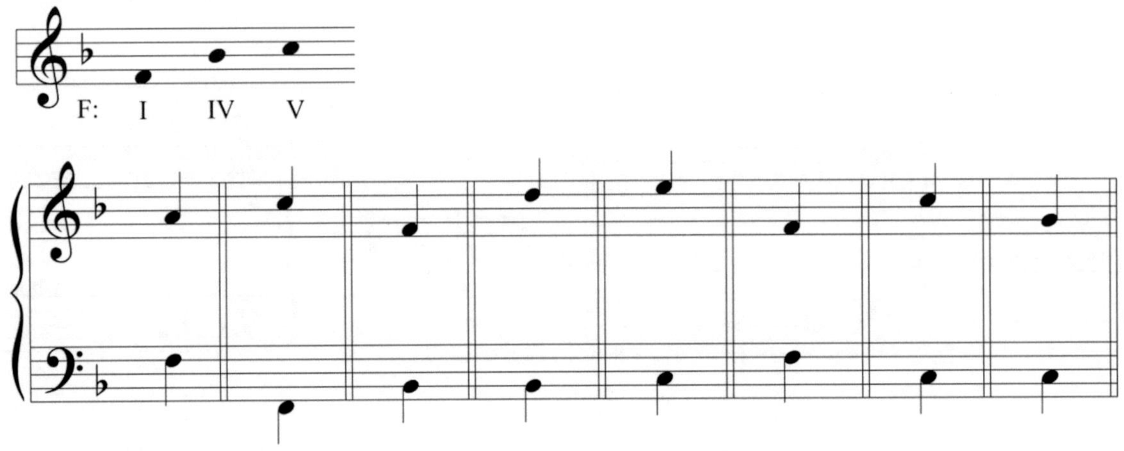

Checklist✓

- Write a chord plan including roman numerals and solfa names
- Highlight the root of each chord – remember this will always be the bass note
- Use the root twice, i.e. double it in another voice
- Space the voices with no more than an octave between each adjacent voice, except for the tenor and bass
- The tenor often has to use ledger lines, especially if the soprano is high
- The root will always be in the bass but remember the upper voices will vary

Exercise 1.7

Complete each chord plan. Add roman numerals below the bass notes. It is good practice to choose the soprano part before adding alto and tenor parts.

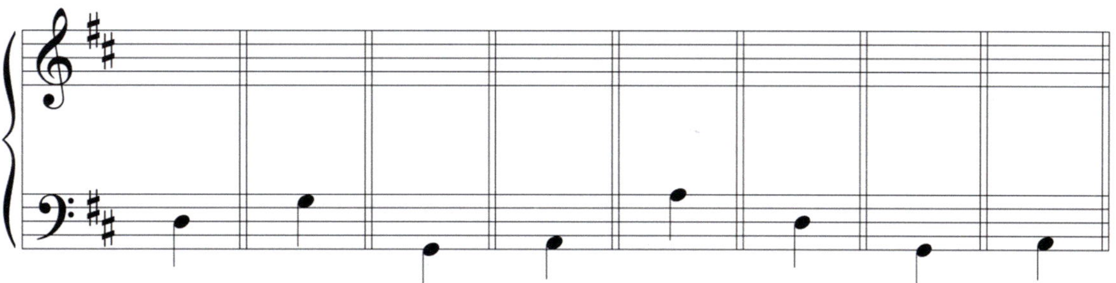

Exercise 1.8

Complete each chord plan, then arrange each of the following chords for SATB. Begin by writing the root of each chord in the bass, followed by the soprano, then alto and tenor.

(a)

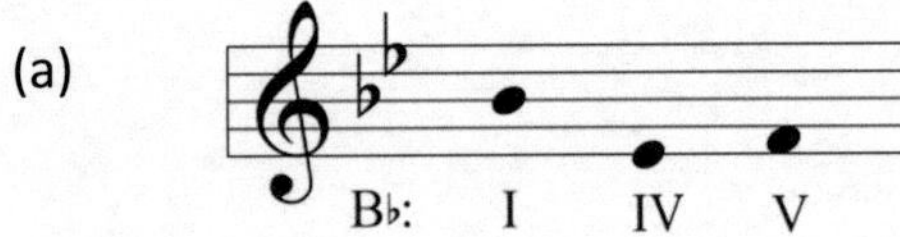

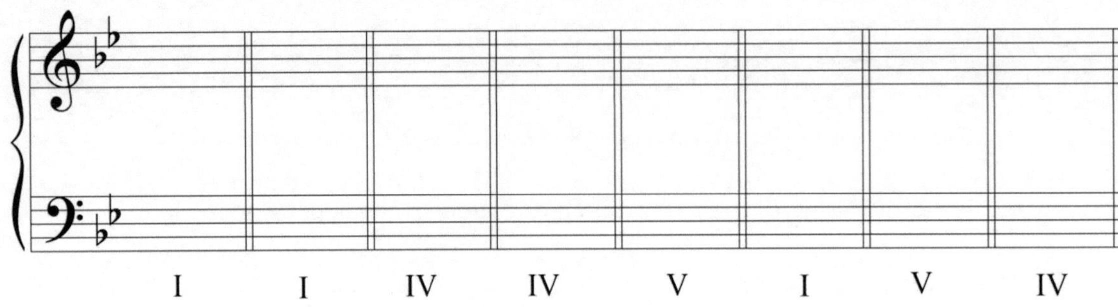

(b)

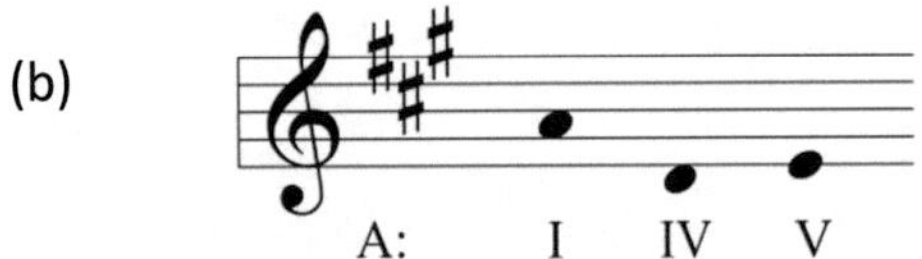

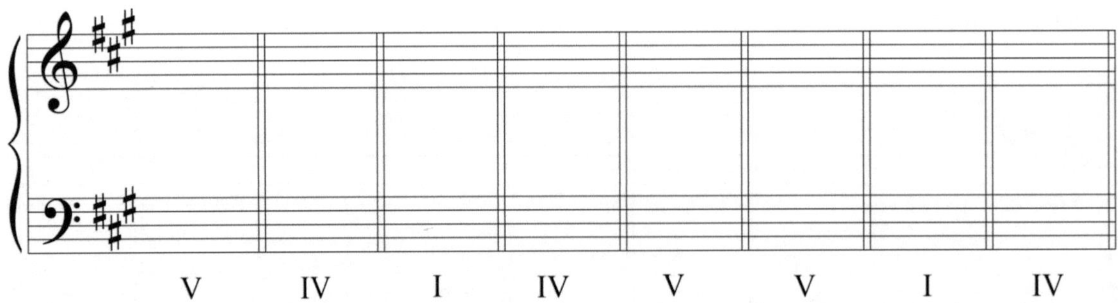

Primary Triads in a Minor Key

These are the primary triads in A minor together with the roman numerals and solfa.

- Notice the lower case roman numerals for the minor chords
- Remember to include the leading note accidental in chord **V** (major chord)

Exercise 1.9

Complete each of the following for SATB by adding alto and tenor parts. The chord plan, roman numerals and solfa are included for you.

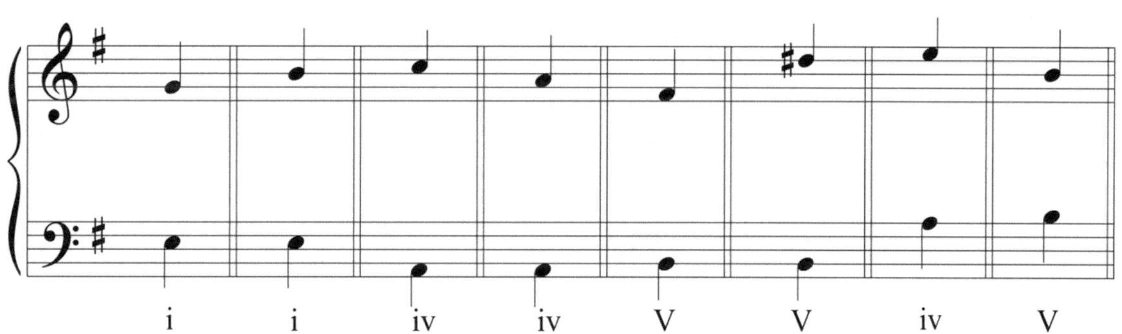

Exercise 1.10

Complete each chord plan, add the roman numerals below the bass and write parts for alto and tenor. Remember to include the accidental in chord **V**.

Exercise 1.11

Arrange each of the following chords for SATB. Begin by writing the root of each chord in the bass, followed by the soprano, then alto and tenor parts.

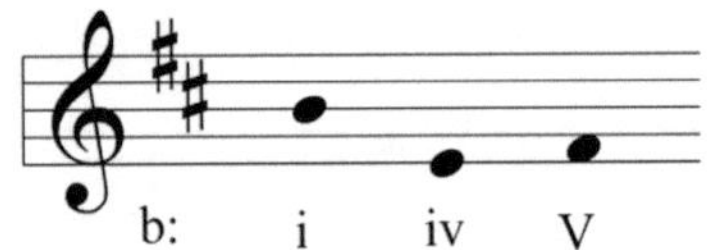

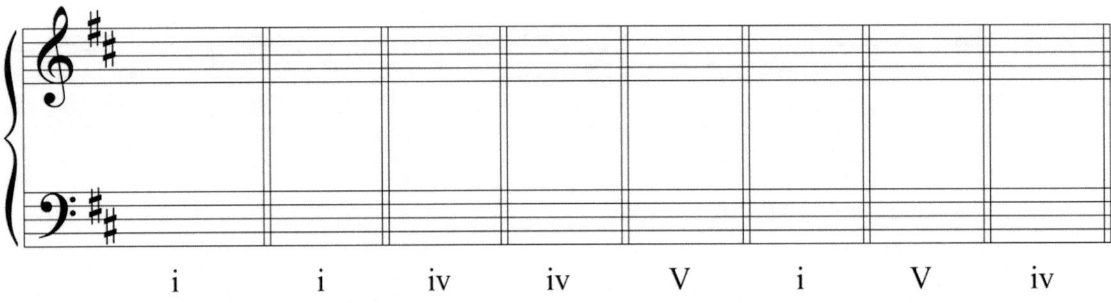

Choosing chords to suit a given soprano

We have emphasised how the root must appear in the bass voice. However, any note of the triad may appear in the soprano part. As a result, chord choices must be made because some notes occur in more than one chord. The easiest way to approach this is by using solfa.

Looking again at the primary chords in C major, we notice that *d* occurs in both chords **I** and **IV**, and *s* occurs in both chords **I** and **V.**

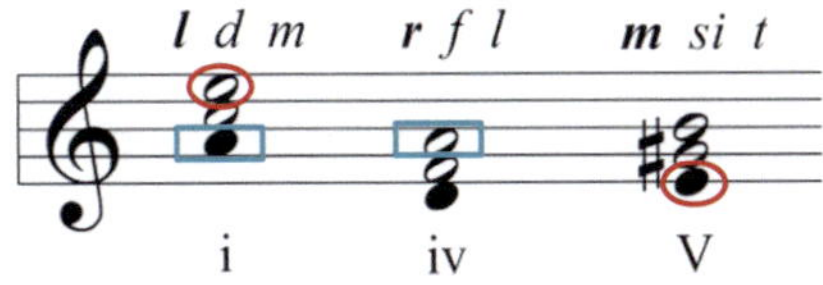

Similarily, in a minor key *l* occurs in both chords **i** and **iv** and *m* in both chords **i** and **V**.

Exercise 1.12

Complete the chord plan, then choose a chord for each of the given soprano notes. Write the root in the bass together with its roman numeral. Then add alto and tenor parts.

CHAPTER 2

CADENCES

Like language, music needs punctuation. As there are different types of punctuation in language so there are different types of cadences in music. Various combinations of chords give specific effects. A cadence of some type generally occurs at the end of every main phrase.

Perfect Cadence	**V – I**	Sounds final	Closed
Imperfect Cadence	**I – V**	Sounds incomplete	Open-ended
Plagal Cadence	**IV – I**	Sounds final	Gently closed

 Audio 2.1

Listen to the well-known melody *'O When the Saints'.* You hear the melody alone with chords included at the main phrase endings – the cadence points.

You will notice that the first phrase sounds incomplete (imperfect cadence **I – V**) while the second phrase sounds final, (perfect cadence **V – I**).

Listen to part of the well-known carol *'It came upon the midnight clear'*. You hear the melody with chords included at the cadence points.

You will notice that phrases 1 and 3 sound incomplete (imperfect cadence **I – V**), while phrase 2 sounds gently closed (plagal cadence **IV – I**) and the last phrase sounds final (perfect cadence **V – I**).

Exercise 2.1/ Audio 2.3

You will hear the melody *'Morning has Broken'* which is harmonised at the phrase endings. Judge each cadence effect as either open or closed – the first one is done for you. For each of the other cadences write either open or closed in the blank boxes.

The Perfect Cadence in a Major Key

When arranging a perfect cadence for SATB begin by completing a chord plan. Then write the roots in the bass part.

Now choose a soprano note for each chord, taking care to create a smooth line as one chord connects to the next. Here are three possibilities.

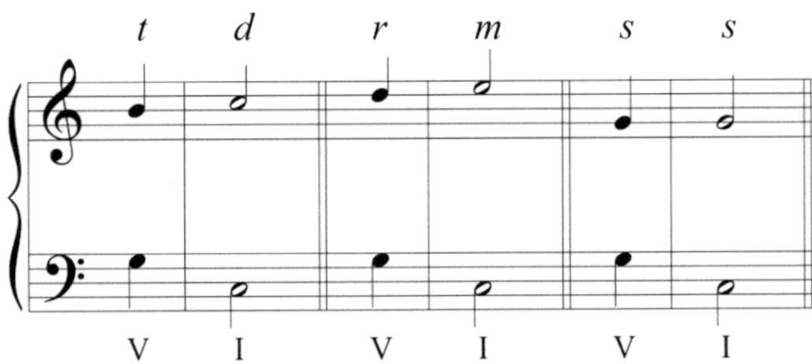

Finally, complete the alto and tenor parts, taking care to create smooth connecting lines.

The easiest way to complete a perfect cadence is to move the upper voices (SAT) as follows: ***t – d; r – m; s – s***. These lines may be swapped between the upper voices for different effects.

Notice there is a common note in both chords, ***s – s***; keep it in the same voice.

Audio 2.4

Listen to Audio 2.4 to hear each of the above. Pay careful attention to the solfa and you will be able to distinguish the individual voices.

In **V – I** the leading note always rises a step to the tonic: ***t - d***

V – I Summary

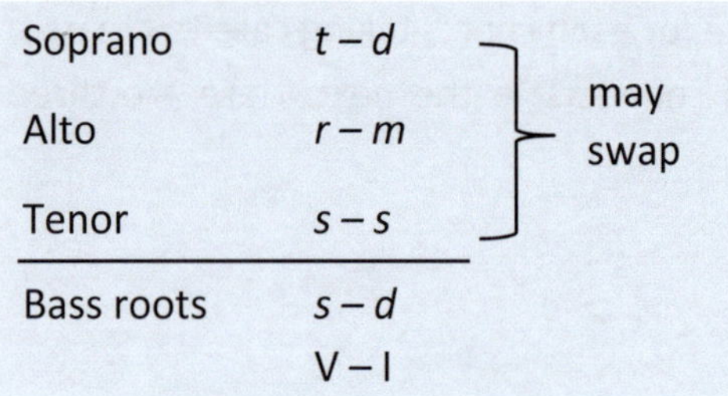

Soprano	*t – d*	may swap
Alto	*r – m*	
Tenor	*s – s*	
Bass roots	*s – d* V – I	

It is often the case that a perfect cadence occurs across a bar line, thus accenting the final chord of the cadence.

Exercise 2.2

Fill in the alto and tenor parts to complete each perfect cadence. Take care with spacing and doubling.

(a) 

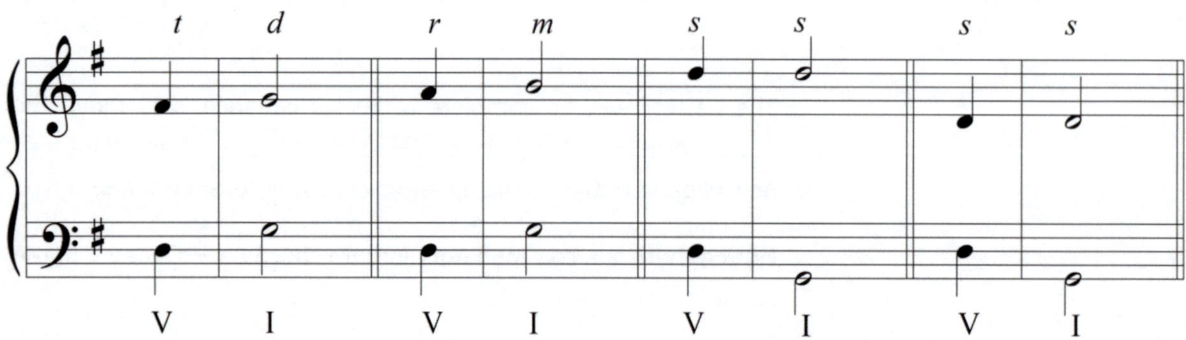

(b)

d m s
s t r
F: I
V

r m t d s s t d
V I V I V I V I

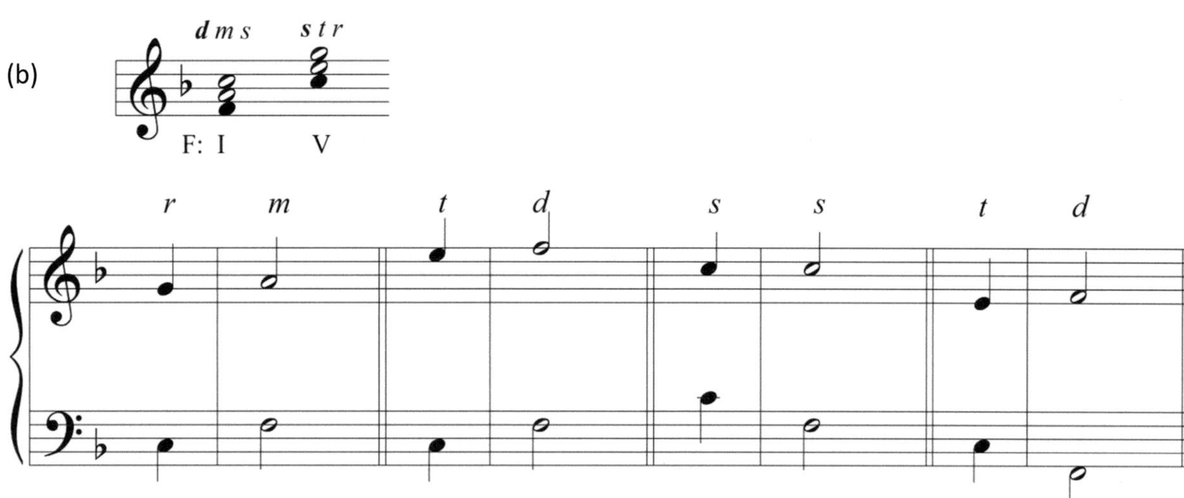

Exercise 2.3

Arrange parts for SAT to complete each perfect cadence. Write a chord plan. Choose the soprano line first. Take care with spacing and doubling when adding alto and tenor lines. Show a variety of arrangements.

(a)

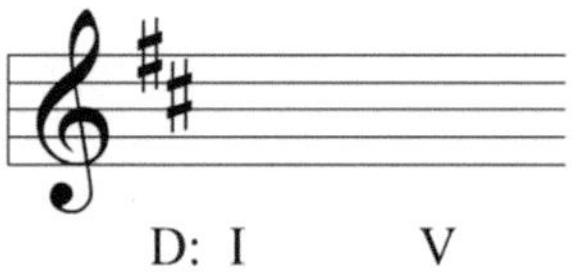

D: I
V

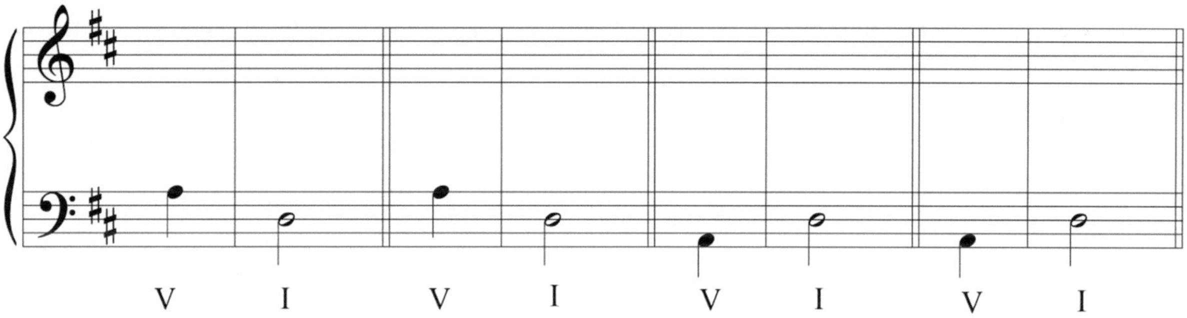

V I V I V I V I

(b)

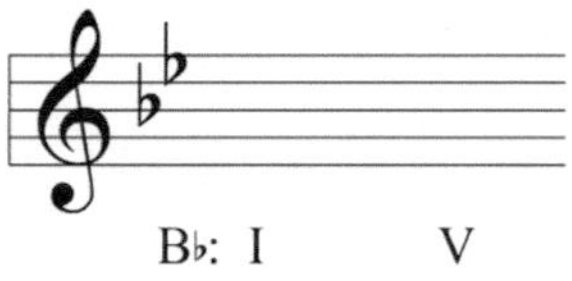

B♭: I
V

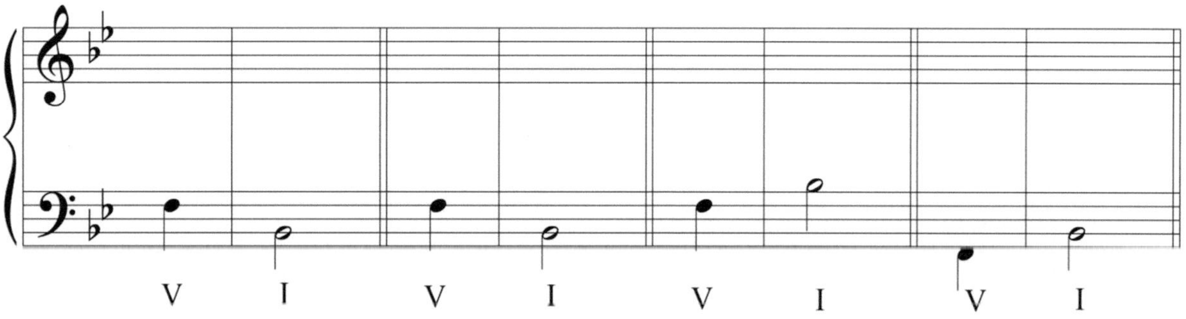

V I V I V I V I

Exercise 2.4

In this exercise the soprano line is given. Arrange parts for ATB to complete each perfect cadence. Begin by making a chord plan, then write the roots in the bass followed by alto and tenor parts.

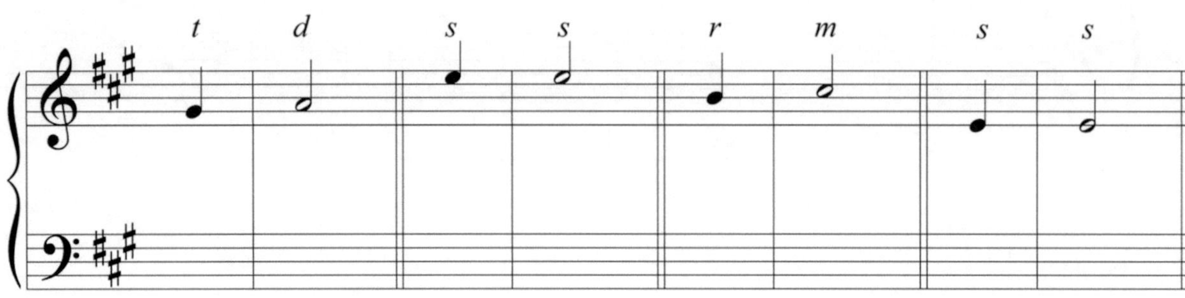

Exercise 2.5

Each of the following melodies ends with a perfect cadence in the boxed area. Make a chord plan, then complete the cadence by writing the roots in the bass, followed by the alto and tenor voices.

(a)

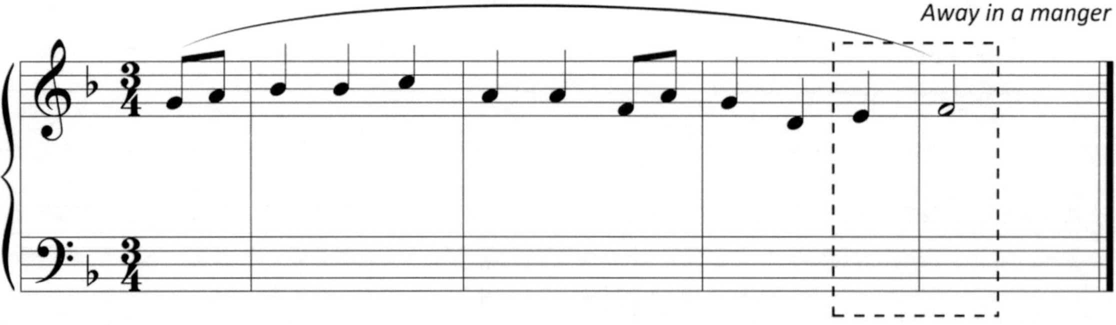

(b)

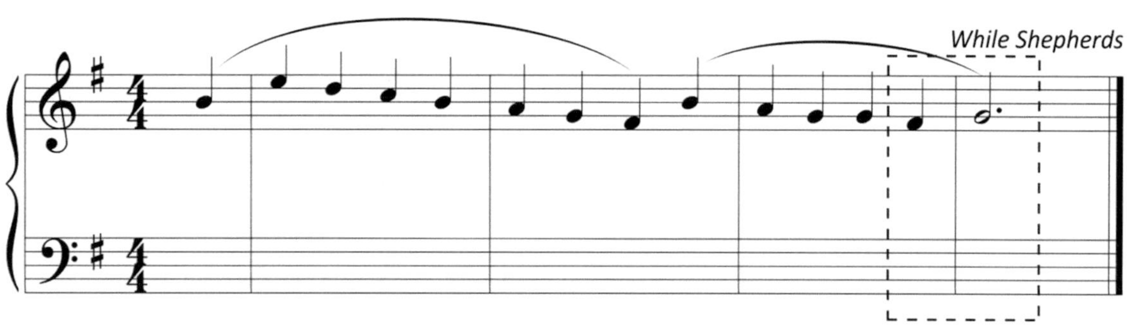

The Perfect Cadence in a Minor Key

The guidelines for writing a perfect cadence in a minor key are the same as those for a major key, but note the difference in solfa. When completing the chord plan always remember to include the leading note accidental in chord **V**. As before, begin by writing the roots in the bass.

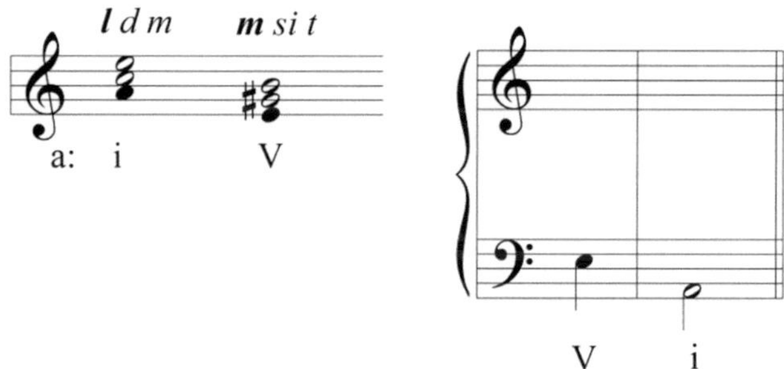

Next choose a soprano note for each chord, taking care to create a smooth connecting line. Here are some possibilities.

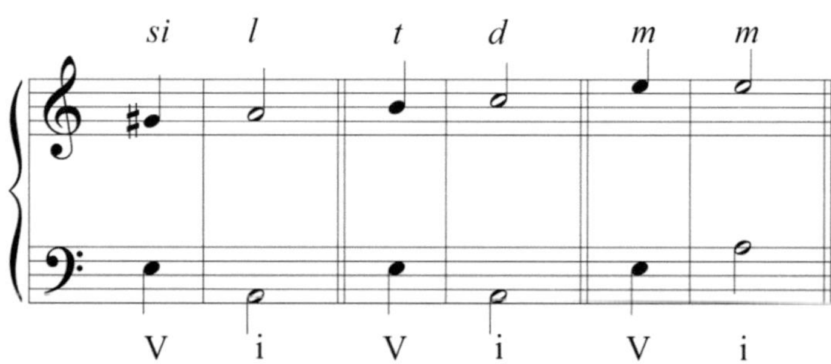

Finally, complete the alto and tenor parts, taking care to create smooth connecting lines.

The smoothest way to complete a perfect cadence in a minor key is for the upper voices to move as follows: ***si – l; t – d; m – m.*** As before, different arrangements can be made by swapping the upper voices.

The common note between both chords is ***m – m***; keep it in the same voice.

Audio 2.5

Listen to Audio 2.5 to hear each of the above. Listen carefully to the solfa to help distinguish between the voices.

The leading note always rises a step to the tonic in **V – i**: ***si - l***

V – i Summary

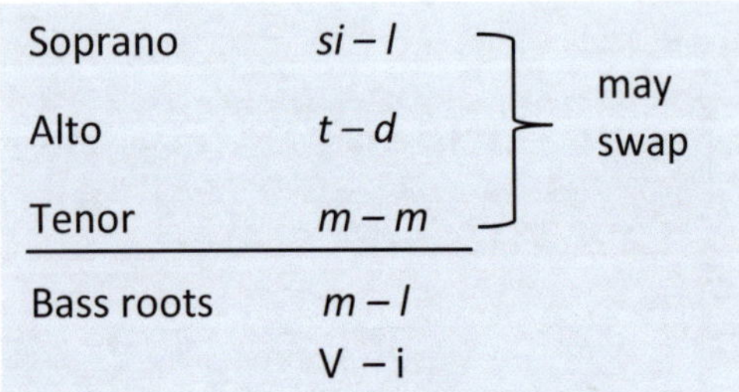

Soprano	*si – l*	may swap
Alto	*t – d*	
Tenor	*m – m*	
Bass roots	*m – l* V – i	

Exercise 2.6

Fill in the alto and tenor parts to complete each perfect cadence. Take care with doubling and spacing.

(a)

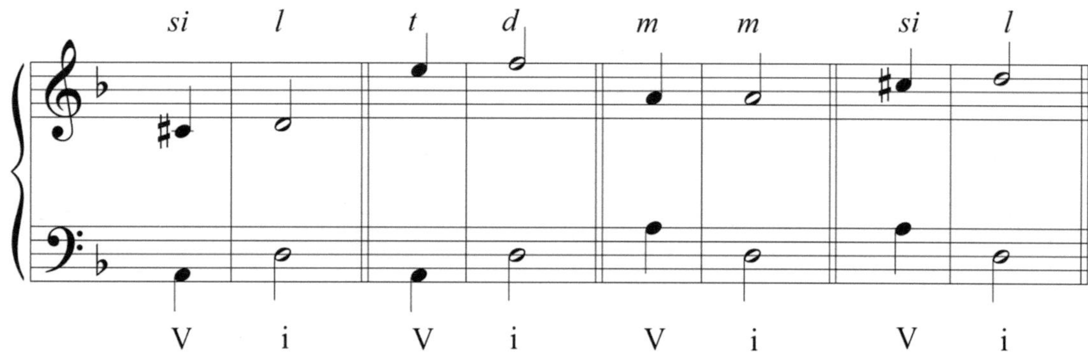

(b)

Exercise 2.7

Complete each perfect cadence by arranging parts for SAT. First make a chord plan, then choose the soprano line using different arrangements. Finally add the inner voices.

(a)

(b)

Exercise 2.8

Harmonise each soprano part to make a perfect cadence. Again, begin by making a chord plan, then write the roots in the bass followed by alto and tenor voices.

Exercise 2.9

This melody ends with a perfect cadence in the boxed area. Make a chord plan, then complete the cadence by writing the roots in the bass and adding the inner voices.

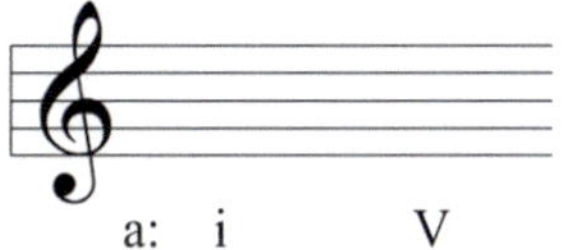

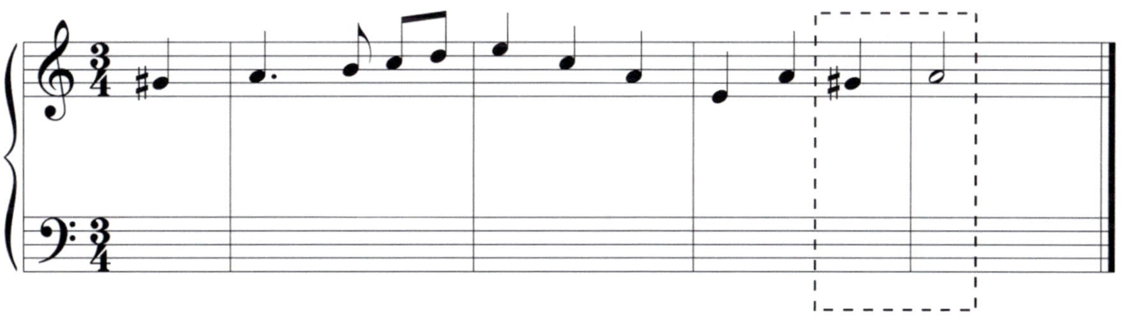

The Plagal Cadence in a Major Key

A plagal cadence gives a more gentle close to a phrase compared to a perfect cadence. The chords used are **IV – I**.

Listen to part of this Scottish folk-song *'Ye Banks and Braes'* to hear the effect of the plagal cadence at the end.

Historically, a plagal cadence was most commonly heard as *'Amen'* at the end of a hymn tune. Nowadays, it is common practice to omit the final *'Amen'*.

Listen to the final phrase of the familiar Crimond tune for *'The Lord's my Shepherd'* with the *'Amen'* included.

A method of working

To write a plagal cadence for SATB, complete a chord plan and write the roots in the bass.

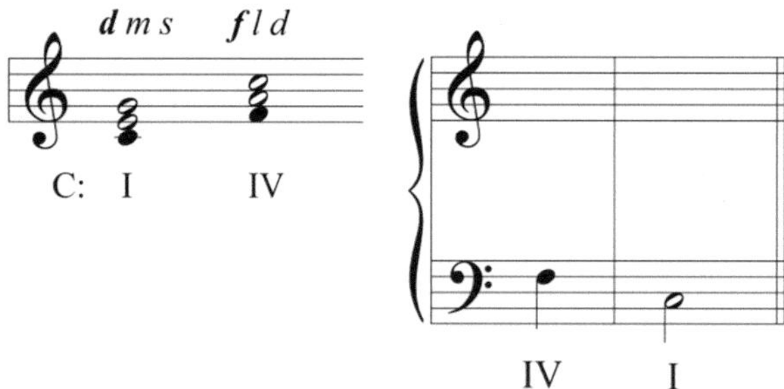

Now choose a soprano note for each chord, connecting as smoothly as possible. Here are some possibilities.

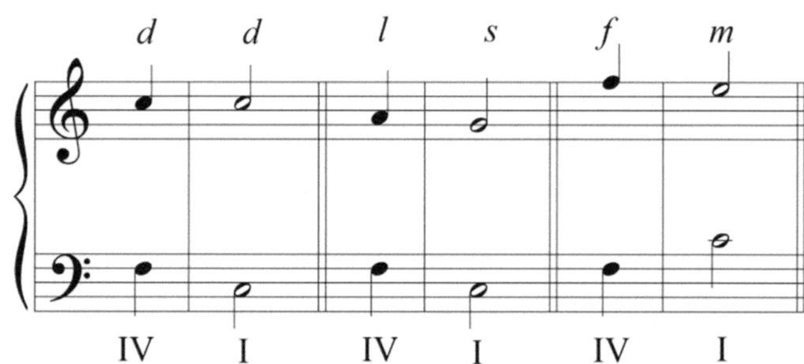

Finally, complete the alto and tenor parts taking care to create smooth connecting lines.

The easiest way to complete a plagal cadence in a major key is to move the upper voices SAT as follows: ***d – d; l – s; f – m.***
These lines may be swapped between the upper voices for different effects.

The common note between both chords is ***d – d***; keep it in the same voice.

Listen to Audio 2.8 to hear each of the above. Follow the solfa to distinguish the movement of the individual voices.

IV – I Summary

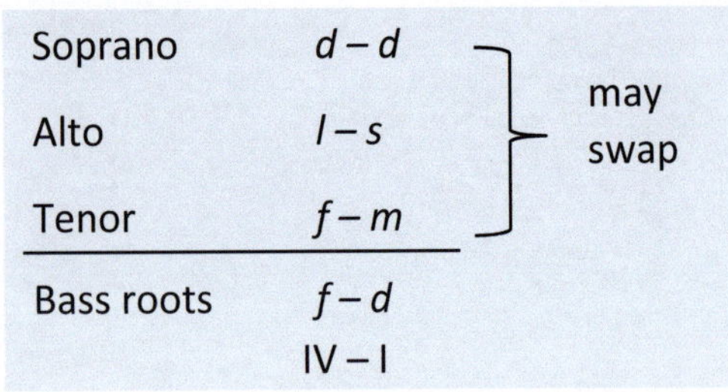

Soprano	*d – d*	may swap
Alto	*l – s*	
Tenor	*f – m*	
Bass roots	*f – d* IV – I	

Exercise 2.10

In the plagal cadences that follow, soprano and bass are given. Complete the alto and tenor parts.

(a)

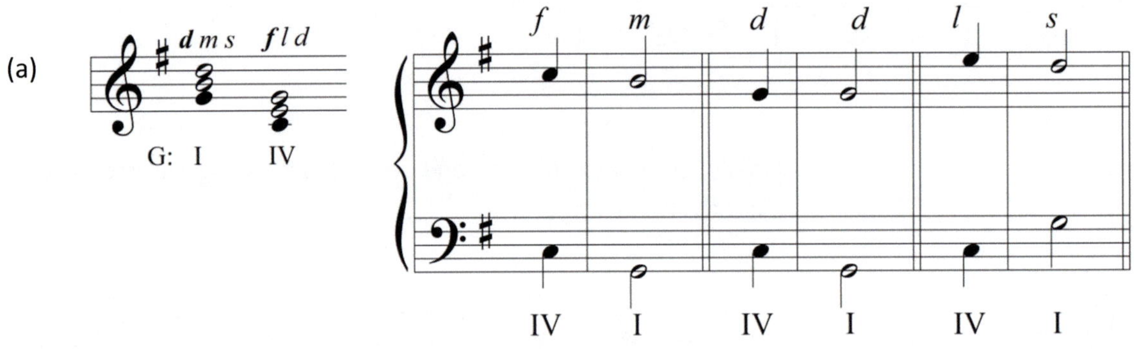

(b)

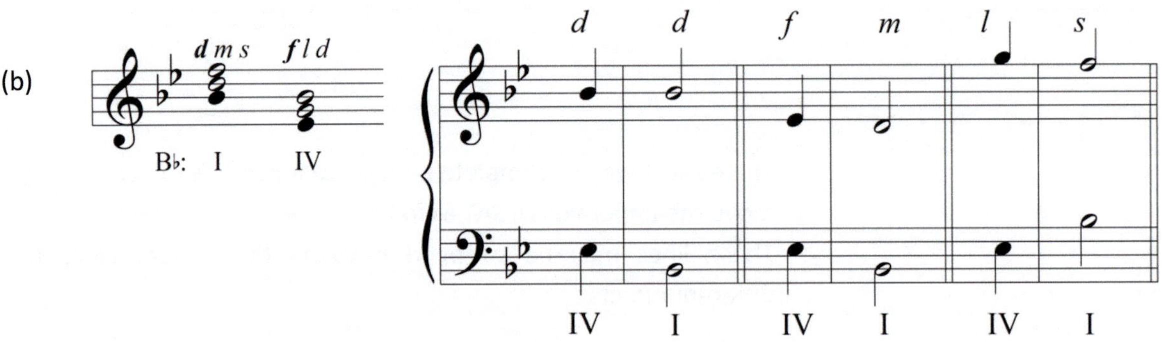

Exercise 2.11

Complete each plagal cadence by arranging parts for SAT. Make a chord plan and write the soprano line first in a variety of arrangements. Then fill in alto and tenor lines.

(a)

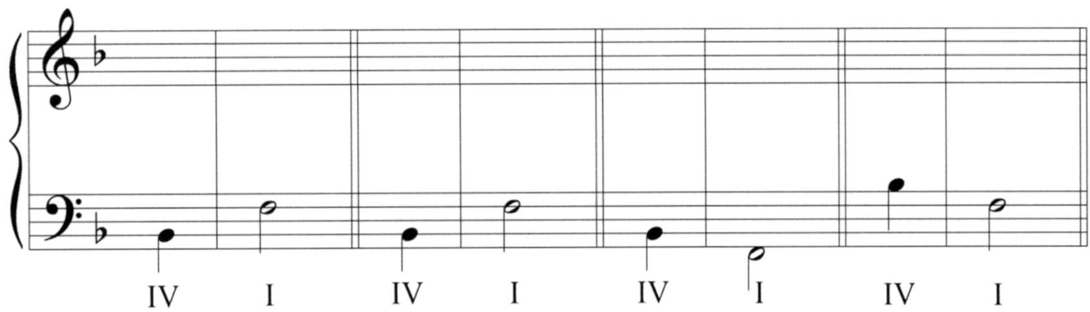

(b)

Exercise 2.12

Harmonise each soprano part to make a plagal cadence. Begin by making a chord plan, then write the roots in the bass, followed by alto and tenor parts.

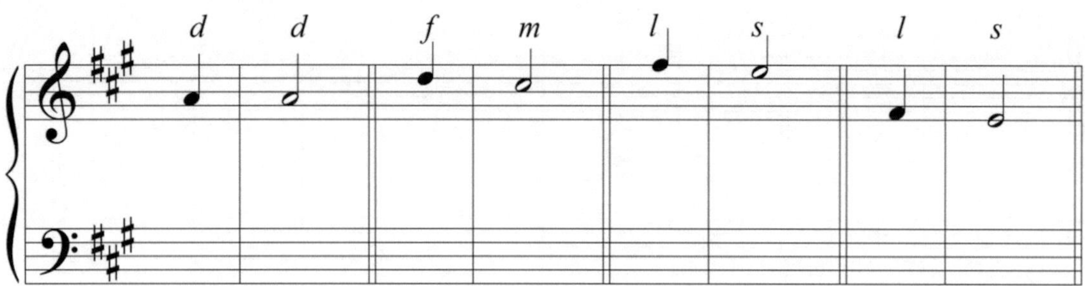

Exercise 2.13

This melody ends with a plagal cadence in the boxed area. Make a chord plan, then write the roots in the bass and complete the inner parts.

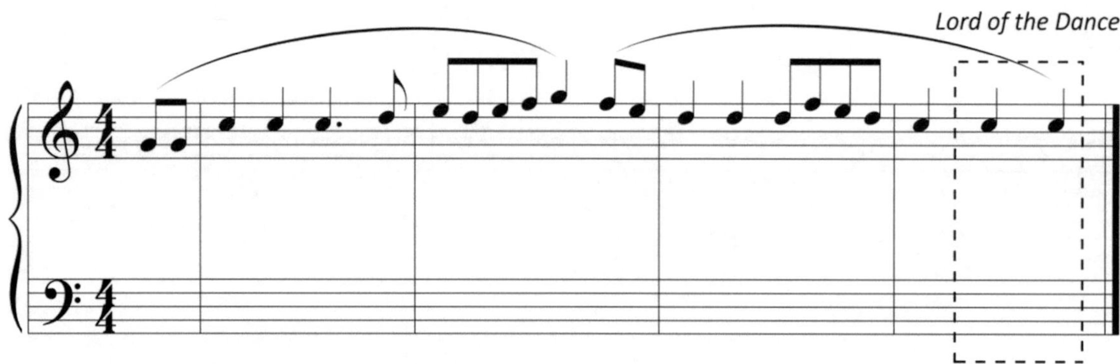

The Plagal Cadence in a Minor Key

Listen to the plagal cadence in a minor key found in the final phrase of the carol *'The Angel Gabriel'*.

When writing a plagal cadence in a minor key, the guidelines are the same as those for a major key but note the difference in solfa.

As before, draw up a chord plan and begin by writing the roots in the bass.

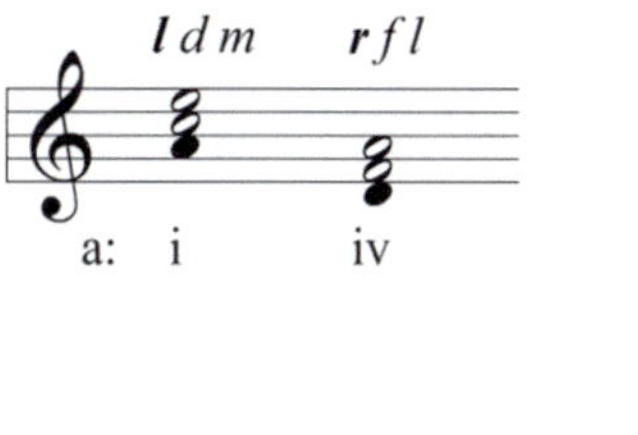

Next choose a soprano note for each chord, taking care to create a smooth connecting line. Here are some possibilities.

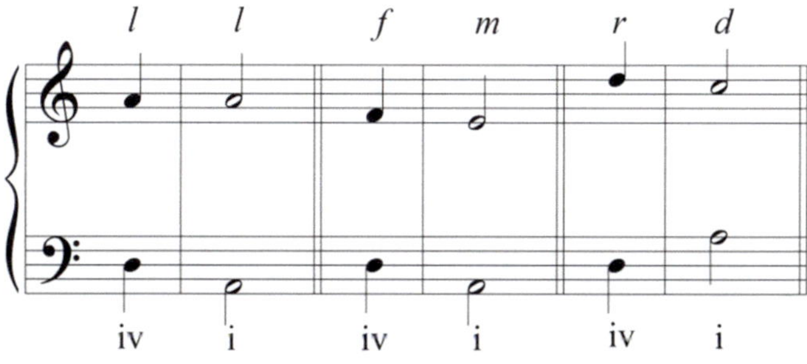

Finally, complete the alto and tenor parts, taking care to create smooth lines.

The easiest way to complete a plagal cadence in a minor key is for the upper voices to move as follows: ***l – l; f – m; r – d.***
As before, different arrangements can be made by swapping the upper lines.

The common note between both chords is ***l – l***; keep it in the same voice.

Listen to Audio 2.10 to hear each of the above examples. Carefully note the solfa to help you distinguish the individual voices.

iv – i Summary

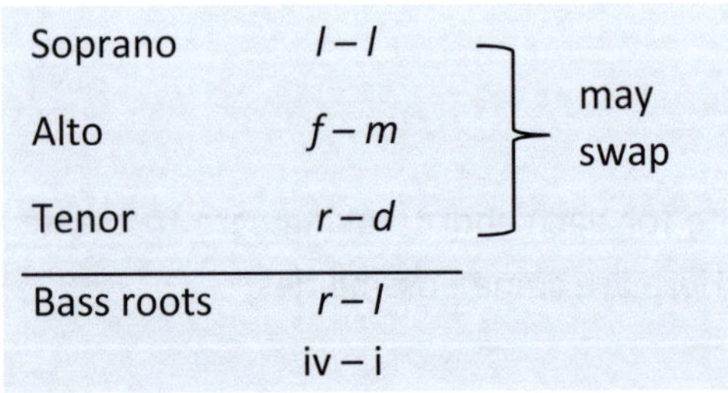

Soprano	*l – l*	may swap
Alto	*f – m*	
Tenor	*r – d*	
Bass roots	*r – l*	
	iv – i	

Exercise 2.14

Fill in alto and tenor parts to complete each plagal cadence. Take care with spacing and doubling.

(a)

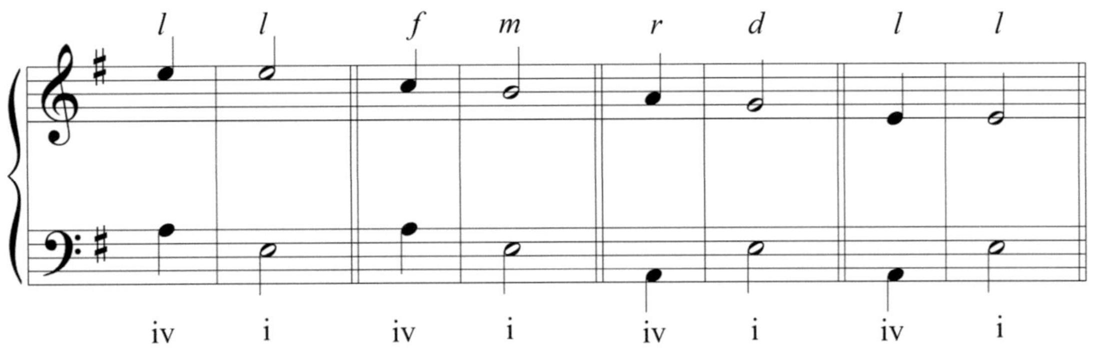

(b)

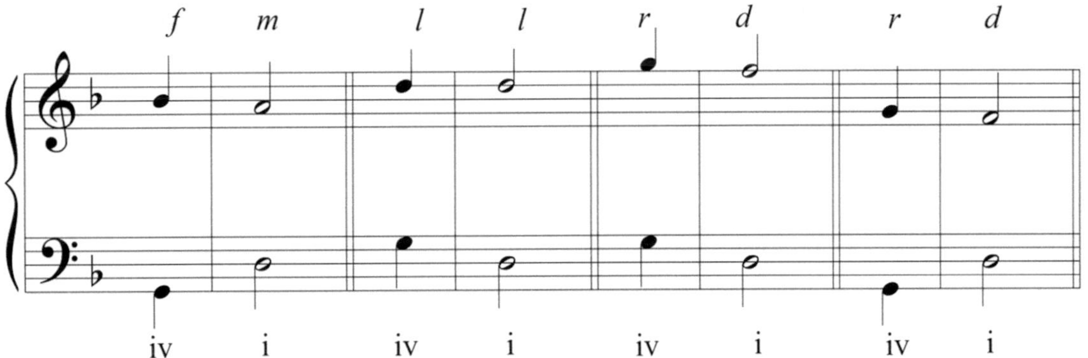

Exercise 2.15

Complete each plagal cadence by arranging parts for SAT. First make a chord plan, then choose the soprano line using different arrangements. Finally add inner voices.

Exercise 2.16

Harmonise each pair of soprano notes to make a plagal cadence. Begin by making a chord plan, then write the roots in the bass, together with their roman numerals. Add the alto and tenor parts.

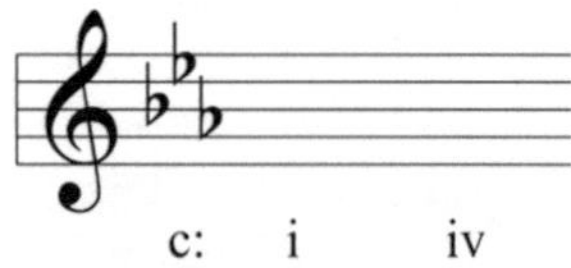

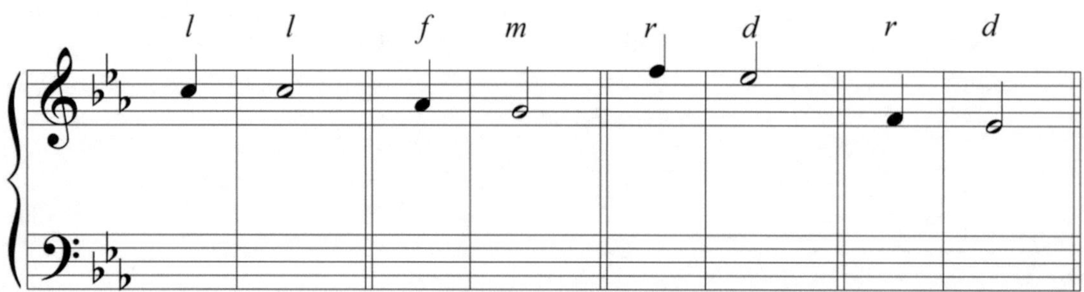

Exercise 2.17

This melody ends with a plagal cadence in the boxed area. Make a chord plan, then write the roots in the bass. Add roman numerals and complete the inner parts.

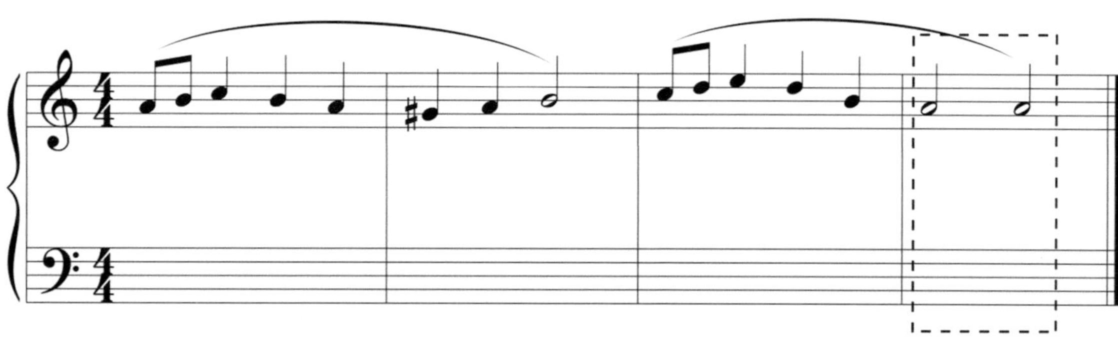

CHAPTER 3

THE IMPERFECT CADENCE

The imperfect cadence gives the phrase an open-ended effect. There are a number of different chord combinations available. The most common being **I – V**. This will be dealt with first.

Listen to part of *'Twinkle Twinkle Little Star'* to hear the imperfect cadence at the end of the third and fourth phrases.

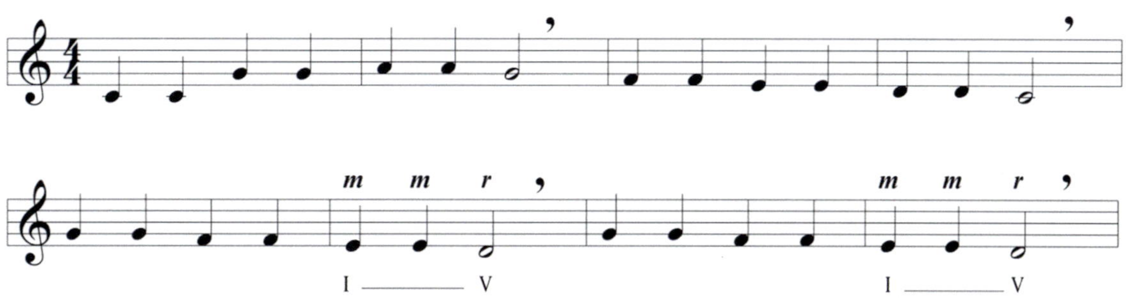

The first phrase of the *'Coventry Carol'* ends with an example of the imperfect cadence in the minor key.

Writing I – V in Major and Minor Keys

You have already written the progression **V – I**. By reversing the movement, you can easily create **I – V**.

Major Keys

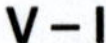

V – I

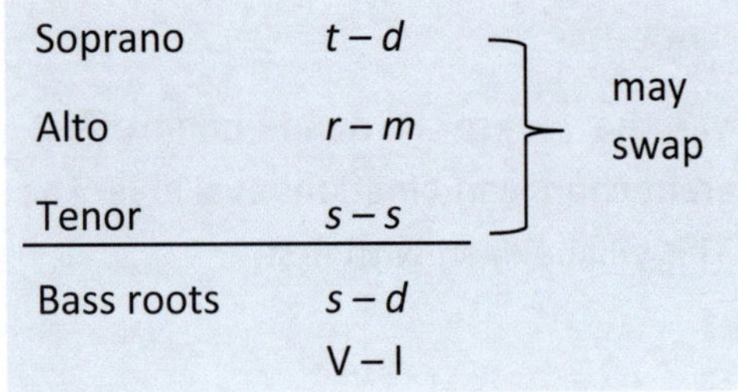

Soprano	*t – d*	may swap
Alto	*r – m*	
Tenor	*s – s*	
Bass roots	*s – d*	
	V – I	

I - V

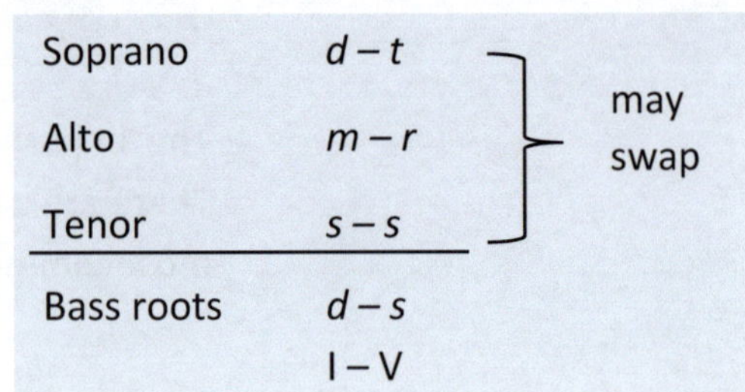

Soprano	*d – t*	may swap
Alto	*m – r*	
Tenor	*s – s*	
Bass roots	*d – s*	
	I – V	

Minor Keys

V – i

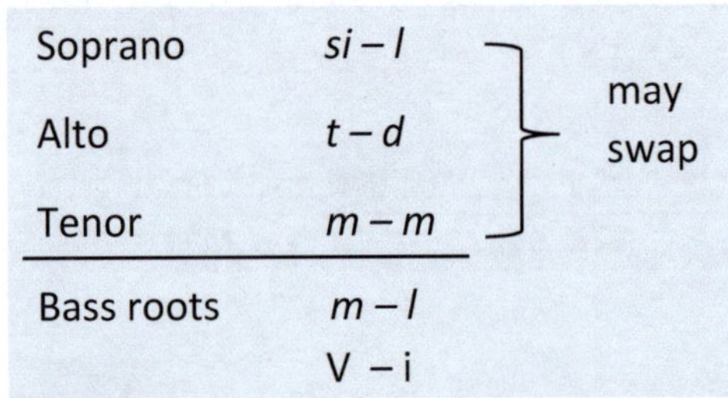

Soprano	*si – l*	may swap
Alto	*t – d*	
Tenor	*m – m*	
Bass roots	*m – l*	
	V – i	

i - V

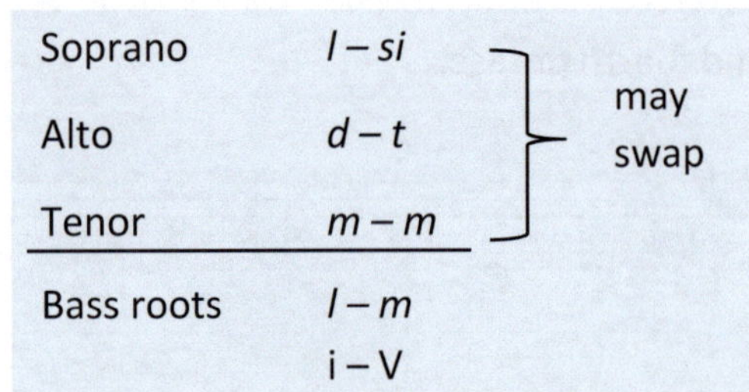

Soprano	*l – si*	may swap
Alto	*d – t*	
Tenor	*m – m*	
Bass roots	*l – m*	
	i – V	

Listen to Audio 3.3 as you follow the examples below.

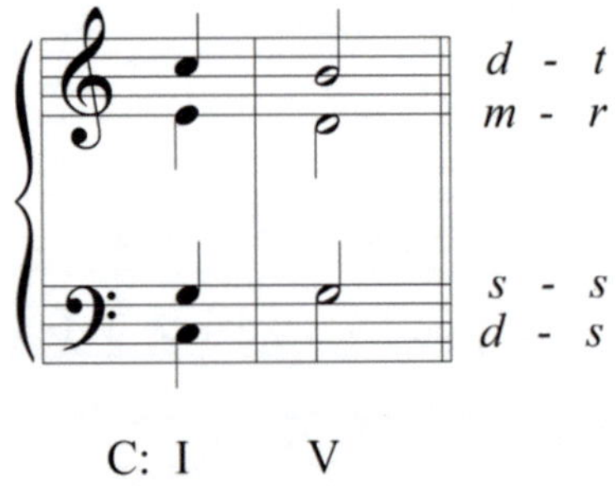

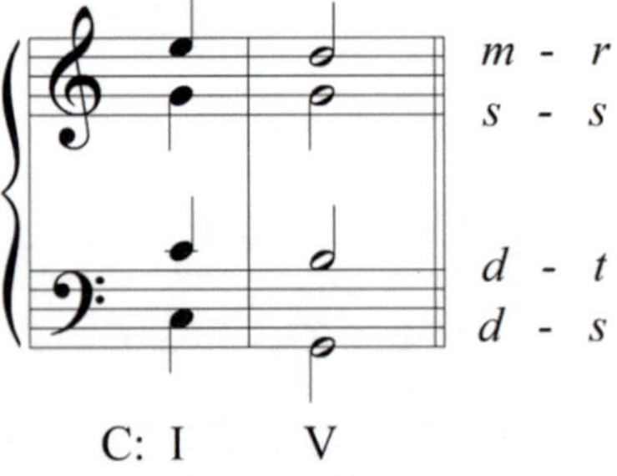

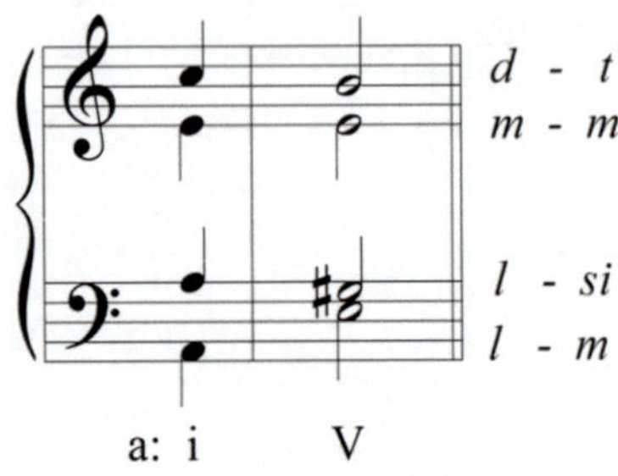

Exercise 3.1

Fill in the alto and tenor parts to complete each imperfect cadence. Be aware of correct spacing and doubling.

(a)

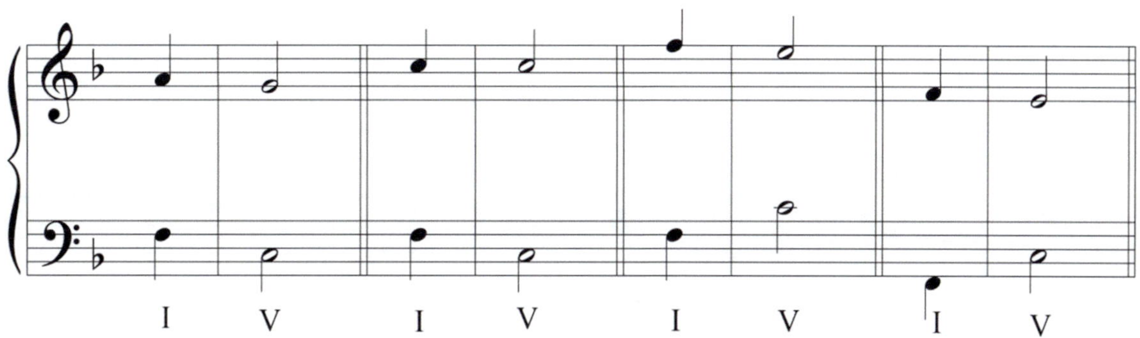

(b)

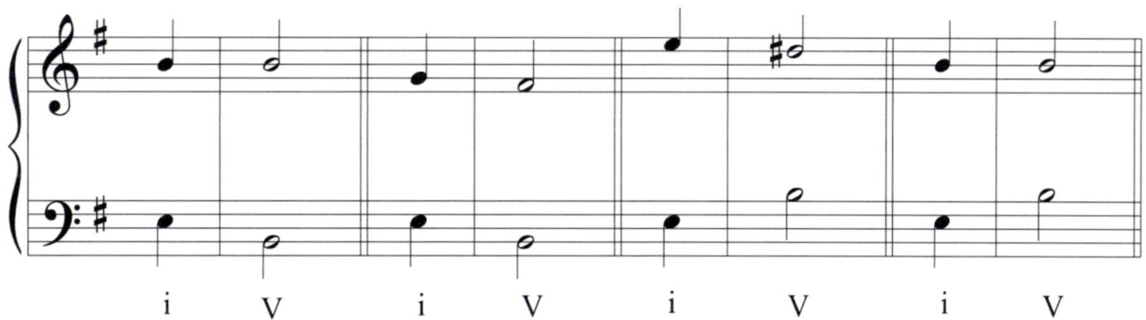

Exercise 3.2

Write parts for SAT to complete each imperfect cadence. Make a chord plan. Choose the soprano part first, showing a variety of arrangements. Include roman numerals in (b).

(a)

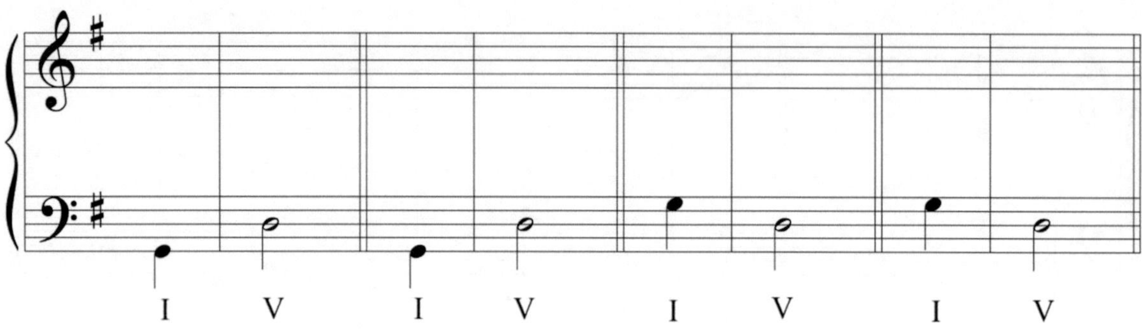

(b)

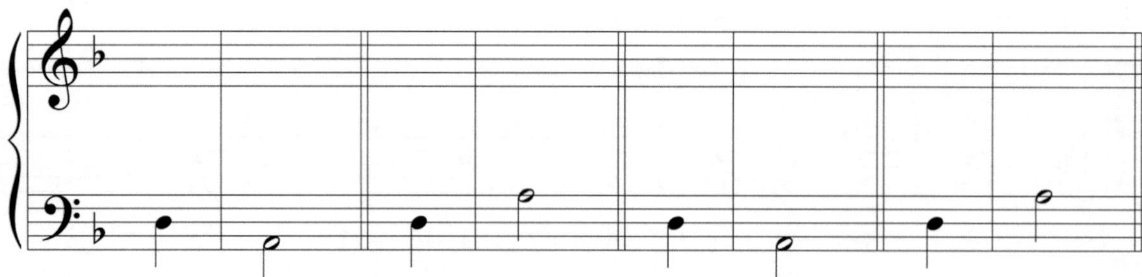

Exercise 3.3

To the given soprano add parts for ATB to form imperfect cadences. Make a chord plan, then write the roots in the bass part adding roman numerals. Finally, add alto and tenor parts.

(a)

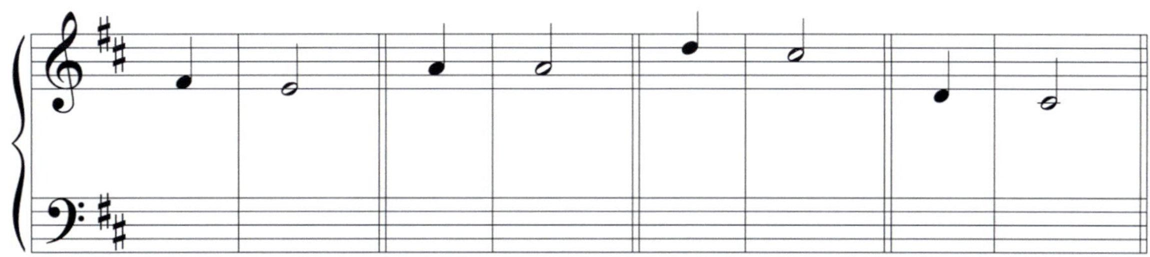

(b)

Exercise 3.4

These phrases end with imperfect cadences in the boxed areas. Make a chord plan. Then write the roots in the bass and complete the alto and tenor parts.

(a)

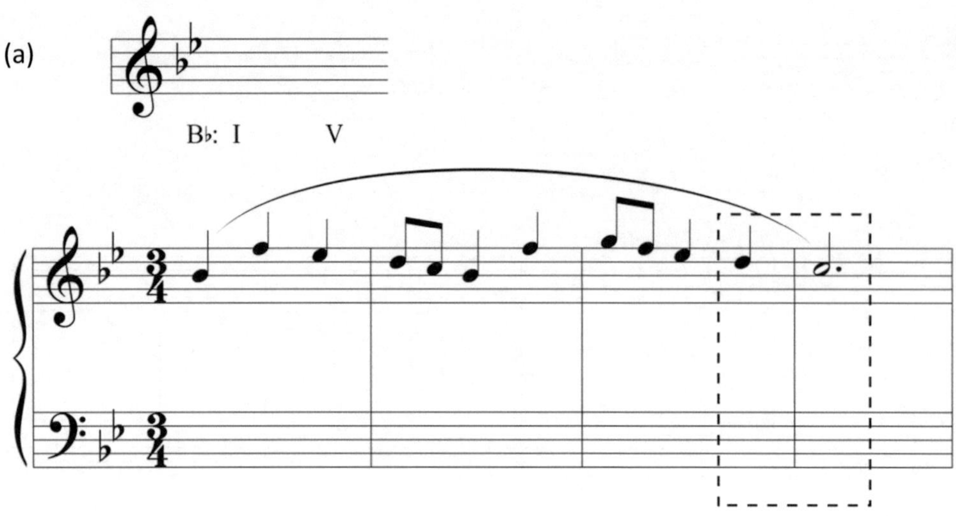

(b)

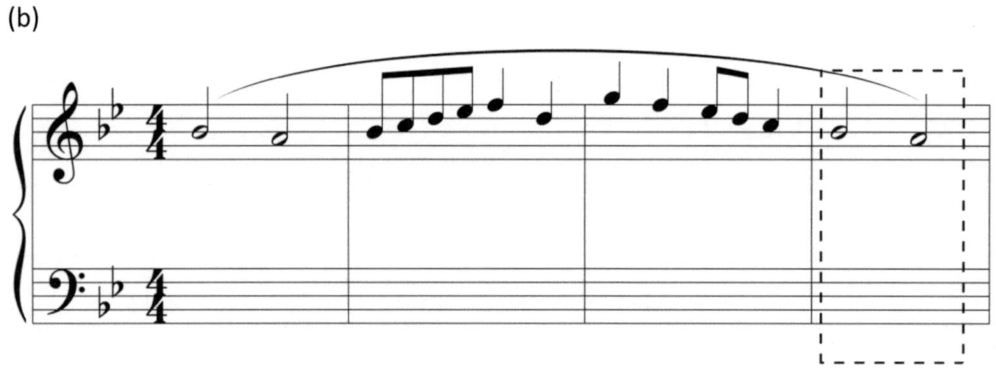

(c)

Writing IV – V in Major and Minor Keys

The chord progression **IV – V** is another way of creating an imperfect cadence.

Listen to Audio 3.4 to hear its effect at the end of this phrase from the Scottish folk-song *'Loch Lomand'*.

When writing **IV – V** the bass roots will rise a step. The easiest way to complete the upper voices is to have them moving **downwards.**

Listen to Audio 3.5. Follow the solfa to hear the movement of the individual voices in the examples below.

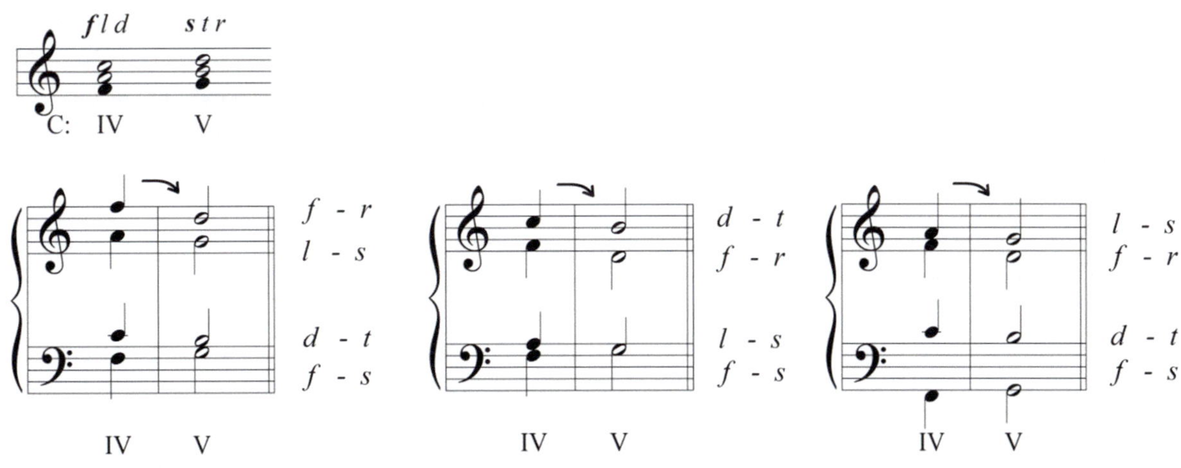

Listen to Audio 3.6 to hear the following **iv – V** progressions in a minor key.

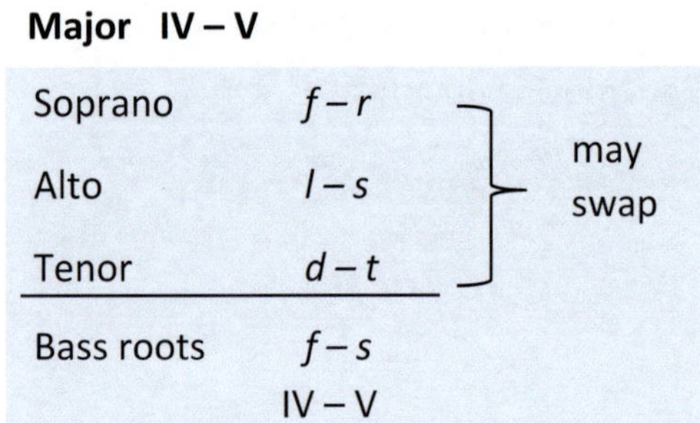

Major IV – V

Soprano	*f – r*	may swap
Alto	*l – s*	
Tenor	*d – t*	
Bass roots	*f – s* IV – V	

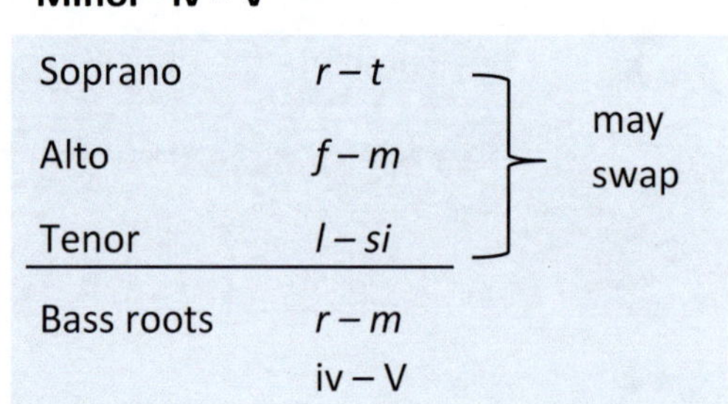

Minor iv – V

Soprano	*r – t*	may swap
Alto	*f – m*	
Tenor	*l – si*	
Bass roots	*r – m* iv – V	

Grammatical Point

As seen in the above layout the movement of **IV – V** has a distinctive shape. The reason for this is to avoid consecutive 5ths (parallel 5ths) and consecutive 8vs (parallel octaves), which weaken these lines.

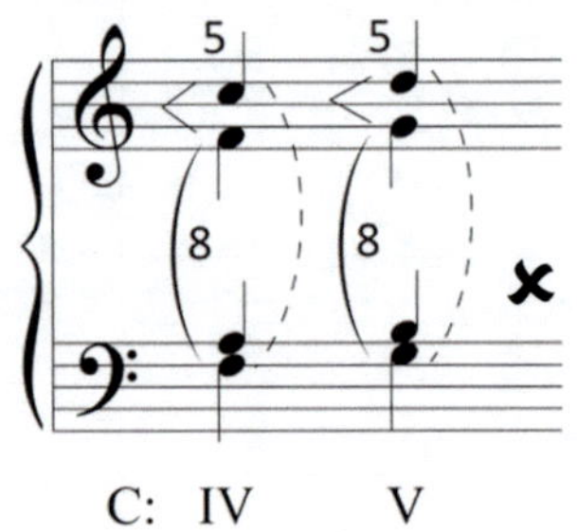

- In this example consecutive 8vs (parallel octaves) are present between bass and alto parts
- Consecutive 5ths (parallel 5ths) are present between soprano and alto parts
- Compound consecutive 5ths (parallel 5ths) are also present between bass and soprano parts

Listen to Audio 3.7. The first incorrect version has an open sound while the correct version sounds more rounded. Follow the music below as you listen.

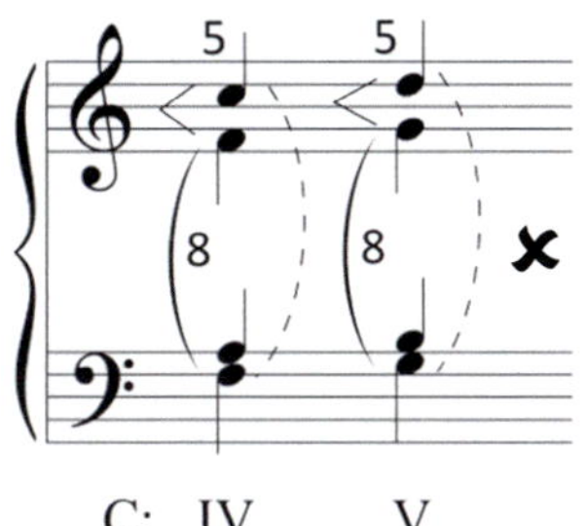

When writing four-part harmony consecutive/parallel perfect 5ths and consecutive/parallel perfect 8vs should be avoided

Exercise 3.5

In the imperfect cadences which follow, soprano and bass parts are given. Complete the alto and tenor parts.

(a)

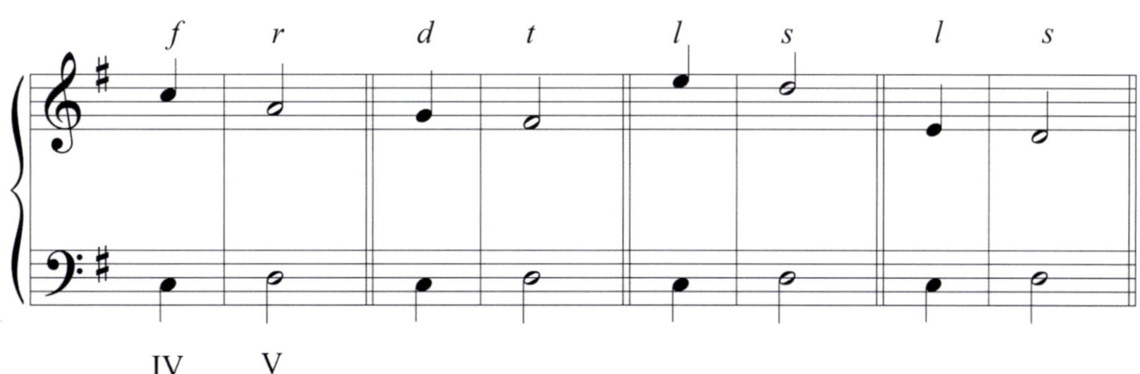

(b)

Exercise 3.6

Complete each imperfect cadence by arranging parts for SAT. Make a chord plan. Write the soprano line first in a variety of arrangements, then fill in alto and tenor voices. Remember the necessary downward movement of all the upper parts.

Exercise 3.7

Harmonise each soprano part using the progression **IV – V**. Begin by making a chord plan. Then write the roots in the bass followed by alto and tenor voices.

(a)

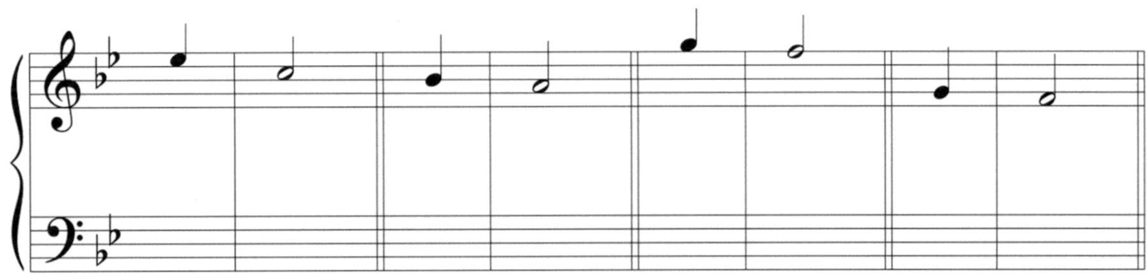

(b)

Exercise 3.8

Study the following melodies. In the boxed areas there are two imperfect cadence possibilities. Make use of both chord progressions you have learnt.

(a)

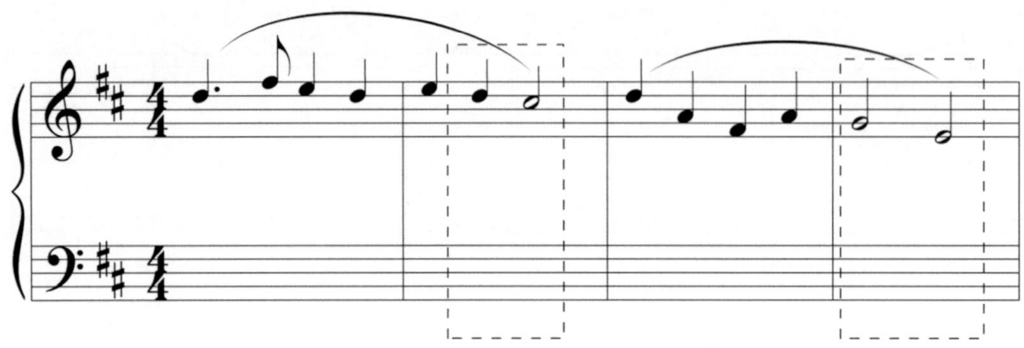

(b)

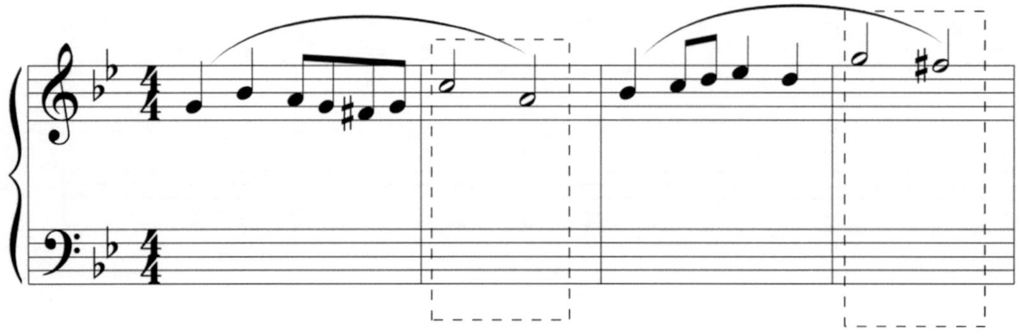

Exercise 3.9

The following exercise contains a mixture of all the cadences covered so far: perfect, plagal and imperfect. Complete each for SATB. Add roman numerals.

Four cadence progressions have now been studied, each with a distinct quality. In general, choose the strongest cadence to close the piece. Use the more open-ended cadences at the other phrase endings.

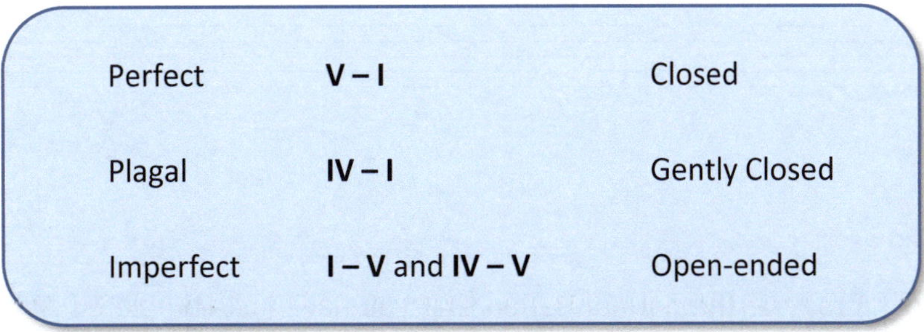

Perfect	**V – I**	Closed
Plagal	**IV – I**	Gently Closed
Imperfect	**I – V** and **IV – V**	Open-ended

Exercise 3.10

In the following melody the cadence chords have been decided for you. Harmonise only the cadences in the boxed areas. Use the guidelines that you have been given.

(a)

Audio 3.8

Listen to Audio 3.8 to hear the harmonisation that you have just completed. While the detail of your inner voices may be different the overall effect of each cadence will be the same.

(b) This is a minor key melody with the cadence chords highlighted in the boxed areas. Complete the harmonisation by adding parts for ATB.

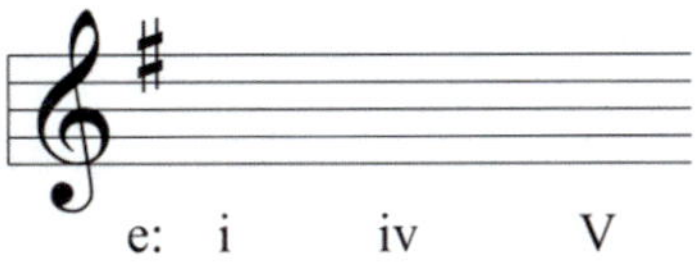

e: i iv V

i V

iv V

iv i

V i

Audio 3.9

Listen to Audio 3.9 to hear the melody harmonised at the cadential points. As before, the inner detail may be arranged differently but the overall sound effect of the cadences will be the same.

Summary

- Write a chord plan including roman numerals and solfa
- Write the root of each chord in the bass part
- Watch the doubling and spacing
- Connect the upper parts smoothly
- Remember in **IV – V** the bass rises and all the other parts fall

CHAPTER 4

WRITING SOPRANO LINES

Thus far we have concentrated only on cadences. Now we will write a series of chord progressions using **I, IV** and **V** to create a complete phrase. The most musical way of approaching this is to focus on the soprano line first. The aim is to create an interesting soprano line which will have some contrast of rhythm to the bass and a well-shaped outline. This is the first step in creating what will ultimately be a full four-part harmonisation.

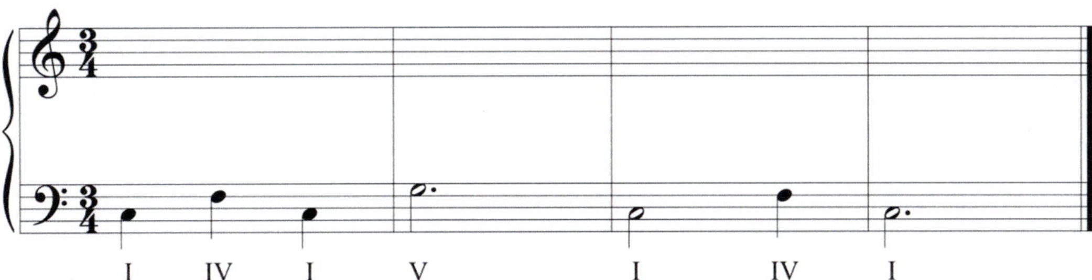

In creating the melody the following steps will secure an interesting and successful shape above the bass.

- Make a chord plan and write the roman numerals below the given bass
- At every chord change take care to connect the soprano smoothly to the next chord

  This means: repeating a note
  or
  moving by step up or down
  or
  moving a 3rd up or down
- However, where the chord is sustained or repeated, the soprano is free to move between any notes of that chord.
- As you sing the melody, include solfa as a tool to ensure a strong musical shaping.

Here are two possible soprano lines above the given bass. Where there is a chord change and the soprano connects smoothly we use this sign ⁄. Where there is no chord change and the soprano moves freely we have used this sign ⁄.

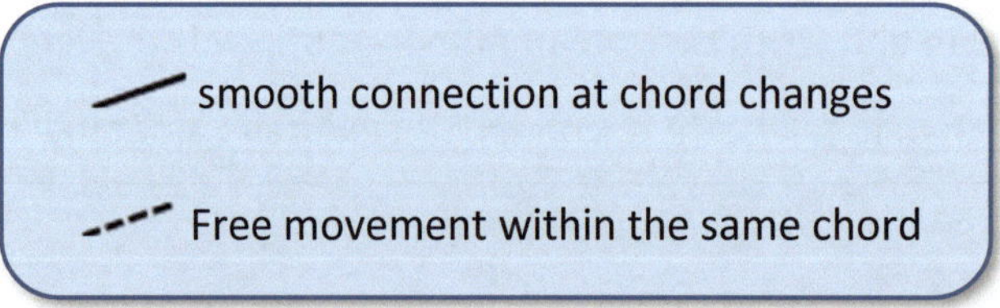

Listen to Audio 4.1 to hear both versions of our simple soprano line.

Here is another example in A major.

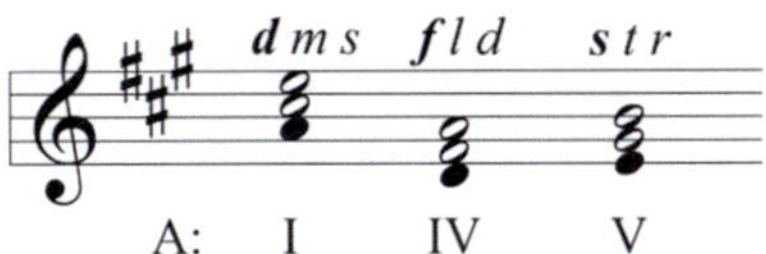

There are two important points to note in the above:

(i) The downward movement over **IV – V**

(ii) The leading note rising to the tonic as the chord changes from **V – I**

Here is another melodic possibility above the same bass line.

* Notice the leading note ***t*** is not rising to the tonic in this instance because there is no chord change on beat 3.

In the final bar the soprano should ideally finish on the root or the 3rd of chord **I** to create a decisive ending.

Listen to Audio 4.2 to hear both versions of the soprano line.

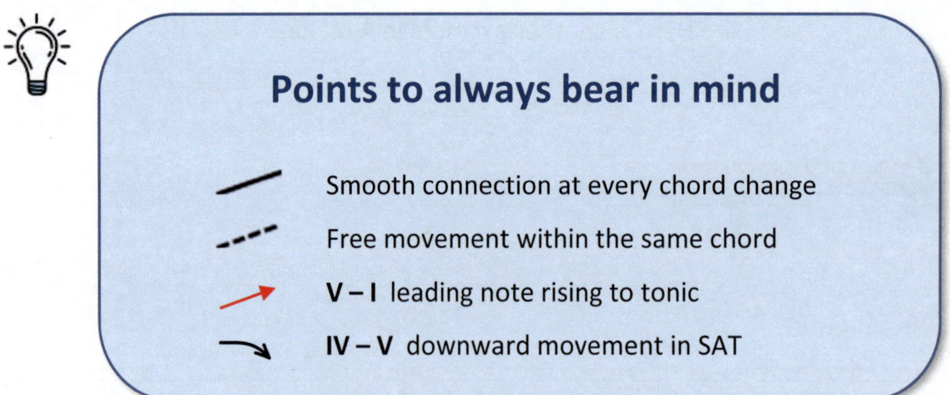

Exercise 4.1

Following the suggestions given, above the given bass write two versions of a soprano line, ending on the root or the 3rd of chord **I**. Complete the chord plan before you begin. Remember to sing with solfa as you write.

(a)

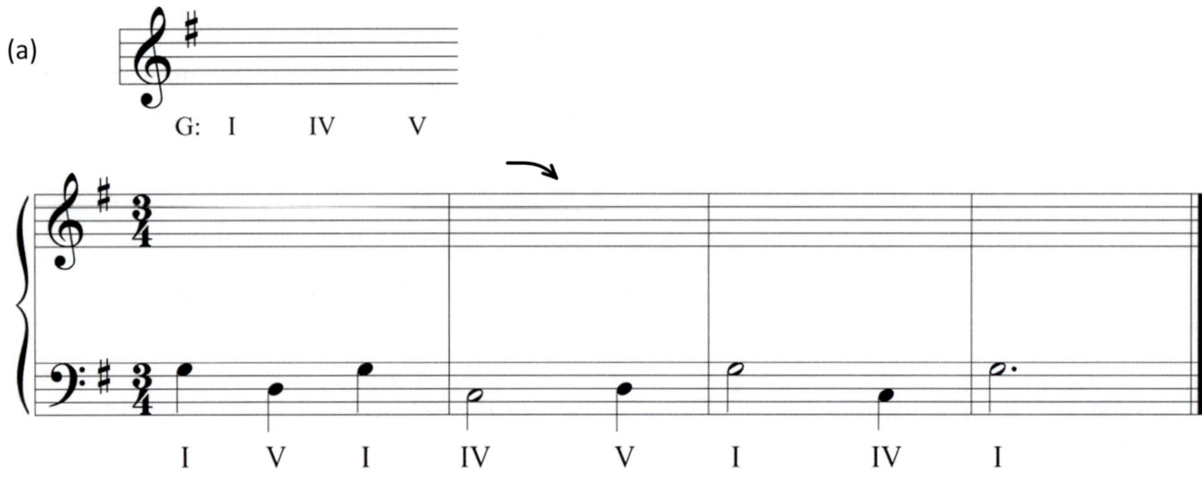

(b)

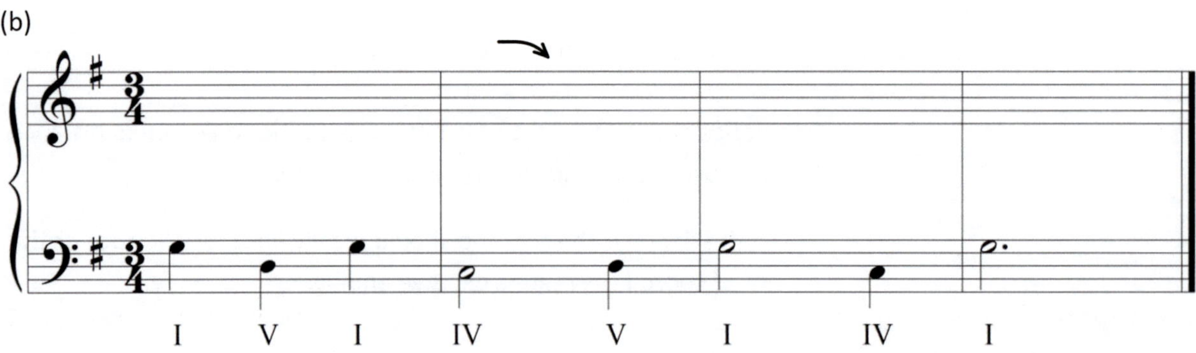

Exercise 4.2

Write two versions of a soprano line above the given bass. Again, complete the chord plan and add roman numerals before you begin. Remember to sing using solfa.

(a)

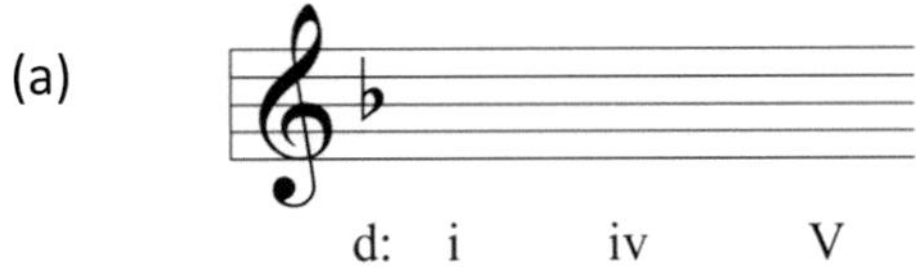

(b)

Passing Notes

Very few melodies will use chord notes only. Simple decoration will add both rhythmic and melodic interest. A passing note 'passes' between any two chord notes a 3rd apart, creating stepwise movement either up or down.

Notice that the passing note (circled in green) is on the weak part of the beat – the second of a pair of quavers.

Occasionally a passing note may take up a whole unaccented beat.

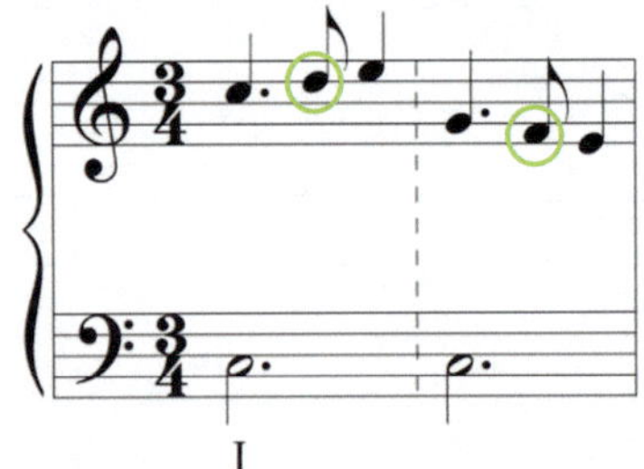

An interesting variation is to make use of a dotted rhythm.

A passing note moves by step between notes of the same chord or notes of different chords.

Approaching Exercises

The following steps can be a useful approach to achieve a musically flowing soprano line.

Begin by writing the framework of the melody using only chord notes.

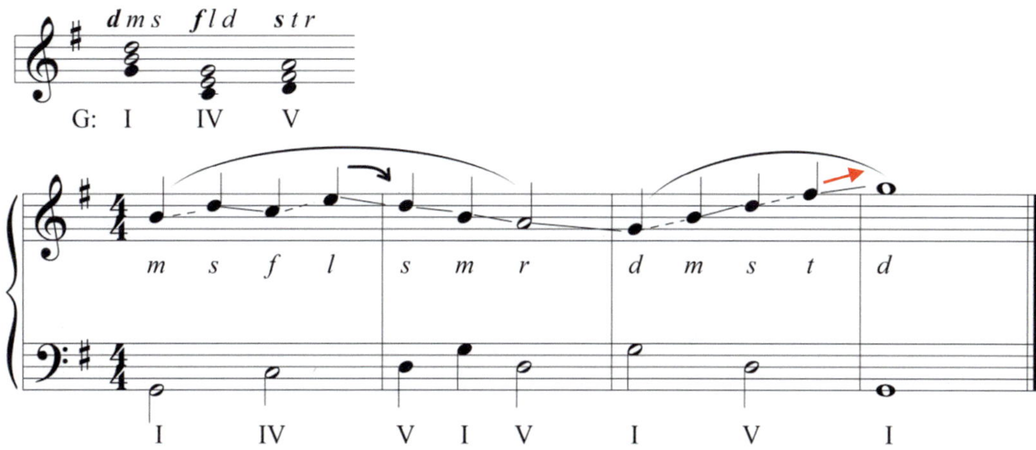

Now, some passing notes are added to give a better flow to the melody.

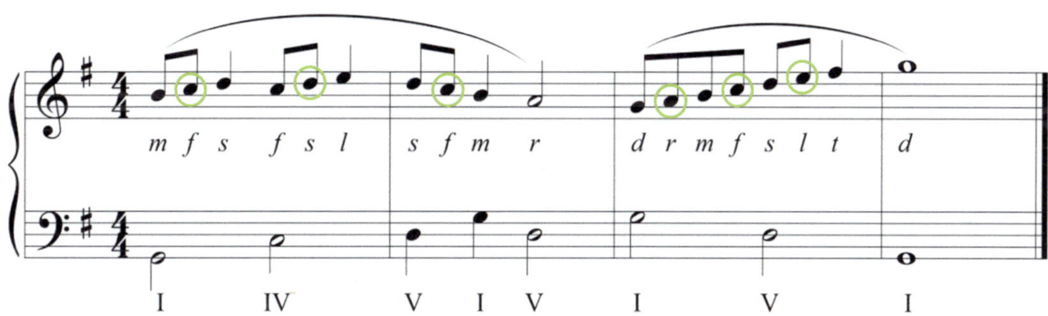

 Audio 4.3

Listen to Audio 4.3 to compare both versions. Notice the added interest created by the passing notes.

Here are two examples in F major. The first shows the basic framework using chord notes only. The second adds passing note decoration.

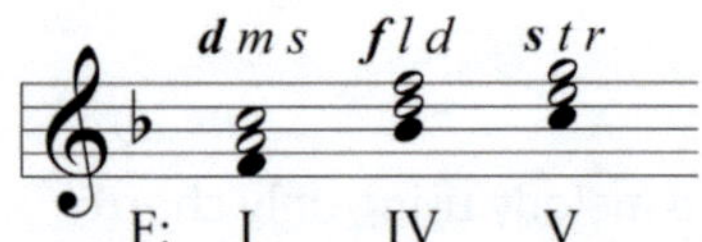

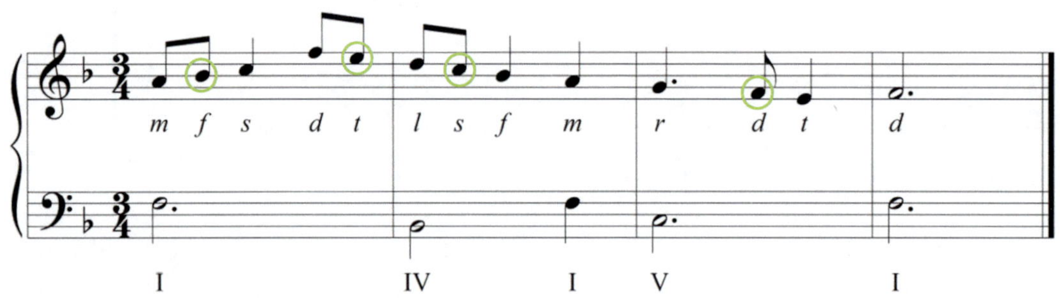

Listen to Audio 4.4. Notice the extra melodic interest in the second version.

Checklist✓

- Make a chord plan and write roman numerals below the bass
- Create a framework by using chord notes only
- Smooth connection at chord changes
- Free movement within the same chord
- **V – I** leading note rising to tonic
- **IV – V** downward movement in SAT
- Add solfa and sing as you write
- Decorate by adding passing notes

Exercise 4.3

Add roman numerals. Then write a soprano line above each of the given bass lines.

Working in $\frac{6}{8}$

The harmonic rhythm in compound time is usually:

When adding passing notes the rhythm is as follows:

This example in G major begins by creating a framework melody using chord notes only. Then decoration is added.

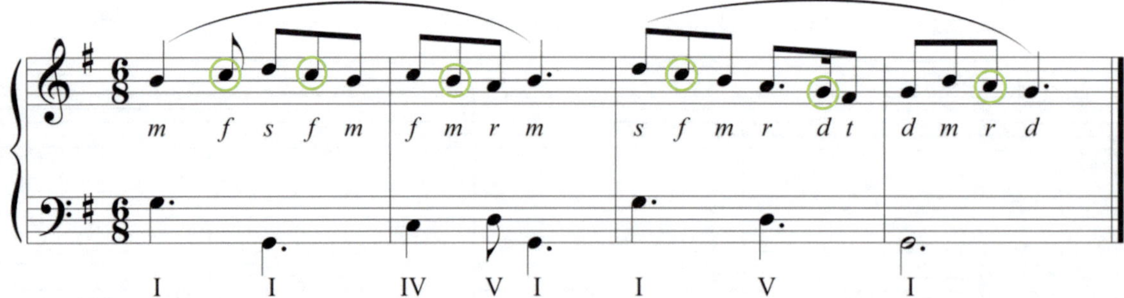

Listen to Audio 4.5 comparing both versions.

Exercise 4.4

Add roman numerals below the bass. Create a soprano line above each of the given bass lines. Apply the suggested steps outlined earlier. Remember to sing as you write.

(a)

(b)

Minor Key

Let us follow the same basic steps when writing a soprano melody above a given bass in the minor key.

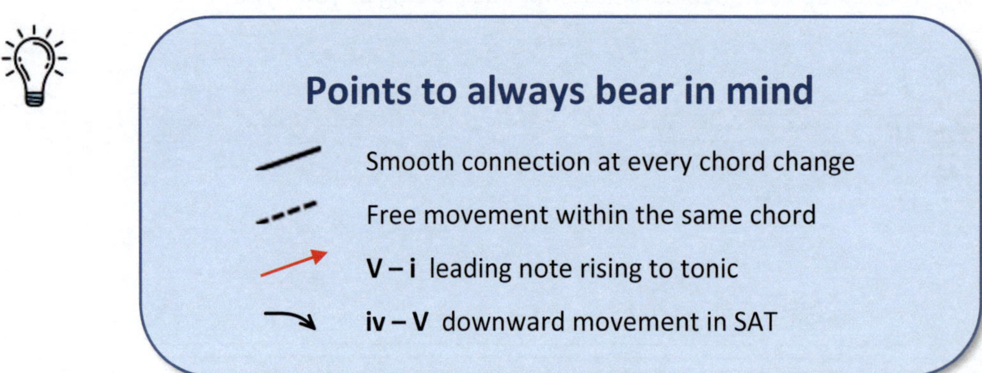

As before, we begin by creating a melodic framework above the bass using chord notes only.

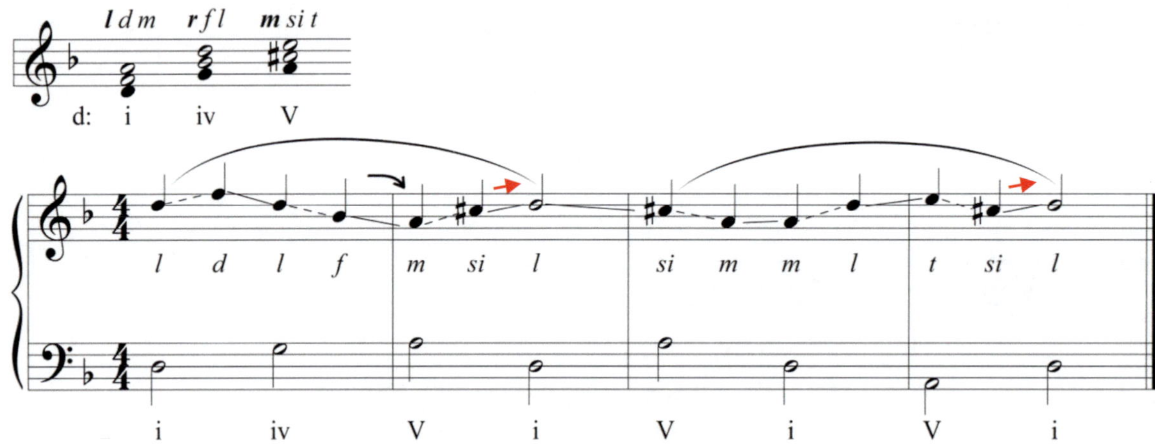

Notice in bar 2 that the leading note rises to the tonic as the chord changes, but in bar 3 its movement is free because there is no chord change following it on beat 2.

Here is another possibility above the same bass.

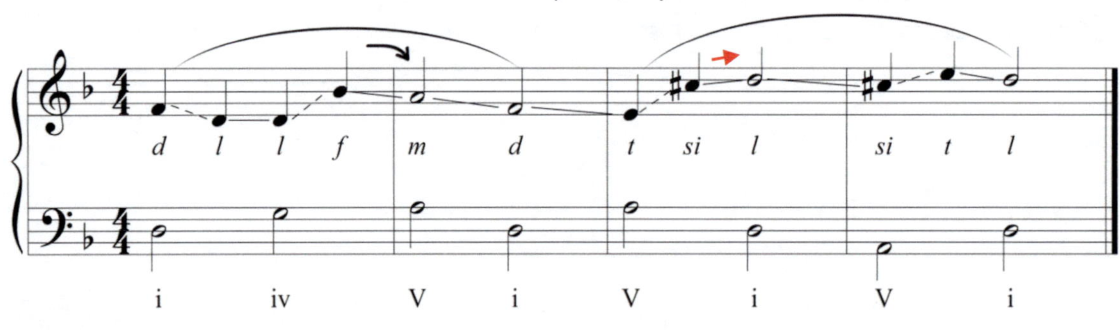

Listen to Audio 4.6 to hear both versions.

Passing Notes in the Minor Key

Passing notes in the minor key are equally effective in creating musically flowing lines. The only special consideration is when using the 6th and 7th notes of the scale as passing notes. Here, we want to avoid an augmented 2nd interval. Take the earlier example in D minor and consider how to approach this.

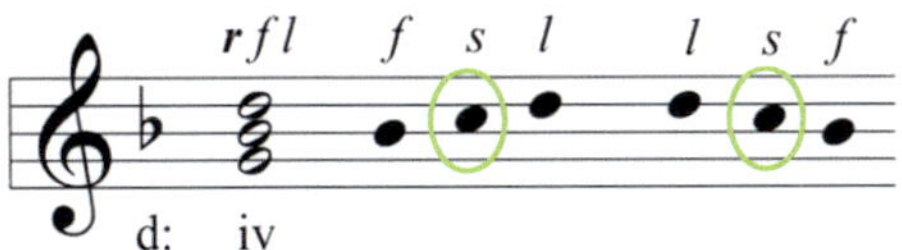

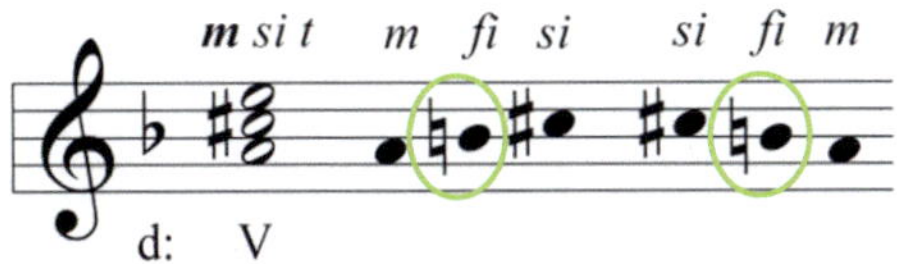

- Write a chord plan
- Plot in the available passing notes between the relevant chord notes
- The passing note between ***f*** and ***l*** is ***s***
- The passing note between ***m*** and ***si*** is ***fi***
- This is the case whether you are ascending or descending

Below is the simple and decorated D minor example.

Audio 4.7

Listen to Audio 4.7 paying particular attention to ***s*** and ***fi*** as passing notes in the second version.

This is an example in compound time in the minor key; first showing the framework and then the decorated version.

Audio 4.8

Listen to Audio 4.8. Pay particular attention to the passing notes in the second version.

Exercise 4.5

Write musically shaped soprano lines above each of the given bass lines. Follow the pointers already given. Always add roman numerals.

(a)

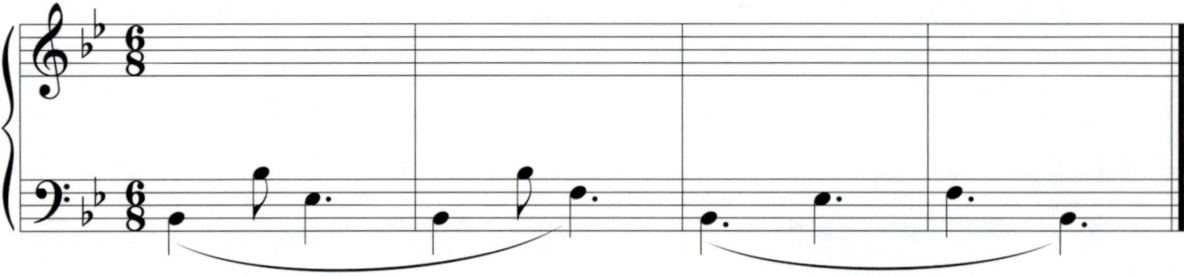

(b)

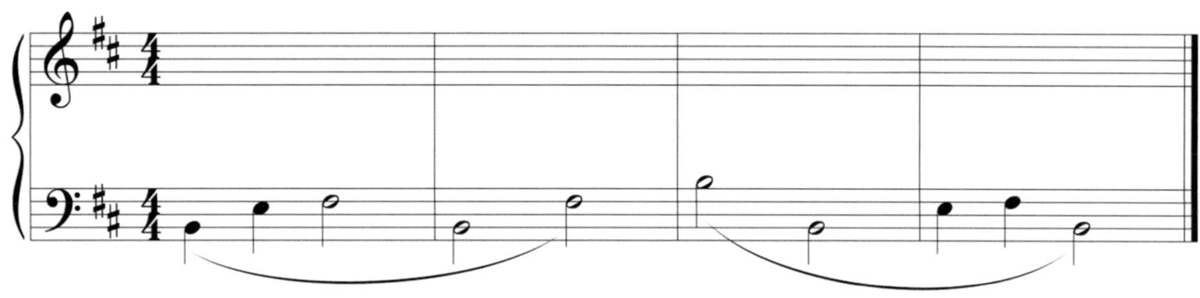

(c)

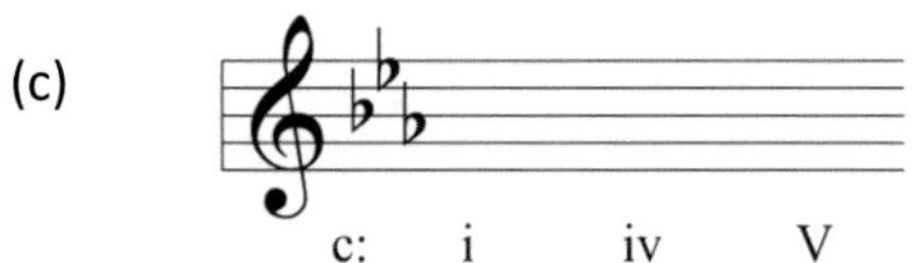

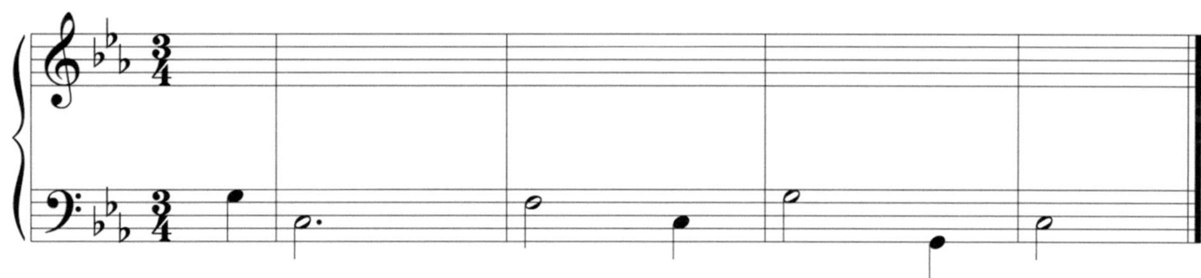

Auxiliary Notes in the Major Key

Another way to decorate the soprano line is to include the **occasional** auxiliary note. Examples below are highlighted in blue.

- There are two types: upper and lower
- They occur between repeated pitches
- They are on the weak part of the beat, as with passing notes.

First, a framework melody is created.

Now decorate by adding some auxiliary notes.

- Look ahead when choosing which auxiliary note to use (upper/lower). In general, if the melody rises use the lower auxiliary; if the melody falls, use the upper auxiliary.

- Notice the G minim in bar 3, as printed again below. It may be broken up to include both an auxiliary and a passing note. This gives good flow to the line.

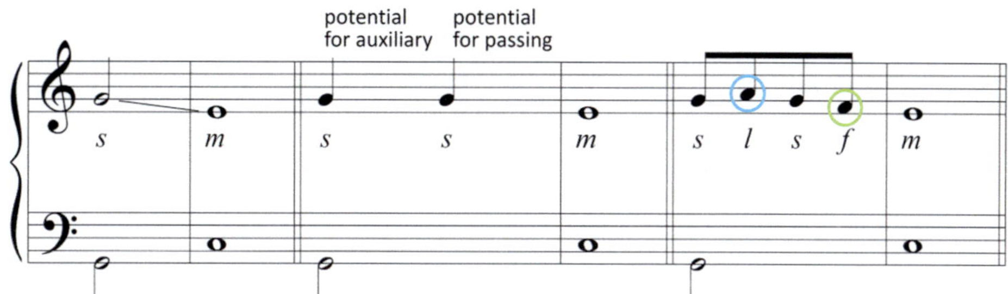

Listen to Audio 4.9 to hear all previous examples.

This is an example in compound time. First a framework melody is created above the bass line.

Now decoration is added using a mixture of passing and auxiliary notes.

Listen to Audio 4.10 comparing both versions.

Exercise 4.6

Melodic frameworks are already given above each bass line. Rewrite, adding auxiliary or passing notes as appropriate.

(a) 

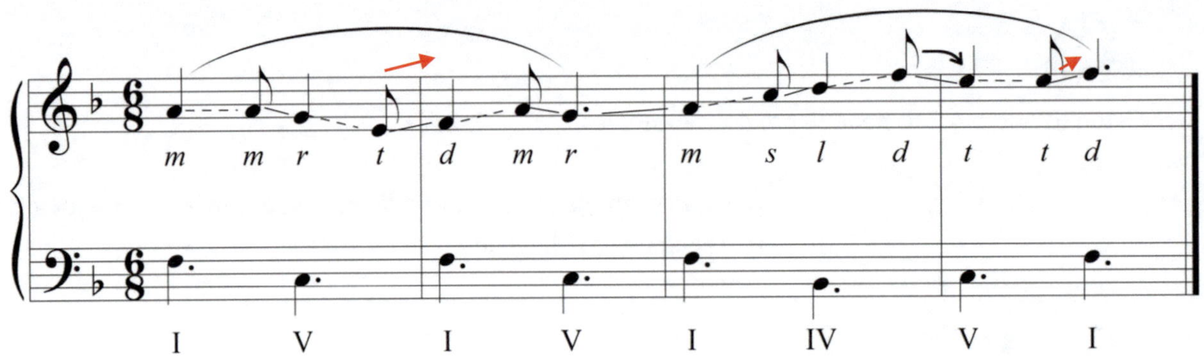

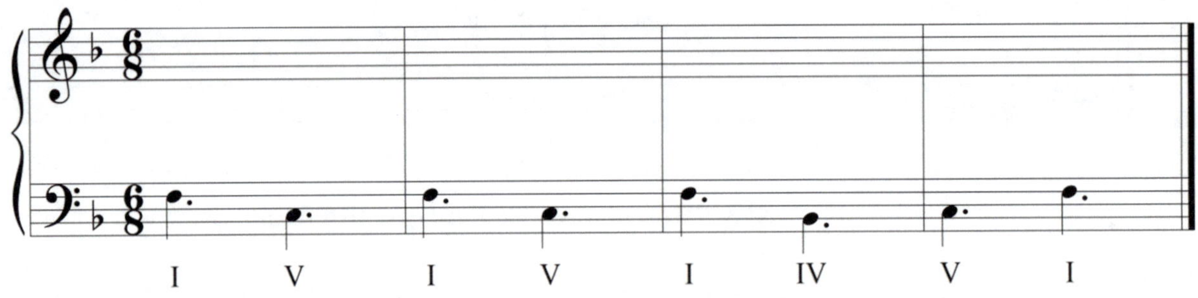

(b)

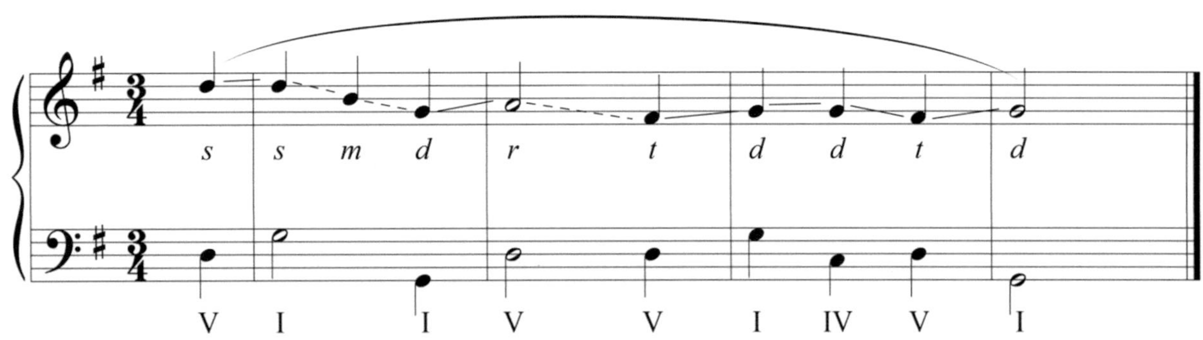

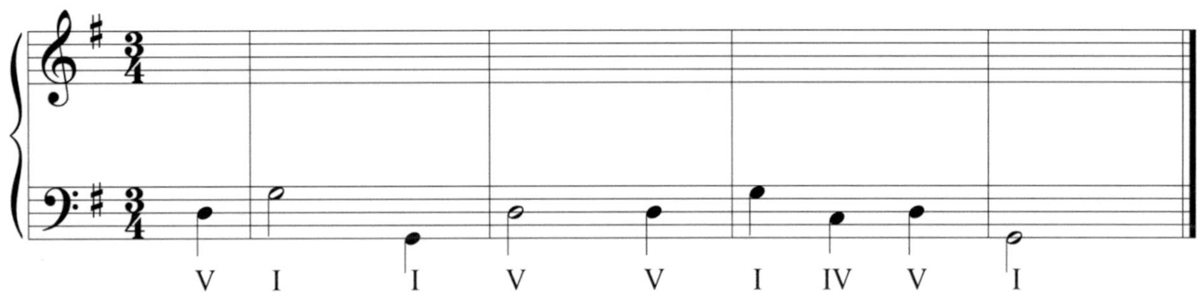

Auxiliary Notes in the Minor Key

As with passing notes, auxiliary notes involving the 6th and 7th notes of the scale need extra care in order to avoid the awkward interval of the augmented 2nd.

The upper auxiliary from ***f*** is ***s***

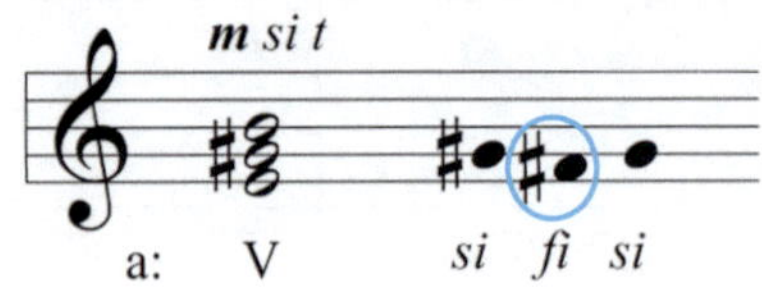

The lower auxiliary from ***si*** is ***fi***

This is an example in A minor, first showing the framework, then the decorated version.

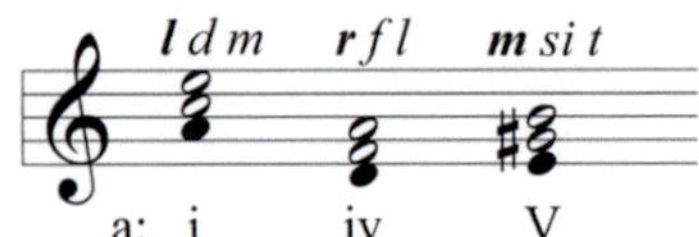

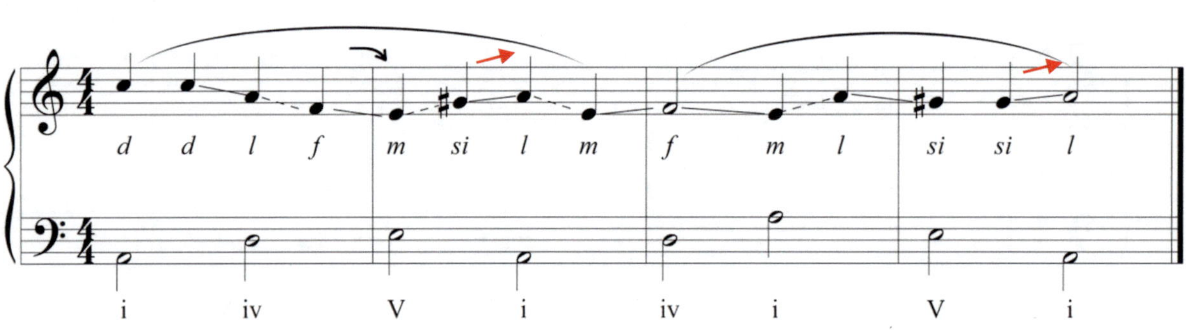

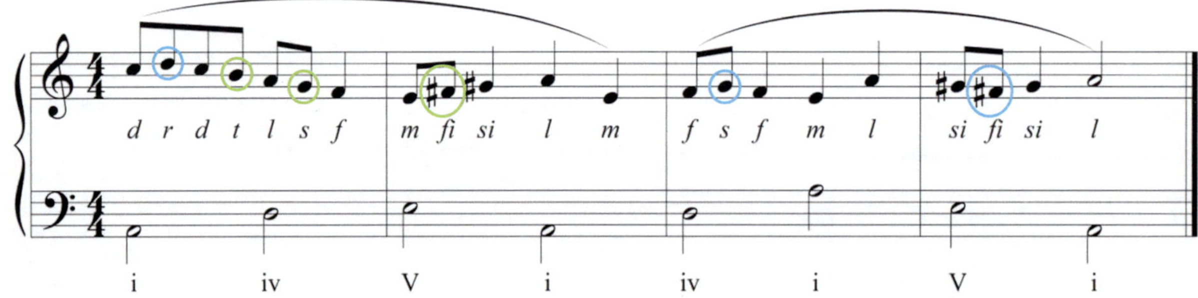

Audio 4.11

Listen to Audio 4.11, compare both versions paying particular attention to ***s*** and ***fi*** as auxiliary notes.

Before this final group of exercises, let us summarise the guidelines.

Checklist ✓

- Make a chord plan and add roman numerals below the given bass
- Plot in a melodic framework, recognising occasions where smooth movement is necessary and freedom of movement is possible
- Include solfa and sing as you write
- Remember the downward melodic movement at the **IV – V** progression and the upward melodic movement when dealing with the leading note to the tonic
- Use decoration to enhance the melodic and rhythmic interest
- Take special care in the minor key when the 6th and 7th notes are involved as decoration

Exercise 4.7

Write musically shaped soprano lines above each of the given bass lines. Decorate with a mixture of passing and auxiliary notes.

(a)

(b)

D: I IV V

I IV I V V I IV V I

(c)

g: i iv V

i i V i iv iv V i iv V i i

(d)

A: I IV V

V I I IV I I V I IV V I

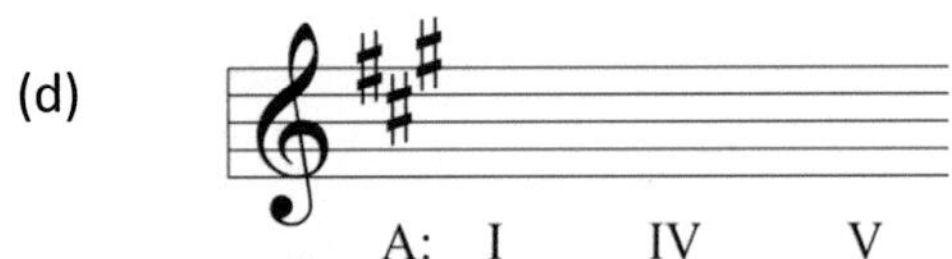

CHAPTER 5

HARMONISING MELODIES

At present **I, IV** and **V** will be used when harmonising a given melody. There are several points to be considered.

1. Which chords to use?
2. How often to change chords?
3. Where to place the chord changes?

Audio 5.1

Begin by listening to Audio 5.1. Sing along with the melody and notice that the obvious passing and auxiliary notes are highlighted.

Next write a chord plan and decide the cadence chords at the end of each phrase. Remember, that at present, the root of the chord will always be in the bass part.

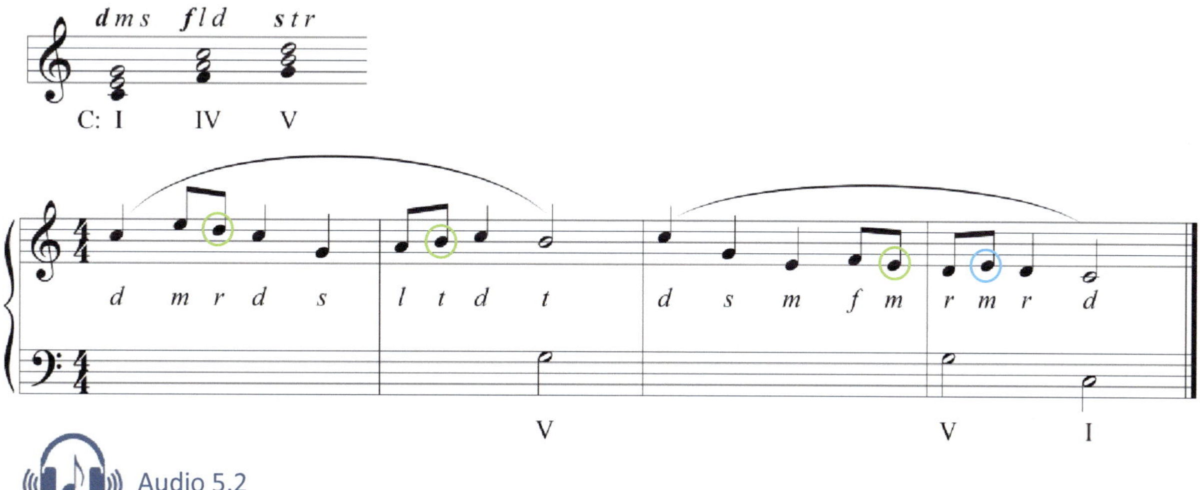

Audio 5.2

As you listen to the above example, notice that the first phrase ends with an imperfect cadence resting on **V** and the final phrase has a perfect cadence **V – I**.

Now, back to the beginning.

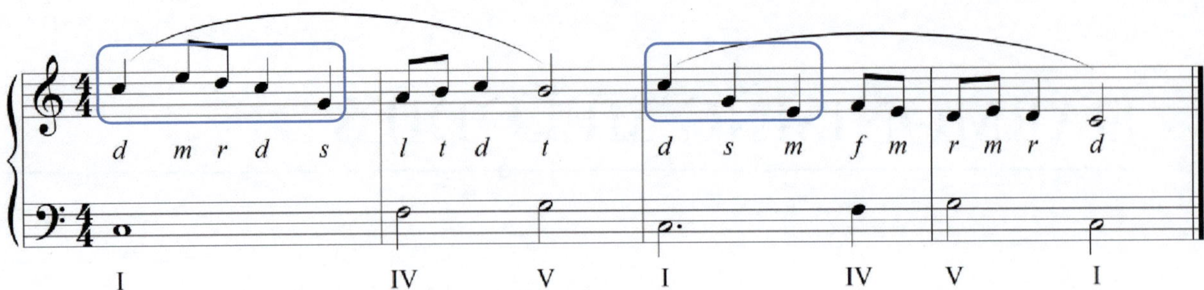

- Arpeggio shapes are often a clue as to the best chord choice. They are highlighted here in bars 1 and 3. The melody in bar 1 uses the tonic arpeggio so chord **I** is the obvious choice. Bar 3 is also based on the tonic arpeggio, again indicating chord **I**.

- To mark the natural accent of the music, chords generally change when moving over a bar line. In bar 2, ***l*** and ***d*** can both be harmonised as chord **IV**, giving the expected change over the bar line and also creating the imperfect cadence as it moves to **V**.

- The melody in bar 3 again has the tonic arpeggio, so chord **I** can harmonise the first 3 beats. Chord **IV** can harmonise ***f*** on beat 4 and lead nicely into the final cadence.

Listen to Audio 5.3 to hear the melody with the complete bass added.

Now consider our original questions.

1. Which chords to use?

   As well as choosing chords which will match certain melody notes, it is equally important to create a sequence of chords which makes musical sense. Imagine you are writing a sentence in English: you can choose appropriate words to build the sentence in a meaningful way, rather than just picking words at random from a dictionary. In musical terms, our chord choices must relate to one another to create logical harmonic progressions. Chords **I, IV** and **V** work well together in any combination. The cadential progressions covered so far can also be used freely within the phrase. They are called cadences only when they occur at the end of a phrase.

2. How often to change chords?

   Generally speaking, a lively, busy melody will need fewer chord changes, whereas a slow, lyrical melody will need more changes.

3. Where to place the chord changes?

   The most important chord change should correspond with the first beat of each bar, and other changes should follow the natural division of the time signature.

Special case!

The same chord may end one phrase and begin a new phrase even with a bar line in between, because there is a break in the musical sense.

Begin by listening to Audio 5.4 to hear the following melody in the key of A minor. Sing along with the solfa. The passing and auxiliary notes are already highlighted.

Now write a chord plan and decide the cadence chords.

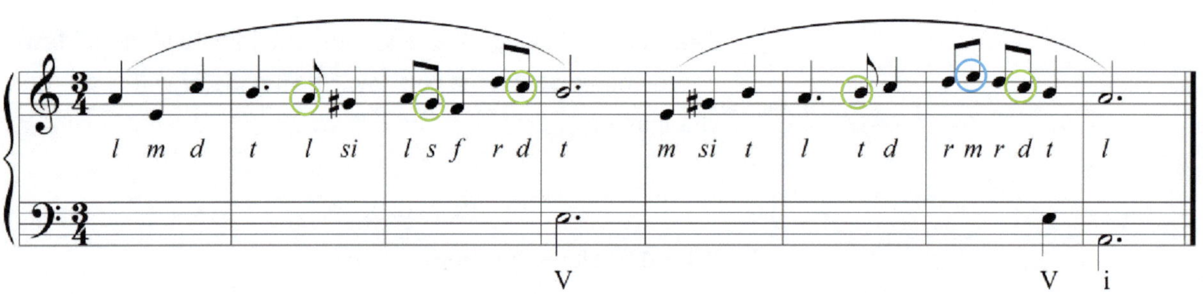

Notice in several bars, the arpeggio shaping which will suggest the most appropriate chords at these points.

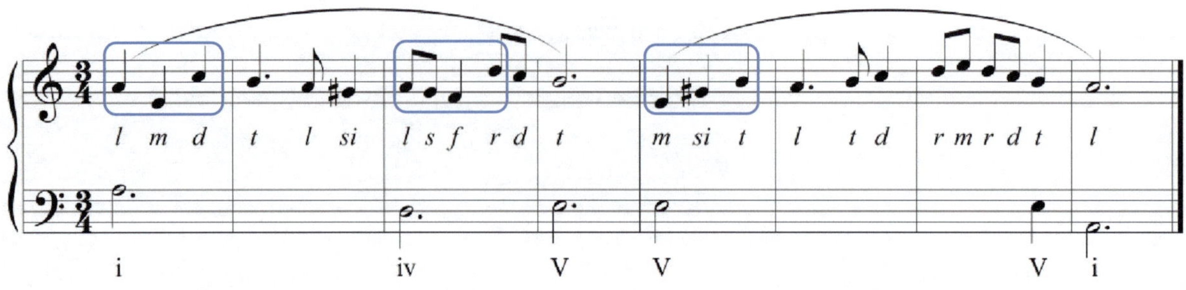

To complete the harmonisation

- The ***t*** and ***si*** in bar 2 are part of chord **V**
- The ***l*** and ***d*** in bar 6 are part of chord **I**
- The ***r*** in bar 7 is part of chord **IV**

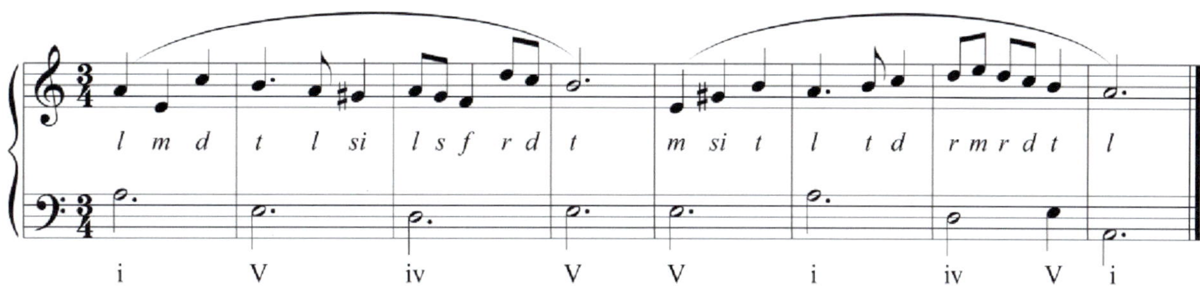

 Audio 5.5

Listen to Audio 5.5 to hear the completed bass line. Notice that the chords generally change over the bar line. The exception is between the two phrases.

 Audio 5.6

Listen to Audio 5.6 to hear another worked example in A minor. Study the points below.

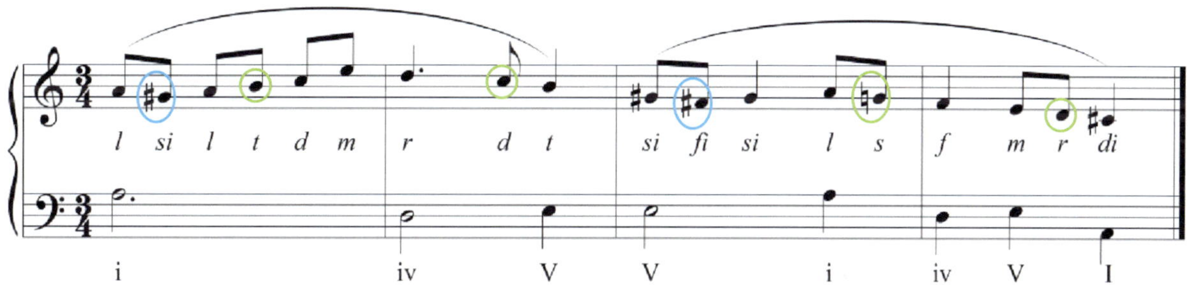

- Notice the increase in the rate of chord change as we approach the final cadence – this has the effect of driving the music forward to a strong conclusion.
- Did you notice the bright sound at the end? This is called a Tierce de Picardie (Picardy 3rd). The 3rd of chord **I** is raised a semitone creating a major sound. This is used frequently at the **end** of pieces in the minor key.

Exercise 5.1

Sing each of the given soprano melodies. Choose chords to harmonise by writing in the bass part. Solfa, arpeggio shapes and decoration have been highlighted to help you. Remember to form a cadence at the end of each phrase.

(a)

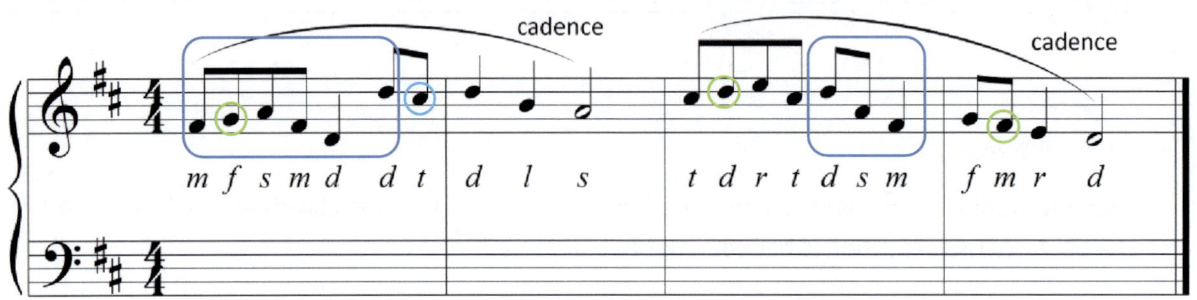

Numerals ____________________

(b)

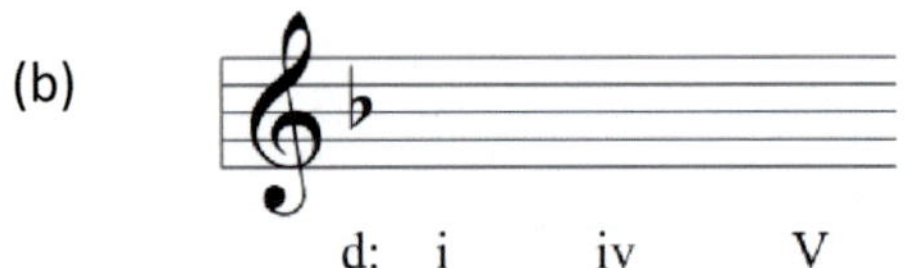

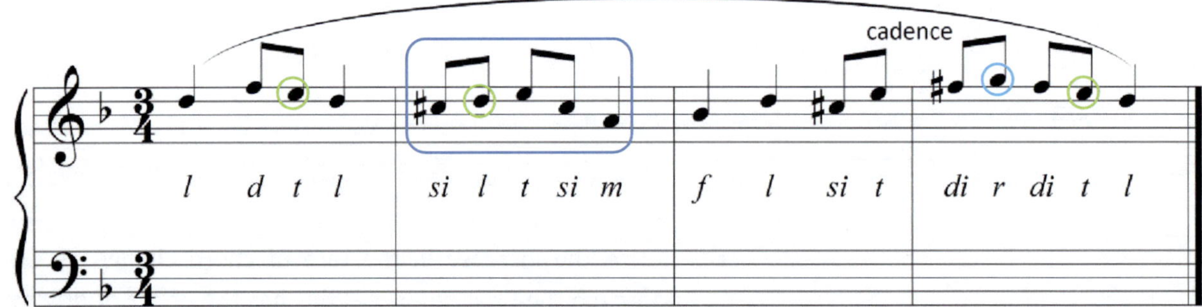

Numerals ____________________

(c)

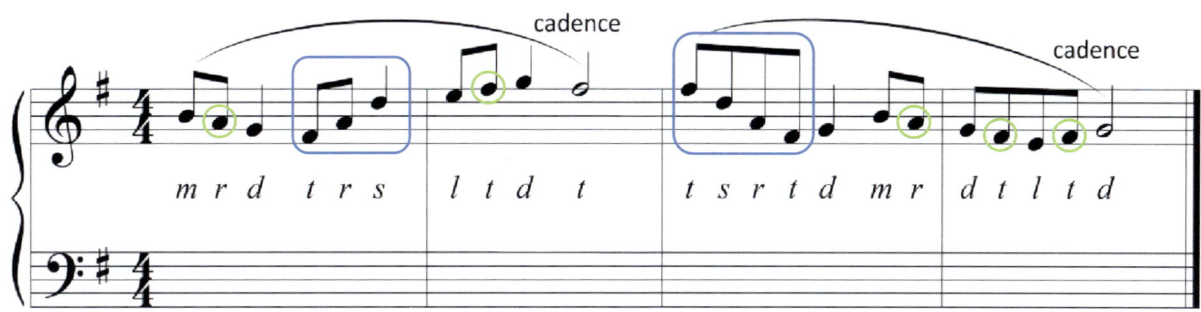

Numerals ____

(d)

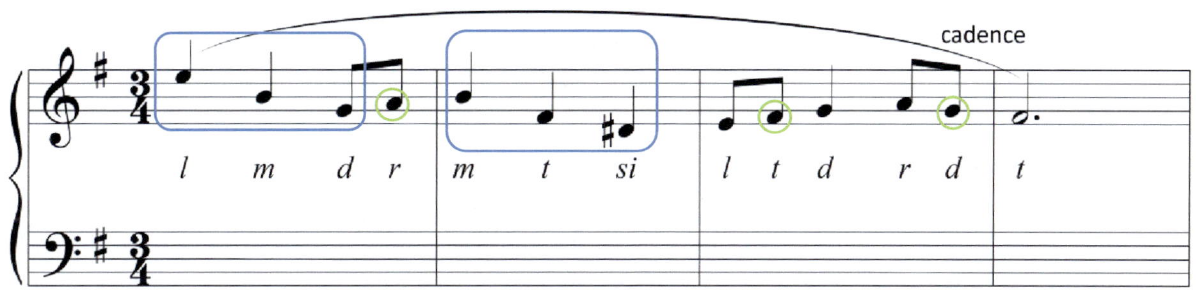

Numerals ____

____

Harmonising in $\frac{6}{8}$

The harmonic rhythm in compound time is likely to be:

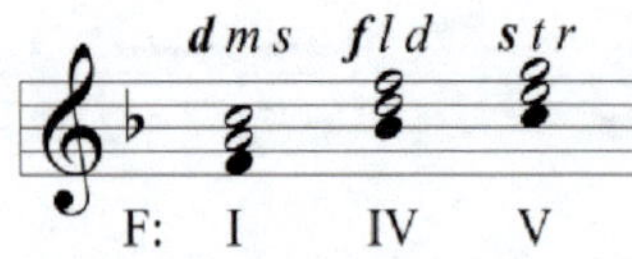

Study the worked example in F major noting the points made below.

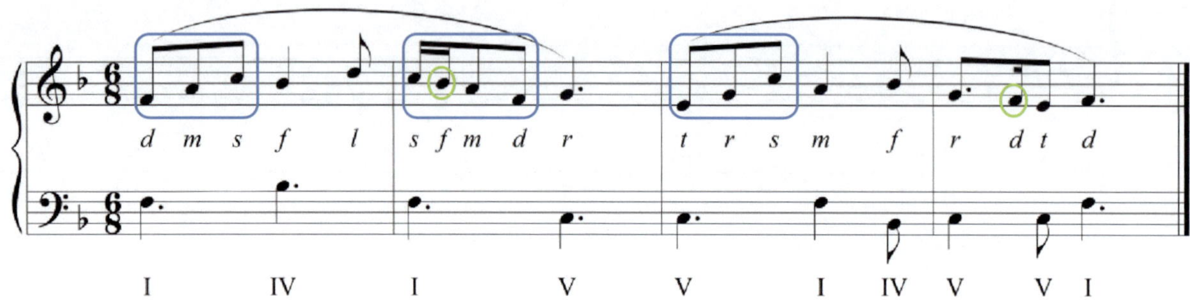

- Notice the highlighted arpeggio shapes
- The rate of chord change increases towards the final cadence
- The chords change over the bar line except between the phrases

 Audio 5.7

Listen to Audio 5.7 to hear the above compound time example.

Checklist ✓

- Always begin by singing the melody – use solfa
- Circle obvious passing and auxiliary notes
- Pinpoint arpeggio shapes
- Plot in cadences
- Be aware of the accents in the music and normally change chords over the bar line to emphasise this
- Watch out for the possibility of the Tierce de Picardie in the minor key

Exercise 5.2

Add a bass to harmonise each melody following the guidelines given.

(a)

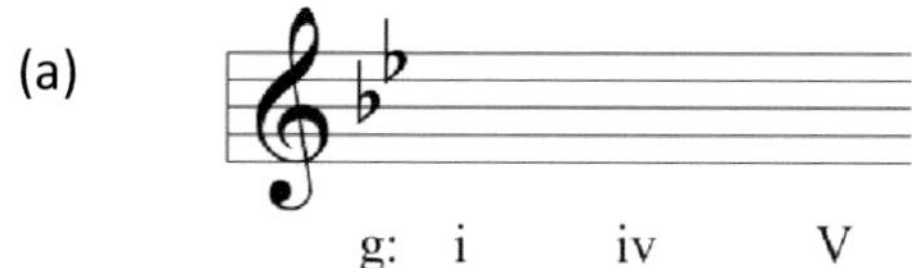

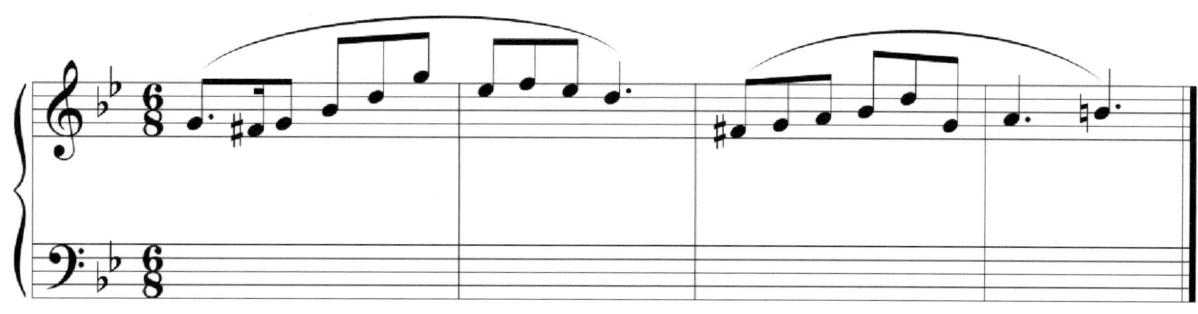

Numerals ___

(b)

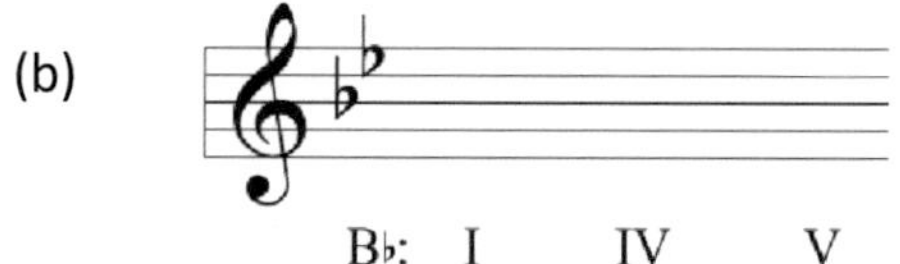

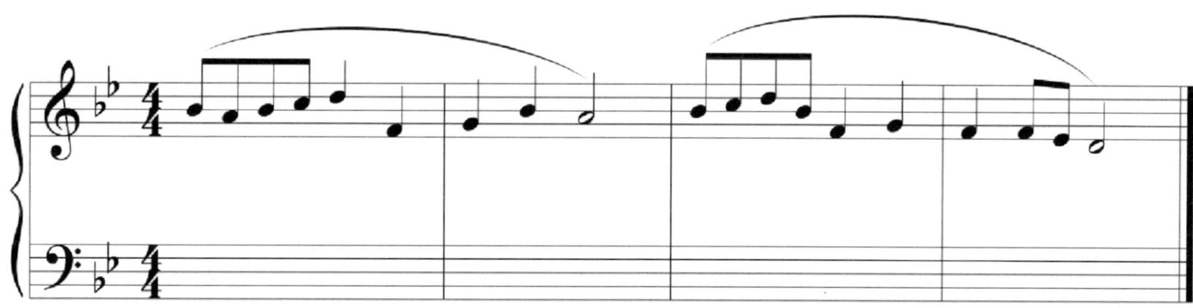

Numerals ___

(c)

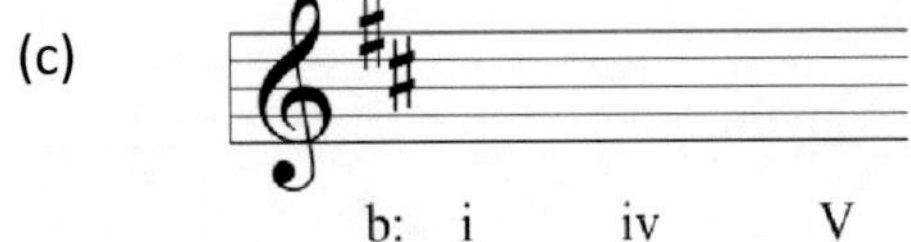

Numerals ____

(d)

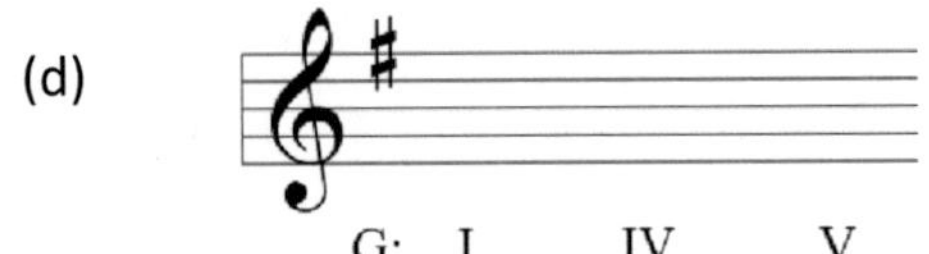

Numerals ____

(e)

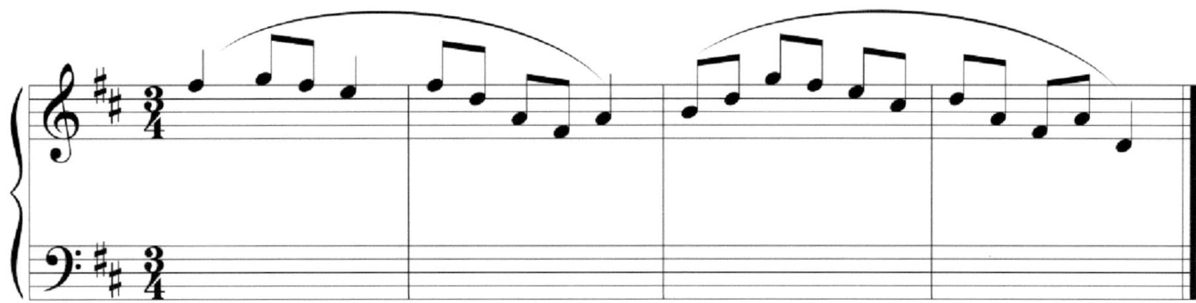

Numerals ____________________

(f)

Numerals ____________________

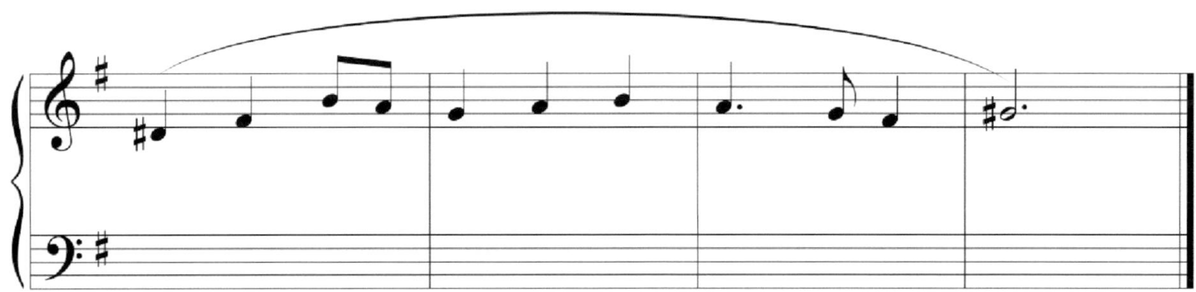

____

CHAPTER 6

ADDING INNER VOICES - Alto and Tenor

So far the focus has been on the soprano and bass lines. Now the harmony is filled in by adding parts for alto and tenor voices. The term **part-writing** refers to the movement of each vocal line. In this chapter the soprano and bass lines are given. At the outset, the soprano will be simplified to facilitate ease of movement in the inner voices.

Audio 6.1

Begin by listening to the soprano and bass of this short example.

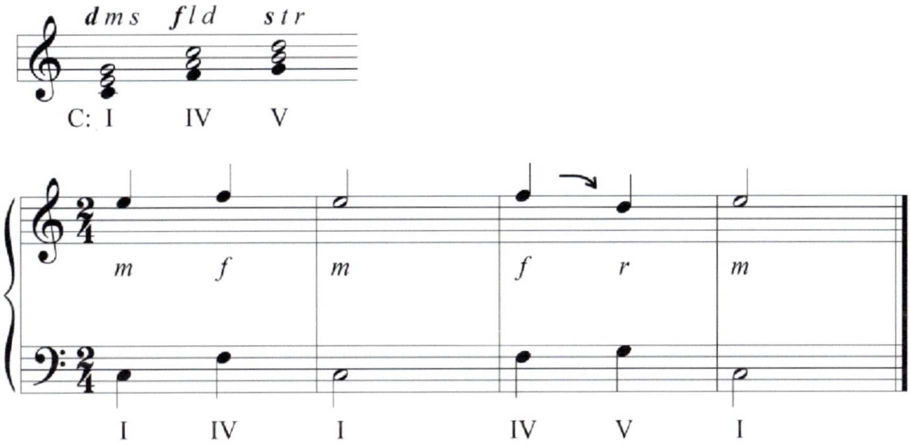

When approaching the inner parts, aim to connect all the upper voices smoothly when moving from one chord to the next chord change. This means:

- Repeating a note that is common to both chords
  or
- Moving by step either up or down
  or
- Moving a 3rd either up or down

Let us add alto and tenor parts.

- Looking along the alto line, notice how smoothly the notes connect.
- Now look along the tenor line – the same smooth connection occurs with common notes repeated in the same part.
- In bar 3, notice that **all** upper parts are falling in **IV – V**.
- In the final cadence **V – I** the leading note rises to the tonic as expected (tenor ***t* – *d***)

Listen to Audio 6.2 to hear the completed harmonisation above.

The next example works with a more active soprano line which will bring up new considerations.

Listen to Audio 6.3 to hear the given soprano and bass parts.

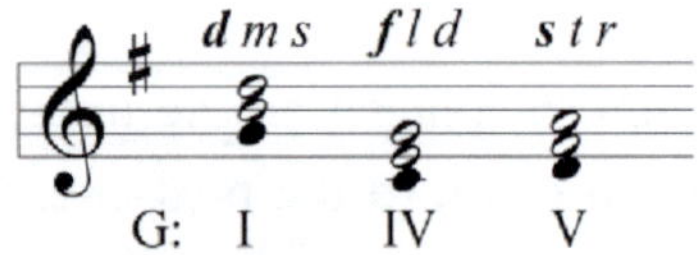

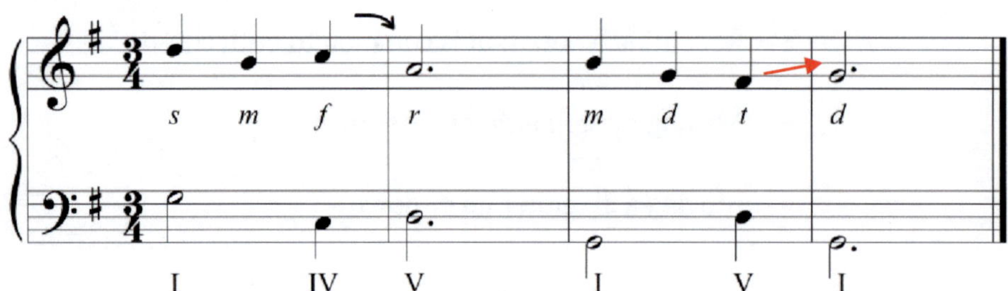

Here alto and tenor parts are added.

When the soprano moves over the same chord it is necessary to freely ***re-arrange*** the inner parts. Ensure that all notes are present on each beat and take care with doubling and spacing. This can be seen in bars 1 and 3.

Audio 6.4

Listen to Audio 6.4 to hear the basic four-part harmonisation above.

Now decoration is added to enhance the soprano line.

(A)

Audio 6.5

Listen to Audio 6.5 to hear the decorated version.

It is rare that there is only one solution when harmonising. Here the first two beats could be arranged differently as follows:

The alto is sustained.

Both alto and tenor parts move to lower pitches on beat 2.

If the second option is chosen, this will have a knock-on effect on the part-writing which follows.

Listen to Audio 6.6 where you hear example B. Compare it with example A in Audio 6.5. Example A has a lighter effect (with alto and tenor on higher pitches) whereas example B has a slightly rounder quality (with alto and tenor on lower pitches).

This is an example in the minor key with a flowing soprano line.

Listen to Audio 6.7 to hear the given soprano and bass parts.

As we consider adding alto and tenor lines there are a few points to be noted:

- The re-arranging necessary at ┌- - - - - ┐
- The downward movement needed at **IV – V**
- Smooth connection at all chord changes

 Audio 6.8

Now listen to Audio 6.8 to hear the completed harmonisation. Pay particular attention to the smooth movement for SAT at all chord changes.

Exercise 6.1

Study the given soprano and bass parts, then add alto and tenor parts following the guidelines given.

(a)

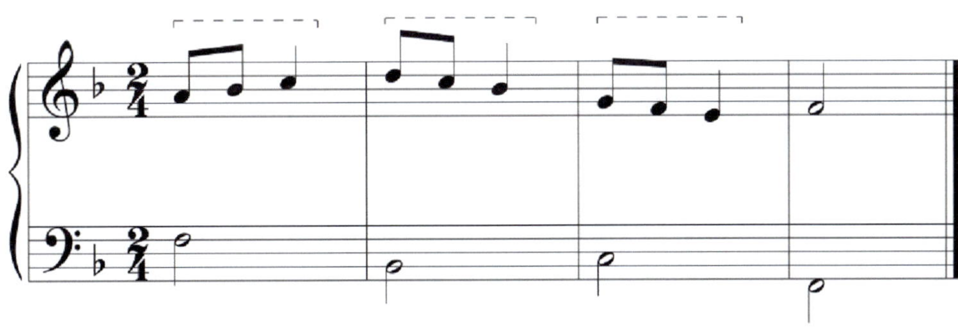

Numerals ____________________

(b)

Numerals____

(c)

Numerals____

(d)

Numerals____

Listen to Audio 6.9 to hear the next worked example. Then study the points which follow.

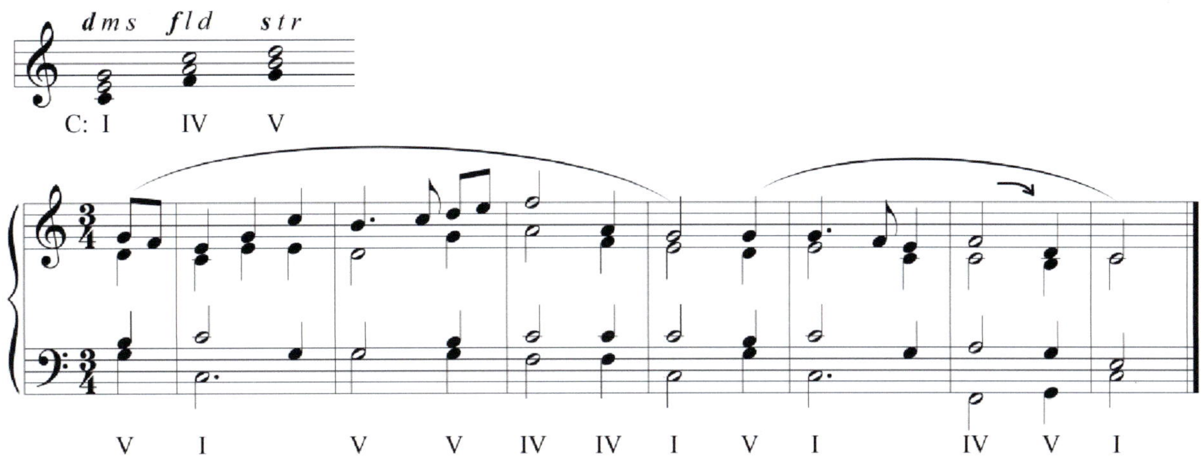

Upbeat: If a melody begins with an upbeat it may be left unharmonised. However, if a chord is chosen it is likely to be chord **V**.

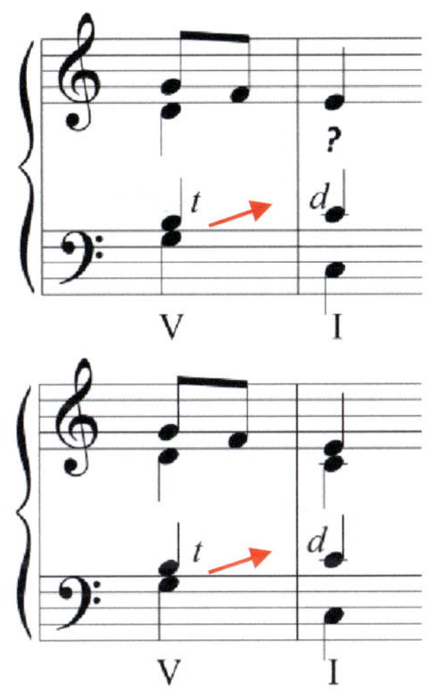

Tripled root: In the first pair of chords the leading note rises to the tonic as expected (***t - d***). There is a question as to the movement in the alto – it must connect smoothly, so it also moves to the tonic (***r – d***). The result is ***three roots in chord I and no 5th.***

The last pair of chords in the final cadence is also arranged in this way.

The **3rd** should never be omitted, it is this note that gives a chord its major or minor quality.

V – IV (bar 2 – 3): This is **IV – V** in reverse! As the bass falls a step all the other parts rise.

An unwelcome passing note (bar 6): Although there is an opportunity to include a passing note in the soprano, by doing so, consecutive 5^{ths} (parallel 5^{ths}) would be formed with the tenor line and therefore it is best left out.

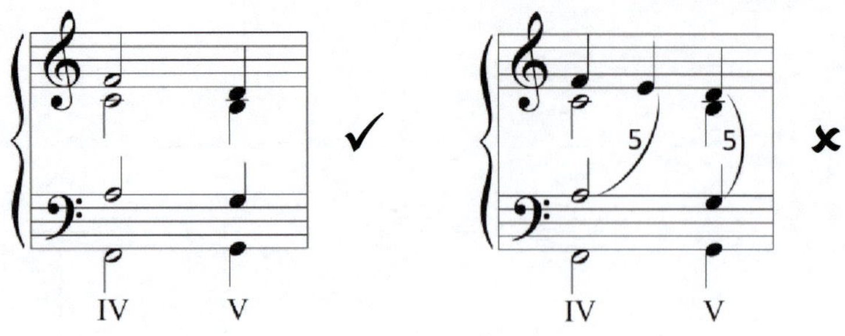

Grammatical Point

Here the soprano and bass parts are given to which the alto and tenor parts are to be added.

This solution is problematic because in the second chord the tenor part drops below the previous bass note.

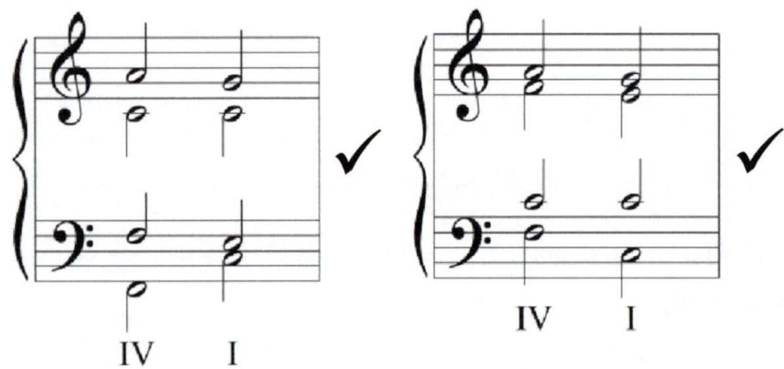

To solve the difficulty, create more space between the tenor and bass parts by either dropping the bass an octave or swapping the alto and tenor parts.

This problematic crossing/overlapping of parts should be avoided. It tends to occur where a unison is involved – take care!

Always think of branching out in both directions following a unison.

However, in this arrangement there is no crossing/overlapping of parts since the tenor in the second chord sits at the **same pitch** as the previous bass part.

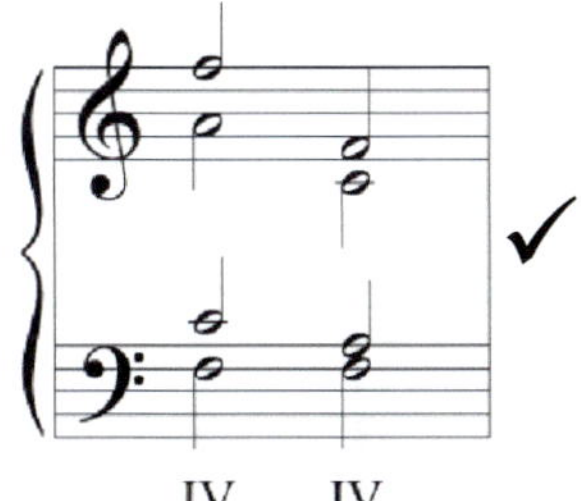

Furthermore, if there is **no chord change** and the harmony remains the same, the crossing/overlapping of parts is not problematic as we are simply re-arranging/re-organising the **same** group of sounds.

Checklist✓

- Sing the soprano line using solfa
- Add the roman numerals below the bass
- Connect smoothly at all chord changes – look for notes in common
- Re-arrange freely when a chord is sustained or repeated
- Normally all the chord notes should be present – occasionally the 5th may be left out and the root tripled
- Never omit the 3rd
- **IV – V** SAT ↘
- **V – IV** SAT ↗

Exercise 6.2

Complete the following harmonisations by adding alto and tenor parts. Bear in mind the various points highlighted previously.

(a)

Numerals ____

(b)

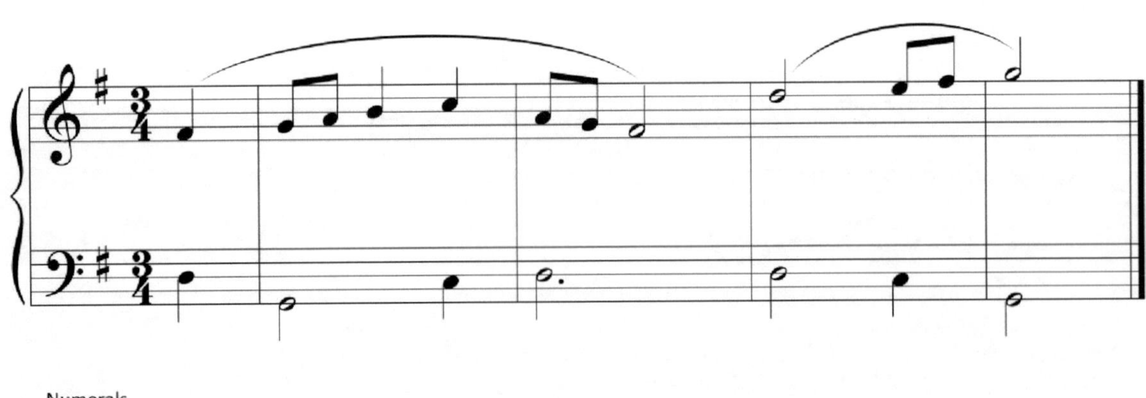

Numerals ____

(c)

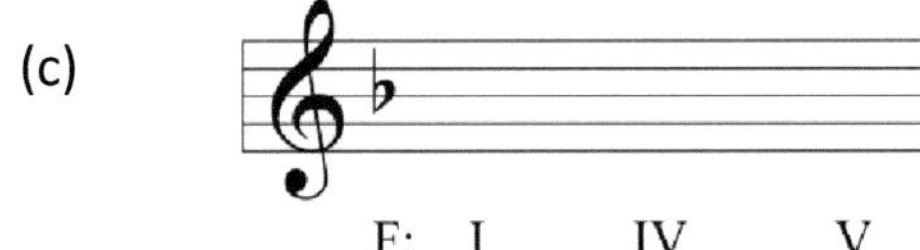

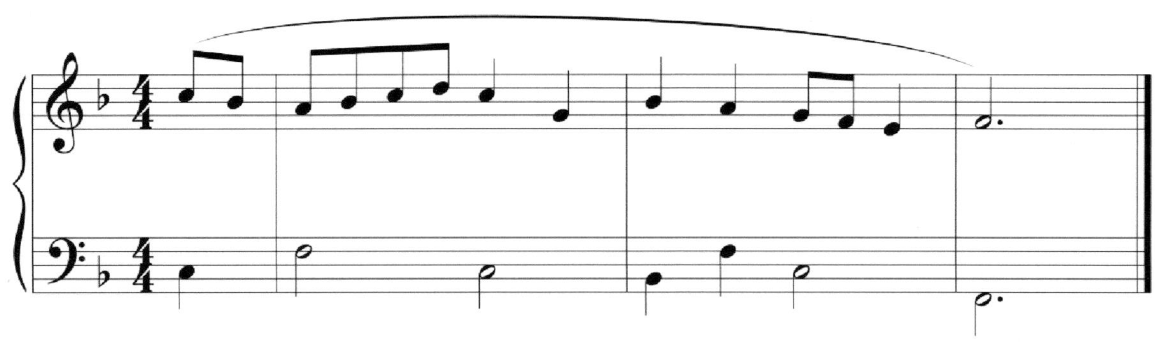

Numerals____

(d)

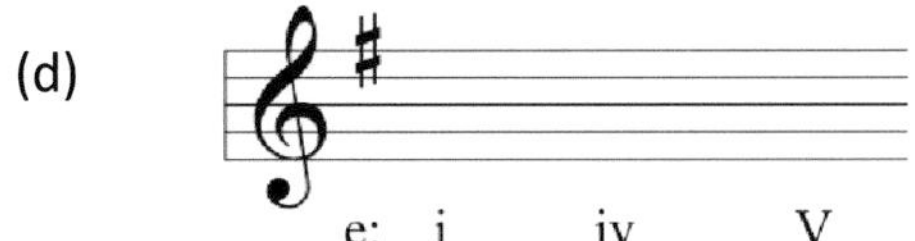

Numerals____

(e)

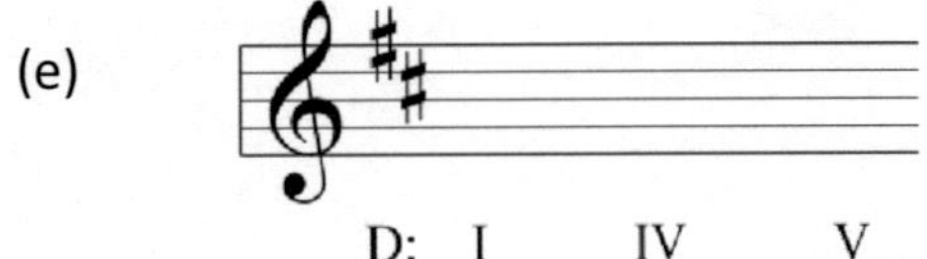

Numerals____

(f)

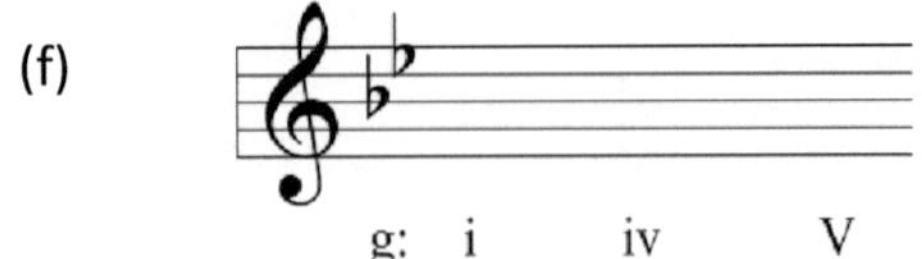

Numerals____

Analysis

So far chords have been used in relation to a vocal setting. However, in the following analysis exercises you will encounter this harmonic knowledge in a variety of textures; piano music and string quartet. You will come across harmonic vocabulary that you have not yet studied. However, we have highlighted specific chords relating to the harmonic content covered in the preceding chapters. The analysis is linked to aural/visual observation where you will hear the harmonic material in original works. The extracts are taken from Baroque, Classical and early Romantic literature.

The texture and layout of vocal music varies from that of instrumental music. In the latter, it is common to find chords arranged for any number of parts by duplicating notes at different pitches. You may encounter the following textures as highlighted below.

You are already familiar with this type of layout for voices – chord **I**.

This is also chord **I** arranged for piano. The harmony occupies a minim beat. The bass sustains the root while the right hand has arpeggio shaping using the notes of the chord in a semiquaver rhythm.

This is chord **I** followed by chord **V** in minim values. The bass indicates the position of the harmony while the right hand pitches spell out the chord notes. The right hand uses a typical piano texture i.e. a wide arpeggiated spread moving from bass through to high treble.

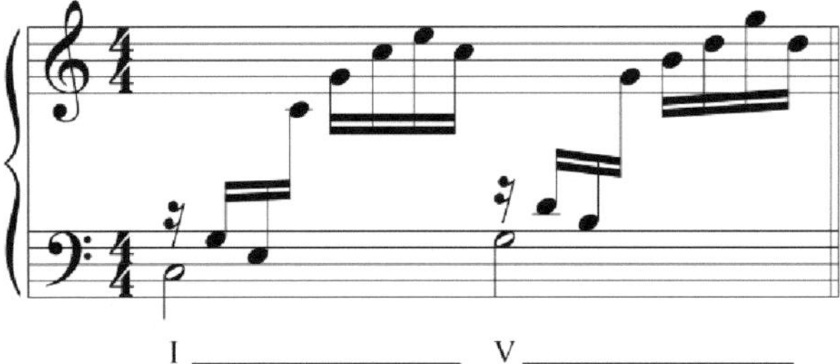

Another common texture is melody (RH) and accompaniment (LH). In this example the harmony changes every bar as follows: **I – V – I**. This style of accompanying bass line principally has the main note of the chord on the strong beat followed by remaining notes of the chord on subsequent weak beats. Most importantly, it is the lowest sounding note which determines the position of the chord. The right hand adds melodic interest using chord notes only in bars 1 and 2, while bar 3 introduces auxiliary and passing notes.

String quartet is normally presented in open score with the viola written in the alto clef. In the early stages it may be helpful to rewrite the music in short score using treble and bass only, for ease of reading. Again, the lowest sound determines the position of the chord.

In each of the following extracts you are asked to identify highlighted harmony which uses chords **I, IV** and **V** in root position. You will be asked to write the roman numerals on the score below each highlighted area. You may listen to each audio extract as often as you wish.

Audio 6.10

The following extract is the opening section of an Allegro from the Suite in G major, HWV 441 by Handel. It contains descending arpeggio shapes based on chords **I, IV** and **V**. Write the roman numerals below the highlighted areas on the score.

Allegro Handel

mp mf

dim. p

This is the opening of a Waltz in A minor Op. 124, No. 4 by Schumann.

a) Identify using roman numerals the chords in the highlighted areas.

b) Name the type of cadence formed at the end of the extract: _______________

The following is an extract from Mozart's Piano Sonata in F major K 280. The Adagio is the 2nd movement and is in the key of F minor.

a) Indicate using roman numerals, the chords in bars 1, 3 and 8.

b) Identify the circled notes as either passing or auxiliary.

Bar 1 _________________ Bar 3 __________________

This lively piece 'Knight Rupert' Op. 68, No. 12 by Schumann is in the key of A minor.

a) Identify using roman numerals the chords used in the highlighted areas.
b) Name the type of cadence in each case.

Bar 4 ______________ Bar 8 ______________

Below is an extract from the 1st movement of Clementi's Sonatina in D major, Op. 36, No. 6.

a) Identify the chords in the highlighted areas using roman numerals.
b) Name the type of cadence at the end of the extract:__________________

Below are two extracts from Ecossaises in B minor, D 783 by Schubert. These sections of the music are in the key of D major.

a) In both A and B identify using roman numerals the highlighted chords.

b) Name the cadence which occurs at the end of each extract:

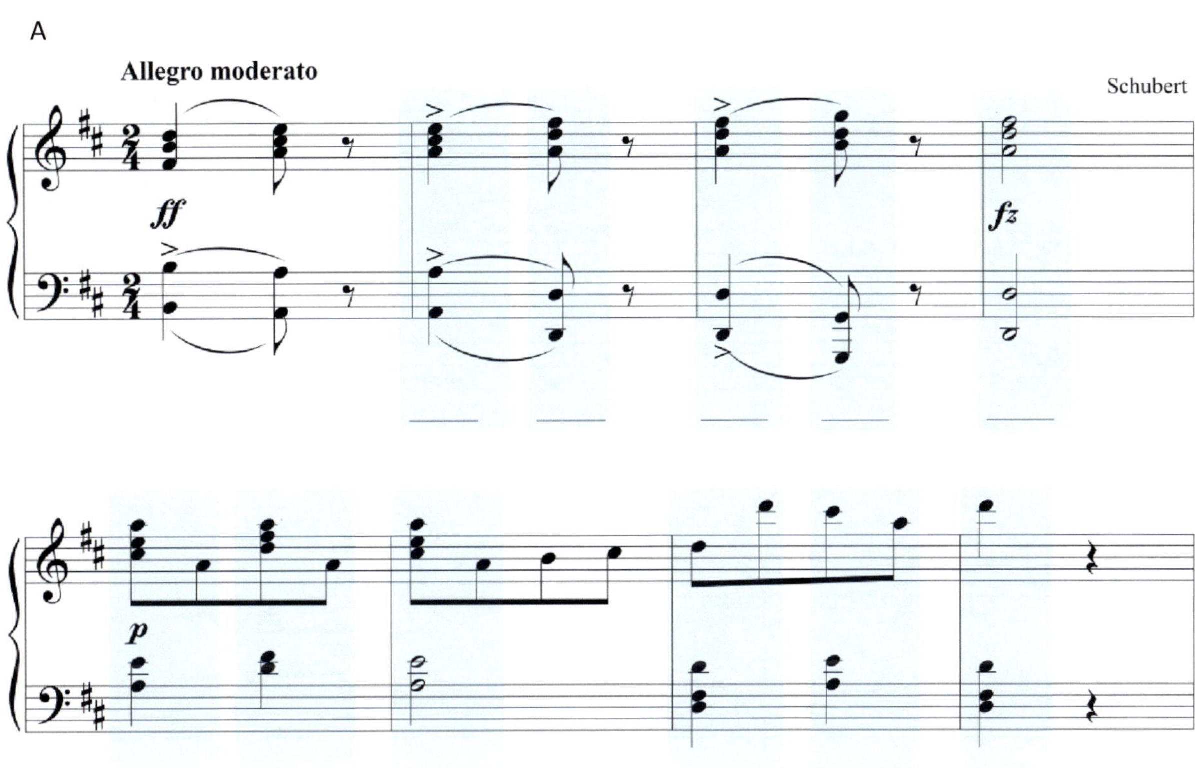

B

Audio 6.16

The following extract is from the 1st movement of Haydn's String Quartet in A major Op. 2, No. 1.

a) Identify using roman numerals the chords in the highlighted areas.

b) Name the cadence which occurs at the end of the extract:_______________

Allegro

Haydn

The extract below is from the 2nd movement of Haydn's String Quartet in A major Op. 2, No. 1.

a) Identify using roman numerals the chords in the highlighted areas.
b) Name the cadence which occurs at the end of the extract:_______________

Menuet

Haydn

CHAPTER 7

THE DOMINANT SEVENTH - V_7

Listen to Audio 7.1. You will hear an extract from the familiar barbershop song, *'Sweet and Lovely'* by Norman Starks. The harmonised extract stops on a familiar rich sounding chord – this is called the dominant seventh.

To produce **V_7** simply add another 3rd on top of the chord.

As there are four notes in the chord, no doubling is required at present. As in any root position chord, the root must be in the bass while the remaining three notes are interchangeable in the upper parts.

Listen to Audio 7.2 to hear the various arrangements of the dominant 7th chord in C major.

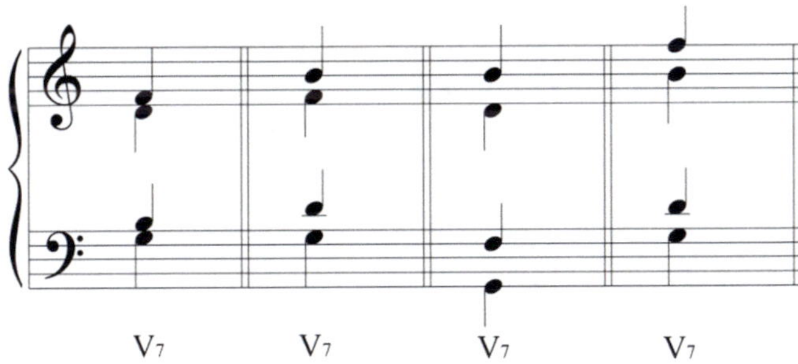

Adding the 7th produces a certain tension in the chord which needs to resolve. There are two dissonant notes which need resolution:

t rises to ***d:*** The leading note rises to the tonic

f falls to ***m***: The 7th of the chord falls a step

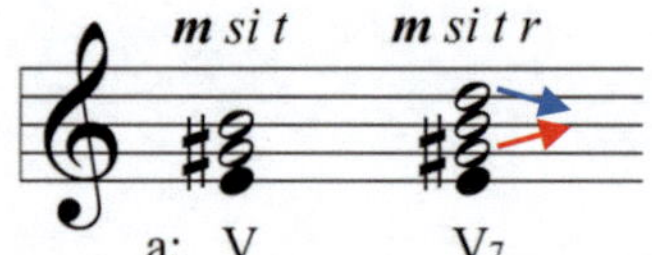

This is **V7** in the minor key.

Similarly, the resolutions are as follows:

si rises to ***l:*** The leading note rises to the tonic

r falls to ***d:*** The 7th of the chord falls a step

Furthermore, in the minor key, no doubling is required at present. The root must be in the bass while the remaining three notes are interchangeable in the upper parts.

Exercise 7.1

Add the alto and tenor parts to complete these dominant 7th chords.

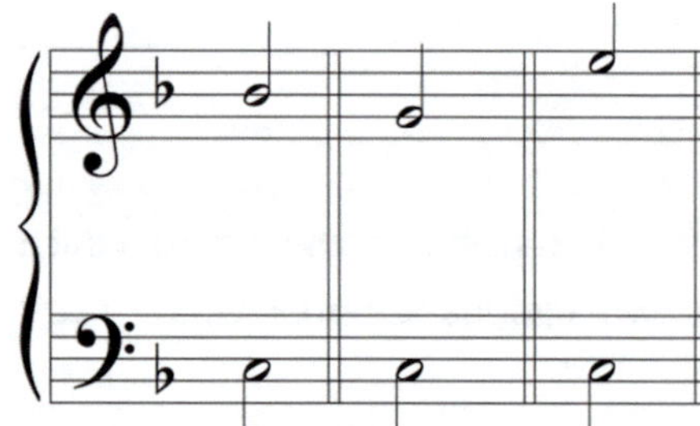

Writing a melody with V7

When chord **V** is used in the given bass we now have the option of including the 7th which may appear in the melody line. See the worked example below.

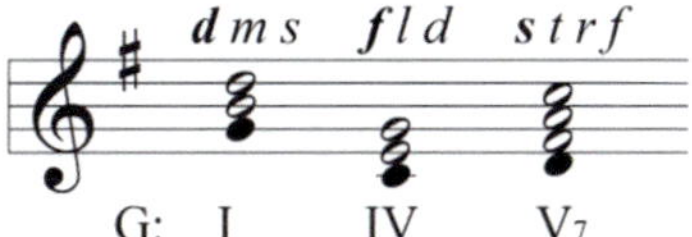

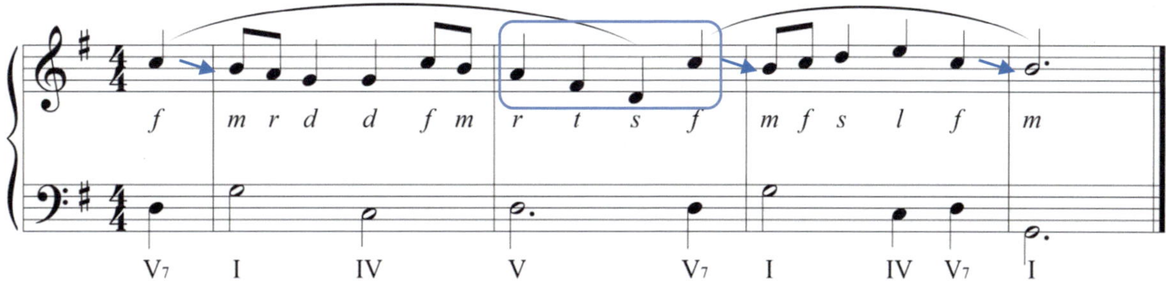

- Notice that the 7th (highlighted with the blue arrow) is included in the chord of **V** three times. It always resolves by falling a step ***f* – *m*** in the next chord.
- Bar 2 is interesting in that the use of **V7** expands the possible arpeggio shape and opens up the melodic range.

 Audio 7.3

Listen to Audio 7.3 to hear the above example.

Below is an example in the minor key. The treatment of **V7** is the same as in the major key.

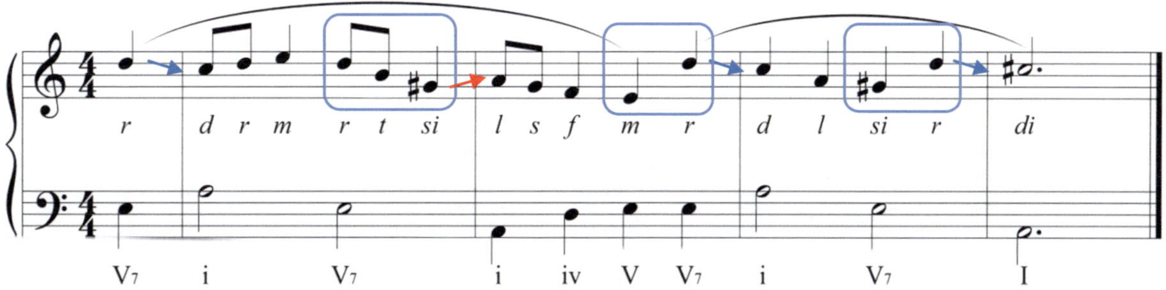

- Highlighted are three different presentations of the **V7** shape. While working **within** the **V7** chord there is freedom of movement between all its pitches, so intervals of a minor 7th and a diminished 5th may occur.
- The 7th of the chord always resolves by falling a step ***r – d*** in the next chord.

Listen to Audio 7.4 to hear the above example.

Exercise 7.2

Add a soprano line to each of the given bass lines. Look for opportunities to use the dominant 7th.

(a)

Numerals____________________________

(b)

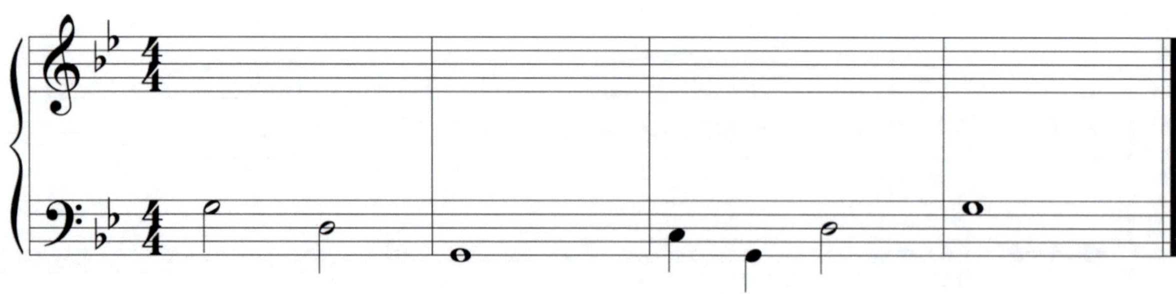

g: i iv V7

Numerals____________________________

(c)

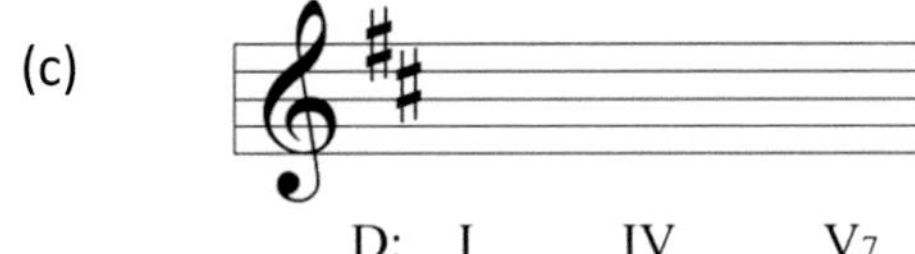

Numerals____

(d)

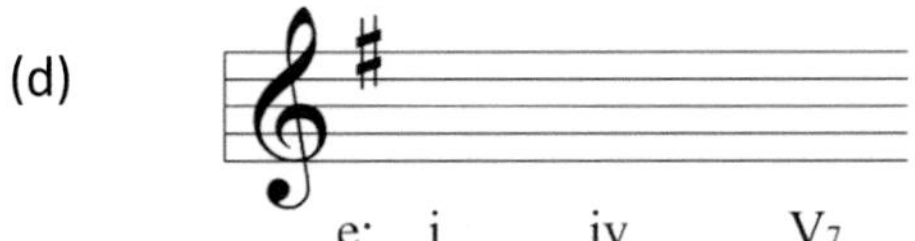

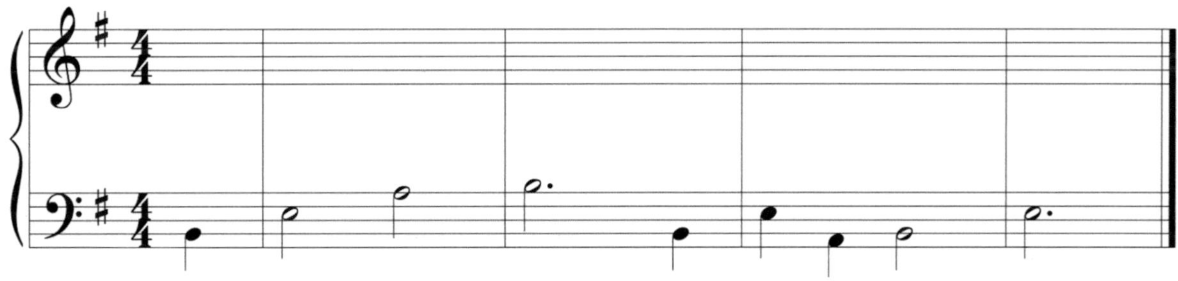

Numerals____

Harmonising a melody with V7

Two clues help you spot opportunities where **V7** can be included.

1. Various arpeggio shapes within ***s – t – r – f*** (***m – si – t – r*** minor key).
2. The melodic shape ***f – m*** (***r – d*** minor key).

This is a worked example.

- The arpeggio shapes are highlighted: bar 2 indicates **V7** while bar 5 indicates chord **I**.
- The movement ***f – m*** → suggests **V7 – I**

Listen to Audio 7.5 to hear the above example.

Exercise 7.3

Add a bass line to harmonise each melody. There are several helpful guidelines included. Don't forget to sing the melody!

(a)

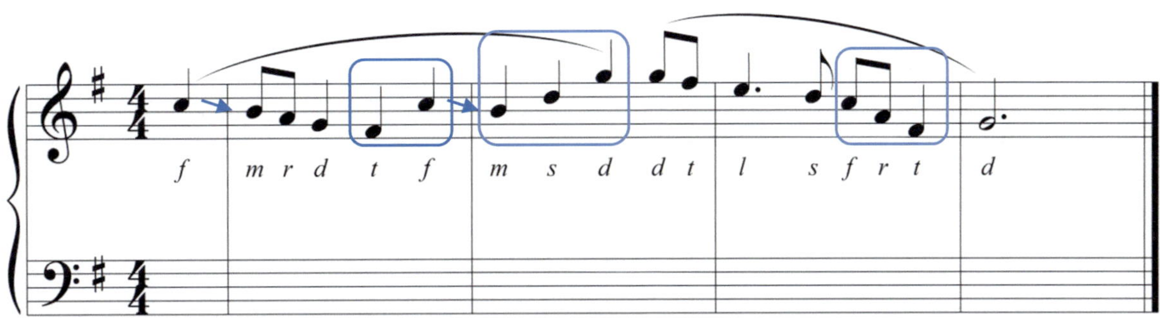

Numerals____

(b)

Numerals____

(c)

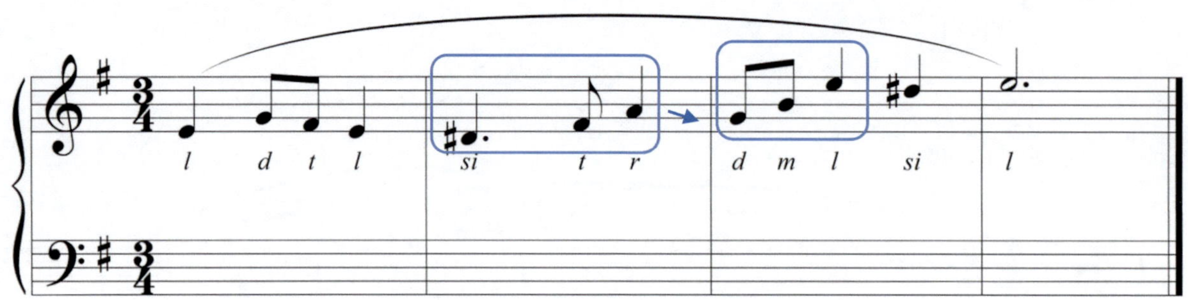

Numerals____

(d)

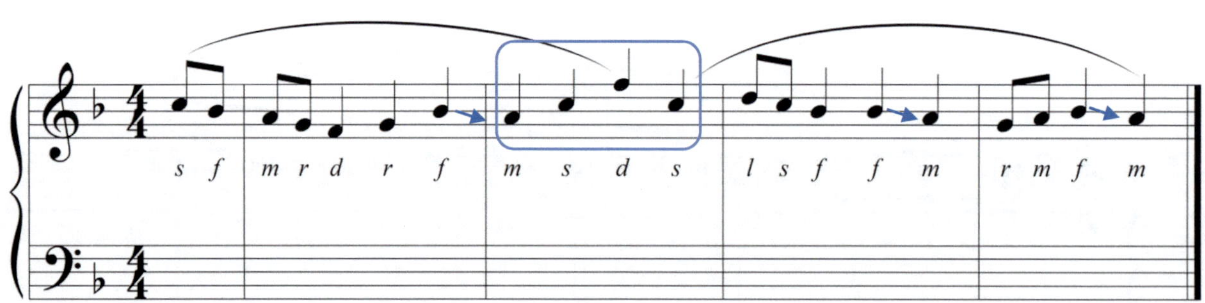

Numerals____

Adding alto and tenor parts with V_7

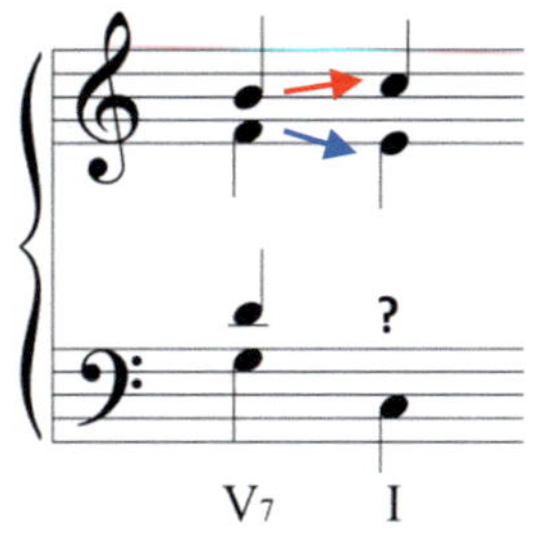

In writing **V_7 – I,** ***t*** rises to ***d*** and ***f*** falls to ***m*** as expected. There is a question about the movement of the other voice.

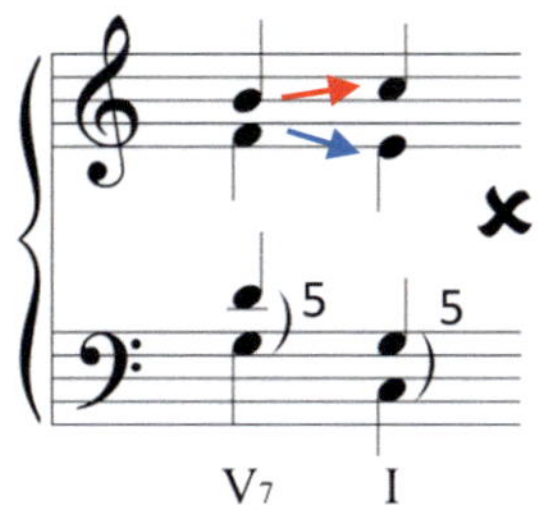

If all notes are included, the problem of consecutive 5^{ths} (parallel 5^{ths}) will arise.

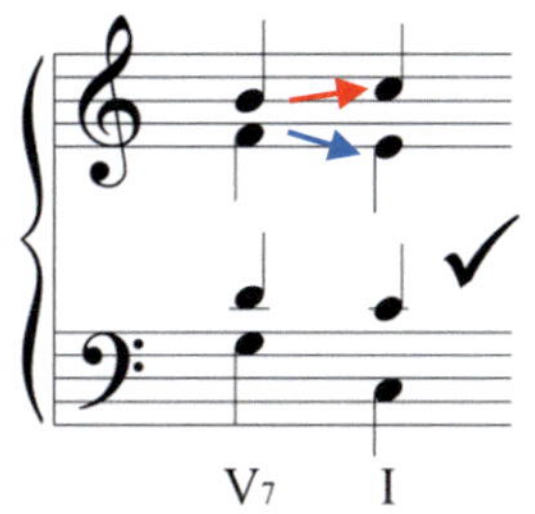

Solution 1 Leave out the 5th in chord **I** and triple the root.

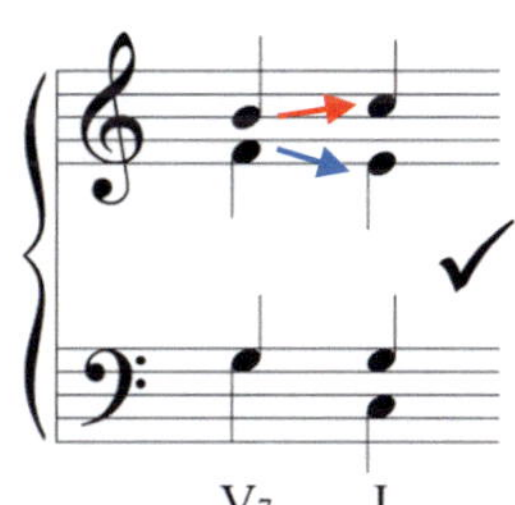

Solution 2 Alternatively, leave out the 5th in chord **V_7** and double the root. In this case all notes are present in chord **I**.

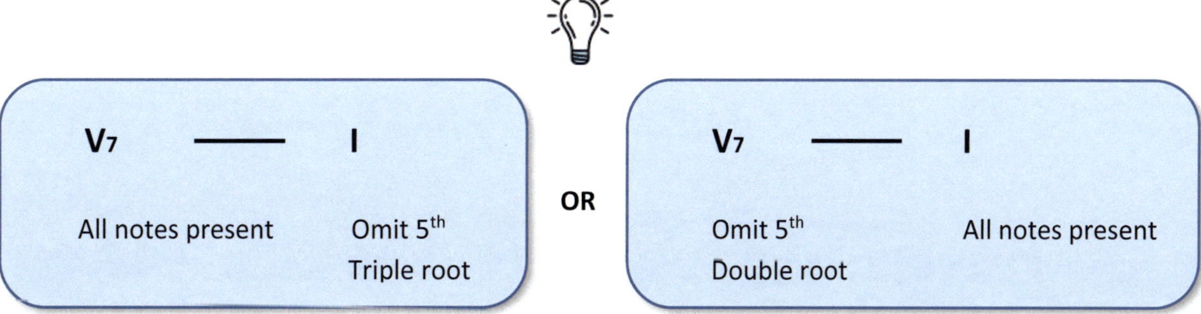

Exercise 7.4

Add alto and tenor parts to complete these progressions using **V7**.

(a)

(b)

In the next example the focus is on adding alto and tenor parts. Begin by studying the soprano and bass lines and then the full four-part harmonisation which follows.

A few points to notice...

- In the tenor part the 7th is added on the quaver upbeat, giving rhythmic interest and a sense of forward motion.
- In the soprano and alto on beats 3 and 4 (bar 1) there appears to be a problem of consecutive 5ths. However, a perfect 5th followed by a diminished 5th is acceptable.
- The 7th is not used at the imperfect cadence (bar 2) as the phrase must be self-contained, i.e. the 7th should resolve within the same phrase.
- In the final bar, the 7th is freely transferred from the soprano to the tenor while the chord remains the same. It then resolves from its final location in the tenor line.

Listen to Audio 7.6 to hear the two-part version followed by 7.7 for the full harmonisation.

Exercise 7.5

Complete each harmonisation by adding alto and tenor parts taking care to resolve **V7** correctly. Include roman numerals and solfa.

(a)

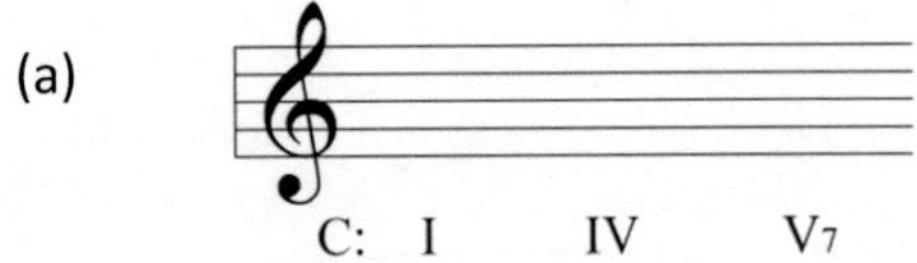

Numerals____

(b)

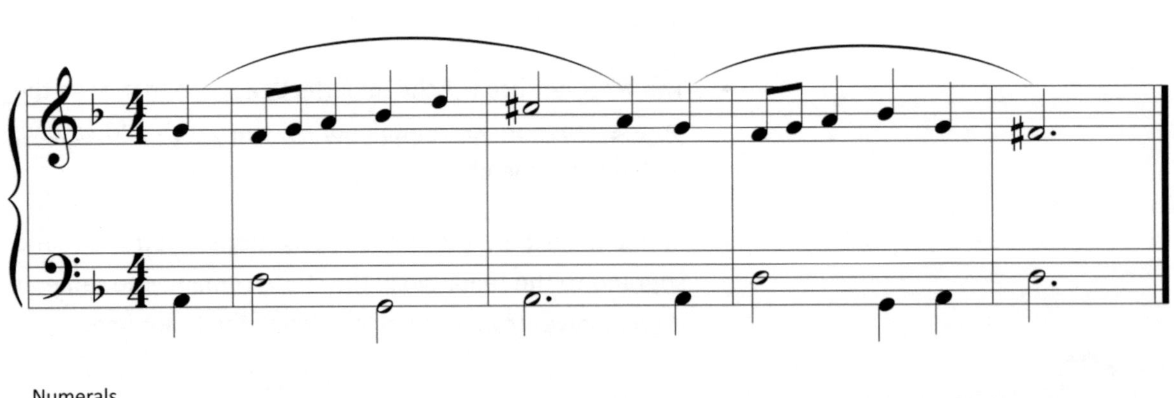

Numerals____

(c)

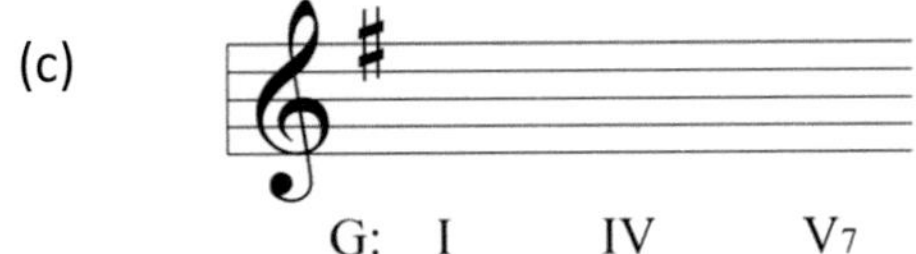

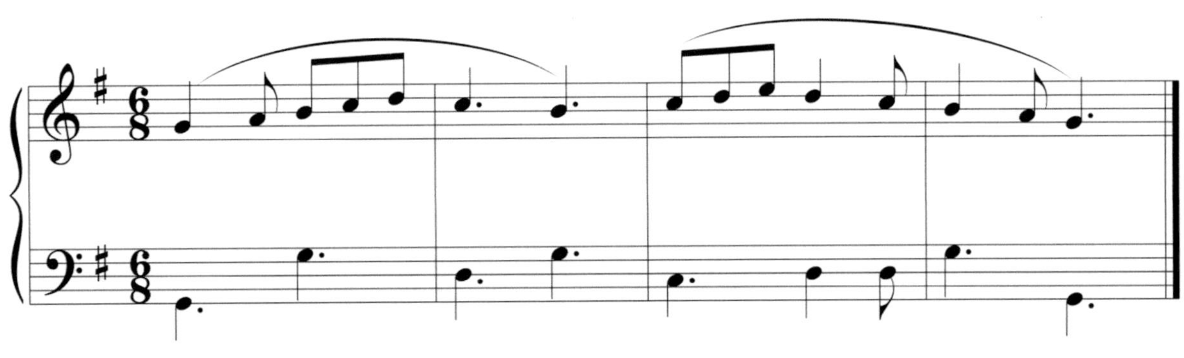

Numerals____

(d)

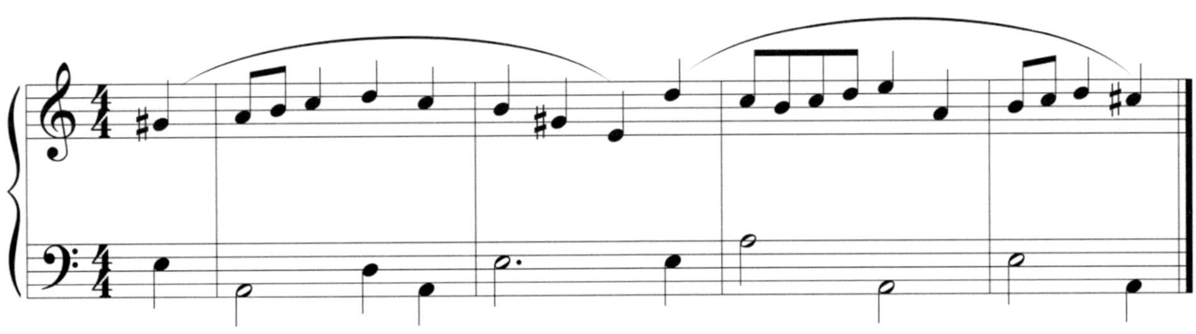

Numerals____

CHAPTER 8

ADDING MORE CHORDS

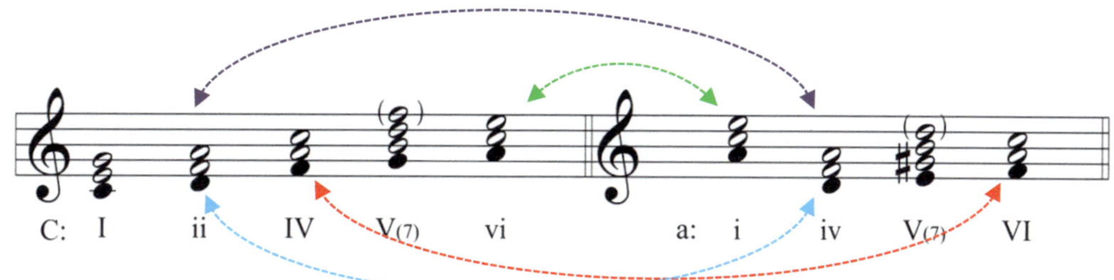

Some chords are common to both major and their relative minor keys. Take a close look at the diagram above and notice the similarities in sound, but the necessary changes in roman numerals. This extends the range of chords as follows:

I, ii, IV, V(7) and **vi** in major keys

and

i, iv, V(7) and **VI** in minor keys

A new Imperfect Cadence

ii – V is another way of creating an imperfect cadence. This will be used only in a major key at present. As with any chord progression the upper voices must connect smoothly. These are some possible arrangements.

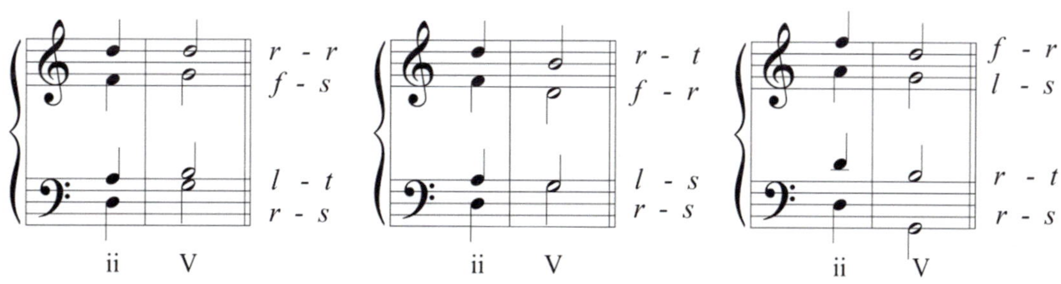

Listen to Audio 8.1 to hear the above arrangements of the new **ii – V** progression.

The Interrupted Cadence

A new cadence is created by using chords **V – VI**. This is called the **interrupted cadence**.

Listen to an extract from 'The Magic Flute' by Mozart. Notice the surprise effect of the interrupted cadence at the end of the first short phrase. This is created because the ear anticipates chord **I** to follow chord **V**, but instead **V** diverts to **vi**. The second phrase closes with the familiar perfect cadence.

Look at the detail of the part-writing in the new cadence.

In **V – vi** the roots rise a step in the bass so the upper parts are expected to fall.

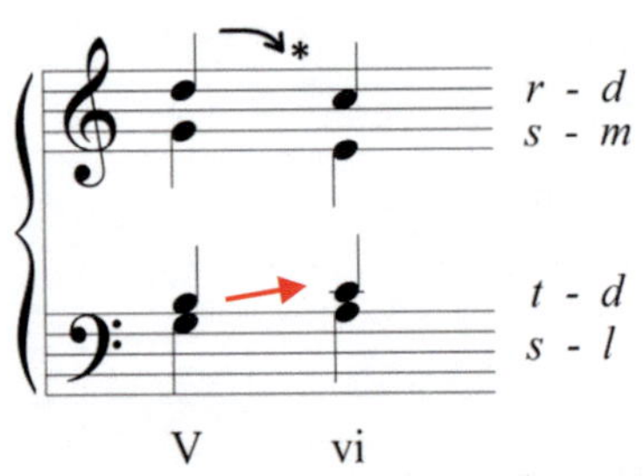

However, the leading note must rise to the tonic. As a result, in chord **vi** the 3rd is doubled rather than the root.

The layout is similar in the minor key.

* Watch out for this symbol to alert you to the special movement of the upper parts in **V – VI:**

Bass rises, leading note rises, other parts fall.
Double the 3rd in chord **VI**

Exercise 8.1

Complete these cadential progressions by adding alto and tenor parts.

(a)

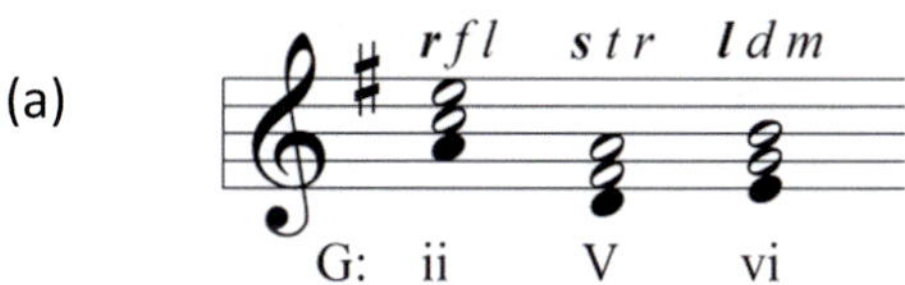

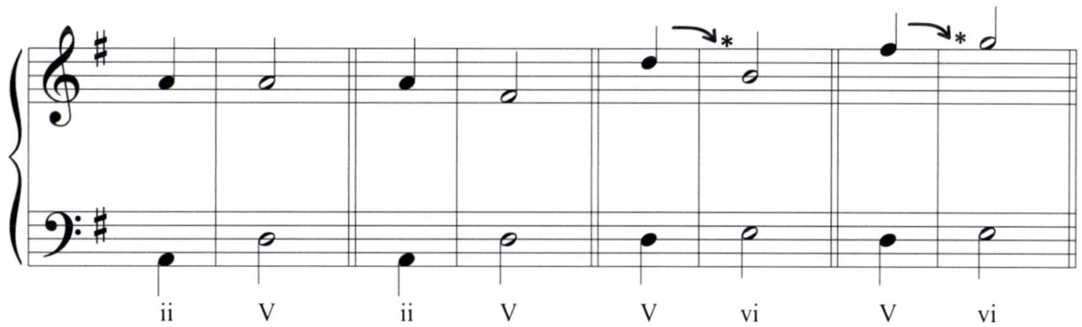

(b)

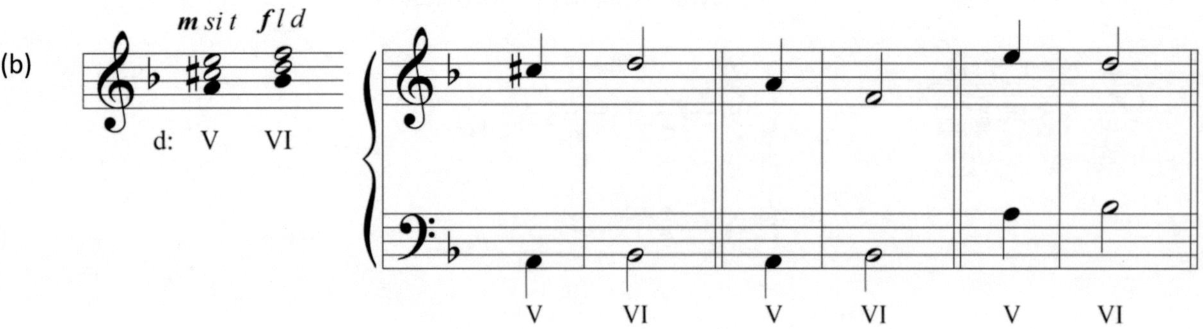

(c)

Exercise 8.2

Add soprano, alto and tenor parts to the given bass to complete these cadential progressions in various arrangements. Include roman numerals and cadence names.

(a)

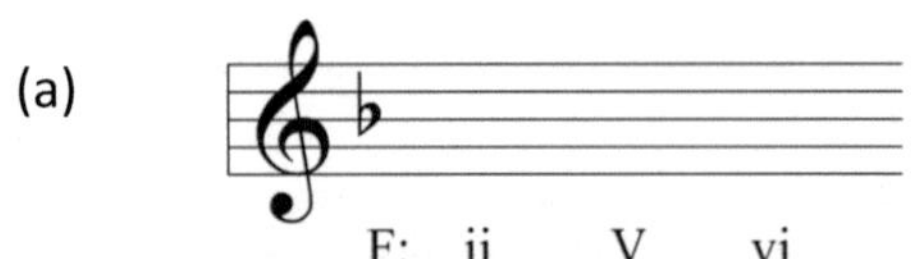

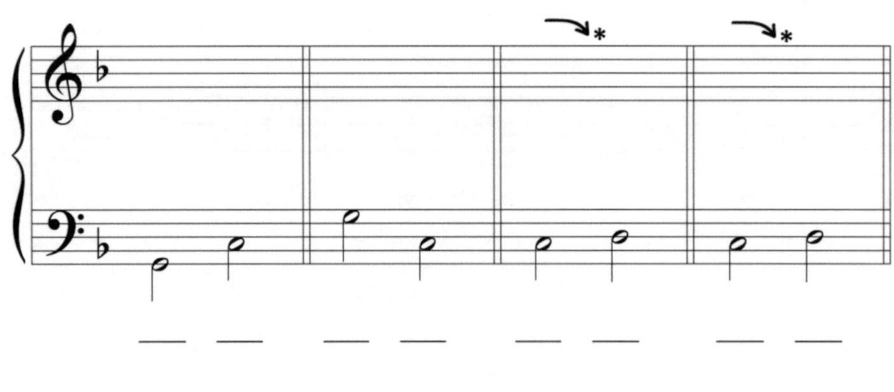

(b)

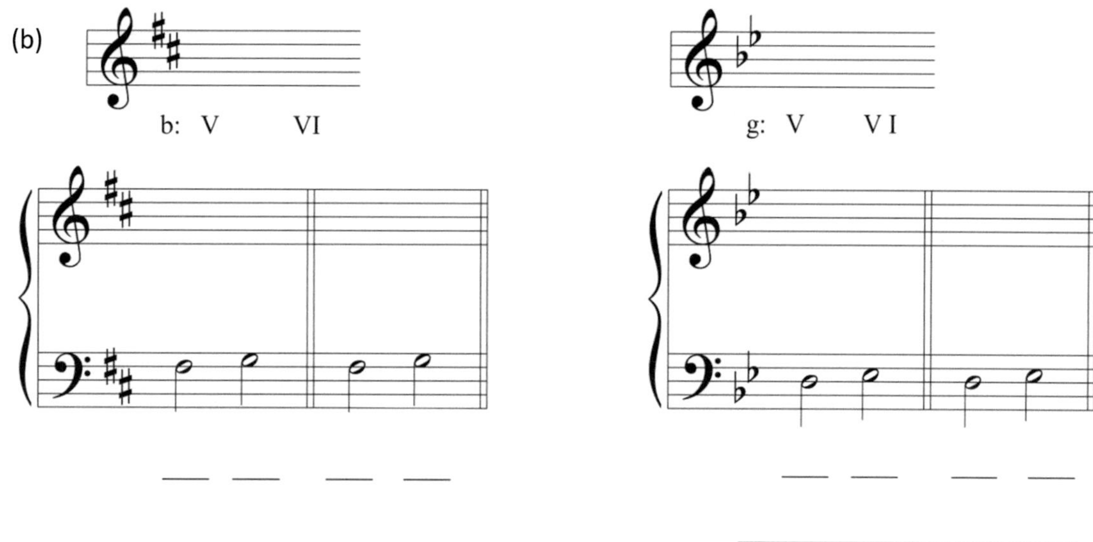

Exercise 8.3

In the following exercises there are four types of cadences in the boxed areas. Harmonise each cadence as indicated by adding alto, tenor and bass parts. Add roman numerals.

(a)

(b)

a: i iv V VI
l si l m r d
Plagal
l l si t r d t l
Interrupted
m r m d l t l si
Imperfect
l s f m m r d t t di
Perfect

Writing a soprano line

Roots falling a third

A given bass line may now include some new progressions. Progressions with roots falling a 3rd are particularly useful: **I – VI**, **VI – IV** and **IV – ii** (**ii** relating to major keys only).

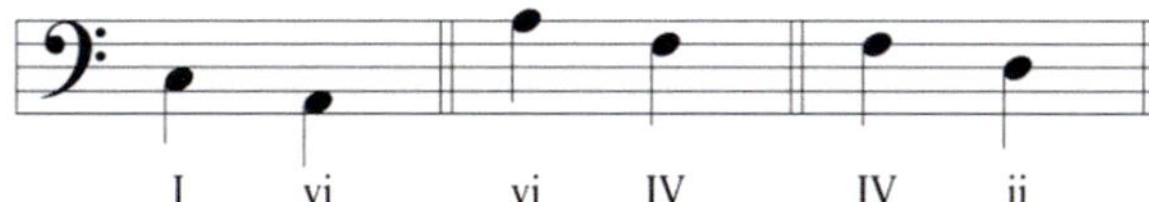

Consider the movement of the soprano part in these new progressions. If all parts move in the **same direction** the problem of consecutive 5ths and octaves may arise and must be avoided.

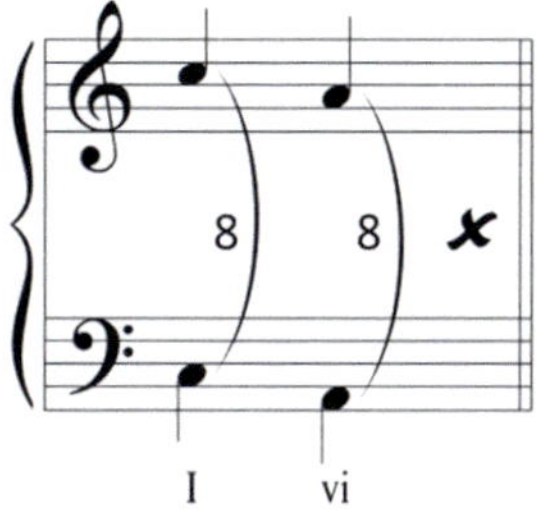

Soprano and bass begin with an octave and move to another octave.

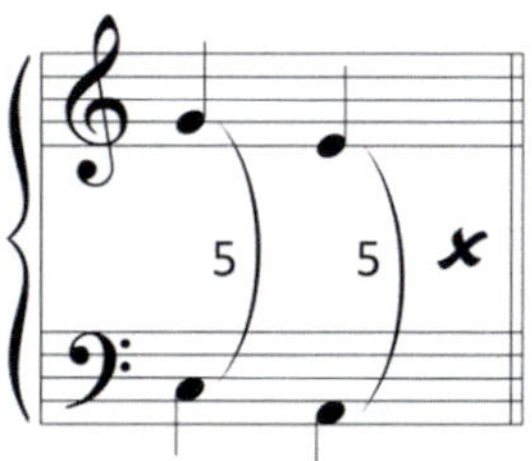

Soprano and bass begin with a perfect 5th and move to another perfect 5th.

Although moving in the same direction, soprano and bass are a 3rd apart – so no problem!

Roots falling a 3rd will always have two notes in common. These common notes **may** form the soprano line.

Alternatively the soprano may move in contrary motion to the bass.

This applies to all progressions where roots fall a 3rd .

Roots rising a step

In the progression **I – ii**, the bass rises a step so all upper parts fall as expected.

This is a bass line which includes some of the new progressions in the major key.

Helpful symbols!

👓	Roots falling a 3rd – watch carefully!
↘*	**V – VI** reminder of movement of upper parts
↘	**IV – V, I – ii** upper parts fall

When the new progressions appear they are highlighted by these symbols. These can be a useful reminder to take special care with the shaping of the lines.

A melody line is now added.

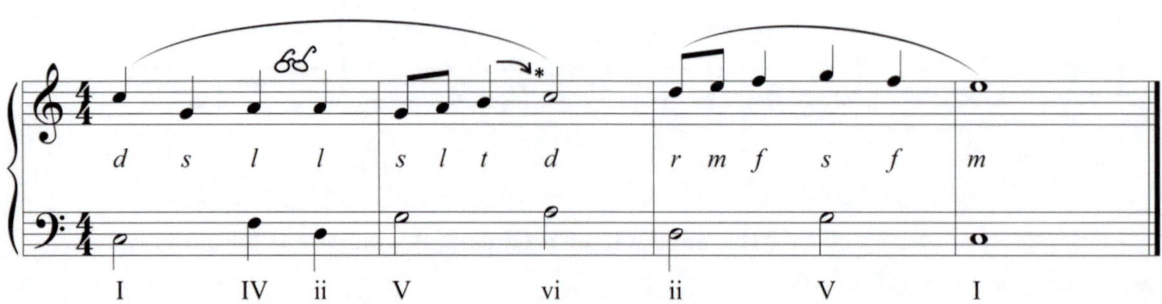

This is another possible melody above the same bass.

And another...

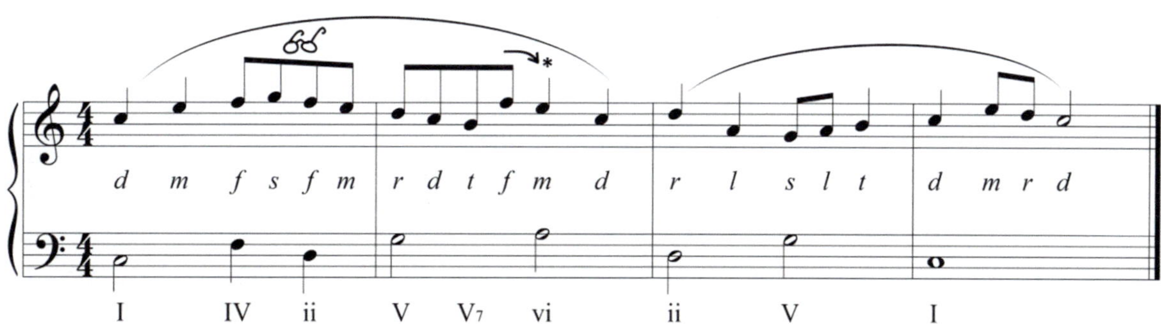

Listen to Audio 8.3. You first hear the above bass line alone, followed by the three possible melody lines.

There is great freedom in writing a melody line above a given bass if we bear two essential points in mind.

- Where the chord is repeated or sustained there is freedom of movement, giving the opportunity to open up the melodic range
- Where there is a chord change, connect smoothly

This is a bass line which includes some of the new progressions in the minor key.

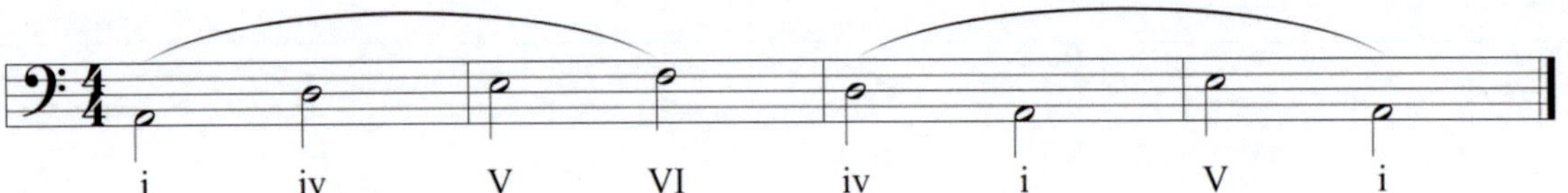

We now show two possible melody lines. The symbols are helpful reminders.

Listen to Audio 8.4. You first hear the above bass line alone, followed by the two possible melody lines.

Exercise 8.4

In these exercises the roman numerals are given and the symbols are included as useful reminders. Write a melodic soprano line for each.

(a)

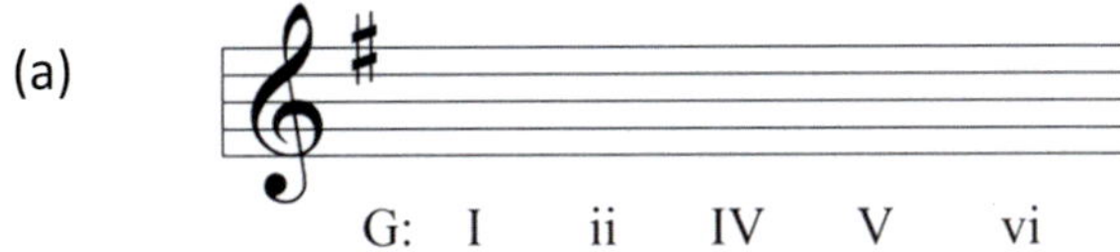

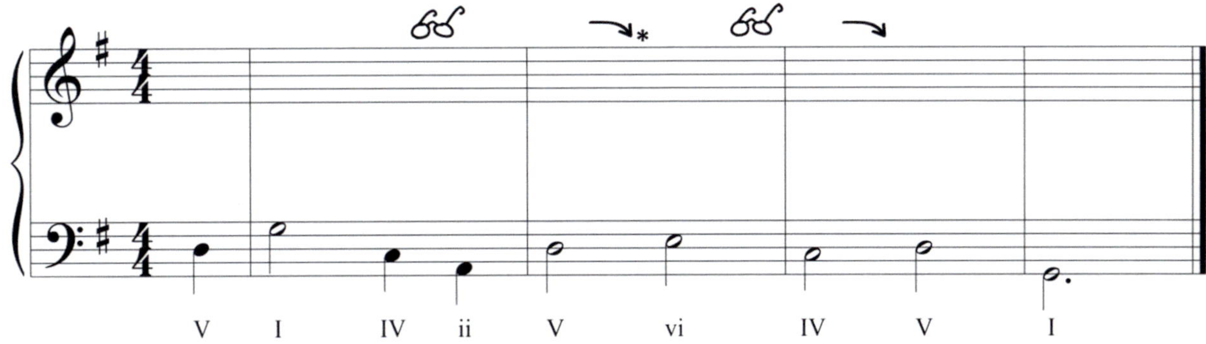

(b)

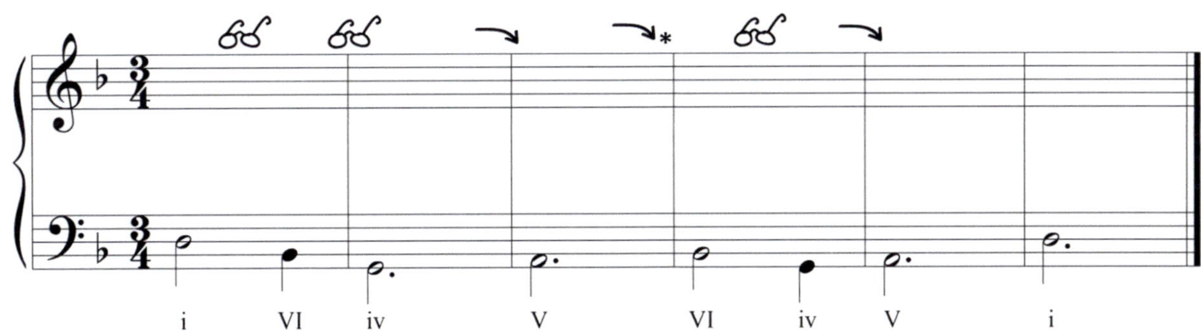

Exercise 8.5

Create a musically shaped soprano line above each of the given bass lines. When adding the roman numerals take note of any particular progressions discussed earlier. Add the symbols as reminders of appropriate movement. Always remember to sing as you write.

(a)

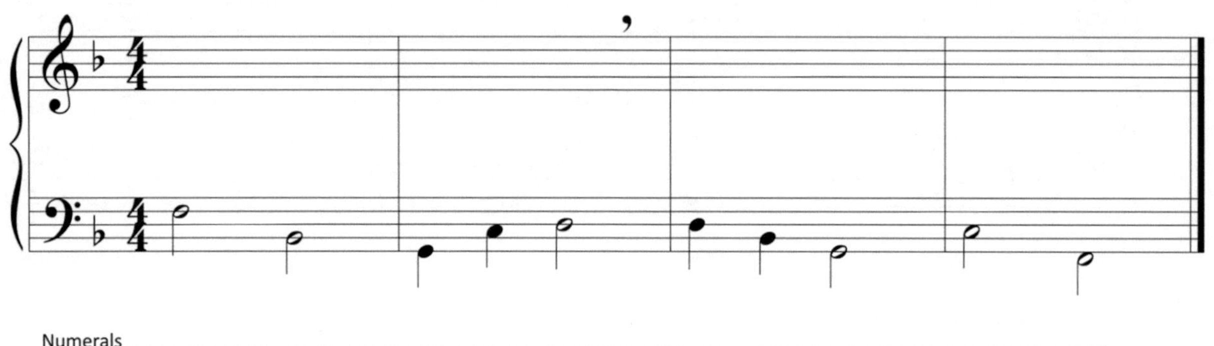

Numerals____

(b)

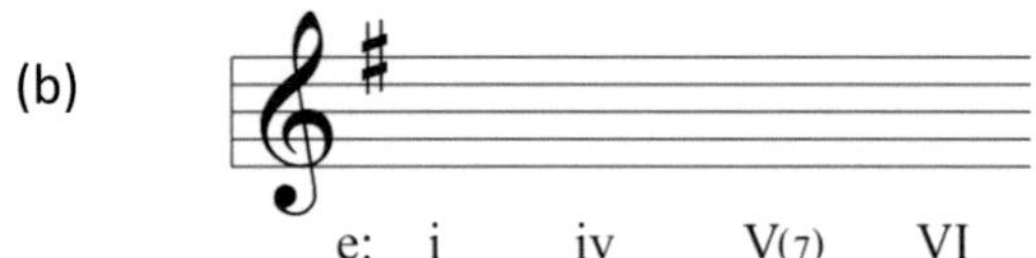

Numerals____

(c)

Numerals____________________

(d)

Numerals____________________

Harmonising a melody including ii (major key) and VI

This is a melody first harmonised using **I, IV** and **V7**, then re-harmonised to include chords **ii** and **vi**.

Listen to the final phrase of *'O little town of Bethlehem'*, comparing the two harmonisations. Notice the extra tonal colour and added interest afforded by chords **ii** and **vi** in the second harmonisation.

Many new chord combinations are now possible. It is useful to group them in the following way.

Roots falling a 5th (based on **V – I**) – Very Strong

V I vi ii I IV ii V

Roots falling a 4th (based on **IV – I**) – Strong

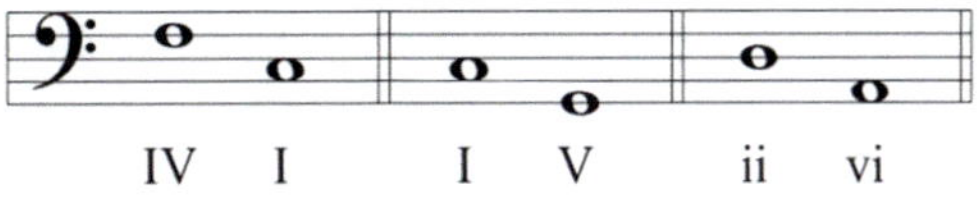

IV I I V ii vi

Avoid **V – ii** as the leading note in chord **V** cannot resolve

V ii ✗

Roots falling a 3rd – Very effective

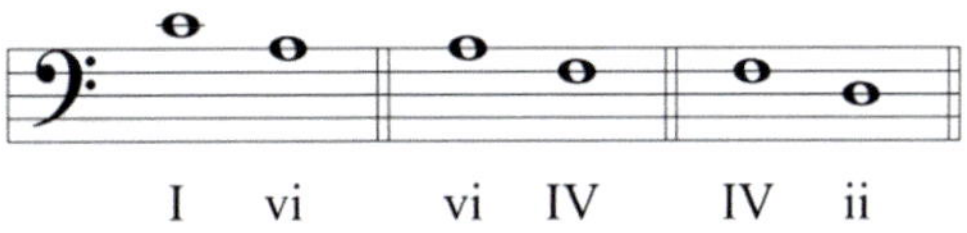

I vi vi IV IV ii

Roots falling a 2nd – Limited

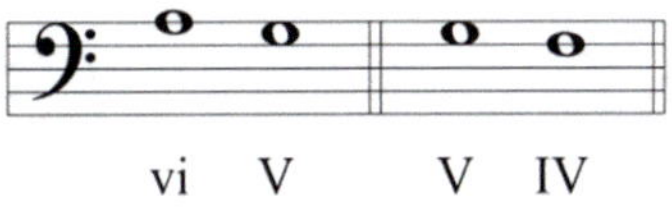

vi V V IV

Avoid **ii – I** – Weak

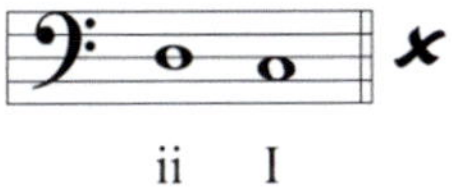

ii I ✗

Roots rising a 2nd – Useful

I ii IV V V vi

Roots rising a 3rd should generally be avoided – stylistically untypical in the Classical idiom.

Remember that progressions involving chord **ii** will only be used in a major key at present.

Look for clues in a given melody to help you spot opportunities to incorporate the new progressions.

- Arpeggio shapes suggest a single chord.

- Repeated notes suggest changes of chord for interest.

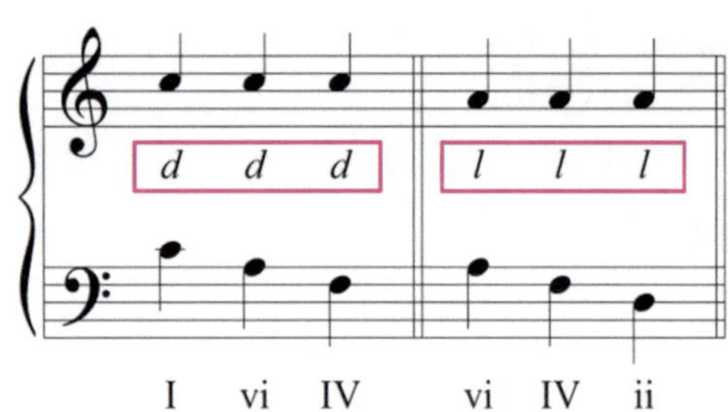

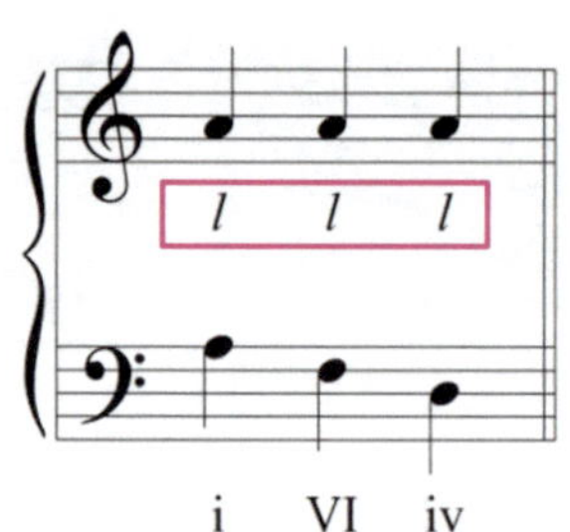

- ***f* – *m*** (***r* – *d*** minor key) can be harmonised effectively by any of the following: **IV – I**, **V7 – I**, **V7 – VI**.

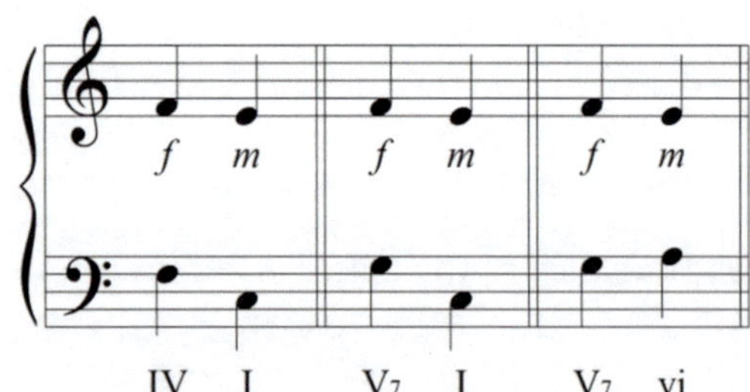

- At cadential points where the melody moves ***r – r – d*** or ***l – t – d*** (major key), the progression **ii – V – I** or **ii – V – vi** is particularly strong.

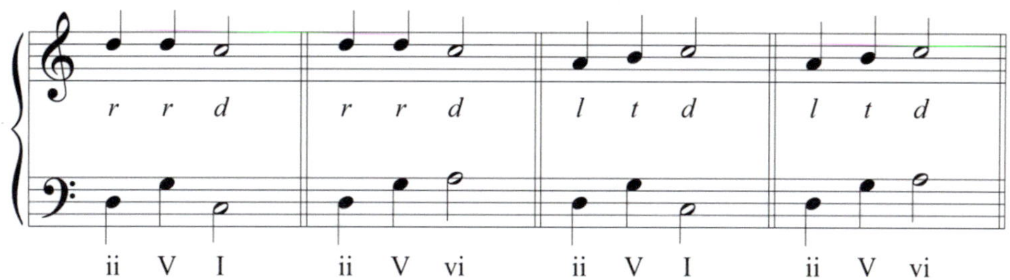

These are two worked examples. Study the points made below.

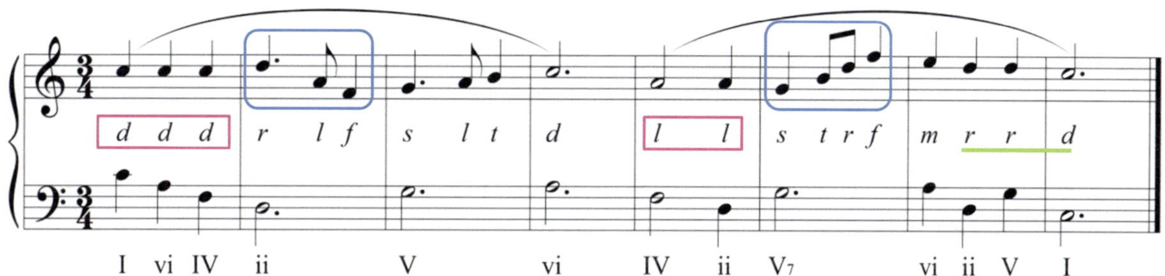

- The repeated pitches in bars 1 and 5 use changes of chord
- The arpeggio shape in bar 2 suggests chord **ii** and in bar 6, chord **V7**.
- The ***r – r – d*** at the final cadence uses **ii – V – I** to give a decisive ending

Listen to Audio 8.6 to hear the above example.

This is another example in A minor.

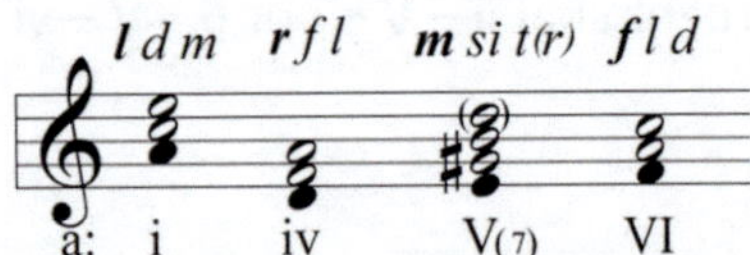

- The repeated notes in bar 1 use a change of chord
- The arpeggio shape in bar 3 suggests chord **VI**
- The repeated notes across the bar line between bars 3 and 4 call for an essential change of chord

Audio 8.7

Listen to Audio 8.7 to hear the soprano and bass lines.

Exercise 8.6

Sing each of the given melodies. Choose chords to harmonise by writing the bass line. Include roman numerals.

(a)

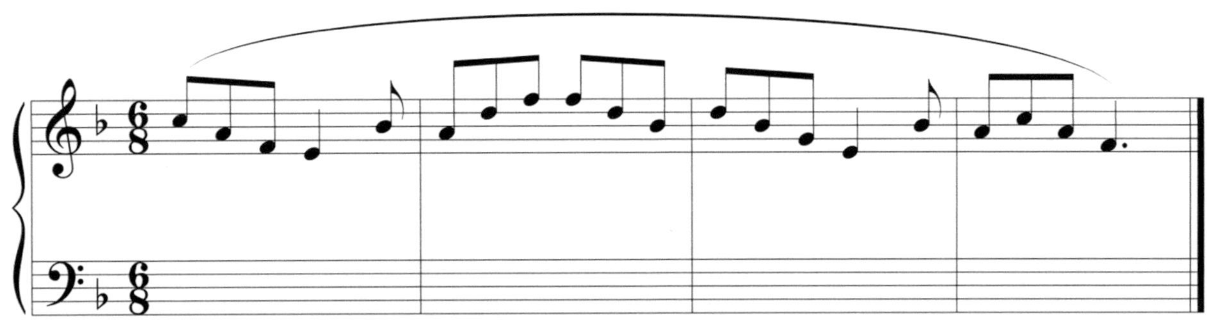

Numerals____

(b)

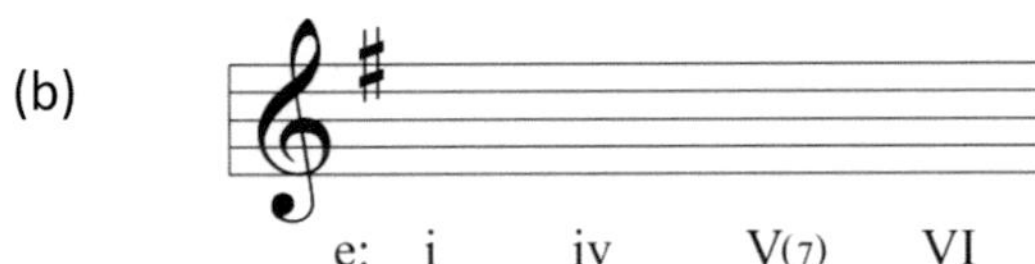

Numerals____

(c)

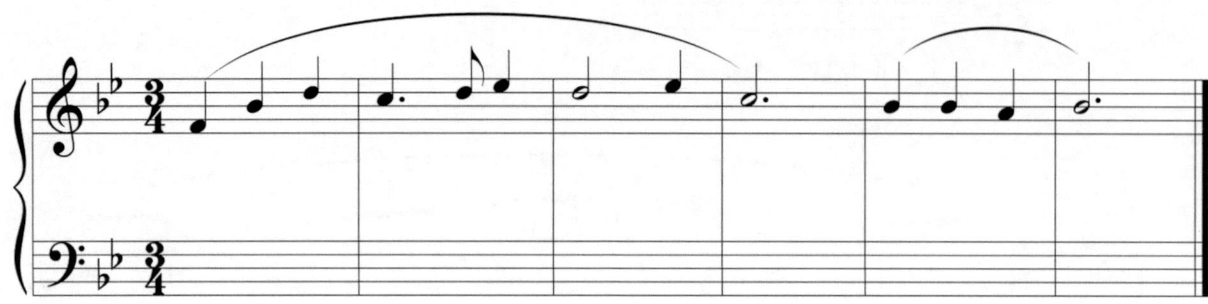

Numerals____

(d)

Numerals____

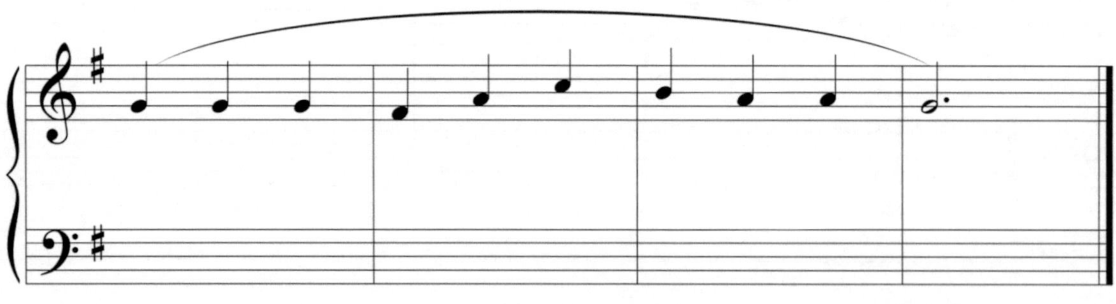

____

(e)

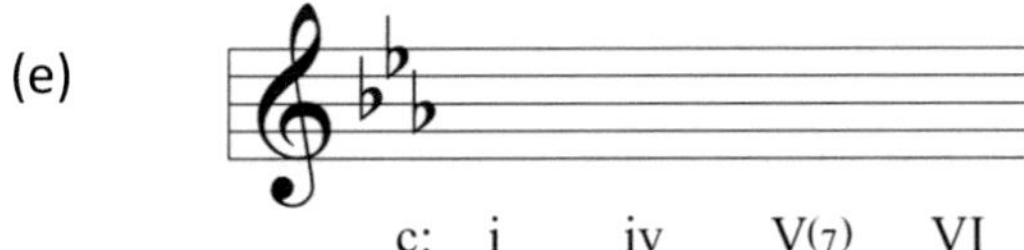

Numerals____

(f)

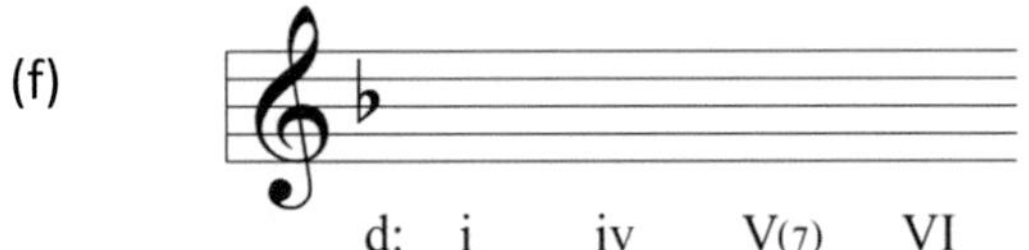

Numerals____

Adding inner voices

Now consider the movement of the inner voices in progressions where the bass roots fall a 3rd. If **all** parts fall a 3rd, the problem of consecutive 5^{ths}/parallel 5^{ths} and octaves occurs.

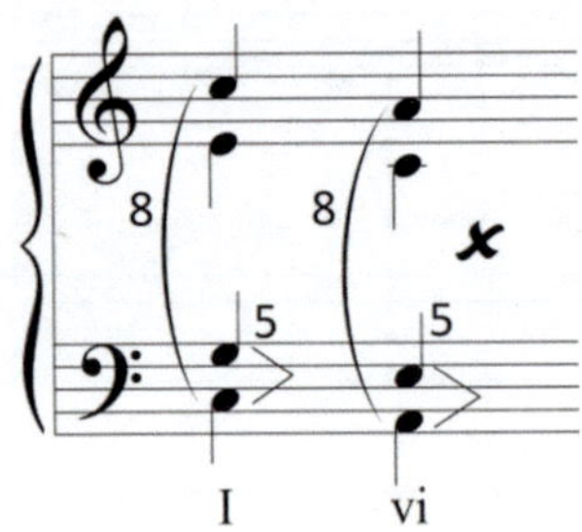

Listen to Audio 8.8.

- The soprano and bass sing their lines - you will hear consecutive (parallel) octaves
- The tenor and bass sing their lines - you will hear consecutive (parallel) 5^{ths}
- When all four parts sing their lines together, the consecutive 5^{ths}/parallel 5^{ths} and octaves can still be heard. Notice how open and hollow the sound is.

Consecutive/parallel 5^{ths} refers to consecutive/parallel **perfect** 5^{ths}

In the progressions **VI – IV** and **IV – ii**, the roots fall a 3rd. Because **all** parts fall a 3rd in these arrangements, the same problematic consecutive 5^{ths} and octaves occur.

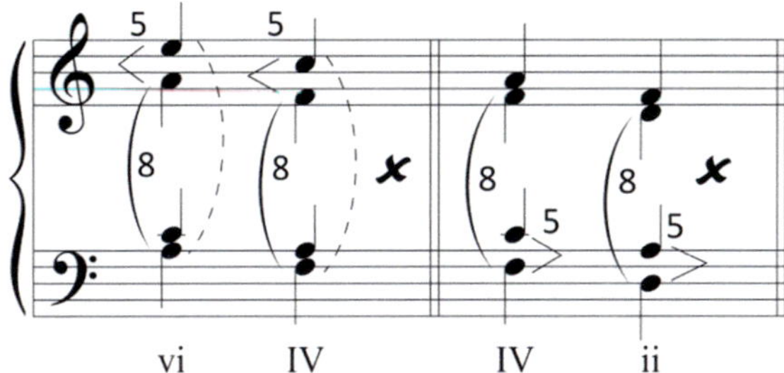

Here is a simple solution!

Keep common notes in the same part to eliminate consecutive 5^{ths} and octaves.

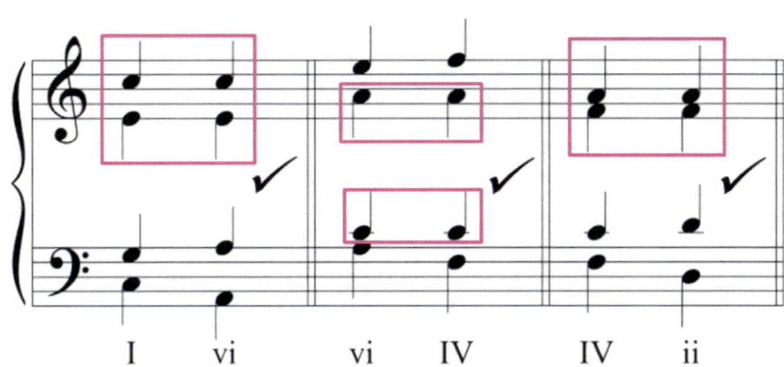

Audio 8.9

Listen to Audio 8.9. Notice how much stronger and fuller the sound is when consecutive 5^{ths} and octaves are avoided.

Here is another solution!

Soprano and bass are moving in 3^{rds} - so no problem yet!

When alto and tenor parts are added take special care – they must **not** also drop a 3rd, otherwise the problem of consecutive 5^{ths} and octaves will occur.

Watch out for roots falling a $3^{rd.}$. The foolproof solution when adding the upper parts is to keep the **common notes** in the same voices.

Roots rising a step

In **I – ii** (major key only), the bass roots rise by step so **all** other parts will fall as expected.

To avoid consecutive 5ths and octaves all four parts should **not** move by the same interval in the same direction

The progression V7 -VI

V – VI has already been studied; remember the leading note rises to the tonic while the other parts fall, doubling the 3rd in chord **VI**.

Notice in **V7 – VI** there is very little difference in the movement. The 7th resolves as expected.

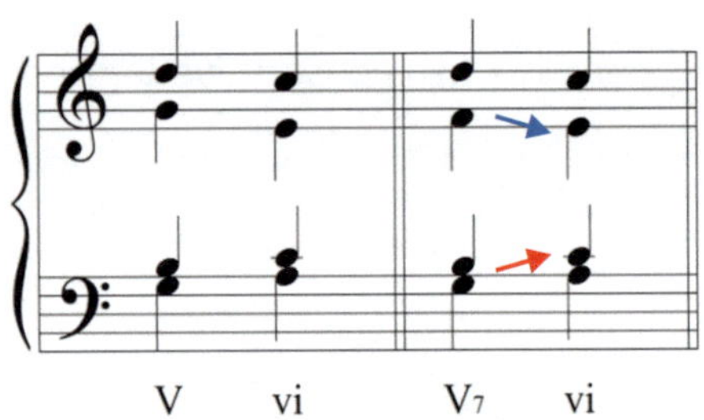

Checklist✓

Roots rising a step:	Upper parts fall ➘
V – VI:	Leading note rises, remaining upper parts fall, double the 3rd in **VI** ➘ *
Roots falling a 3rd:	All parts should **not** move in the same direction – keep common notes in the same voices

Study these two worked examples to see the progressions in context.

Listen to Audio 8.10 to hear the C major harmonisation above.

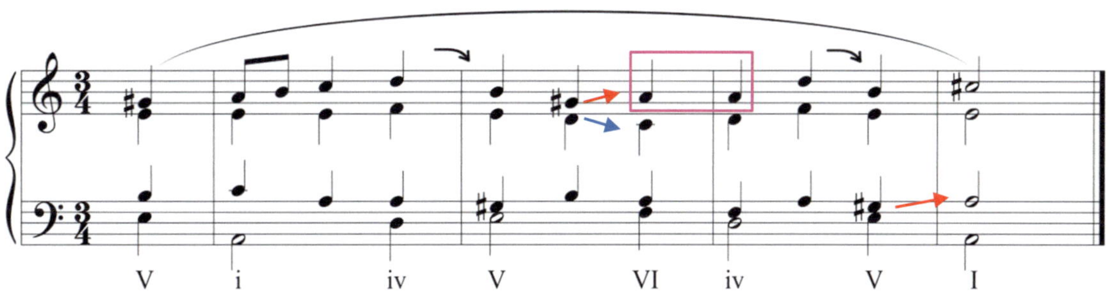

Listen to Audio 8.11 to hear this harmonisation in A minor.

Exercise 8.7

In these exercises the soprano and bass parts are given. As you add the roman numerals below the bass, sketch in the appropriate symbols as helpful aids. Complete alto and tenor parts.

(a)

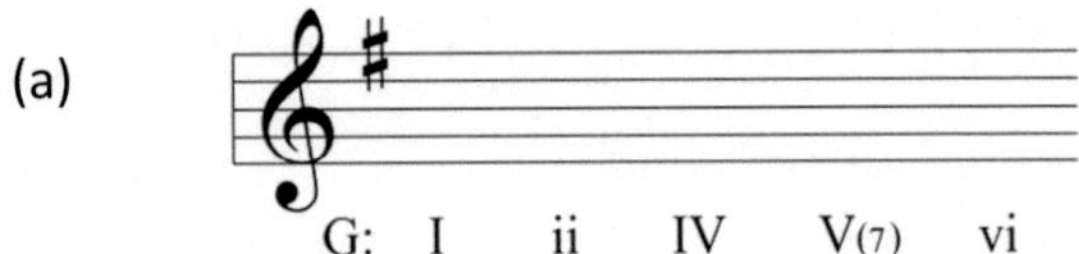

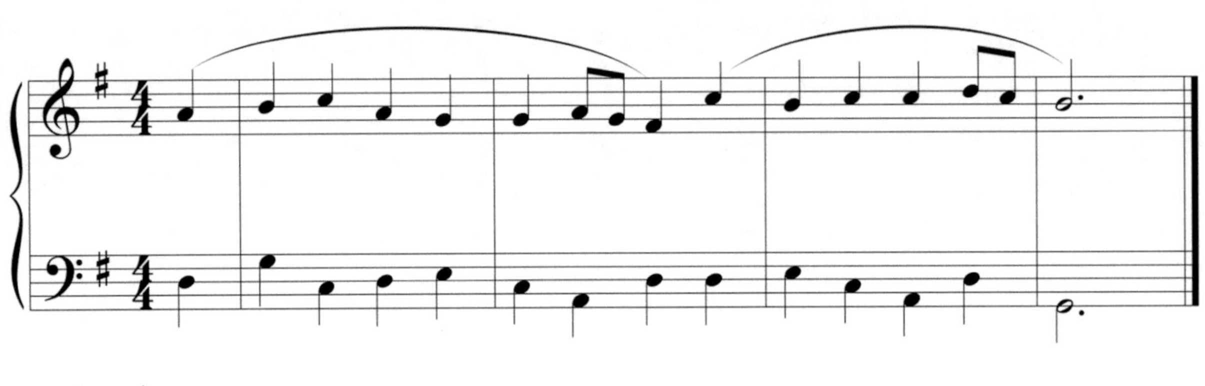

Numerals____

(b)

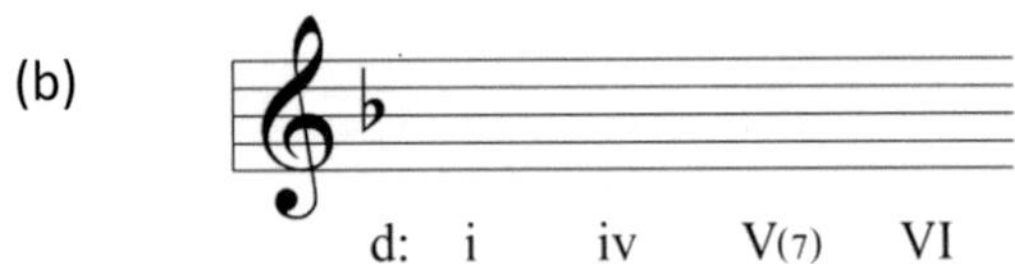

Numerals____

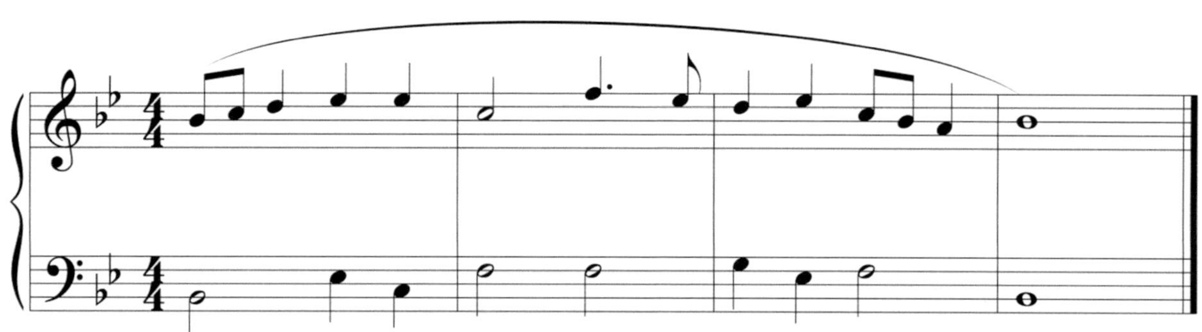

Numerals____

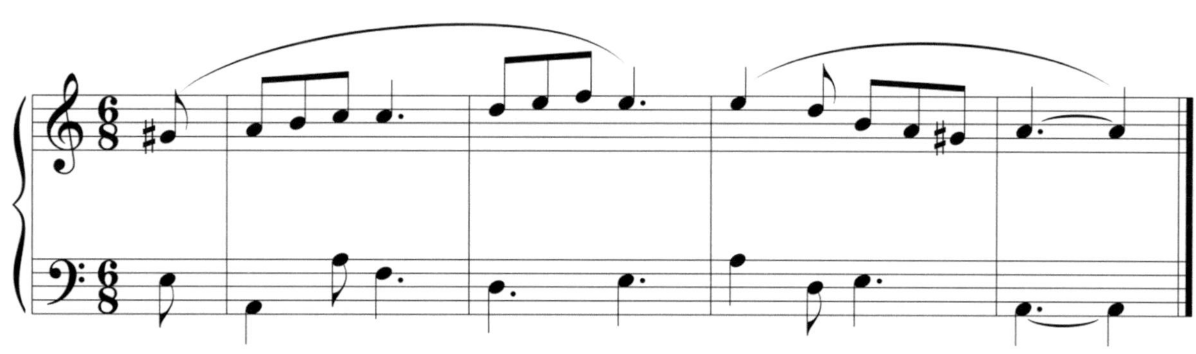

Numerals____

CHAPTER 9

DECORATION

Unaccented Passing Notes

You are already familiar with passing notes in the soprano line. With the addition of the new progressions, passing notes are also possible in the bass line.

This is a worked example from chapter 8.

When roots fall a 3rd in the bass there is an opportunity to include passing notes – this gives a more flowing bass line. This is the above exercise with passing notes added in the bass line.

 Audio 9.1

Listen to Audio 9.1 to hear both versions.

This is a worked example in A minor from chapter 8. Gaps of 3[rds] in the bass create possibilities for passing notes.

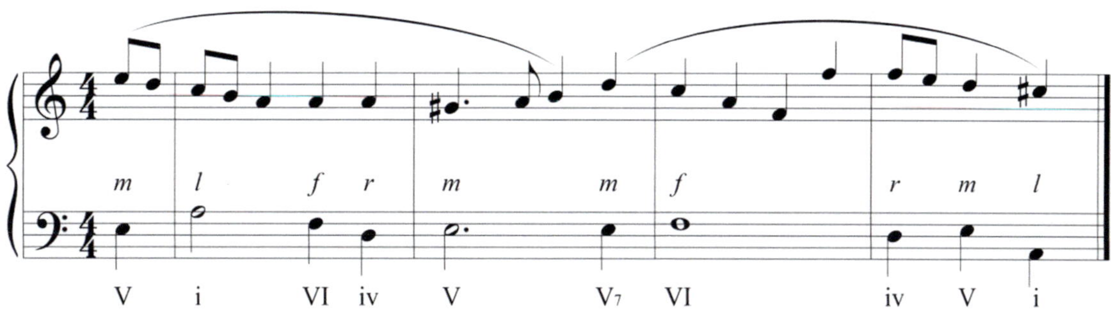

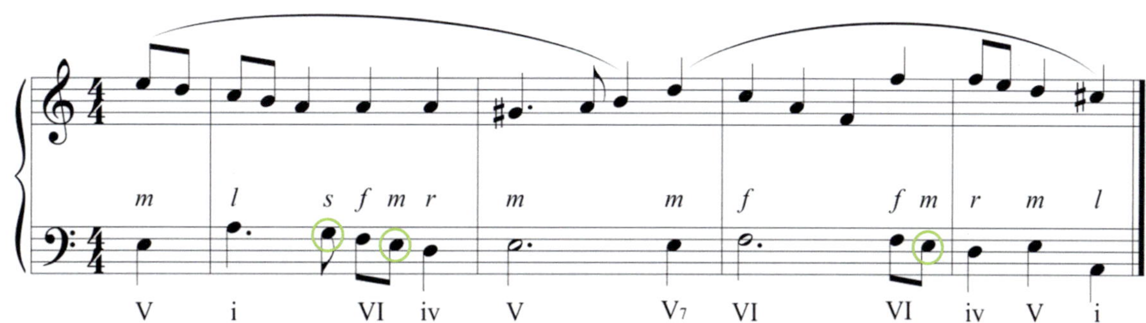

In bar 1:

- The passing note G is written as a quaver value to avoid clashing with the chord note A in the soprano on beat 2
- The passing note E slots in as a quaver

In bar 3:

- The passing note E is delayed until the last quaver of the bar to avoid a clash with the chord note F in the soprano on beat 4

Listen to Audio 9.2 to compare both versions.

Don't strike an unaccented passing note directly with a chord note

Exercise 9.1

Add roman numerals and rewrite the bass line to include some passing notes.

(a)

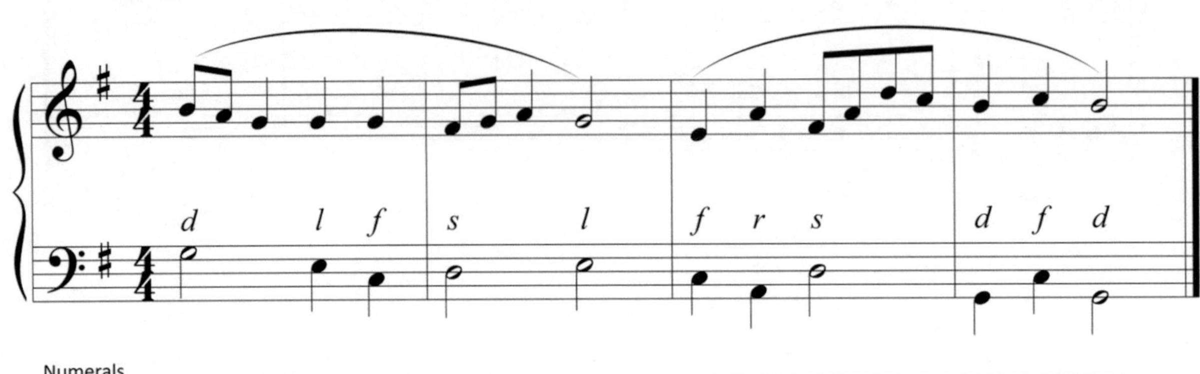

Numerals ______________________________

(b)

Numerals ____

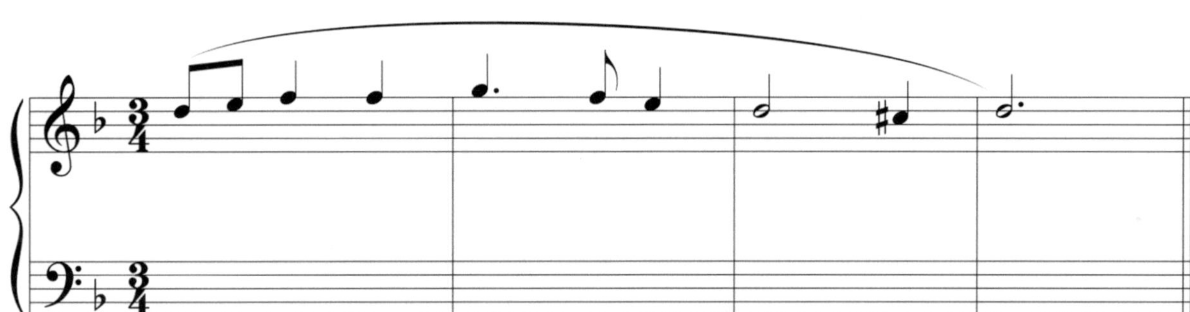

For a fuller texture, passing notes may be used in any two voices simultaneously. In order to blend they should form **3**^{rds} or **6**^{ths} when moving in the same direction.

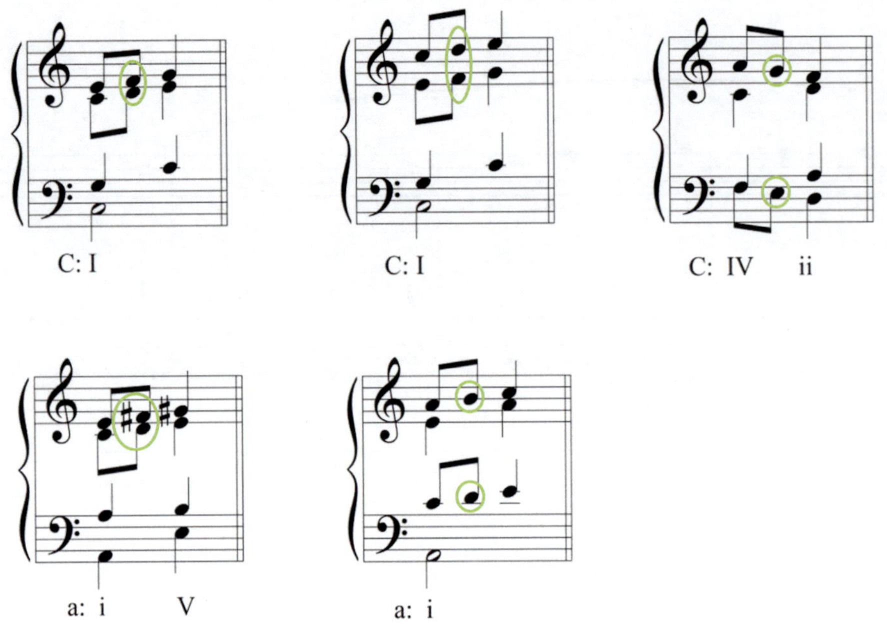

It is possible to use two passing notes in contrary motion provided that both passing notes have the same letter name.

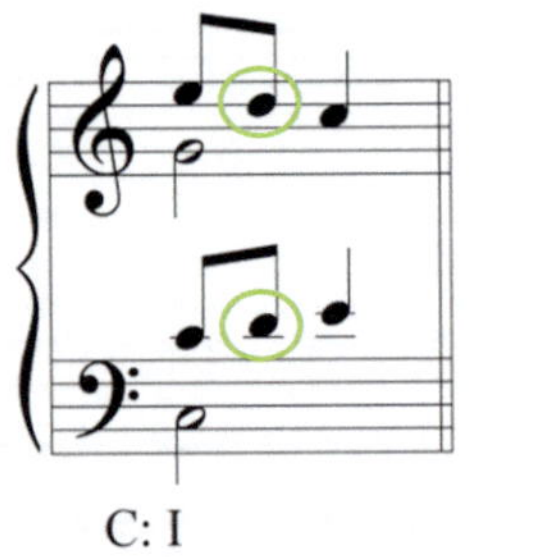

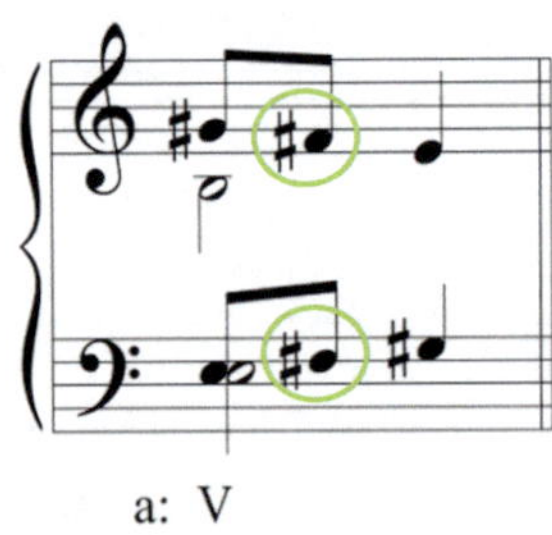

Auxiliary Notes

You are already familiar with using auxiliary notes in the soprano line. They may also move in pairs. The best arrangement is to form **3rds** or **6ths** in the **same direction.**

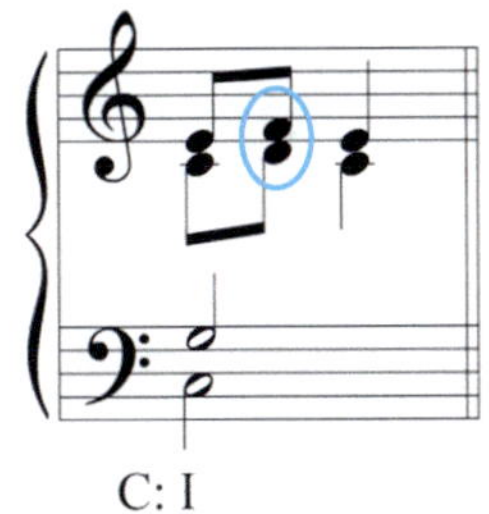

Below is a worked example with a lot of added decoration creating a full and interesting texture.

Listen to Audio 9.3. Follow the music and circle all the decoration. You may listen several times.

A point to note

- In bar 2 (beats 2-3), a passing note has not been added in the soprano since it would create consecutive perfect 5ths with the alto.

Exercise 9.3/  Audio 9.4

Listen to this harmonised melody in A minor. Again, follow the music and circle all decoration.

Further points to note…

- In bar 2, the contrary motion passing notes in the soprano and tenor have used an effective staggered rhythm. This rhythm is used again in bar 6.
- The final tonic chord extends over 2 bars. The double auxiliary notes are intentionally delayed until the 3rd beat to facilitate returning to the chord notes on the downbeat of the final bar.

Remember... don't include a passing note if it creates parallel 5$^{ths.}$.

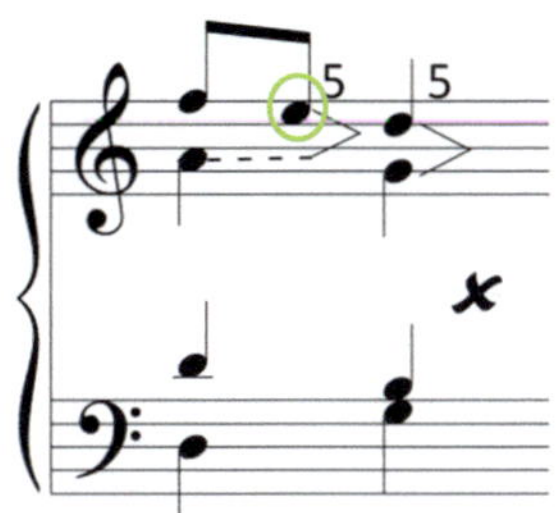

Finally, if the fundamental progression is incorrect, the addition of a passing note won't fix it!

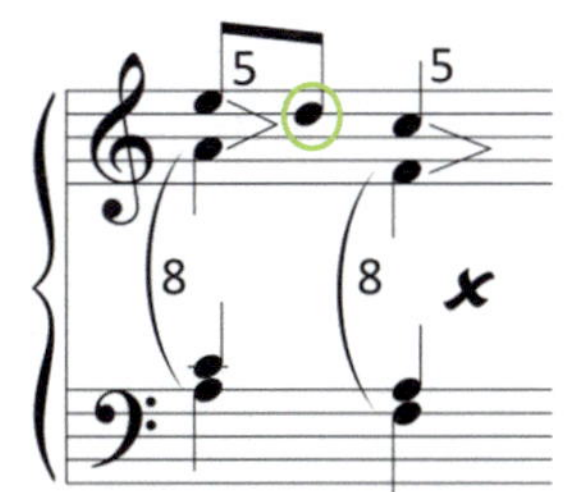

Parallel 5^{ths} still remain!

Checklist ✓

- Only decorate in two voices simultaneously – not three!
- Passing notes in the same direction – 3^{rds} and 6^{ths}
- Passing notes in contrary motion – same letter name
- Auxiliary notes in the same direction only – 3^{rds} and 6^{ths}
- Double decoration should be of the same type – don't mix auxiliary and passing notes
- Don't include a passing note if it creates consecutive 5^{ths}

Exercise 9.4

Add roman numerals to each of the following exercises. Then rewrite each to include decoration. There will be some opportunities to use decoration in two voices at the same time.

(a)

Numerals ____________________

(b)

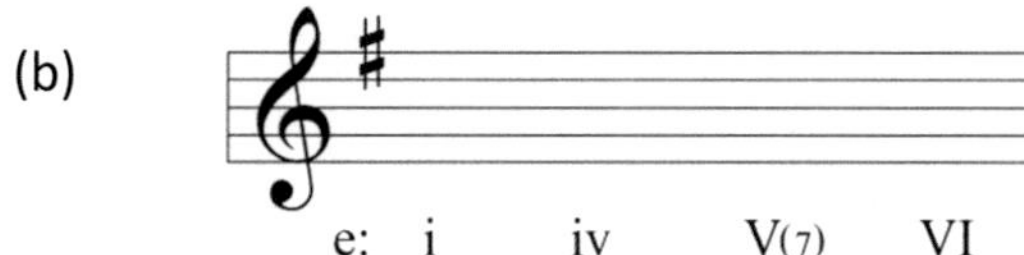

Numerals ____

(c)

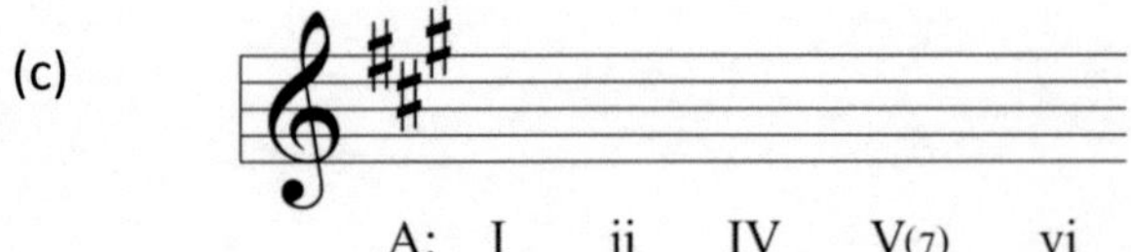

Numerals ____

(d)

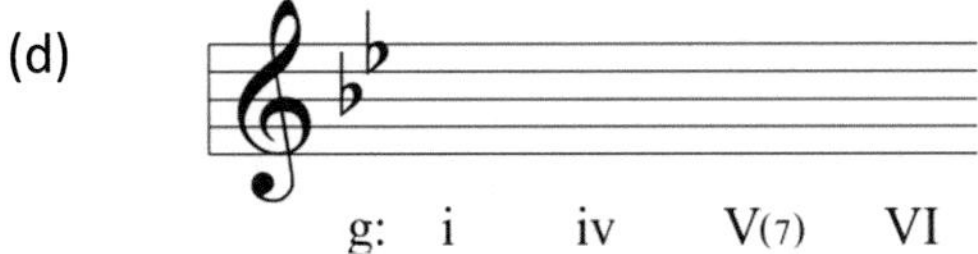

Numerals ____

CHAPTER 10

FIRST INVERSION CHORDS: Ib

So far the chords have been limited to root position. By introducing first inversions the chords are given more flexibility and allow a more flowing bass line. Overall, the sound is more blended and subtle.

In a first inversion, the 3rd of the chord is now in the bass voice and a small **b** is attached to the roman numeral.

Figured bass: This is a method of calculating the intervals from the bass note to the upper parts of the chord.

- A root position is made up of a 3rd and a 5th above the bass. However, because the chords are so common, in practice no figures are actually shown.
- A first inversion is made up of a 3rd and a 6th from its bass note. However, in practice it is generally abbreviated to **6**.

In four-part writing the doubling is the same as before; continue to double the root, but remember that the root is no longer in the bass.

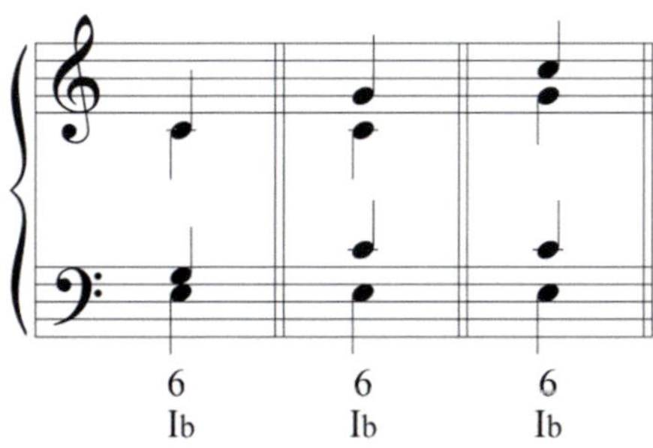

Exercise 10.1

Complete these first inversion chords by adding SAT.

 Audio 10.1

Listen to Audio 10.1. You hear a short harmonised phrase using root positions only. This is followed by the same phrase, substituting some root position tonic chords with first inversions marked *. These lines now have greater fluidity, creating a slightly more sophisticated shape.

 Audio 10.2

Now listen to Audio 10.2 to hear a harmonised phrase in the minor key. The first version uses only root position chords while the second substitutes some of the root position tonic chords with first inversions. Compare both harmonisations.

Ib in a given bass line

Ib is easy to spot in a given bass line since it is the 3rd degree of the scale and chord **iii** is not yet available. Study the bass line below noting the inclusion of **Ib**.

Now we set about writing a soprano line above the same bass. As we know there is great freedom in crafting a soprano line. The essential points to bear in mind are:

- Where a chord is repeated, sustained, or moves to its first inversion, it is an opportunity to open up the melodic range.
- Where there is a chord change, connect smoothly.
- Take care not to double the bass note of **Ib** – remember it is the 3rd of the chord.

Listen to Audio 10.3 to hear the soprano and bass lines.

Exercise 10.2

Add roman numerals below each bass line. In exercises (a) and (b) the figured bass identifies the first inversions. Write a melody for soprano.

(a)

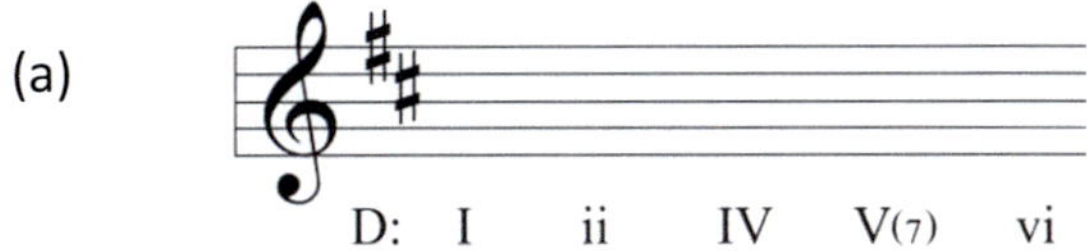

Numerals ______________________________

(b)

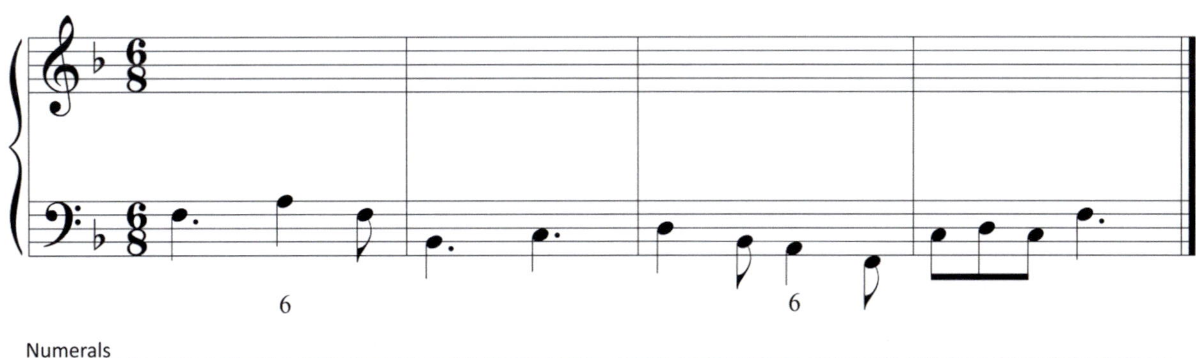

Numerals ______________________________

(c)

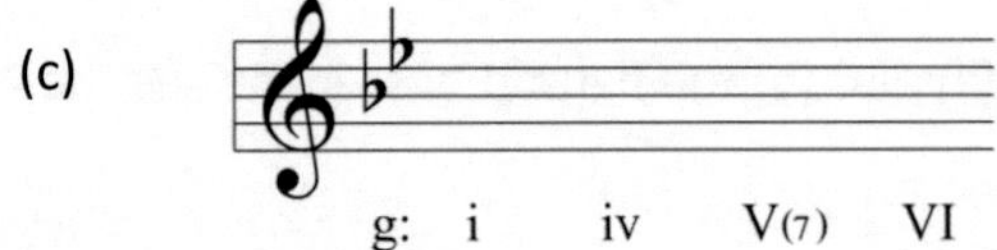

Numerals ____

(d)

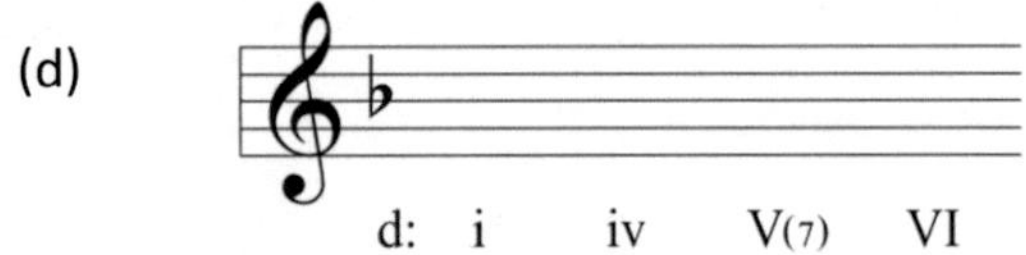

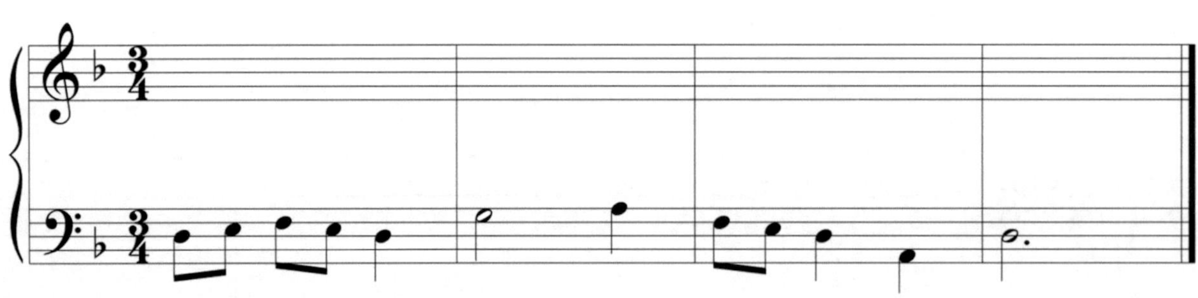

Numerals ____

(e)

Numerals ____

(f)

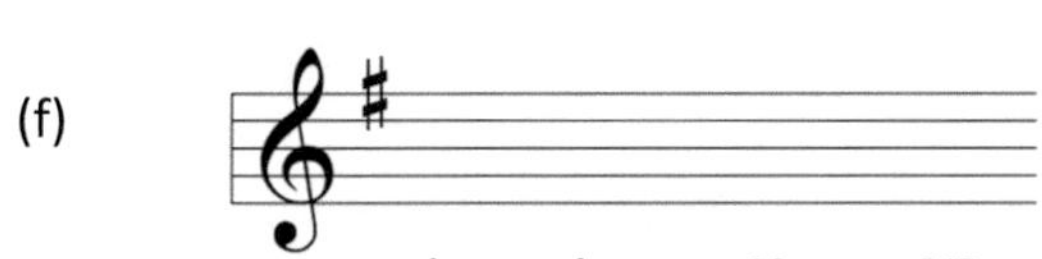

Numerals ____

Harmonising a melody including Ib

When choosing the progressions to harmonise a soprano line, use the same guidelines as before. In situations where chord **I** is chosen, now consider if **Ib** is appropriate. Normally choose **Ib** if it creates a smoother bass line with the chords around it. However:

- Do not use **Ib** as the final chord – it will sound unfinished
- **Ib** is unlikely as the first chord unless there is an upbeat
- Do not use **Ib** if ***m*** (***d*** minor key), is the main melody note in the soprano. It will result in wrong doubling.

Working through the following melody, we first choose the chords in root position.

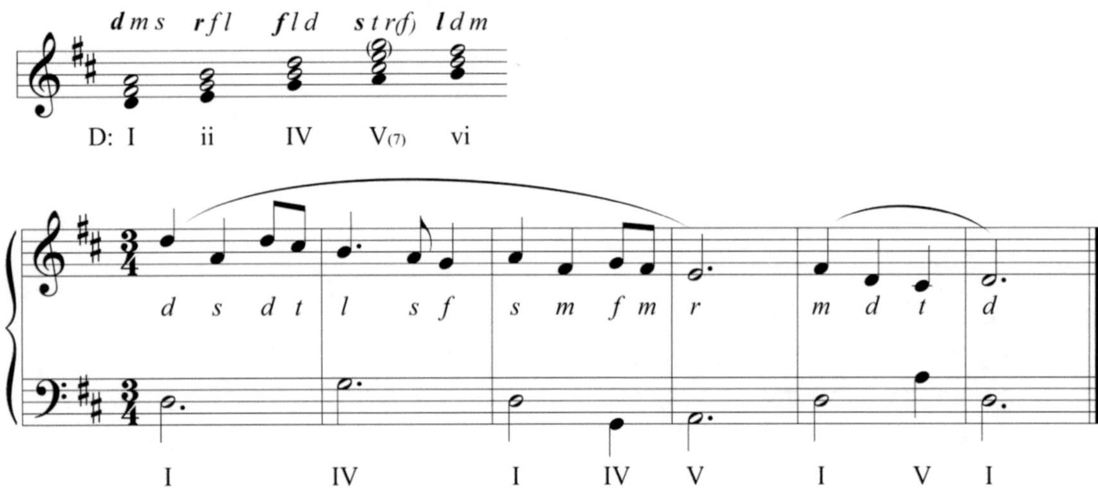

Chord **I** has been chosen four times. Now consider where **Ib** would be appropriate.

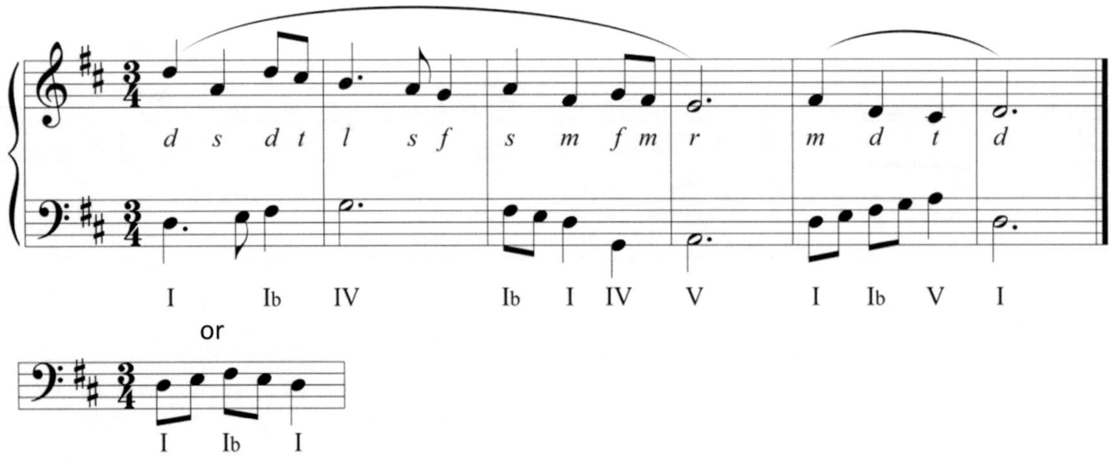

Bar 1: Keep chord **I** in root position for the first strong beat. Move to **Ib** on beat 2 or 3 for bass interest. A further advantage is the addition of passing notes.

Bar 3: Using **Ib** on the first beat creates a smoother bass line from the previous bar. Since beat 2 has ***m*** as the main melody note, move back to root position.

Bar 5: The melody moves ***m – d*** so the bass can move **I – Ib** (***d – m***).

Bar 6: Stay in root position for the final chord.

Audio 10.4

Listen to Audio 10.4 which begins with the version using root position chords only. It is followed by the re-working which includes **Ib**. Notice the more active bass line.

This is a minor key example. Follow the same steps as before, deciding the harmonisation in root position and then reconsidering where to use **Ib**.

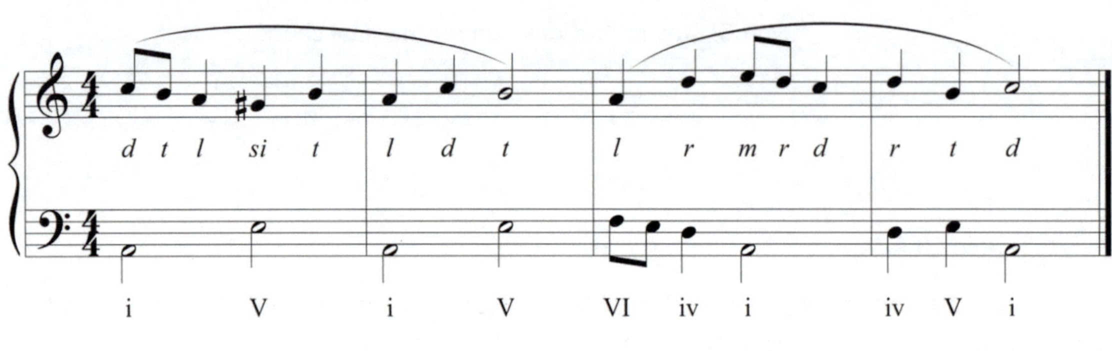

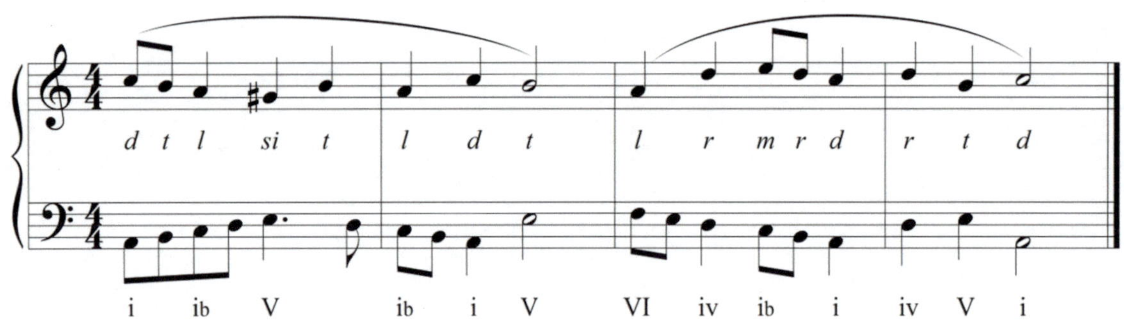

Bar 1: The move to **ib** on beat 2 with the addition of the passing notes creates a flowing shape.

Bar 2: The ***l – d*** movement in the melody line affords the possibility of **ib – i** (***d – l***), in the bass part.

Bar 3: **ib** on beat 3 creates a smooth scalic bass line.

Listen to Audio 10.5 to compare both versions.

Approach the next group of exercises by applying the following sequence as you work.

Checklist ✓

- Add solfa and sing the melody
- Choose your progressions initially in root position
- Where chord **I** has been chosen consider **Ib** if it creates a better flow
- Don't use **Ib** as the final chord
- Don't use **Ib** if ***m*** (***d*** minor key) is in the soprano part

Exercise 10.3

Harmonise each soprano melody by adding the bass line.

(a)

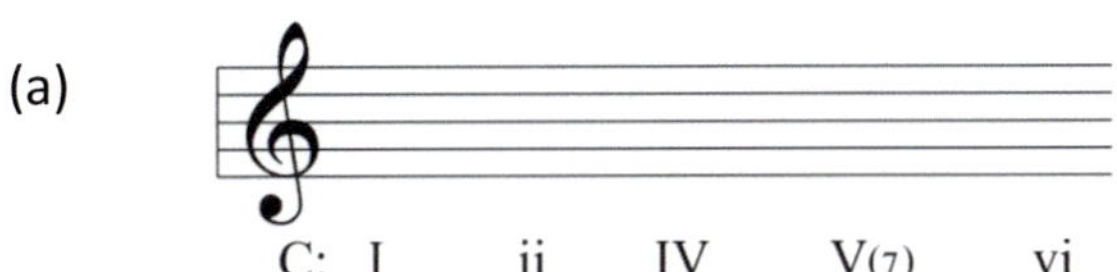

Numerals____

(b)

Numerals____

(c)

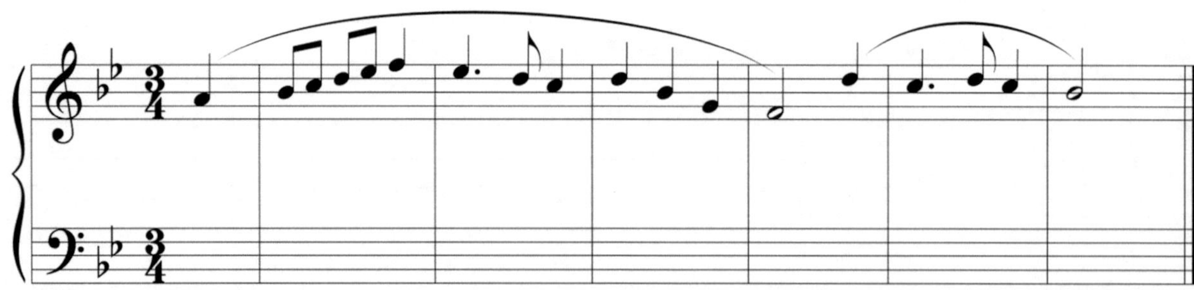

Numerals____

(d)

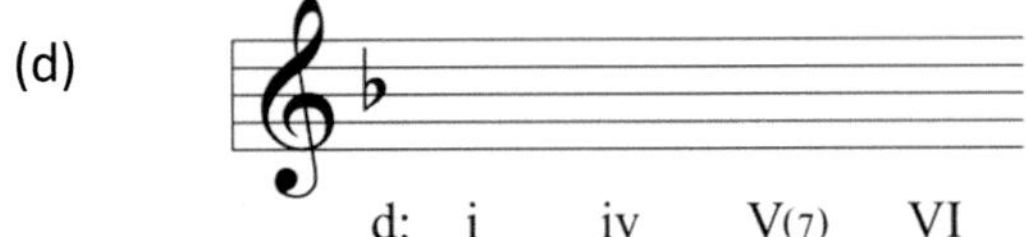

Numerals____

(e)

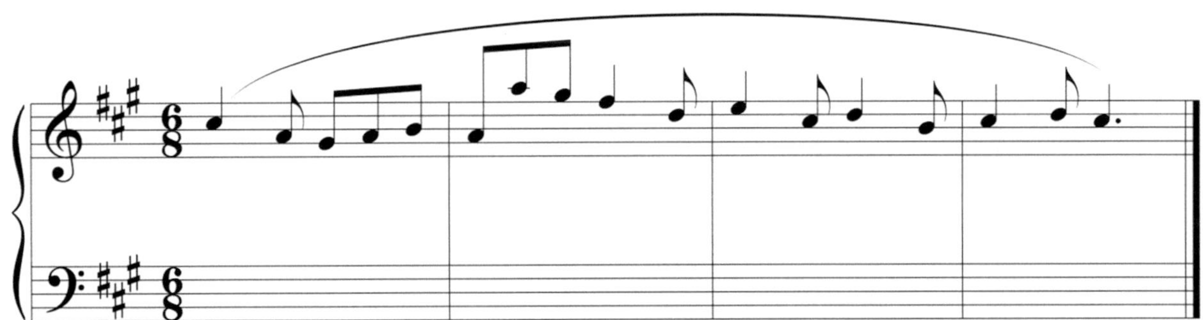

Numerals____

(f)

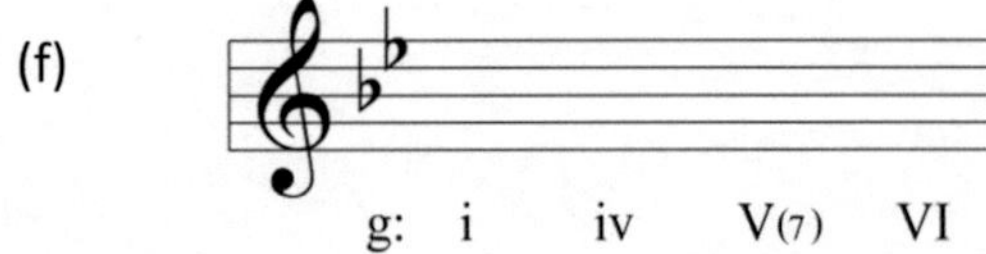

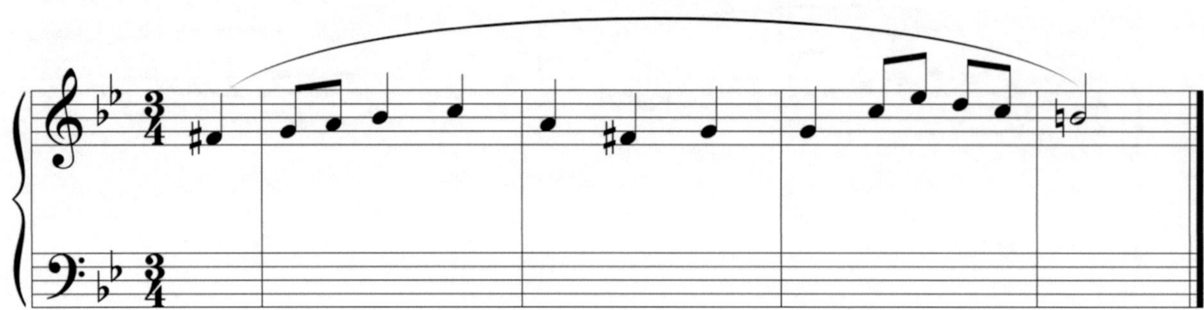

Numerals____

(g)

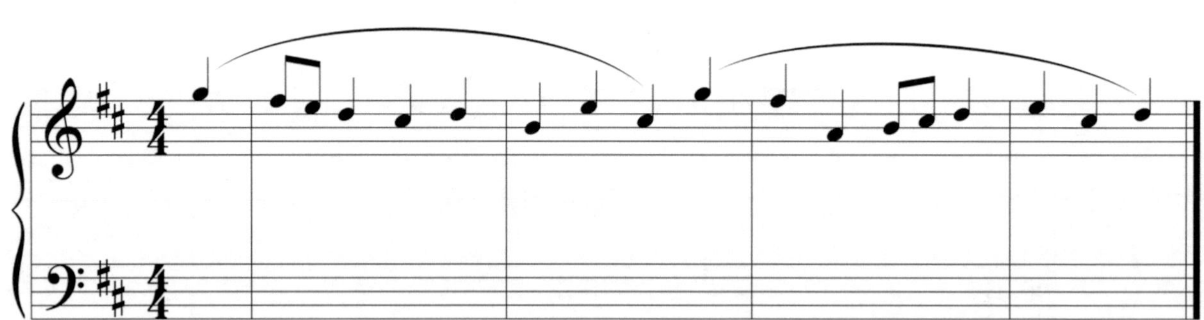

Numerals____

Part-writing with Ib

Compare the part-writing in the following examples.

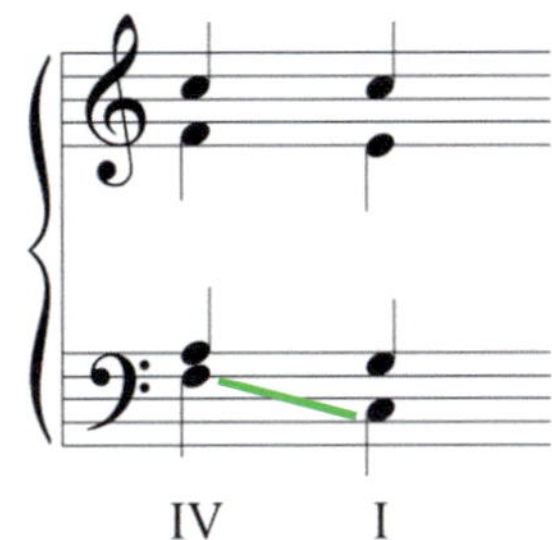

These root position chords show the smoothest possible connection for the upper three voices.

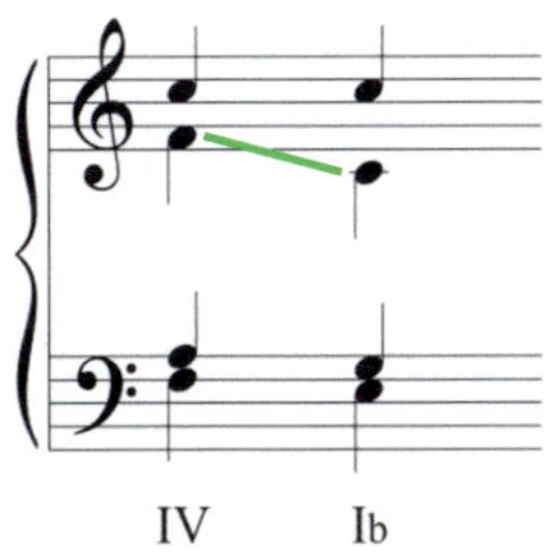

When chord **I** in arranged in its first inversion, notice how the original bass leap (highlighted in green) has transferred to one of the upper voices. The remaining three voices still move smoothly, but they are not necessarily the three **upper** voices.

Here is another solution in which **all** parts are smooth.

Here are consecutive octaves in contrary motion. The use of **Ib** eliminates them.

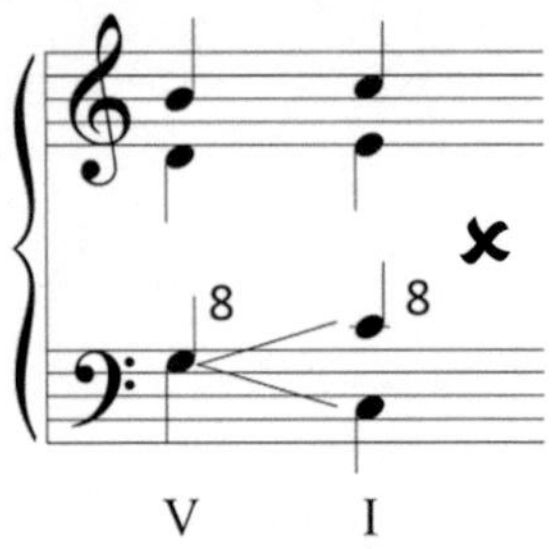

The unison followed by the octave between tenor and bass voices is also considered to be consecutive octaves. However, the movement is corrected by using **Ib**.

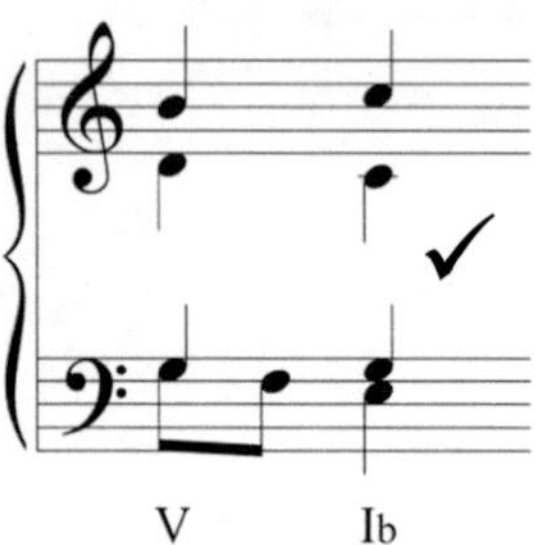

You are already aware that crossing/overlapping of parts is not an issue if the chord remains the same (chapter 6).

This is also the case if moving between two positions of the same chord.

At a chord change aim to have **any** three voices smooth

This is a worked example in F major.

At all chord changes at least three voices are observing smooth movement. Looking carefully at the detail in bar 2, a new possibility of doubling emerges. The 5th is doubled in chord **ii**. This is to avoid consecutive 5^{ths} which would otherwise occur between beats 1 and 2 in tenor and alto voices.

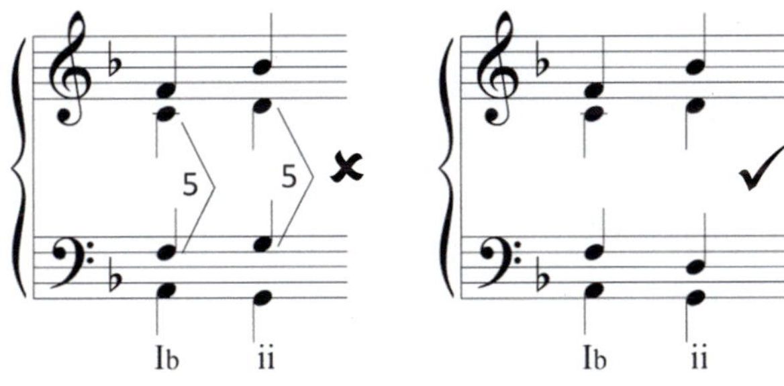

The 5th of any chord may be doubled to facilitate good part-writing

Listen to Audio 10.6 to hear the above four-part harmonisation.

This is a worked example in A minor.

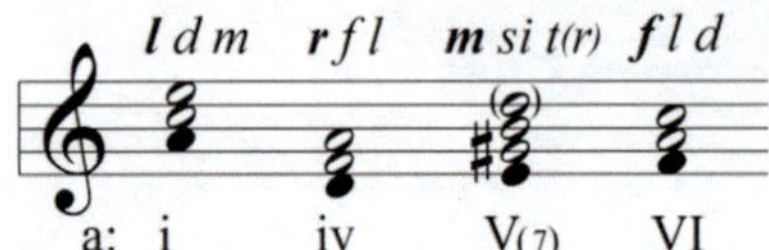

- At the opening, **V – ib** has been chosen to avoid consecutive octaves between soprano and bass parts which would have occurred if both chords were in root position.
- In bar 3 each chord change manages to have all voices smooth.

Listen to Audio 10.7 to hear the four-part harmonisation.

Checklist ✓

- Sing the given material and add solfa
- Use **Ib** to create a smoother bass where appropriate
- In figured bass **6** indicates a first inversion chord
- Aim to have at least three parts smooth at every chord change
- The 5th of any chord may be doubled where necessary
- Don't use **Ib** as the final chord
- Don't use **Ib** if ***m*** (***d*** in minor key) is in the soprano part

Exercise 10.4

In the next group of exercises the soprano and bass lines are given. Add the roman numerals. The use of **Ib** is identified by the figured bass in (a) and (b). Complete each harmonisation by adding alto and tenor parts.

(a)

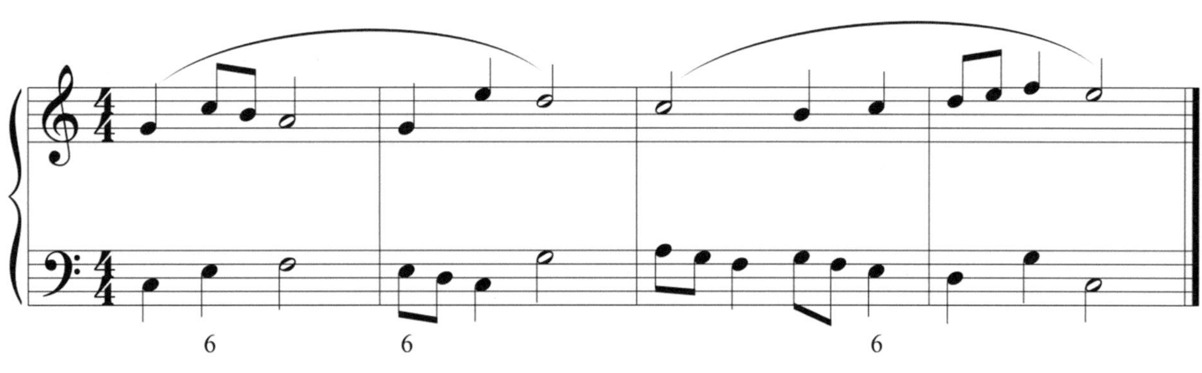

Numerals____

(b)

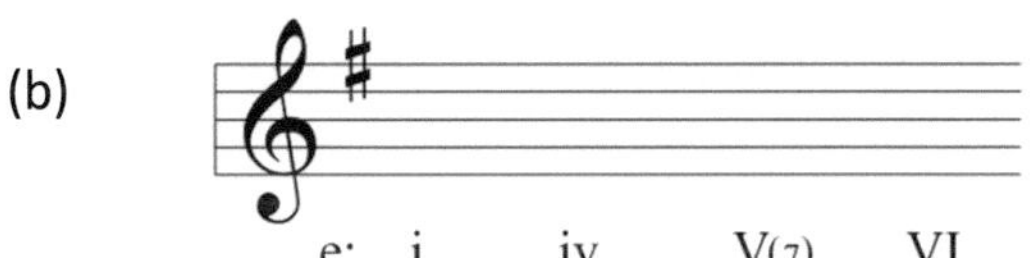

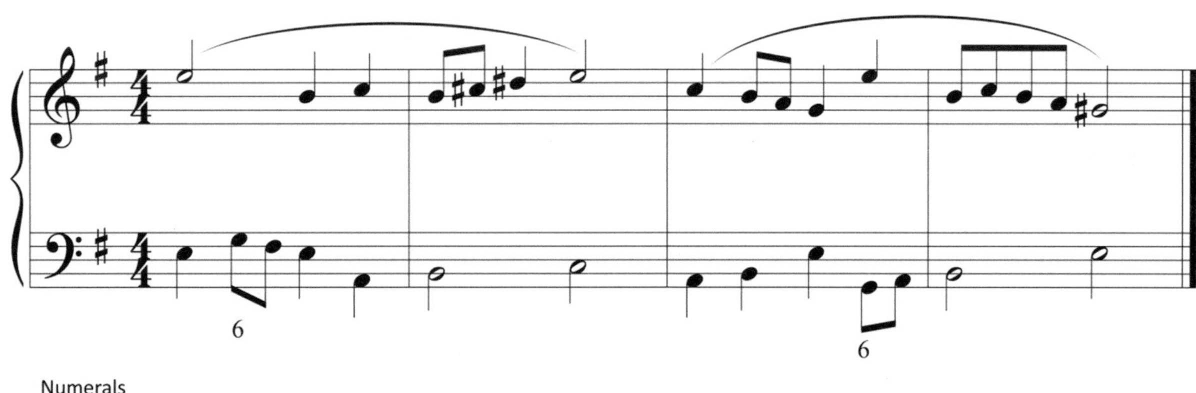

Numerals____

(c)

Numerals____

(d)

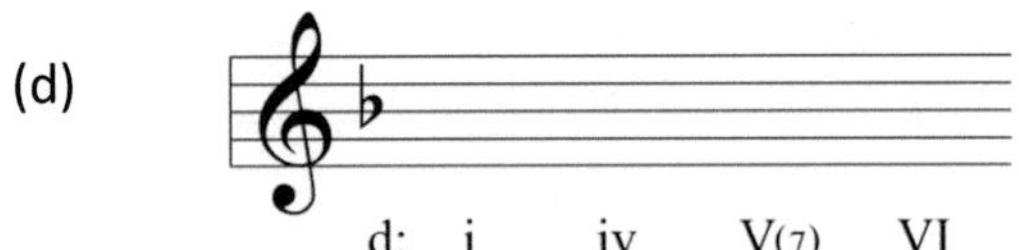

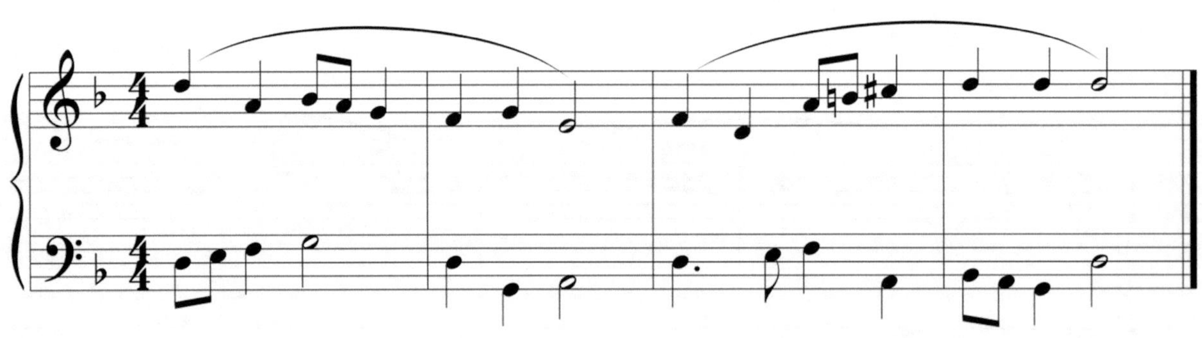

Numerals____

(e)

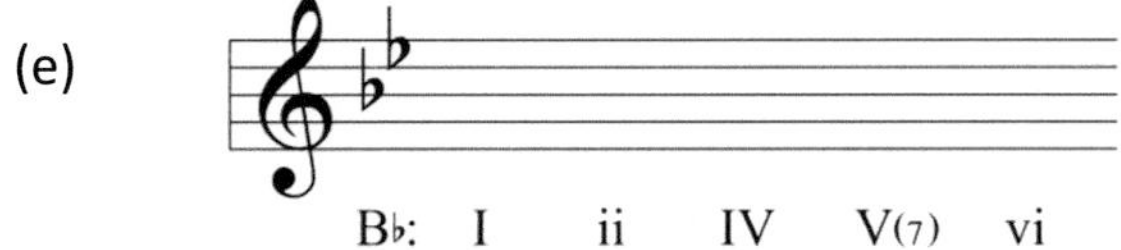

Numerals____

(f)

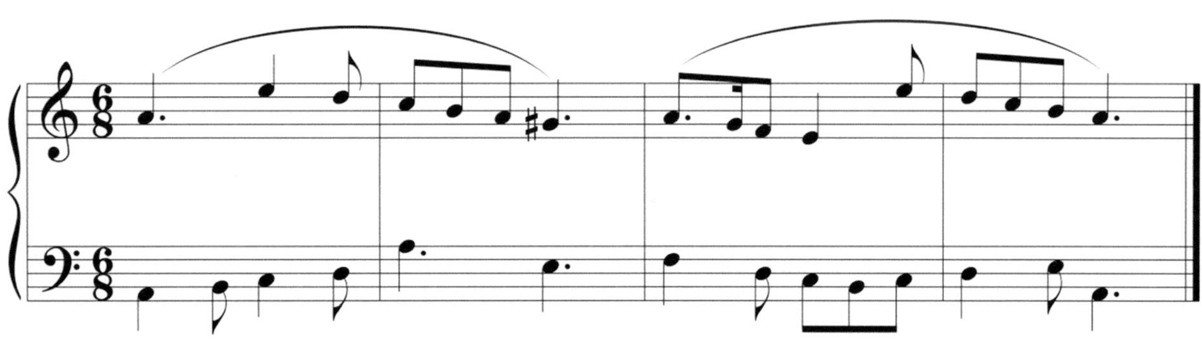

Numerals____

CHAPTER 11

INTRODUCING Vb

Vb can be used as a variation of **V** as appropriate, offering a new bass note and the possibility of smoother connection with the chords around it. As with any first inversion, the root is doubled. Here are a few examples in C major and A minor.

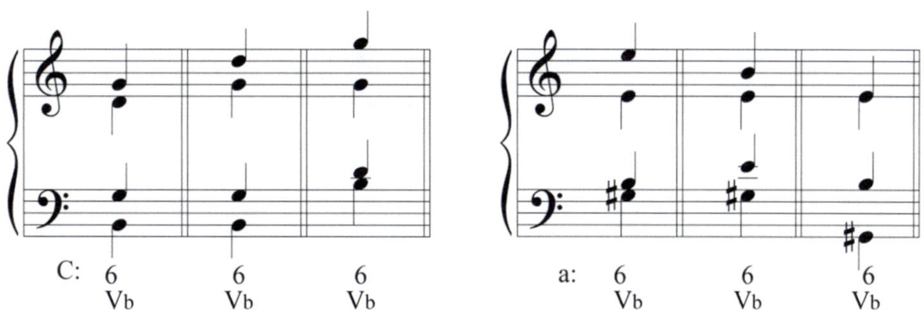

Exercise 11.1

Add roman numerals below these chords. Then complete adding SAT.

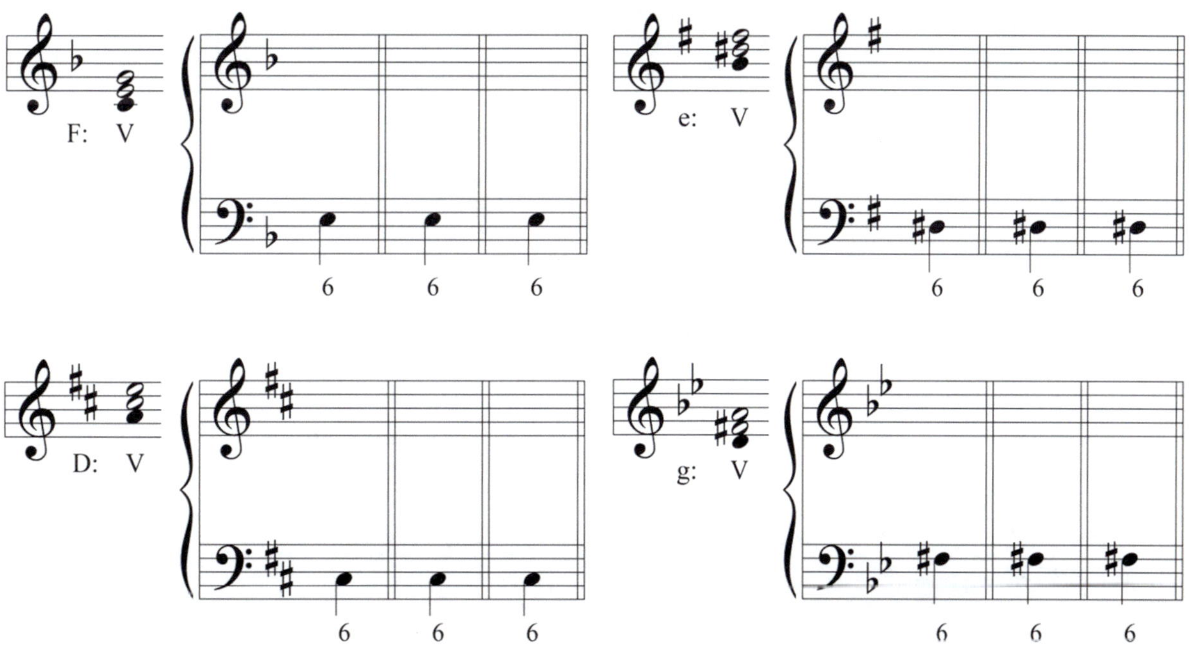

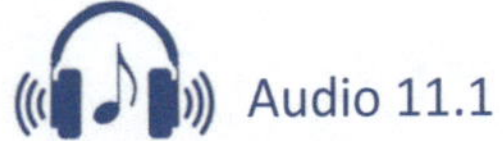

Listen to Audio 11.1. You hear a short harmonised phrase using chord **V** in root position only. This is followed by the same phrase substituting some root positions of **V** with **Vb** marked *.

Audio 11.2

Now listen to Audio 11.2. This minor key harmonisation is also presented in two versions. The first uses **V** in root position, the second substitutes **Vb** where marked *.

Vb in a given bass line

The bass note of **Vb** is the leading note of the key, and is easy to spot in a given bass line since chord **VII** is not yet available.

This is a bass line which makes use of both **Ib** and **Vb**.

Now we set about writing a soprano line.

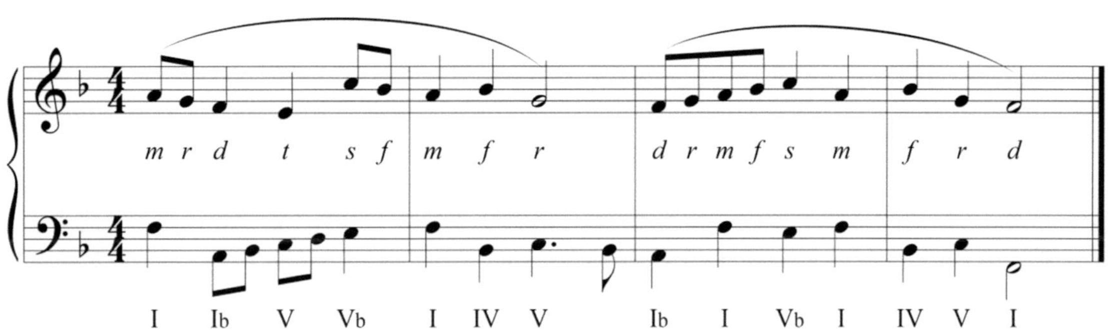

In bar 1, two points to note:

- The large leap between ***t – s*** (beats 3 – 4) is possible since there is no chord change, only a change of position.
- The leading note ***t*** (beat 3) need not resolve as it is transferred into the bass part on beat 4 and then resolves into the following chord **I**.

Using the same bass, this is another possible soprano line.

In bars 2 – 3, note:

- The leap of a fourth, ***r – s*** in the soprano (across the bar line), is possible because of the smooth bass line.

 Audio 11.3

Listen to Audio 11.3 to hear the two contrasted soprano shapings just discussed.

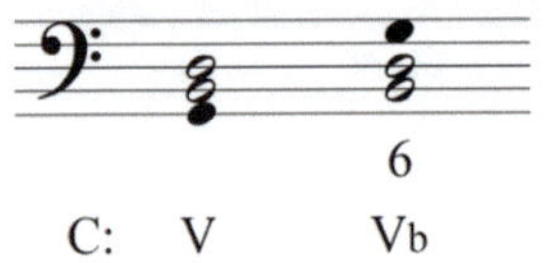

Figured bass: As already stated, a root position chord normally requires no figures, while a first inversion chord is indicated by 6.

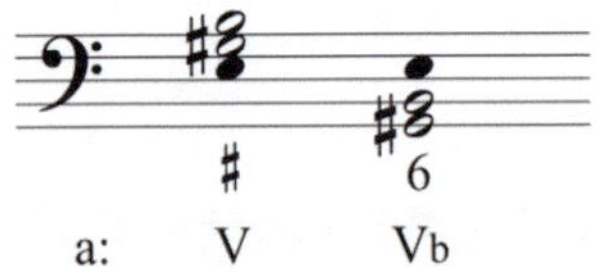

However, in the minor key, in chord **V** root position, the raised 7th accidental is indicated in the figuring. When an accidental appears without a number, it is understood that it always refers to the third above the bass.

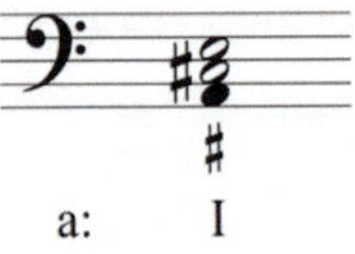

A Tierce de Picardie chord also requires a similar indication in a figured bass.

Exercise 11.2

Sing carefully through each given bass line and circle any obvious passing notes. The figured bass identifies the first inversion chords. Add the roman numerals. Write a melody for the soprano.

(a)

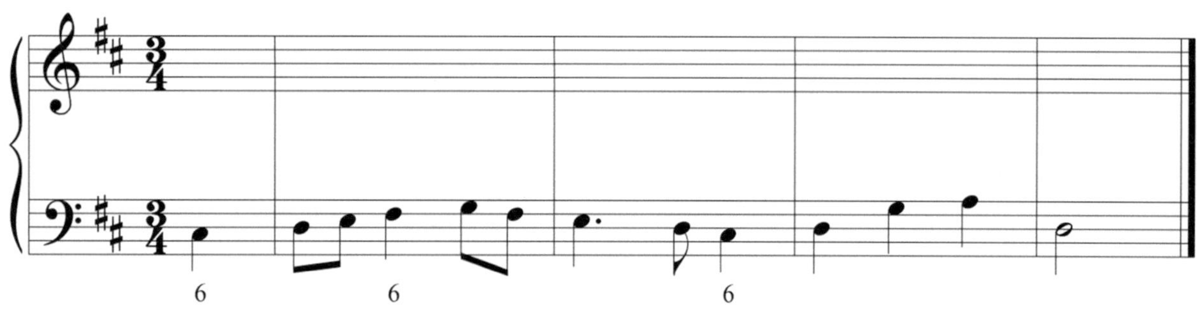

Numerals ____________________

(b)

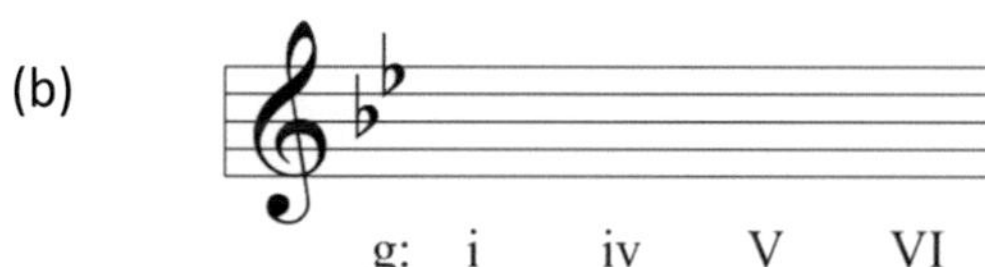

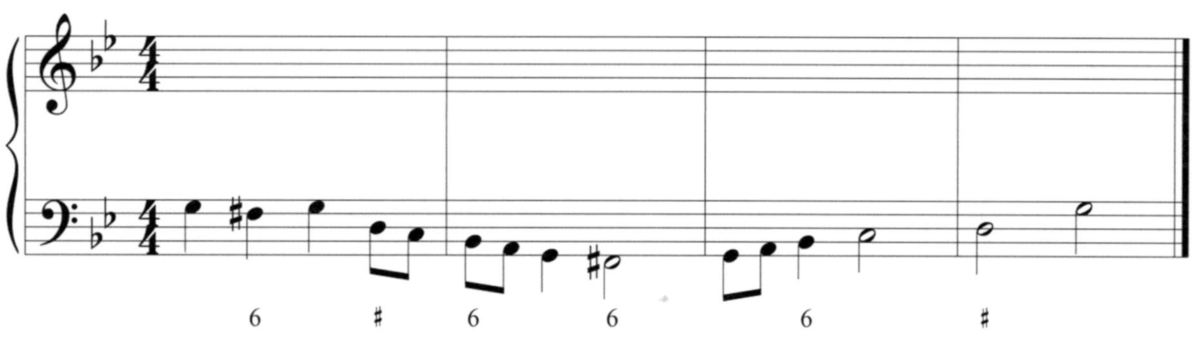

Numerals ____________________

Exercise 11.3

Write a melody for soprano.

(a)

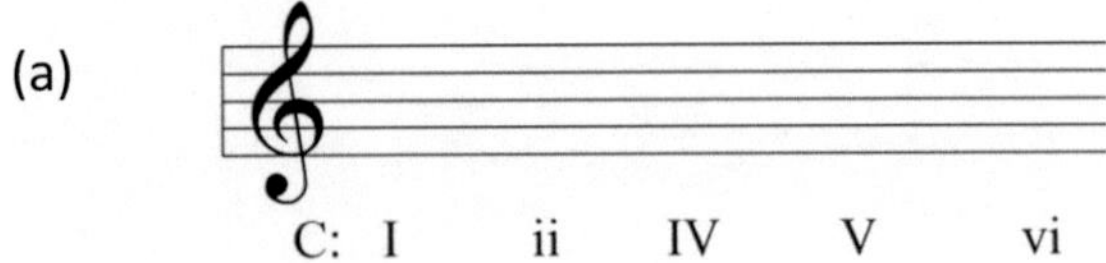

(b)

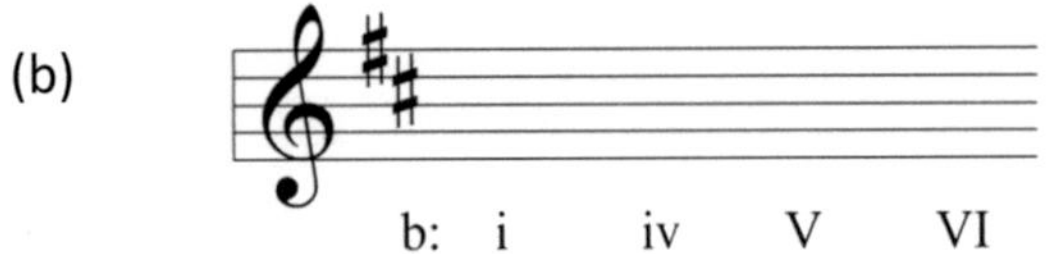

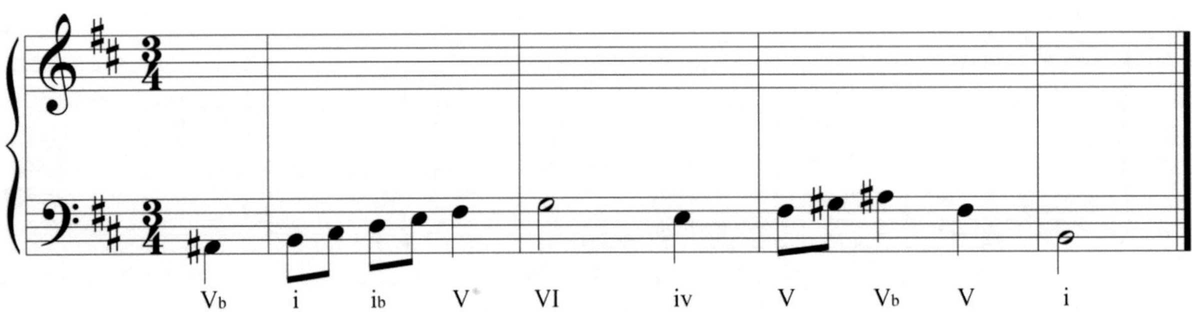

Exercise 11.4

Add roman numerals below each of the given bass lines. Add a soprano melody.

(a)

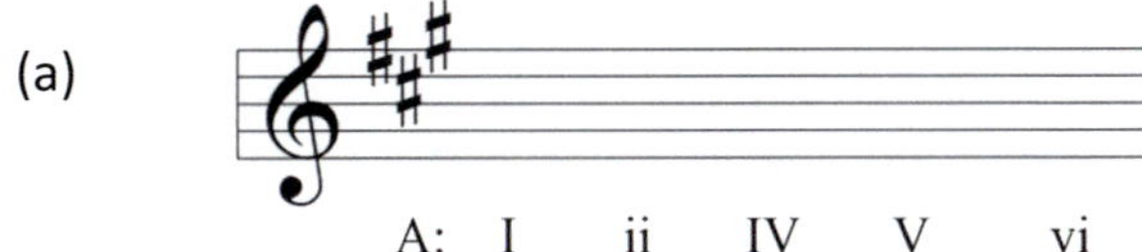

Numerals ______

(b)

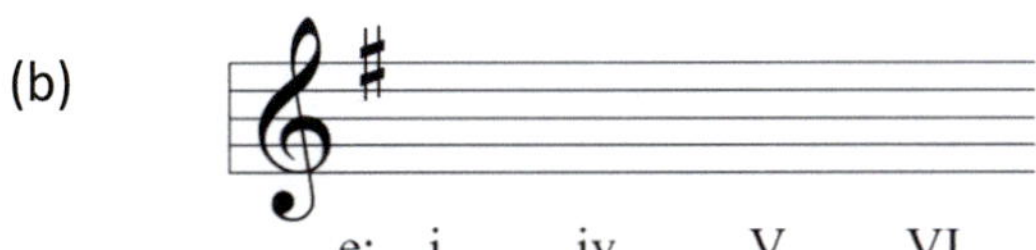

Numerals ______

Harmonising a melody including Vb

The bass note of **Vb** is the leading note. Since the leading note rises a step to the tonic, the logical progression of **Vb** is to **I**. Its other use would be as a variation of **V**.

When harmonising a soprano line it is still useful to plot in the main chord changes in root position. Then, refine your choices by considering appropriate first inversions of chords **I** and **V**. The general aim is to create a smooth flowing bass line.

However, remember the following:

- Where a strong cadential effect is needed, keep chords in root position.
- If the leading note (***t*** – major key, ***si*** – minor key), is the main melody note **Vb** should not be used.

We now work through the following minor key melody, first choosing the chords in root position.

First inversions now improve the shape of the bass line.

Upbeat: The use of **Vb** creates a smoother bass line.

Bar 1: Using **Ib** on beat 2 gives the whole bar a new contour.

Bar 2: The bass is already smooth with the use of **V**. To opt for **Vb** in this instance would be counter-productive resulting in two ungainly intervals. All augmented intervals in any voice should be avoided.

Bar 3: Retain the root position of chord **V** for a strong final cadence.

Audio 11.4

Listen to Audio 11.4 to compare both versions.

This is an example in C major. We follow the same steps as before, deciding the harmonisation in root position and then reconsidering where to use **Ib** and **Vb** as appropriate.

Upbeat: Both root position chords at the opening (**V – I**) sound rather 'cut and dried' whereas **Vb** eases in.

Bar 1: Using **Ib** on beat 2 gives more bass interest.

Bar 2: Leaping to **Vb** on beat 2 connects the bass smoothly into the next chord change.

Bar 3: Option 1 uses **V – I**
Option 2 uses **V – Ib**. Both are viable.

Bar 4: **Vb** works well on beat 1 (as a continuation of the scalic bass), but reverts to root position on beat 2 to allow for a strong final cadence.

Listen to Audio 11.5 to compare both versions.

Exercise 11.5

Harmonise each soprano melody by adding the bass line. Remember always to sing the given line and include the solfa.

(a)

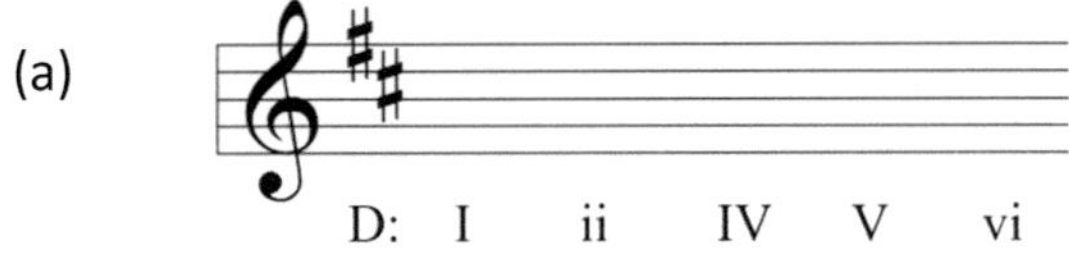

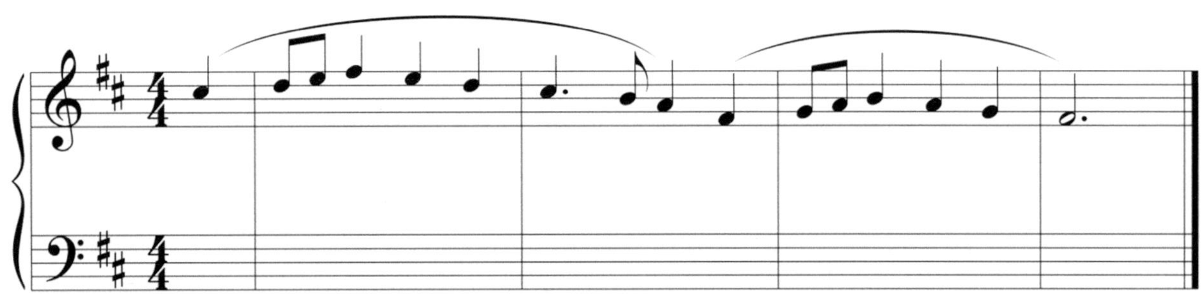

Numerals ______________________________

(b)

Numerals ______________________________

(c)

Numerals ___

(d)

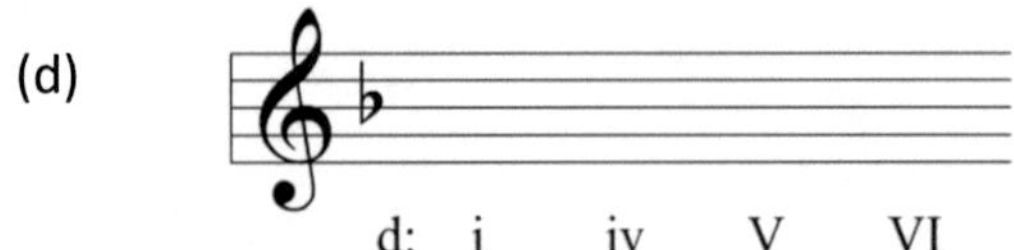

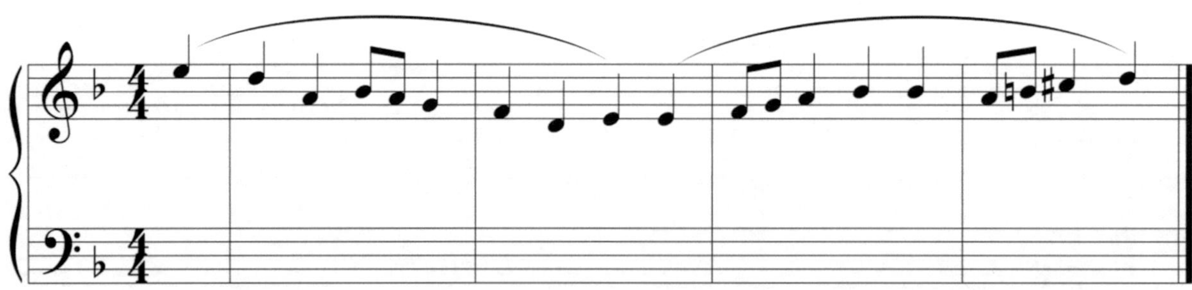

Numerals ___

(e)

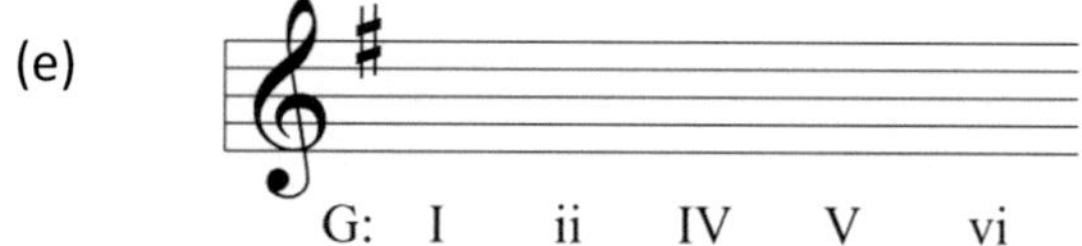

Numerals ____

(f)

Numerals ____

Adding Alto and Tenor

As we introduced **Ib** we stressed the importance of any three voices moving smoothly. Another possibility was the doubling of the 5th of the chord if needed. Both points are relevant when using **Vb**.

This is a worked example in C major.

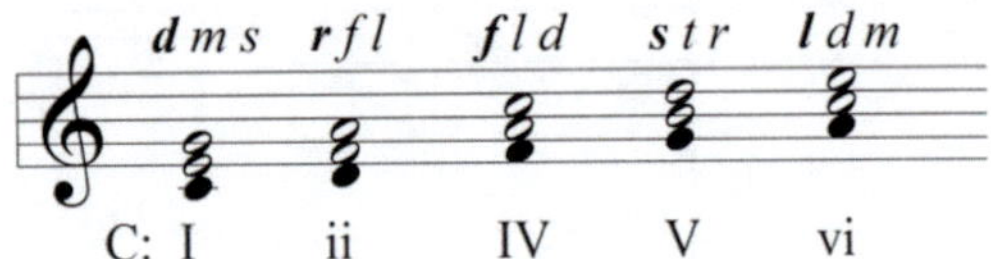

For the most part all the voices are moving very smoothly. However, in bar 2, the movement **Ib – Vb** has a leap in both the bass and tenor parts. Doubling the 5th in **Vb** (in the tenor part), although it would give a smoother line, is not an option here as it results in consecutive octaves with the soprano.

Occasionally, a leap in two parts is workable but always needs to be checked carefully.

Listen to Audio 11.6 to hear the full harmonisation.

This is another worked example in A minor.

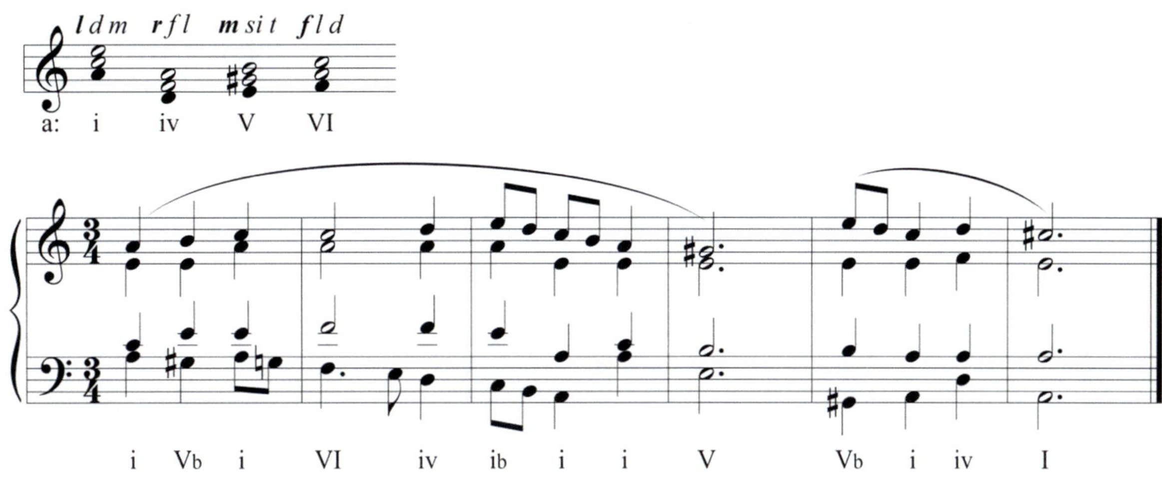

In this harmonisation, notice how smoothly the voices move at chord changes. In bar 3, the 5th has been doubled in **Ib** on the first beat; the doubling of the root would also have been possible at this point.

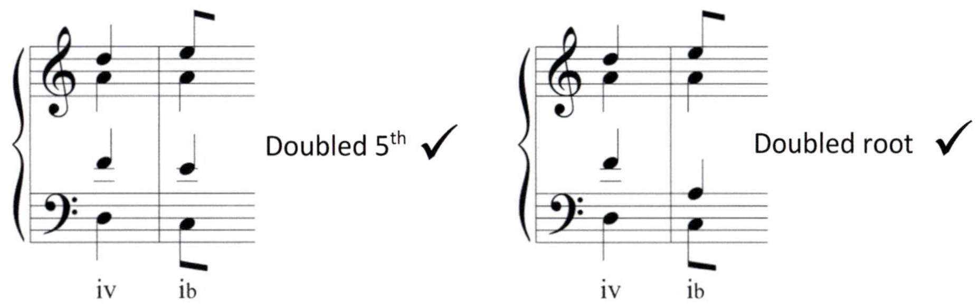

This is another way to arrange the inner voices in the first few bars.

Bar 1: Beat 3 has a different layout which impacts on what follows. Notice that, by the time we reach bar 3, doubling the root in **ib** is now the obvious choice.

Listen to Audio 11.7 to hear both versions.

Exercise 11.6

Add roman numerals and complete the harmonisation by adding parts for alto and tenor.

(a)

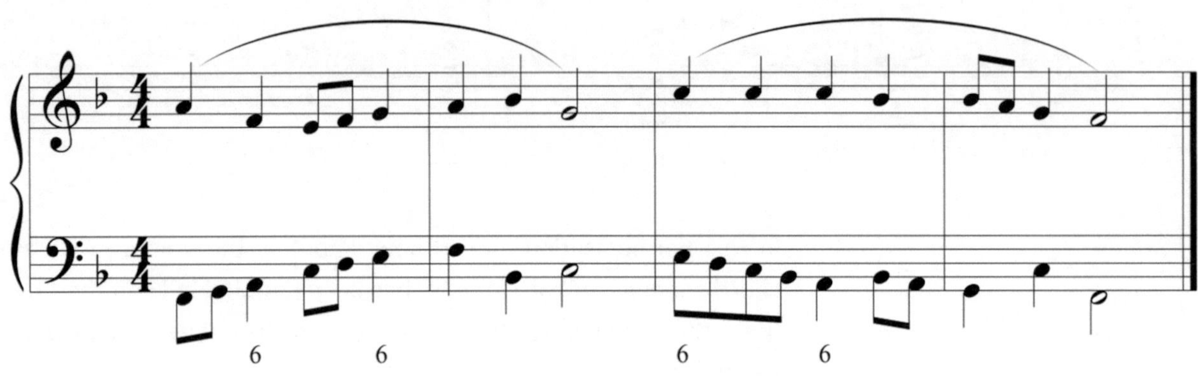

Numerals ____

(b)

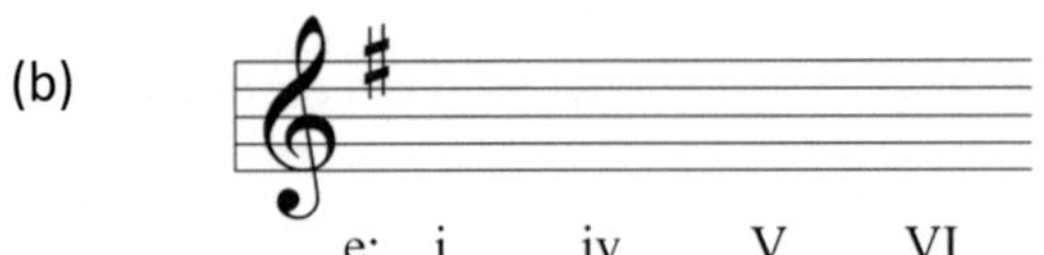

Numerals ____

(c)

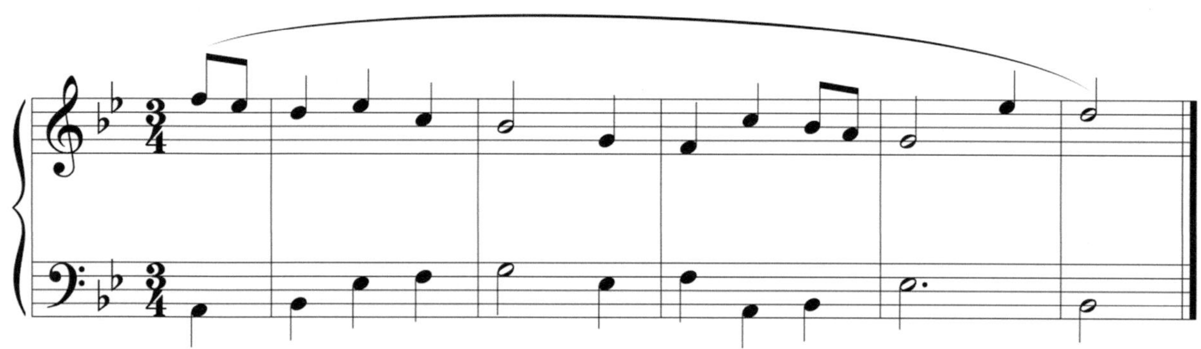

Numerals ____

(d)

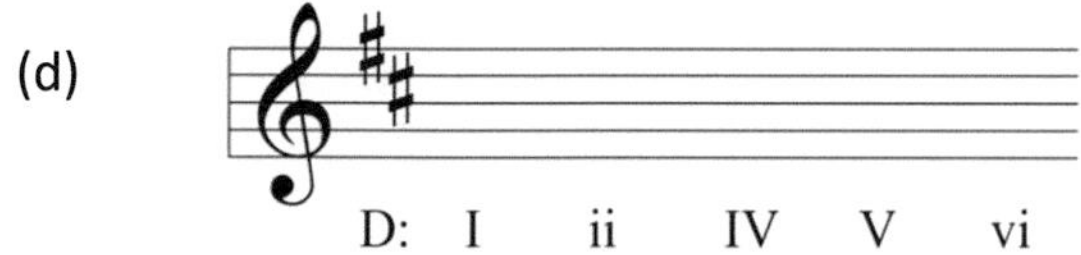

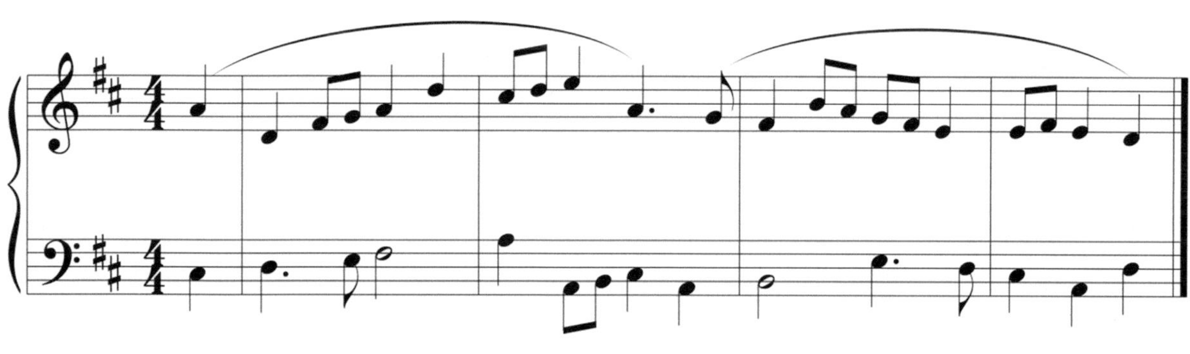

Numerals ____

(e)

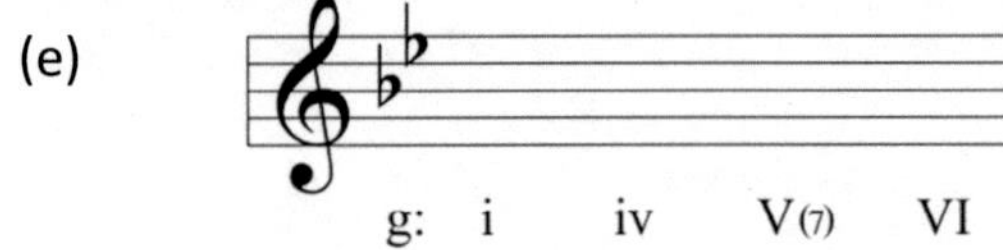

Numerals ____________________

(f)

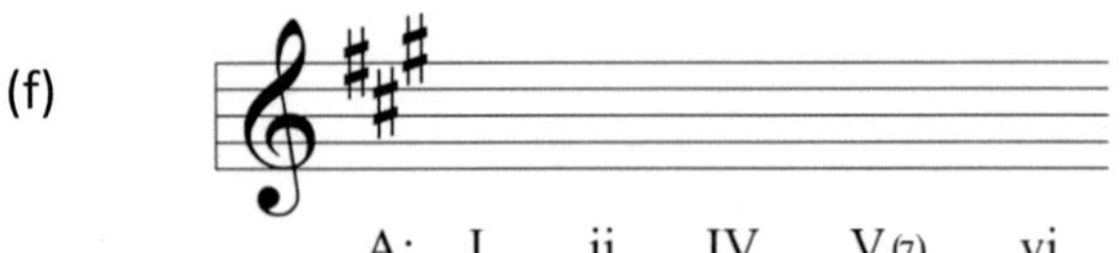

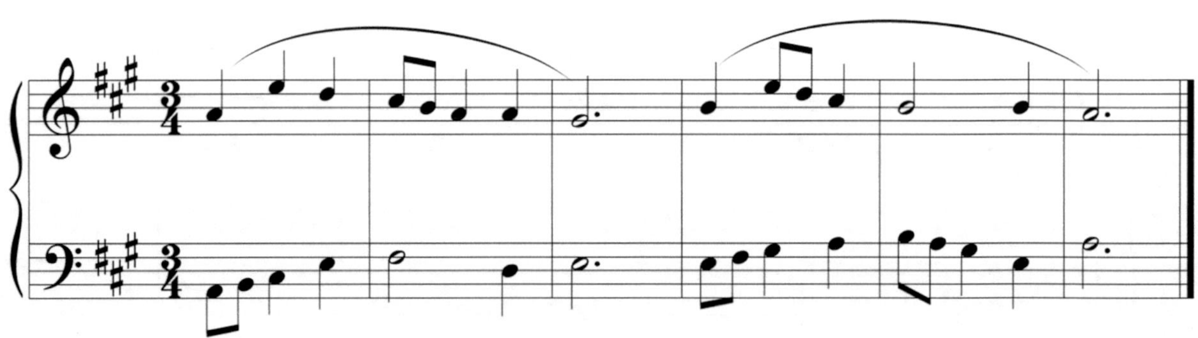

Numerals ____________________

CHAPTER 12

INTRODUCING V7b

The dominant 7th in first inversion - **V7b**, is just as useful as **V7** and gives a richer form of **Vb**.

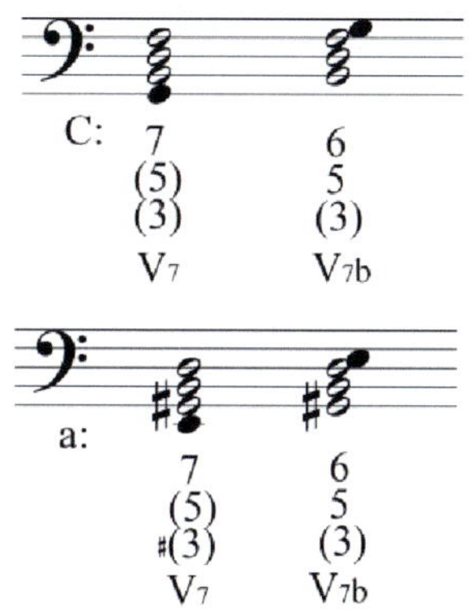

As we know, the figured bass calculates the intervals formed from the bass note to the upper parts of the chord. While all figures are shown here, it is normal practice to abbreviate them by omitting those in brackets.

The only difference with the figuring in the minor key is the indication of the raised 7th accidental in root position.

It can appear as follows:

When an accidental appears without a number it is understood that it always refers to the 3rd above the bass

Using V7b

V7b creates a richer version of **Vb**. All four notes are present in **V7b**. **Vb** resolves to **I; V7b** also resolves to **I** with the leading note rising by step and the 7th falling by step.

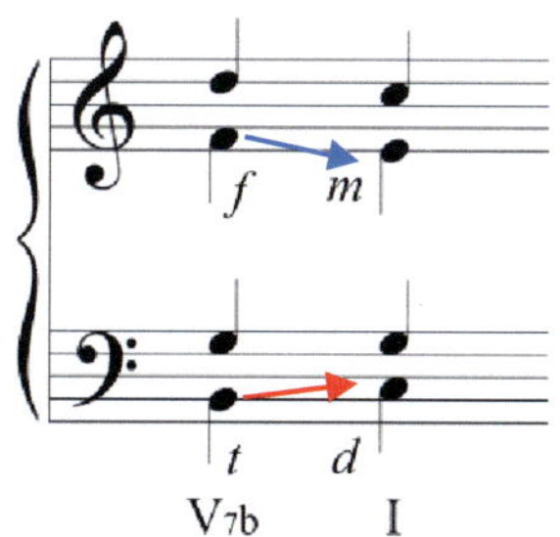

Exercise 12.1

Label the chords according to the figured bass and add parts for SAT.

Harmonising a melody using V7b

There are two clues to help you spot opportunities where **V7b** can be included.

(i) Various arpeggio shapes within ***s – t – r – f*** (***m – si – t – r*** minor key).

(ii) The melodic shape ***f – m*** (***r – d*** minor key).

Take care not to use **V7b** if ***t*** (***si*** minor key), is the main melody note.

This is a worked example used earlier with root position chords.

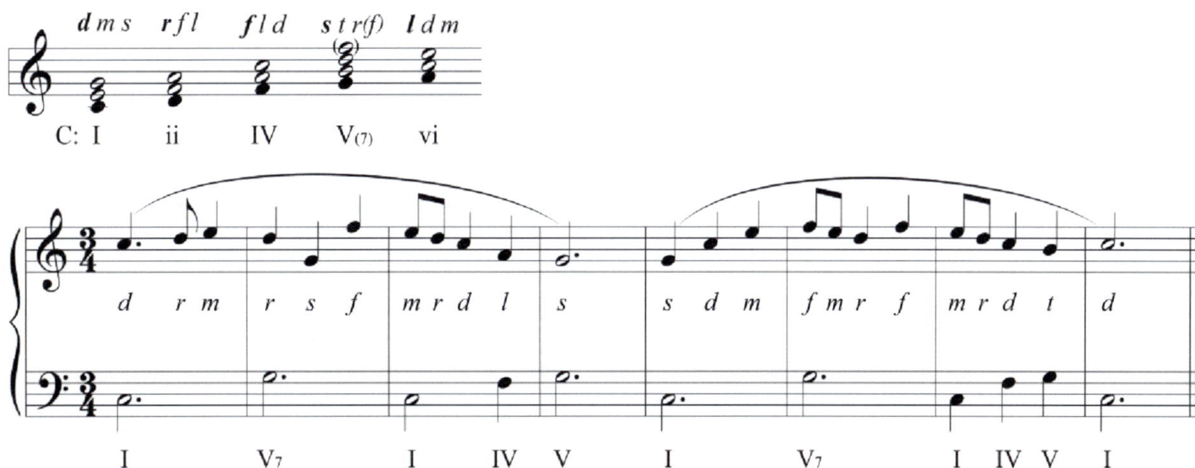

Now reconsider the bass line to include appropriate first inversions of **Ib, Vb** and **V7b**.

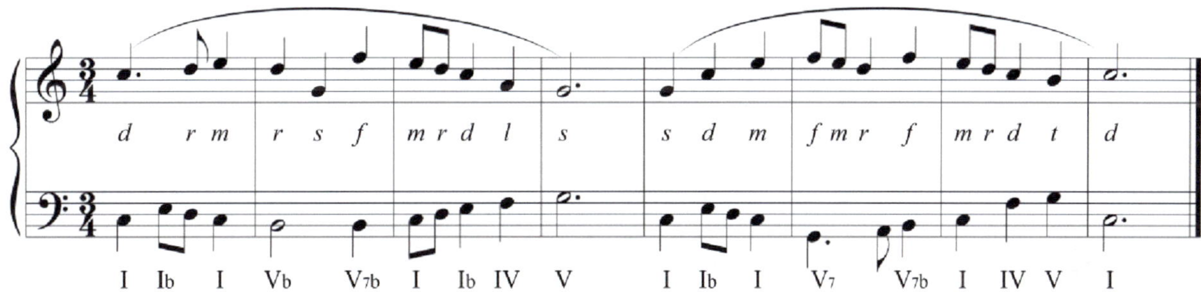

Bar 2: **Vb** and **V7b** give a smoother bass with the chords around them.

Bar 6: The full bar is based around **V7**, so using **V7b** on beat 3 gives the bass more movement. It also connects smoothly to chord **I** in the next bar.

Audio 12.1

Listen to Audio 12.1 to hear and compare both versions.

Exercise 12.2

Add a bass line to harmonise each melody. Begin by singing the melody using solfa. A few pointers are included in (a) and (b) to help you consider **V7b** as a possibility.

(a)

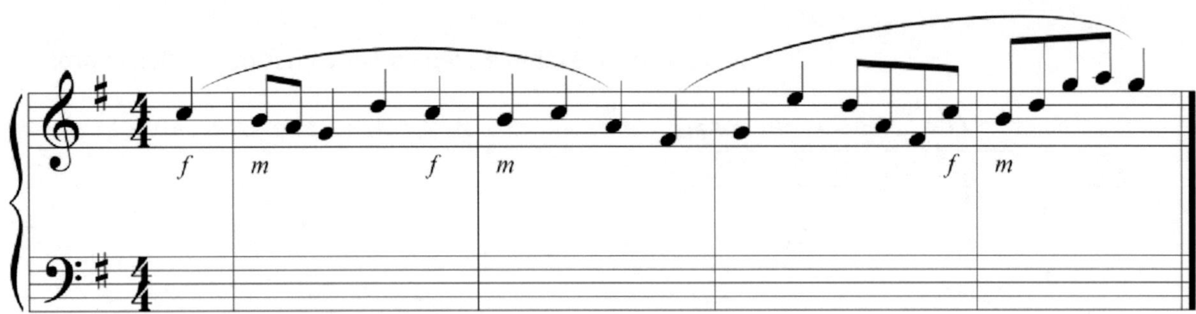

Numerals ____

(b)

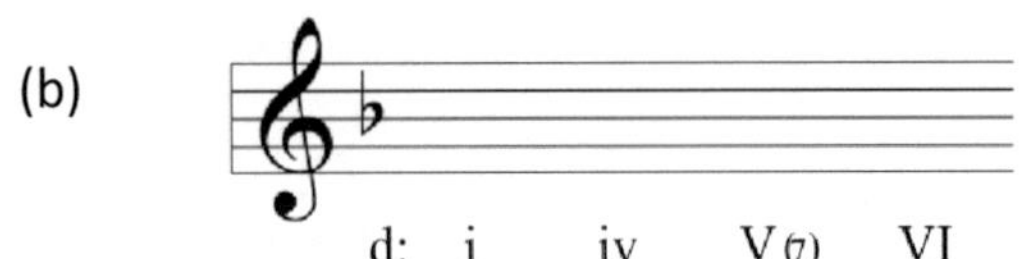

Numerals ____

(c)

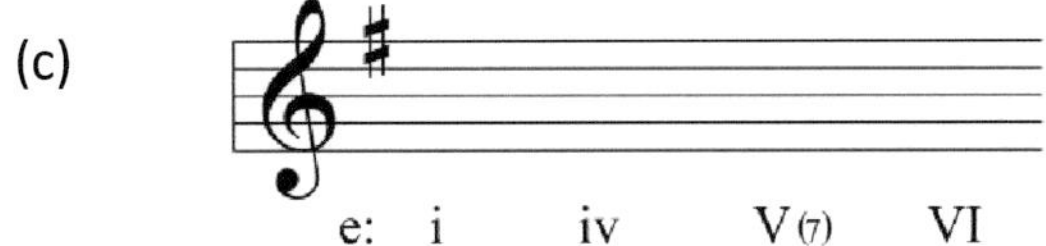

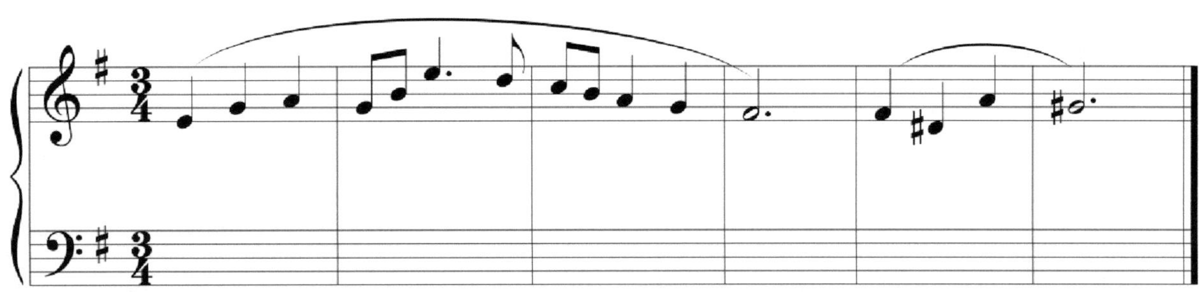

Numerals ____

(d)

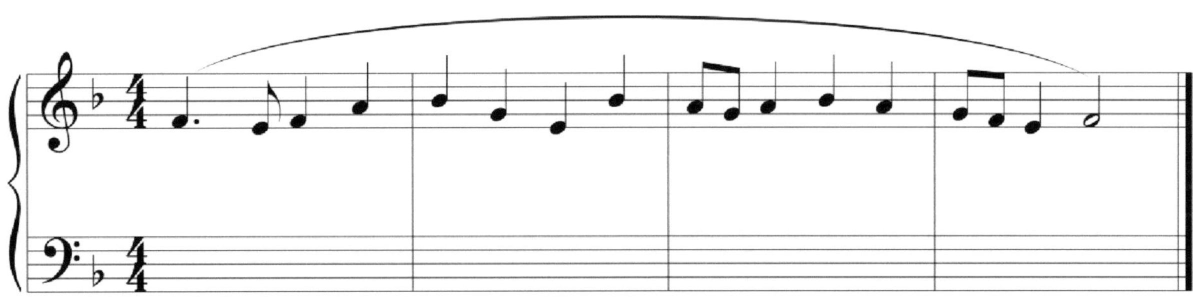

Numerals ____

Adding alto and tenor parts with V7b

This is a worked example in G major.

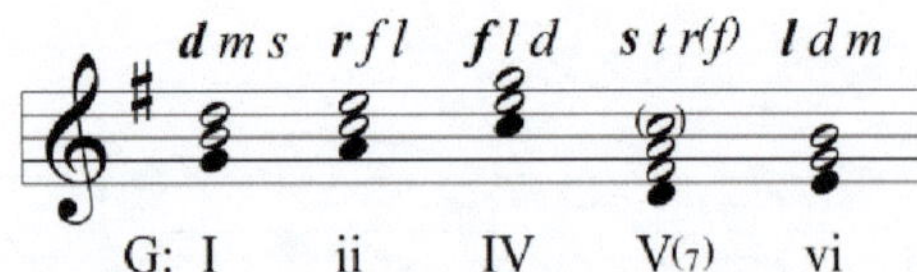

Bar 1, beat 2: Notice how the 7th (*f*) is added after the beat and resolves correctly.

Bar 2, beat 4: All four notes are present in **V7b** with correct resolutions into chord **I** on the following beat.

Bar 3, beat 3: Here **V7b** does not resolve directly, but instead reverts to **V7** with the 7th transferring from soprano to alto. The 7th then resolves in the alto line at the next chord change.

Listen to Audio 12.2 to hear the four-part harmonisation.

Exercise 12.3

Add the roman numerals and complete each harmonisation by adding parts for alto and tenor.

(a)

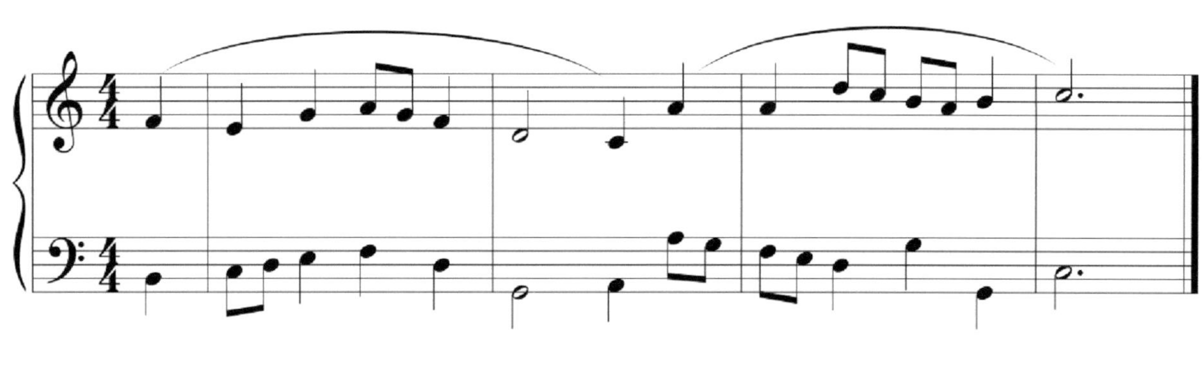

Numerals ____

(b)

Numerals ____

(c)

Numerals ___

(d)

Numerals ___

A quick survey of the dominant 7th

The dominant 7th is a strong versatile chord.

Use it to:

(i) Add richness to the harmony

(ii) Create mobility on a prolonged dominant harmony (i.e. shifting between positions)

(iii) Push the harmony forward as it resolves

Watch the grammar!

Resolutions – the leading note rises a step and the 7th falls a step.

Remember!

(i) The 7th may be transferred within the chord or be added after the beat.

(ii) Melodic intervals needing dominant 7th harmony are:

A leaping 7th ***s – f*** (***m – r*** minor key)
An augmented 4th/diminished 5th ***t – f*** (***si – r*** minor key)

Figured bass:

6	= First inversion
7	= **V7**
6 5	= First inversion **V7b**
♯ ♭ ♮	= Used alone, refers to the 3rd above the bass.

Analysis

In this section you will encounter a variety of musical examples from Dussek to Tchaikovsky. Listen carefully to the extracts before you respond. You may listen as often as you wish.

Audio 12.3

Below is the final section of the Andante Sostenuto in E flat major from Mendelssohn's Christmas pieces. Label the highlighted chords using roman numerals.

Andante sostenuto

Mendelssohn

f *dim.* *p*

pp

This is the opening of Mendelssohn's Song without words in E Major, No. 9 (Op. 30 No. 3).

a) Identify using roman numerals the chords used in the highlighted areas.
b) Name the cadence at the end of the phrase:_______________

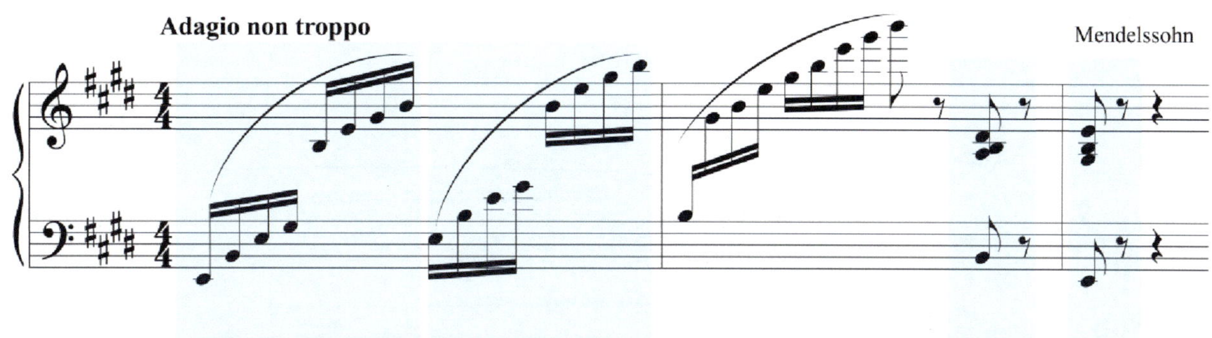

Answer the following questions in relation to the extract from the opening of Beethoven's Bagatelle Op. 119 No. 9.

a) Name the key:______________
b) Identify using roman numerals, the highlighted chords.
c) Name the final cadence:___________________

Study the extract below from the 2nd movement of Mozart's Piano Sonata K 281, and answer the following questions. The key of the movement is E flat major.

a) Identify using roman numerals the chords used in the highlighted areas.

b) Name the final cadence:________________________

Andante amoroso Mozart

Below are two extracts from Dussek's Minuetto in G major from Sonatina Op. 20, No. 1, labelled A and B.

a) In both extracts identify using roman numerals the harmony highlighted.
b) Name the cadence at the end of each extract:____________________
c) In extract B identify the decorative notes circled in the treble as either passing or auxiliary.
Bar 4: A ______________ C _____________ E ____________ Bar 5: E______________

This is part of Tchaikovsky's 'Old French Song' Op. 39 No. 16. Listen carefully and answer the following questions.

a) Name the key:____________________

b) Identify using roman numerals the harmony in the highlighted areas.

c) Name the cadence at the end of the first section (bars 7 - 8):_________________

d) Describe the decorative notes circled in bar 1.

Treble: A____________ C_____________ Bass: C____________ C_____________

Adagio Tchaikovsky

Below is the 1st phrase from Schubert's Ländler, D. 681, No. 1 in E flat major. Listen carefully and answer the following questions.

a) Name the key:____________
b) Identify using roman numerals the harmony in the highlighted areas.
c) Name the type of cadence at the end of the extract:__________________

Audio 12.10

This extract is from the opening of the 2nd movement from Reinecke's Sonatina Op. 47, No. 1. The tonic key is F major. Listen carefully and answer the questions below.

a) Identify using roman numerals the harmony in the highlighted areas.
b) Name the type of cadence occurring in bars 15 – 16:________________

Andantino

C. Reinecke

p

p

This extract is from Schumann's Scherzino (3rd mvt.) from "Carnival Jest from Vienna" Op. 26. This section is in B flat major. Listen carefully and answer the questions below.

a) Identify using roman numerals the harmonic content highlighted.
b) Name the type of cadences occurring in:
   Bar 2: Bar 4:

Below is the opening from Mendelssohn's Allegro non troppo in G major No. 1, from Six Christmas pieces, Op.72.

a) Identify using roman numerals the highlighted chords.
b) Name the type of cadence at the end of the extract: ____________________

The following extract is from the Finale of Haydn's Piano Sonata in D major, Hob. XVI: 37. There are two highlighted areas; the first in the key of D minor, the second in the key of F major.

a) Identify using roman numerals, the highlighted chords.
b) Name the type of cadence formed at the end of each area.
D minor: ____________________ F major: ________________________

Audio 12.14

This extract is from the Finale of Haydn's String Quartet Op. 2, No. 6. Listen carefully and answer the following questions.

a) Identify using roman numerals the highlighted chords.
b) Each pair of chords forms a cadence. Name each cadence.

1.______________ 2.______________ 3.______________

Presto

Haydn

This extract is from the Trio of the 2nd movement of Haydn's String Quartet Op. 2 No. 1. The extract is in the key of A minor. In each bar there is a change of harmony with two changes occurring in bar 7.

a) Identify using roman numerals, the harmony throughout.
b) Name the cadence formed at the end of the extract:____________________

Trio

Haydn

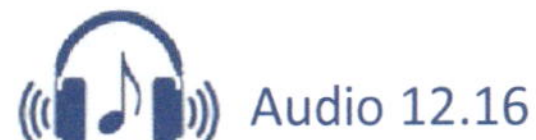

This extract is from the 1st movement of Haydn's String Quartet in C major Op. 9, No. 1. Listen carefully and answer the questions below.

a) Identify using roman numerals, the harmony in the highlighted areas. The pace of the harmony is quite fast as shown by the roman numerals at the start of bar 1.
b) Name the cadence formed at the end of the extract:___________________

CHAPTER 13

ADDING IVb

Think of **IVb** as a variation of **IV**, choosing whichever gives the smoother bass line with the harmonies around it.

A special cadence

In a minor key **ivb – V** creates a particular type of imperfect cadence called a **Phrygian cadence**. This type of cadence is found in the popular Christmas Carol *'God rest ye merry gentlemen'*.

Listen to Audio 13.1. This four-part extract in E minor ends with a Phrygian cadence. Listen to its special qualities.

This is the extracted Phrygian cadence. Notice two essential elements:

the soprano moving ***r – m*** while the bass moves ***f – m***

Remember in chapter 3 the special movement needed in **iv – V** was highlighted (i.e. roots rise a step in the bass while SAT parts fall).

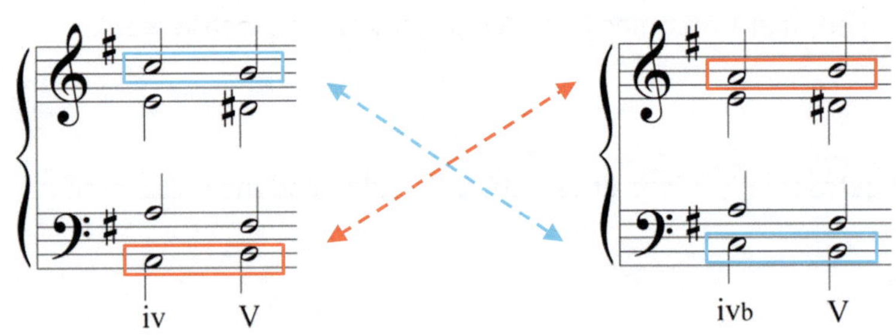

However, in **ivb – V** the rising roots transfer to the soprano, while ATB parts fall.

Bass **roots** rising a step require contrary motion in the upper parts.

When **either** chord is in **first inversion**, contrary motion of the upper parts to the bass is no longer necessary.

Exercise 13.1

Complete these Phrygian cadences in the given minor keys. Remember the two characteristics; the soprano rises ***r – m*** while the bass falls ***f – m***.

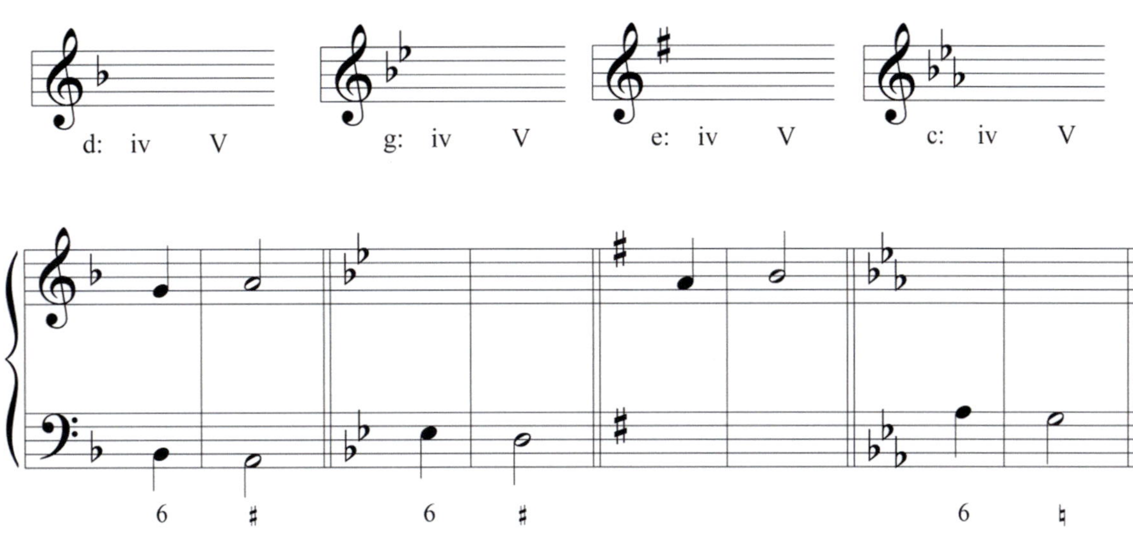

Recognising IVb in a given bass

IVb shares the same bass note as **VI.** Choose whichever gives the strongest progression with the chords around it. Study the following examples.

In this example **IVb** is the better choice. **IV – vi** would be a weaker progression (roots rising a 3rd).

Here **vi** is the better choice allowing a chord change over the bar line (roots falling a 3rd).

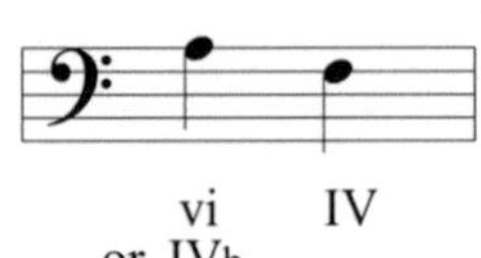

Either **IVb** or **vi** is appropriate here as both chords are within the same bar.

In this instance **IVb** is the better choice, as **vi – I** is weaker (roots rising a 3rd).

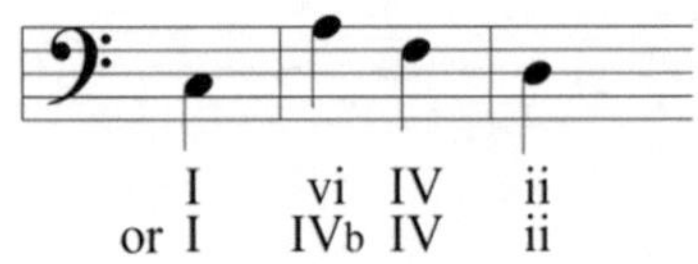

This bass shape offers equal opportunity for using **vi** or **IVb**. Two points may influence your choice depending on context.

(i) **vi – IV** provides a more active harmonic rhythm.

(ii) **IVb – IV** provides a slower harmonic pace with a gentler effect.

All the above progressions are equally effective in both major and minor keys, except those involving chord **ii**.

Study the example below in C major.

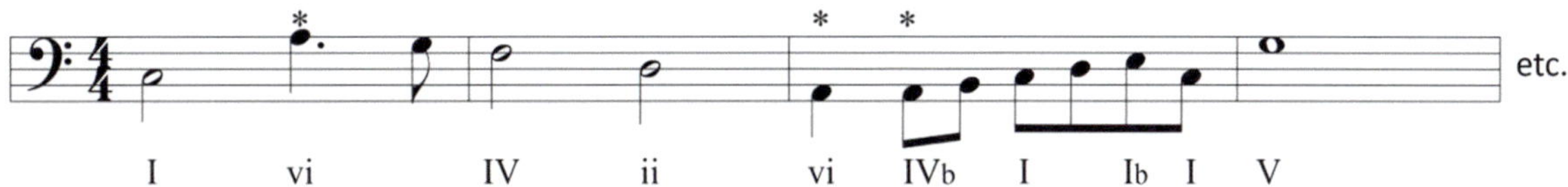

In bar 1 at * chord **vi** is chosen to give a chord change to the following harmony across the bar line.

In bar 3, chord **vi** is chosen on beat 1 as a stronger progression following chord **ii**. It then changes to **IVb** on beat 2 to give a stronger connection to the following chord **I**.

Now we add a possible soprano line using our chosen progressions. The aim is to create as much melodic interest as possible.

Listen to Audio 13.2 to hear our solution.

Exercise 13.2

Carefully study the given bass lines. Choose chords to include some appropriate use of **IVb**. Then add a well-shaped soprano melody.

(a)

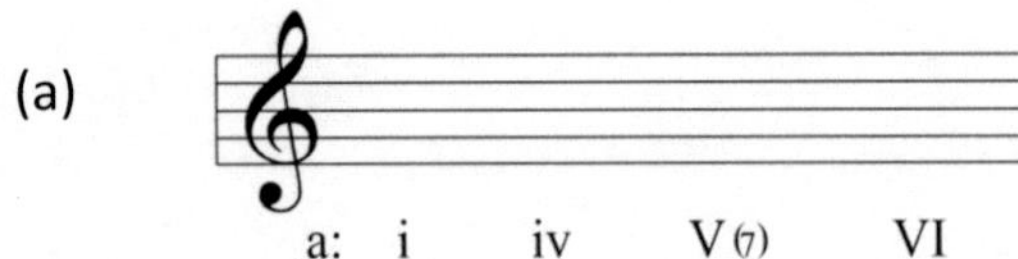

Numerals ______________________________

(b)

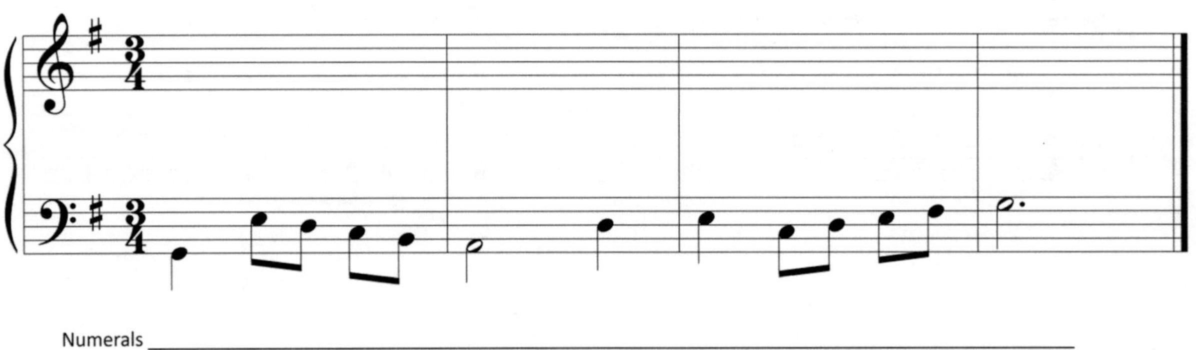

Numerals ______________________________

(c)

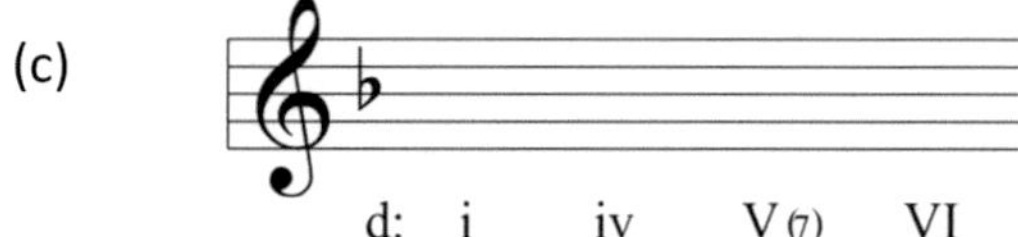

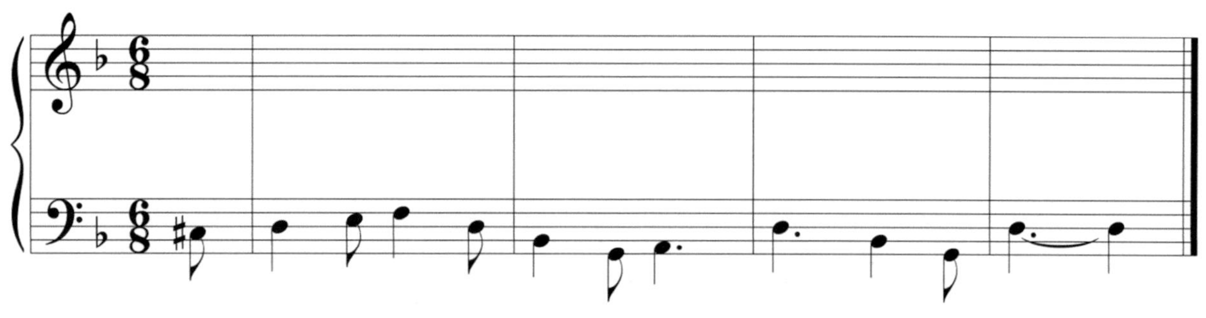

Numerals ______________________________

(d)

Numerals ______________________________

Harmonising a melody using IVb

A few reminders!

1. Add solfa to the melody.
2. Observe cadential points. Watch out for the Phrygian cadence when in the minor key.
3. Plot in likely chords to give a strong harmonic flow. There may be a number of layers in crafting the bass line in order to reach a musical shaping:
    - deciding basic root position chords
    - refining with first inversion possibilities
    - adding passing/auxiliary note decoration

Let us work through this E minor example in stages.

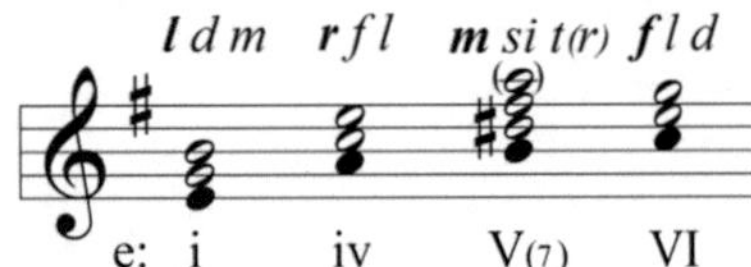

First plot in the cadence points.

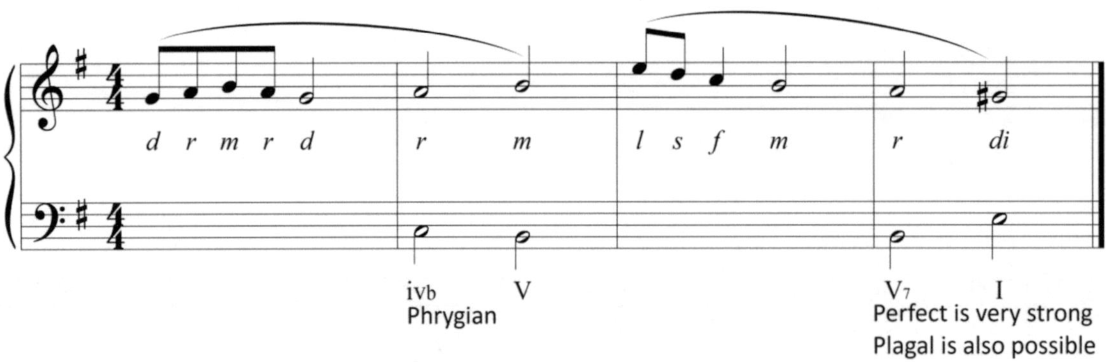

Add the simplest possible bass line in bars 1 and 3.

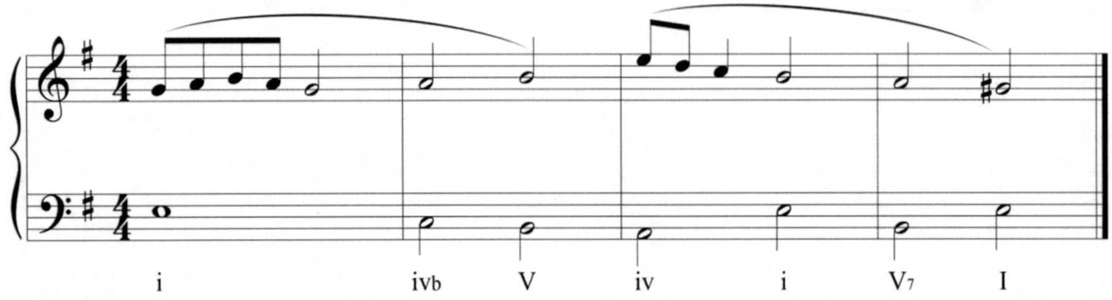

Enhance the bass line by choosing some appropriate first inversion chords.

Consider using an alternative harmonisation to create new colour.

This is another harmonisation for the final cadence.

 Audio 13.3

Listen to Audio 13.3 where you will hear the five previous examples. The step-by-step approach highlights the processes involved in arriving at a successful and interesting solution.

Exercise 13.3

Harmonise each melody by adding the bass line. Make use of the step-by-step suggestions.

(a)

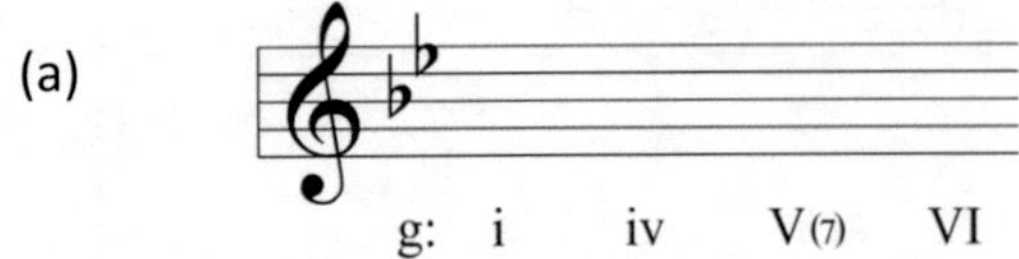

Numerals ______________________________

(b)

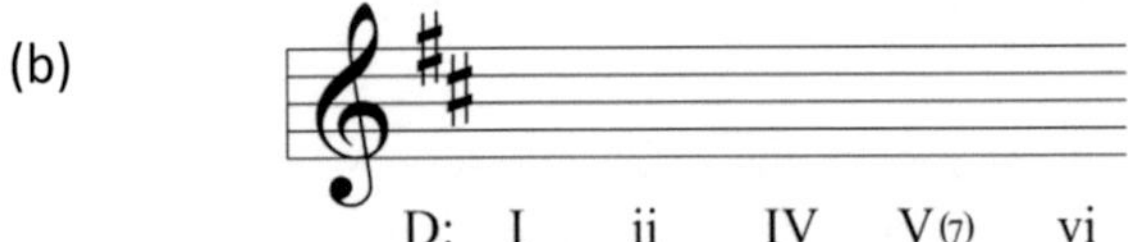

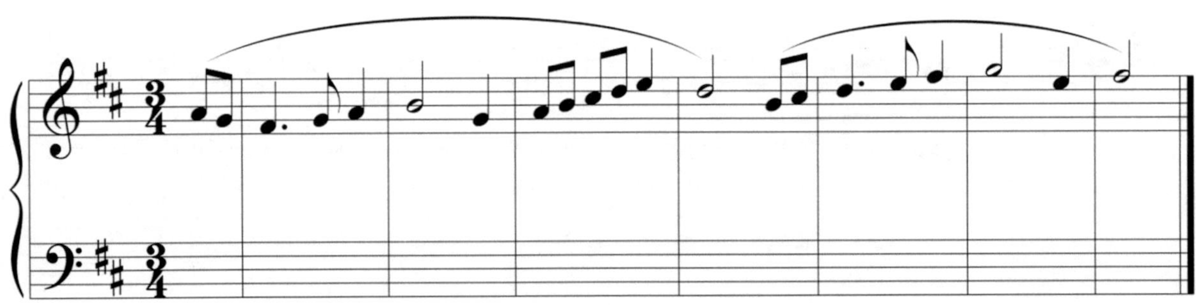

Numerals ______________________________

(c)

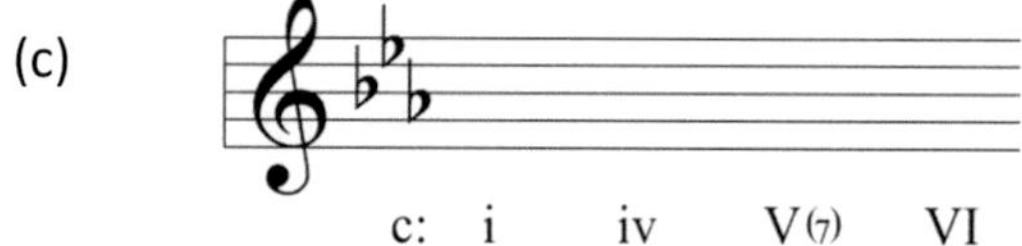

Numerals ____

(d)

Numerals ____

Adding alto and tenor parts

These bass line pitches (***s l t d***) are written with different rhythms, implying different harmonic treatment.

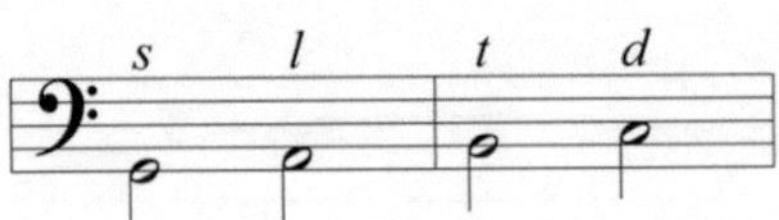

Here the quaver ***l*** is best treated as a passing note.

Here chord changes are needed on the longer values.

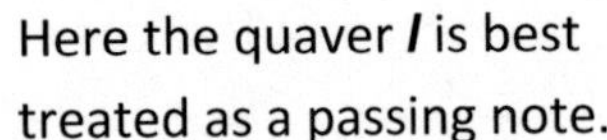

A useful idiom to harmonise this bass shape is **V – IVb – Vb – I**. It is also effective in its descending form as **I – Vb – IVb – V**. At present this will apply only to the major key.

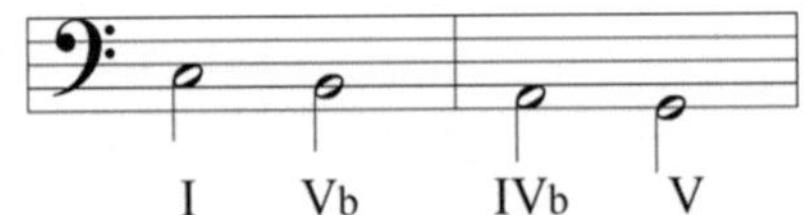

Now take a step back to the basic triads of **IV – V**.

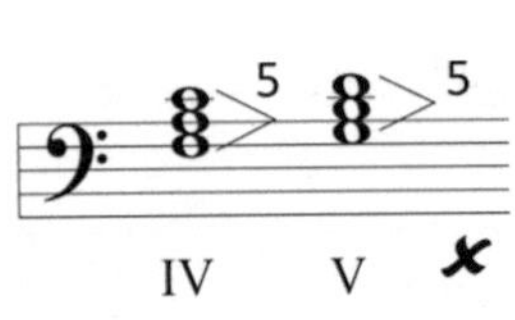

When **both** chords are in root position, we see why contrary motion for the upper parts is necessary to avoid consecutive 5ths and octaves.

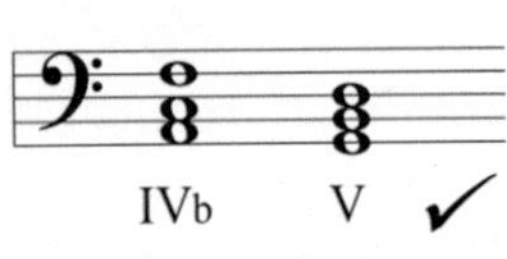

When **either** chord is in first inversion, contrary motion to the bass is no longer necessary.

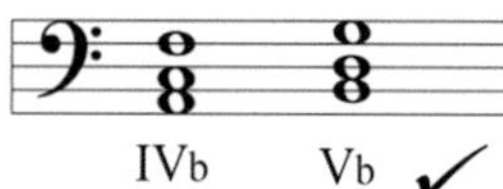

When **both** chords are in first inversion three voices move in the same direction, in a triadic layout.

By copying the triadic layout and transferring the upper notes of both triads into the treble, we have an ideal arrangement for three voices (SA and B).

The question is how to deal with the tenor?

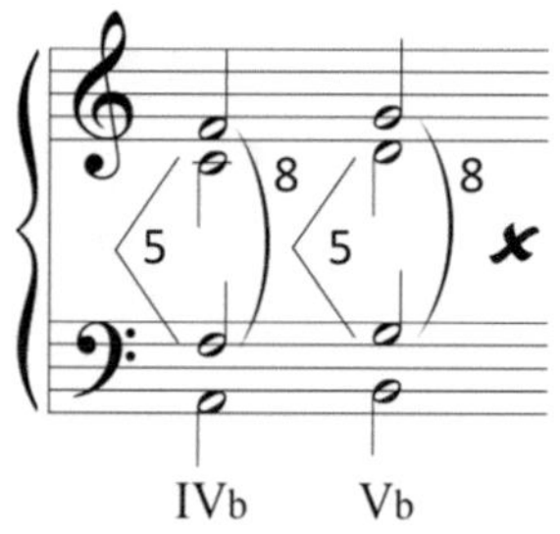

If the roots are doubled in both chords, consecutive 5ths and octaves will be inevitable.

The solution!

Alternate the doubling between the root and 5th of each chord.

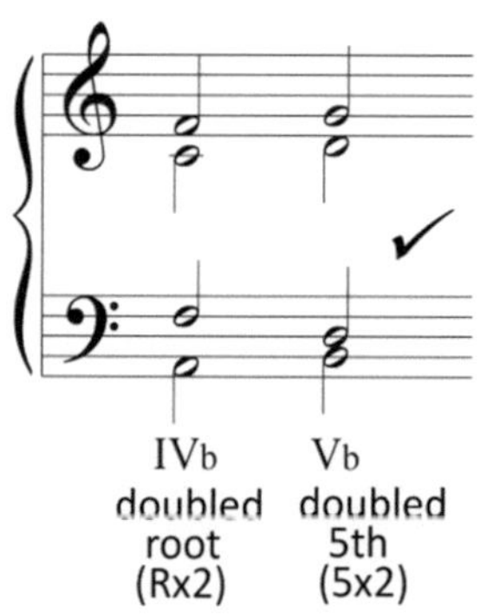

OR

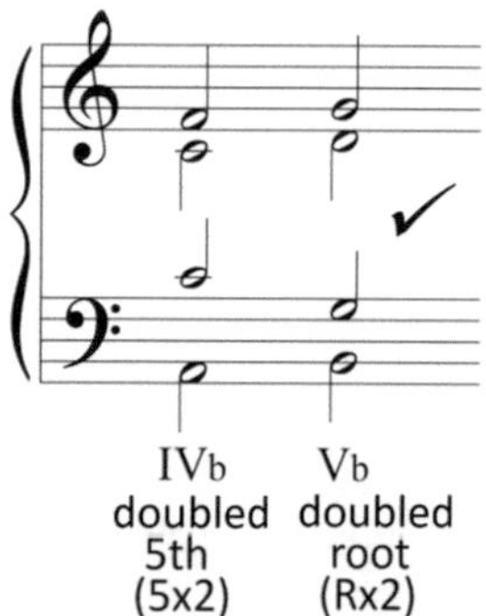

This is the complete idiom in four parts.

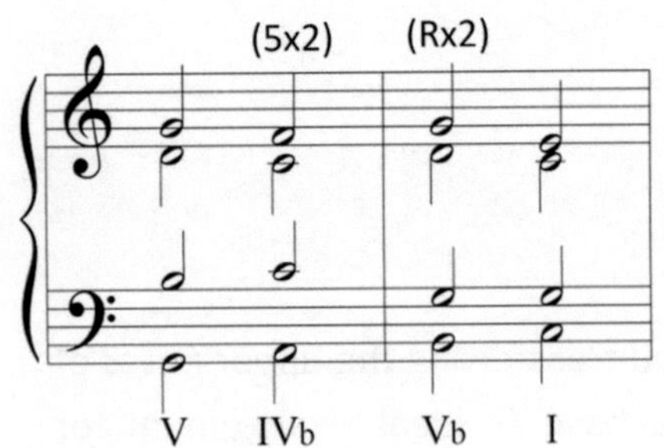

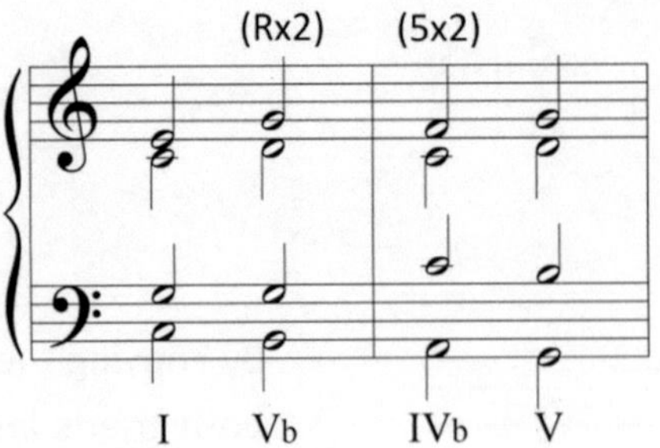

For the present this idiom will be used only in the major key. It is useful to remember this particular soprano shape as it is an indicator that the idiom is suggested: ***s – f – s – m* / *m – s – f - s***

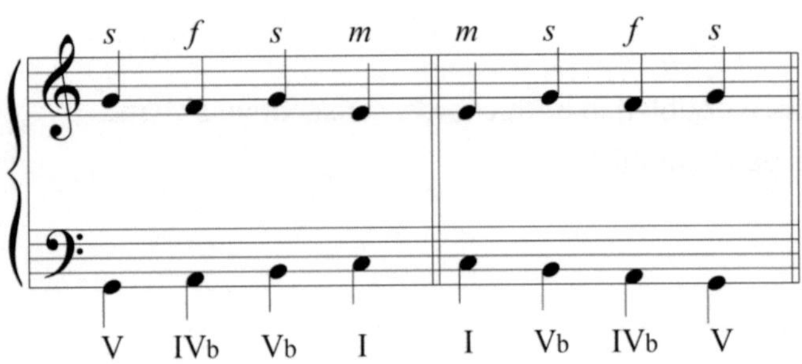

We now set about completing the harmony to the given soprano and bass parts. The solfa is added to highlight the presence of the idiom.

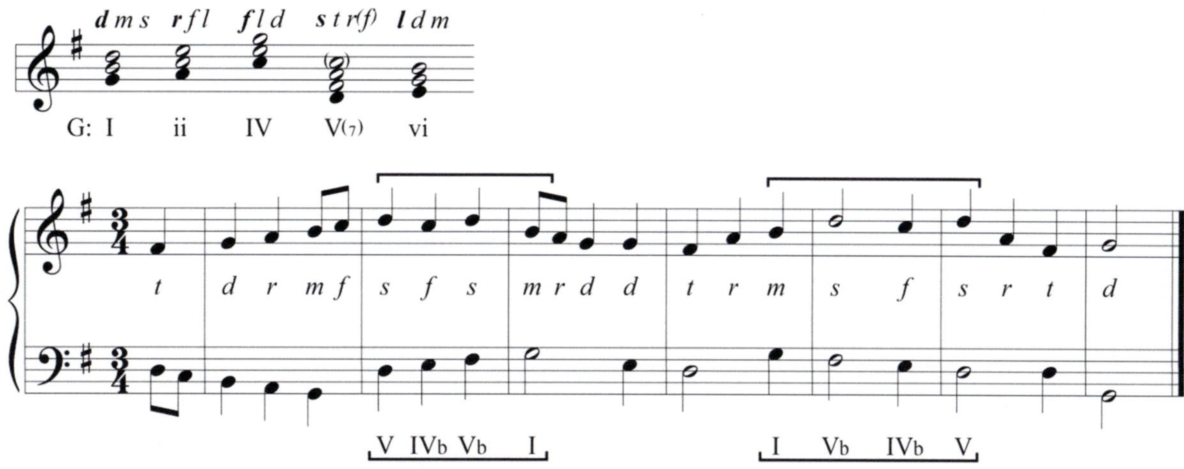

Next we add the remaining roman numerals and commence the inner part-writing.

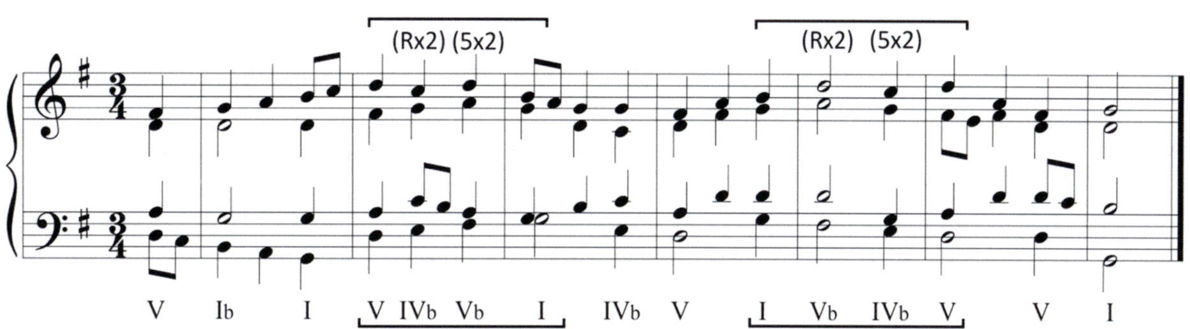

As usual, the aim is to keep three voices moving smoothly at chord changes in order to minimise any grammatical problems. There are two possible arrangements for the inner voices in the idiomatic passages; the alternatives are shown below.

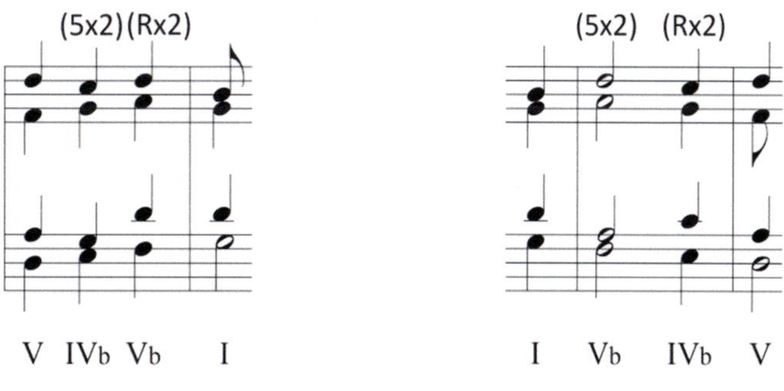

Listen to Audio 13.4. First you hear the two-part version, then the four-part harmonisation.

Exercise 13.4

Complete the following by adding alto and tenor parts. Follow the suggested guidelines. Figured bass is given in the first exercise. Add the roman numerals throughout.

(a)

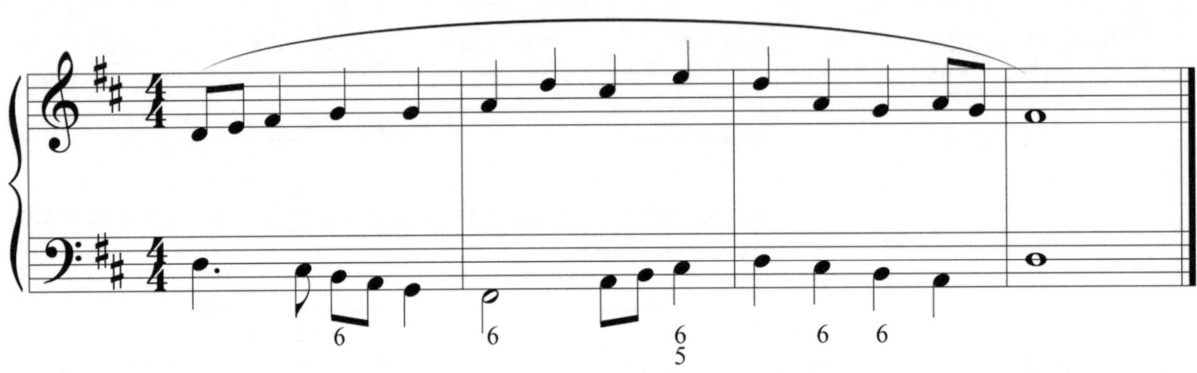

Numerals ____

(b)

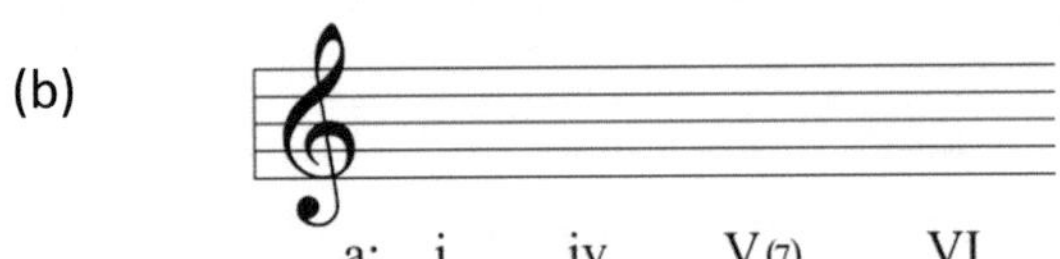

Numerals ____

(c)

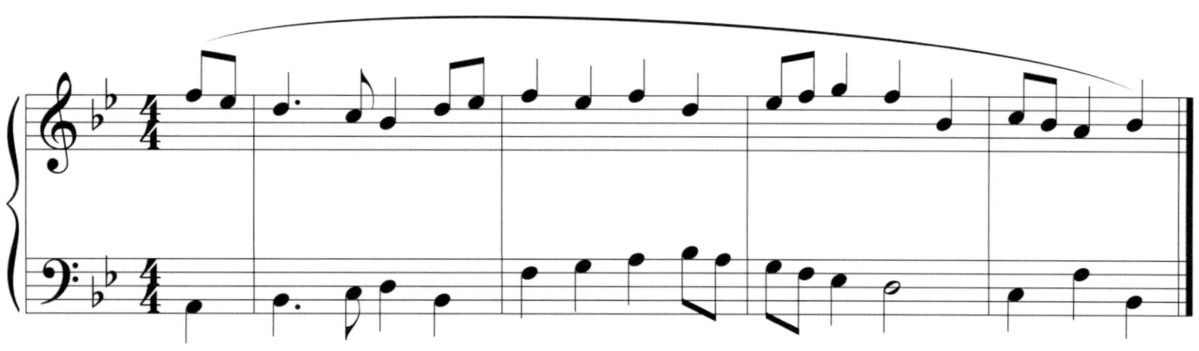

Numerals ______________________________

(d)

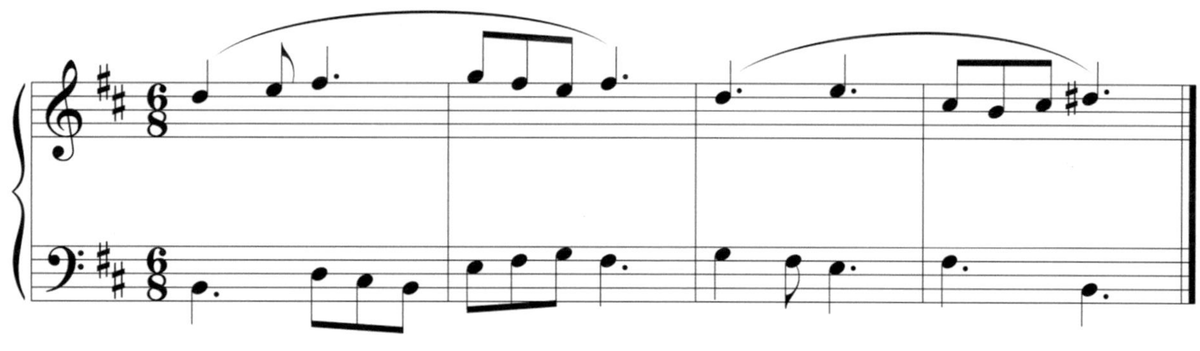

Numerals ______________________________

CHAPTER 14

ADDING VIIb

vii° is a diminished chord in both major and minor keys. A diminished chord is denoted by the small circle symbol. So far, diminished chords have not been used. They are more easily used in first inversion for the following reason:

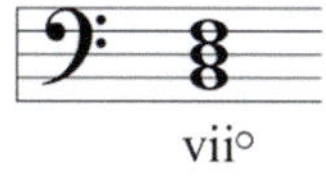

In root position the interval of the diminished 5th between the **bass note** (root) and the 5th is very prominent.

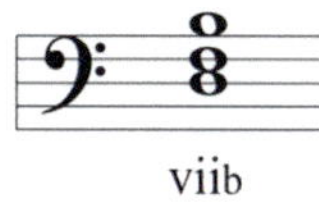

In first inversion there is no dissonant interval with the **bass note**.

Diminished triads favour special doubling. Double the 3rd, since the doubling of the root or 5th would reinforce the dissonance.

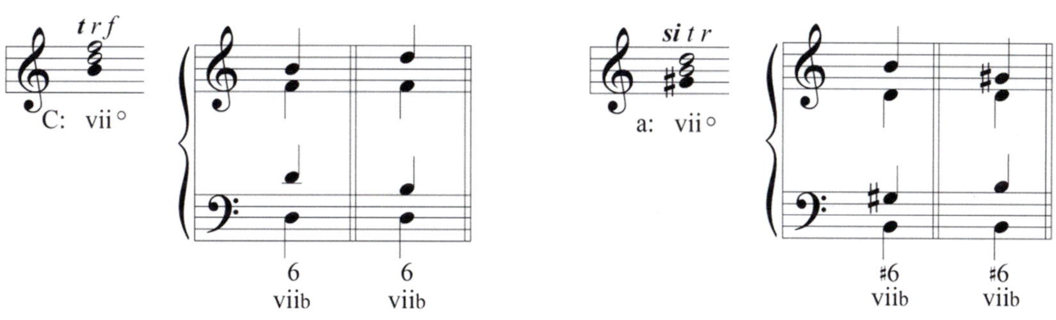

In the minor key example above, the figured bass is presented as ♯6 indicating G sharp which is the leading note of the key.

Exercise 14.1

Write two arrangements of the following **viib** chords for SATB in the named keys.

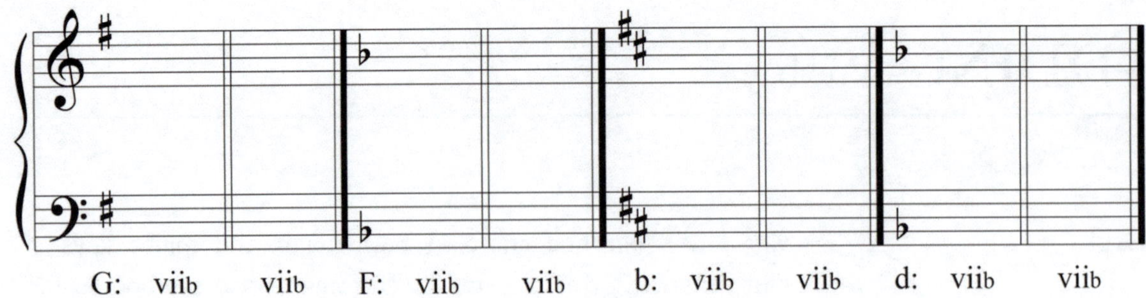

For the moment **viib** will have restricted use. It occurs most commonly between the positions of chord **I** in the following idioms.

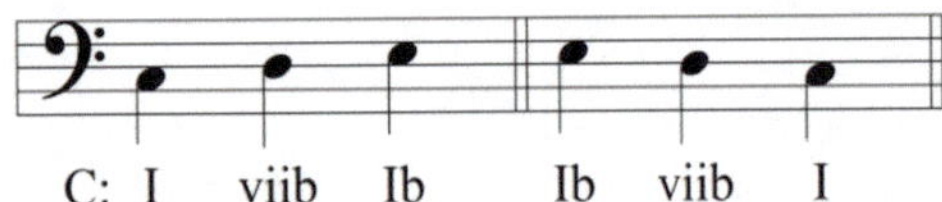

In a four-part arrangement all voices move by step in the following patterns.

(a)

(b)

(c)

(d)

In examples (a) and (b), the 5ths occurring between tenor and alto are not problematic since both are not perfect.

Listen to Audio 14.1 to hear the above progressions in the major key.

These are some minor key arrangements.

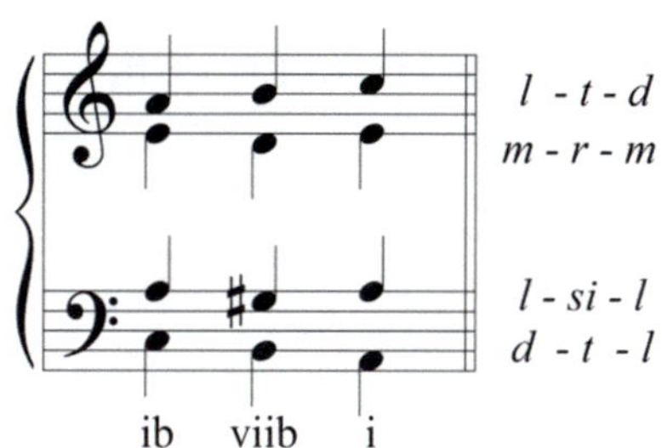

Listen to Audio 14.2 to hear the progressions in the minor key.

In general, notice that one voice always takes the bass notes in a strong contrary motion shape - this is often the soprano. The other strong shape for soprano is ***d – t – d*** (***l – si – l*** minor key).

Major Keys

Soprano	*m - r - d*	may swap
Alto	*s - f - s*	
Tenor	*d - t - d*	
Bass	*d - r - m* I - viib - Ib	

Soprano	*d - r - m*	may swap
Alto	*s - f - s*	
Tenor	*d - t - d*	
Bass	*m - r - d* Ib - viib - I	

Minor Keys

Soprano	*d - t - l*	may swap
Alto	*l - si - l*	
Tenor	*m - r - m*	
Bass	*l - t - d* i - viib - ib	

Soprano	*l - t - d*	may swap
Alto	*l - si - l*	
Tenor	*m - r - m*	
Bass	*d - t - l* ib - viib - i	

* ***s – f – s*** (***m – r – m*** minor key) is the least effective soprano line.

Exercise 14.2

Complete these idioms for SATB. Include roman numerals.

(a)

Numerals ___________________________

(b)

Numerals ___________________________

(c)

Numerals ___________________________

(d)

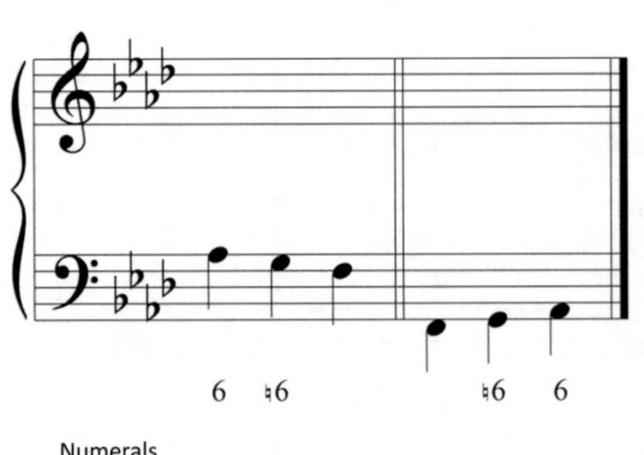

Numerals ___________________________

Because **viib** shares the same bass note as **ii** in a major key, a repeated ***r*** bass can be harmonised as follows.

Common notes in the inner voices may be sustained as in the second example.

Always ensure that **viib** resolves either to **I** or **Ib**

Study the example below, working through the given bass line.

- Bars 1 and 3 present an obvious opportunity to use the idiom
- In bars 2 and 4, ***r*** – ***s*** is harmonised using **ii – V** as **viib – V** is inappropriate.

Now we add a possible soprano line.

- In the idiomatic passages in bars 1 and 3 a typical strong soprano shaping is chosen
- Care needs to be taken to apply contrary motion when roots rise a step (**I – ii** across the bar line between bars 1 and 2)

Listen to Audio 14.3 to hear the two-part solution.

Exercise 14.3

Carefully study the given bass lines. Choose progressions looking out for idiomatic usage of **viib**. Shape the melody as musically as you can.

(a)

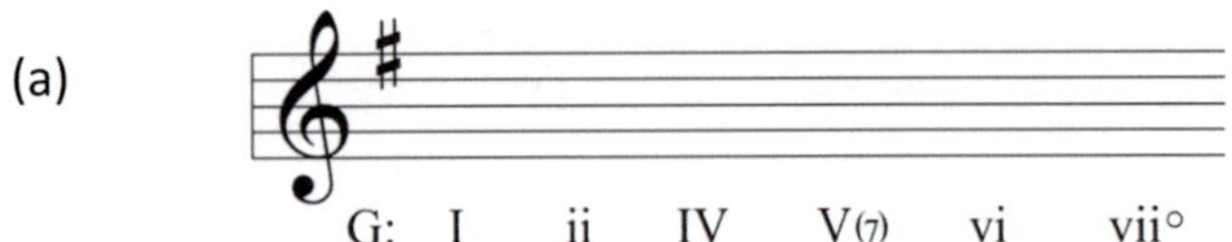

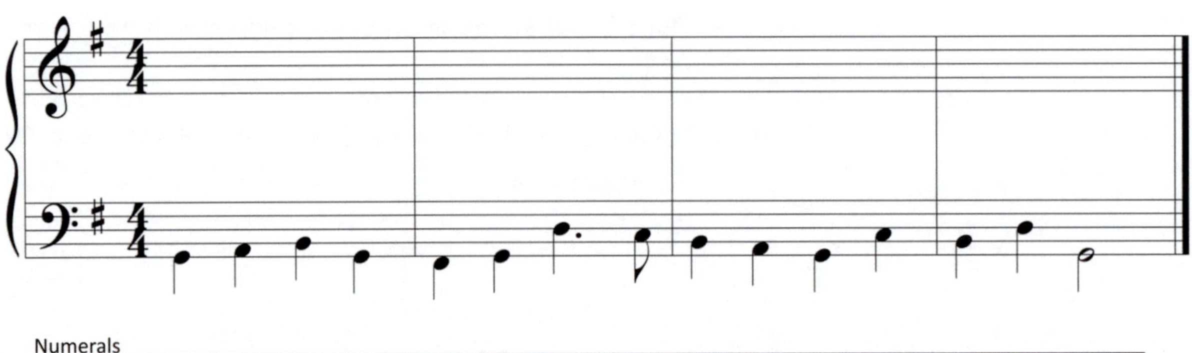

Numerals ____

(b)

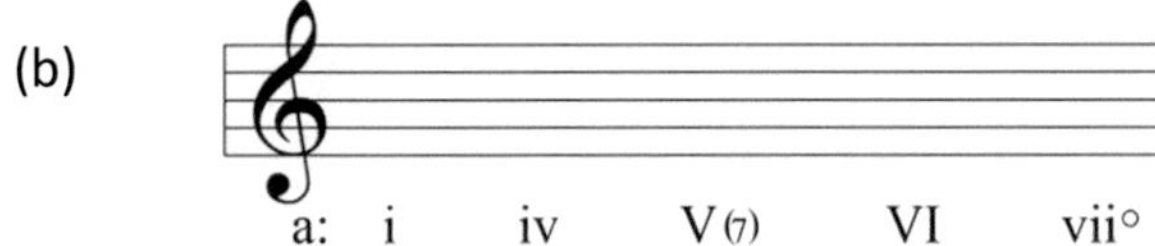

Numerals ____________________

(c)

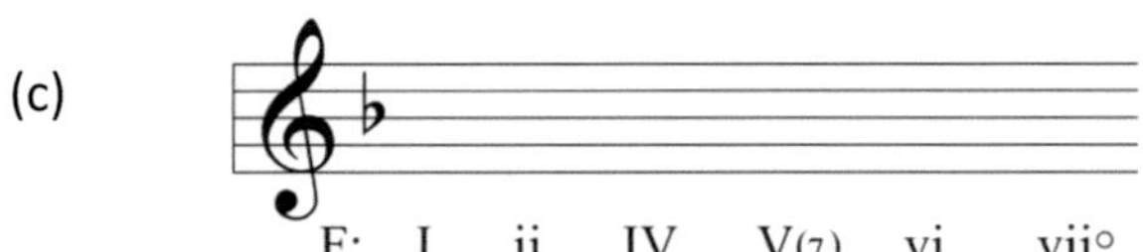

Numerals ____________________

(d)

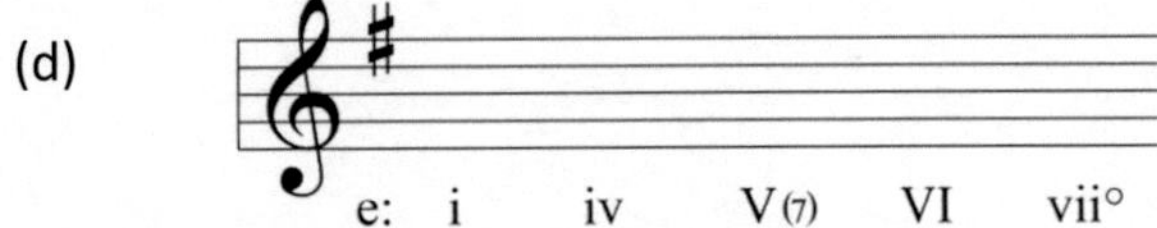

Numerals ____

(e)

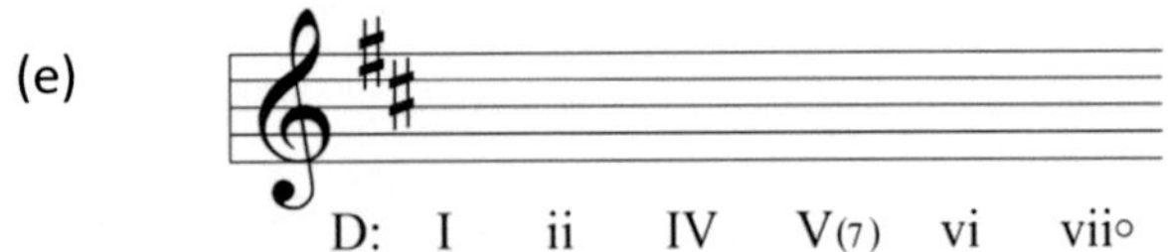

Numerals ____

Harmonising a melody including viib

Let us work through this D minor melody. The first step is to add solfa and highlight any obvious idiomatic shapes.

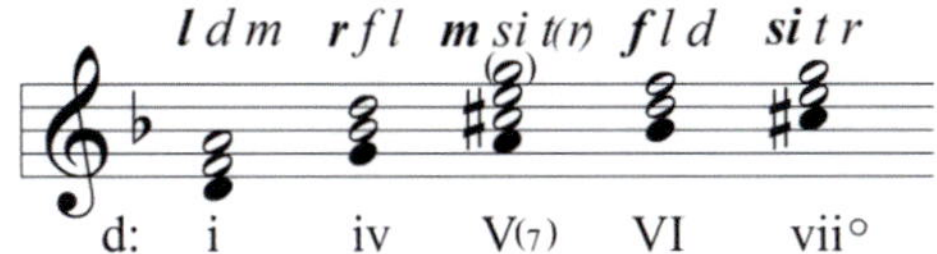

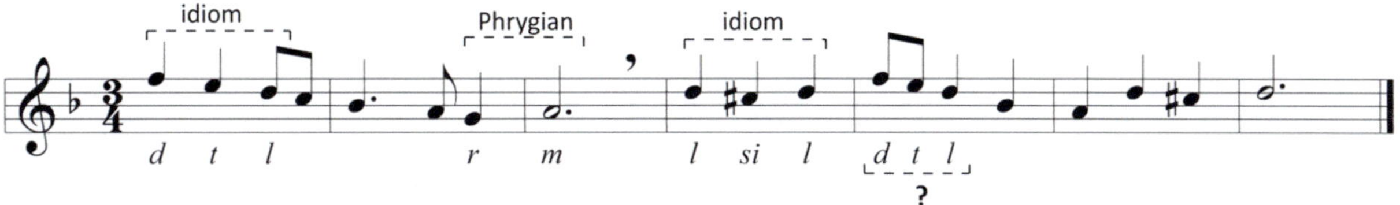

Now plot in a possible bass line.

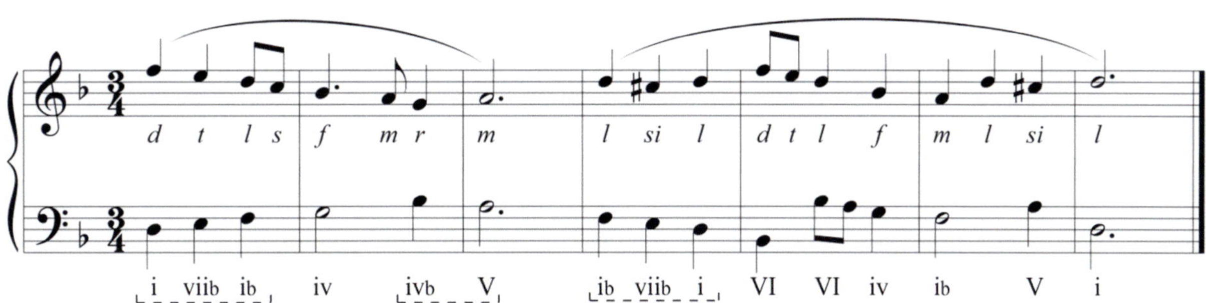

Bar 1: The idiom **i – viib – ib** gives a bass of ***l – t – d*** which moves in contrary motion to the soprano ***d – t – l***.

Bar 2 – 3: An opportunity for the Phrygian cadence!

Bar 4: The soprano ***l – si – l*** can be effectively harmonised by either **i – viib – ib** or **ib – viib – i.** However, in this context **ib – viib – i** is chosen in order to avoid consecutive octaves from the previous chord.

Bar 5: The soprano moves ***d – t – l*** but the idiom is not used, as the quaver ***t*** is best treated as a passing note.

Bar 6 – 7: Notice the soprano moves ***l – si – l.*** However, the idiom is not appropriate at the final cadence.

Listen to Audio 14.4 to hear the worked example.

Exercise 14.4

Harmonise each melody by adding the bass line. Add the solfa and sing the melody. Sketch in possible idiomatic shapings.

(a)

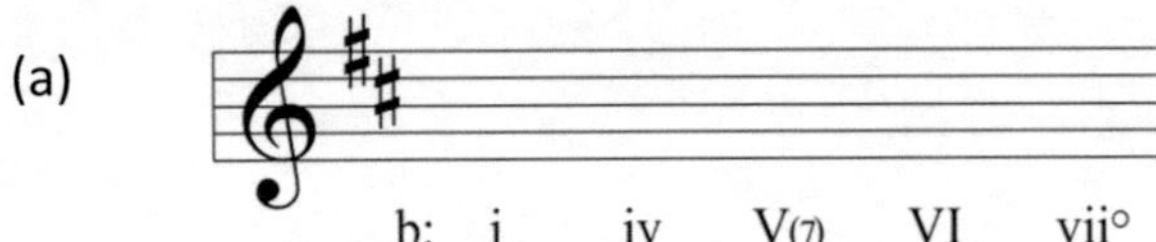

Numerals ____

(b)

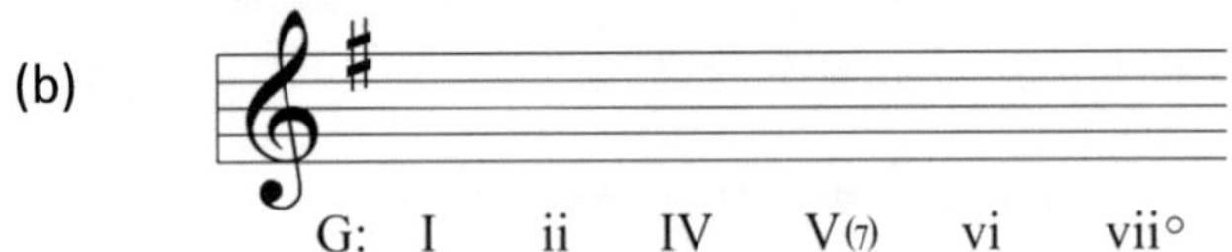

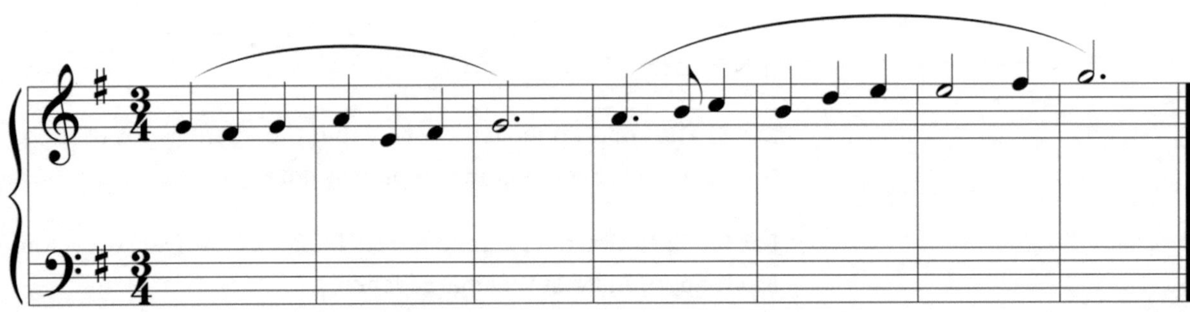

Numerals ____

(c)

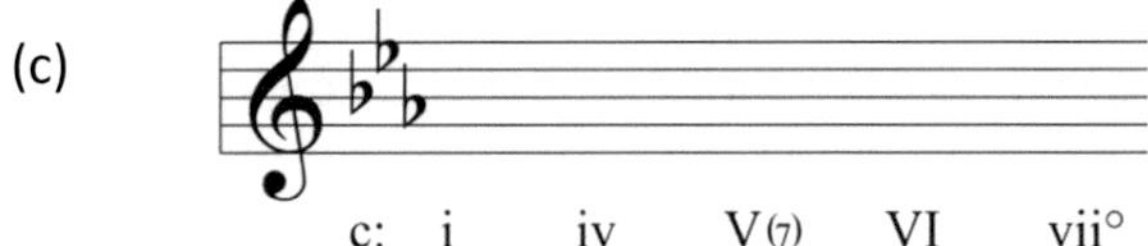

Numerals ____

(d)

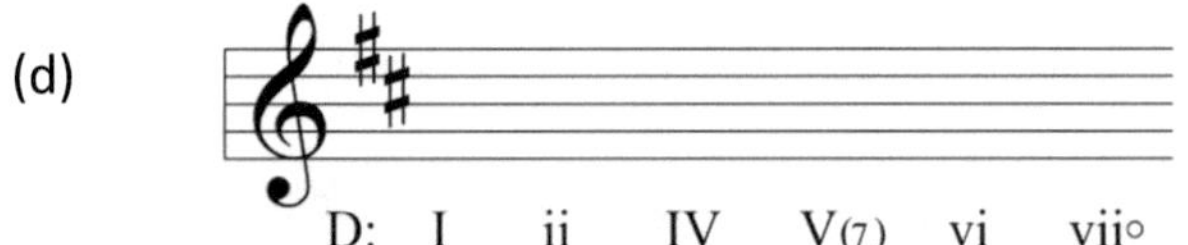

Numerals ____

Adding alto and tenor parts

Taking the previously worked D minor exercise, we now complete the harmony by adding parts for the inner voices.

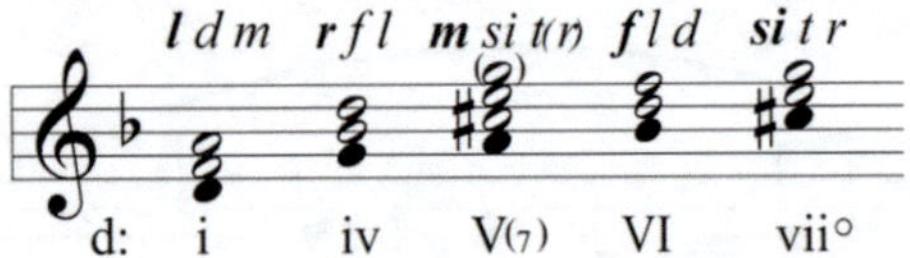

- Notice how the idiomatic passages in bars 1 and 4 follow the best practice of stepwise motion in all voices
- As is usual at all chord changes, three voices normally connect smoothly. However, notice the exception from bar 3 to 4 where soprano and alto both leap more than a 3rd at the chord change. Where this occasionally may happen, carefully check all parts to make sure no grammatical errors creep in.
- In bar 6, beat 1, notice the doubled 5th in the alto part. Although not essential, it enables a smoother alto overall in these few bars.

Listen to Audio 14.5 to hear the full four-part harmonisation.

Exercise 14.5

Study the given soprano and bass lines adding solfa and roman numerals. Add parts for alto and tenor, taking care with the shaping of the lines.

(a)

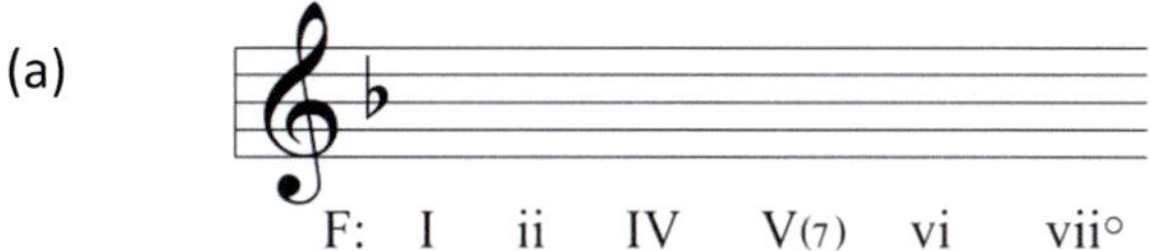

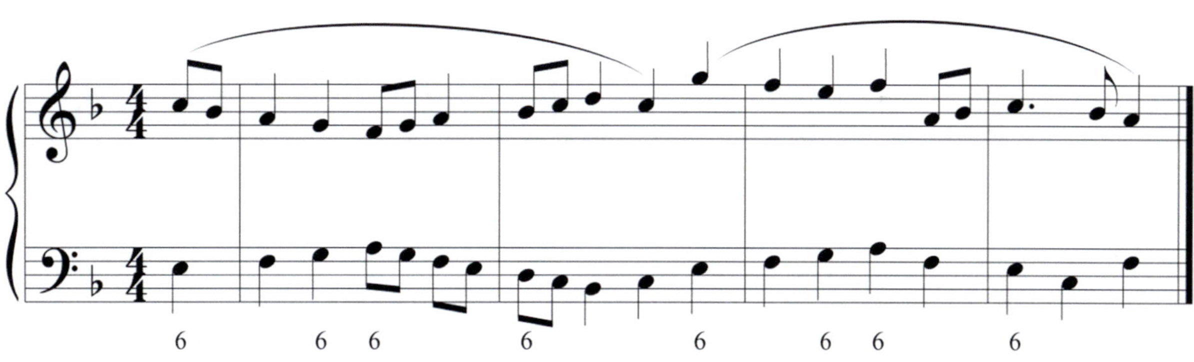

Numerals ____________________

(b)

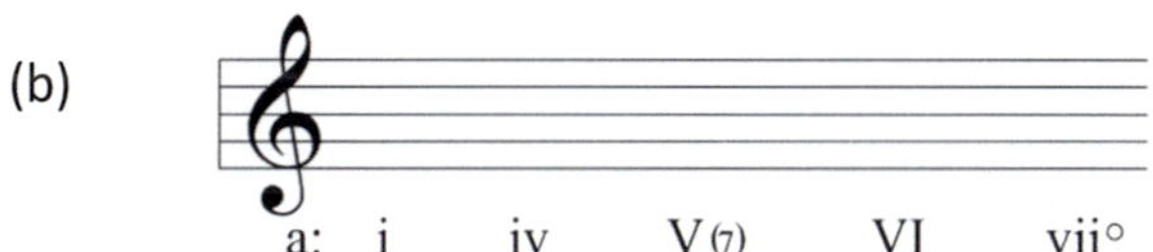

Numerals ____________________

(c)

Numerals ____

(d)

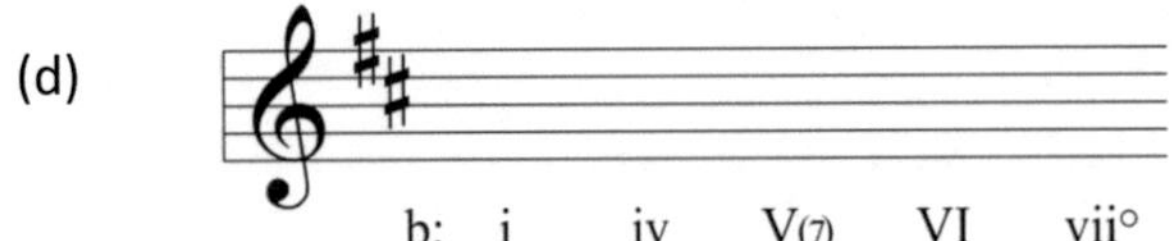

Numerals ____

So far in our workings we have always emphasised the importance of crafting a strong and musically interesting soprano line over a given bass. This should always be in place before contemplating the inner voices. So, when working through exercises the following sequence can prove very valuable.

- Decide appropriate progressions for the given bass
- Shape a musical soprano line. At this point double-check that no grammatical errors have crept in. Modify now if necessary.
- Once satisfied, carefully complete the inner voices. Little further modification should be needed at this point.

Exercise 14.6

Complete the following for SATB.

(a)

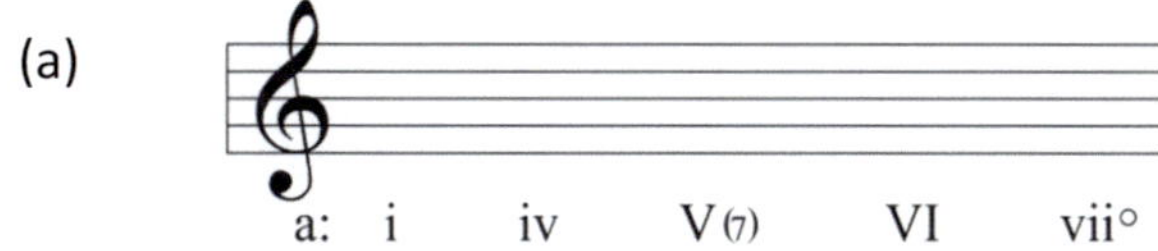

(b)

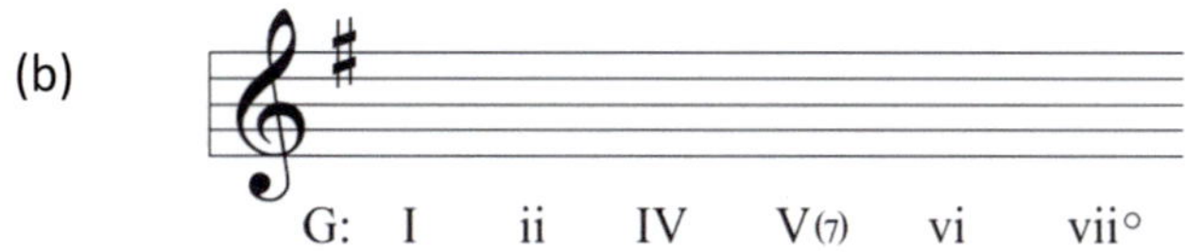

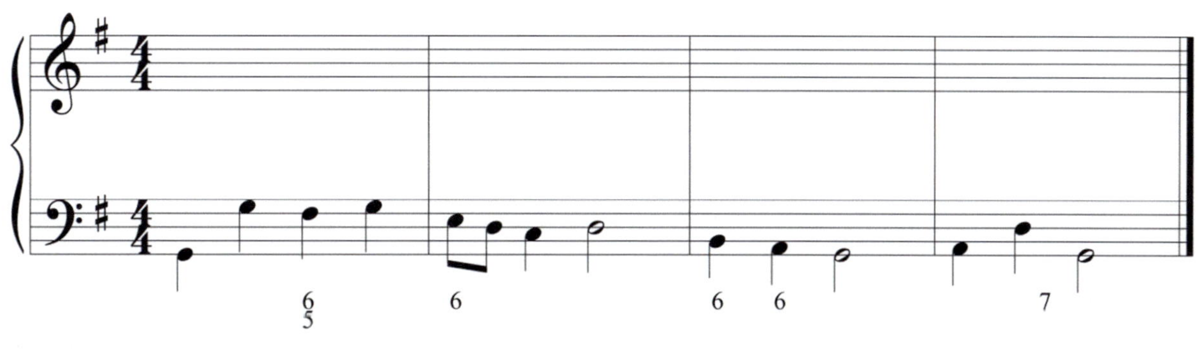

Numerals ____________________

CHAPTER 15

INTRODUCING IIb

In the major key, chord **ii** is a minor chord.

In the minor key, chord **ii** is a diminished chord.

In the major key, chord **ii** is freely available in both root and first inversion.

In the minor key, **ii** is restricted to its first inversion. Because it is diminished, the doubling of the 3rd of the chord is necessary.

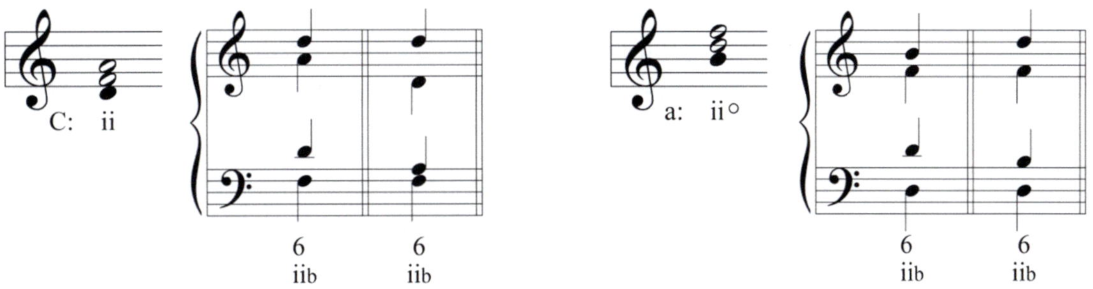

In the major key, **iib** can be used as a variation of **ii**.

In the minor key, **only iib** will be used at present.

The following progressions are effective in major and minor keys:

- **iib** is best followed by **V**
- **iib** and **IV** share the same bass note; choose according to context
- Use **I – iib** or **Ib – iib** in preference to **I – ii**

Listen to this harmonisation to hear the progressions in context. Then study the points made.

- In bar 2, the repeated bass ***f*** lends itself to a change of harmony. **IV – iib** is always preferable to **iib – IV** (i.e. roots falling a 3rd as opposed to roots rising a 3rd).
- In bar 2, there are two other important observations:
  (i) The 3rd is doubled in **iib** when approaching **V**. This is common practice in the major key, and essential in the minor key.
  (ii) In **iib – V**, all upper parts move in contrary motion to the bass. This again is common practice in the major key, and essential in the minor key.
- Bar 3 begins with two first inversion chords by step. Note the triadic layout between soprano, alto and bass. The doubling of the tenor part is crucial to avoid consecutive 5ths and octaves. The solution is always to alternate the doubling. Here the root is doubled in **Ib** and the 3rd in **iib**. Another option is to double the 5th in **iib**.

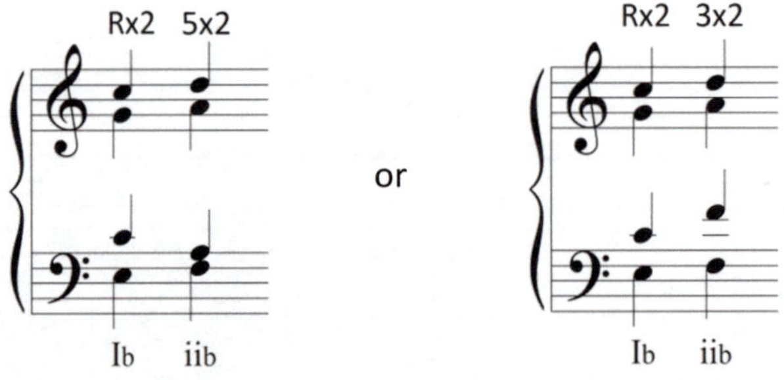

- In bars 3 – 4, as **vi** moves to **iib** over the bar line, both soprano and alto leap more than a 3rd. This is always an occasion to double-check the grammar!
- In bar 4, **iib – V** employs both the expected movement and the doubling.

Audio 15.2

Study this minor key example while listening to Audio 15.2. Pay special attention to the diminished quality of **iib**.

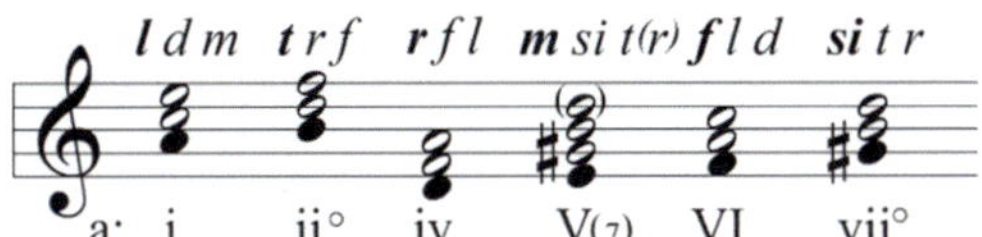

Looking at the detail you will notice features similar to those already discussed in relation to the previous example in the major key.

- Bars 1 – 2: **ib – iib**, two first inversion chords by step, use triadic layout and alternate the doubling.
- Bars 2 – 3 and bars 5 – 6: **iib – V**, soprano, alto and tenor move in contrary motion to the bass.
- Bar 5: Repeated bass using a chord change for interest.
- Bars 7 – 8: To form a final cadence, **iv** (not **iib**) is required.

Exercise 15.1

Carefully study the given bass lines. Add roman numerals. Write a soprano part, taking into consideration the points made earlier.

(a)

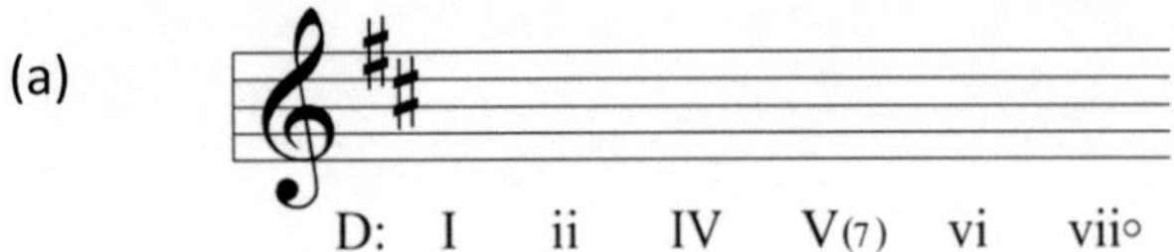

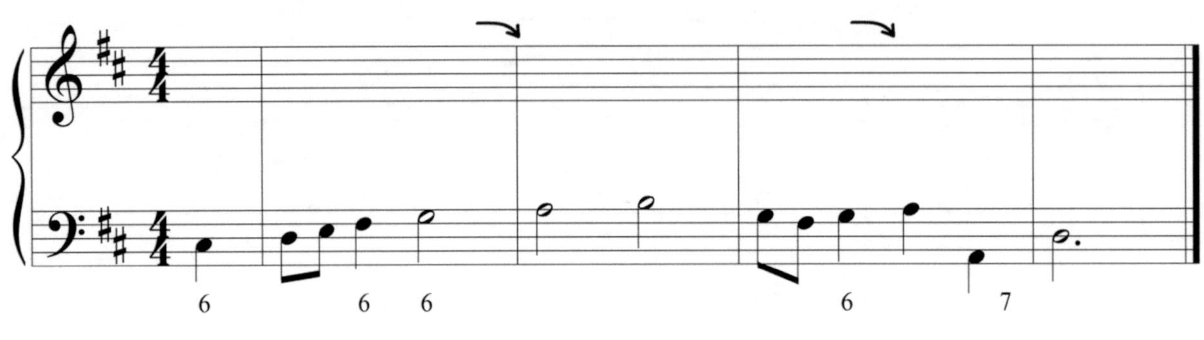

Numerals ______________________________

(b)

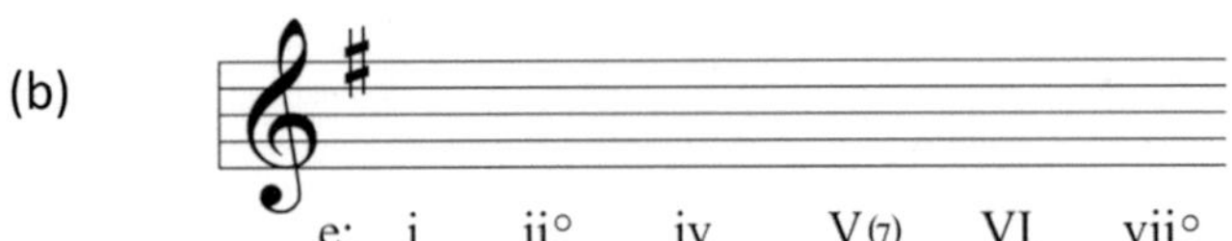

Numerals ______________________________

(c)

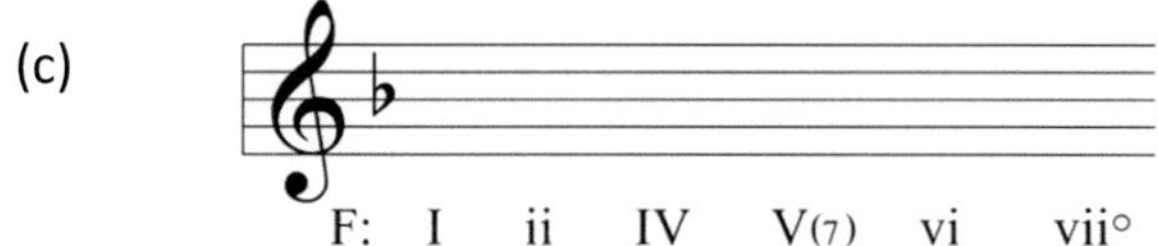

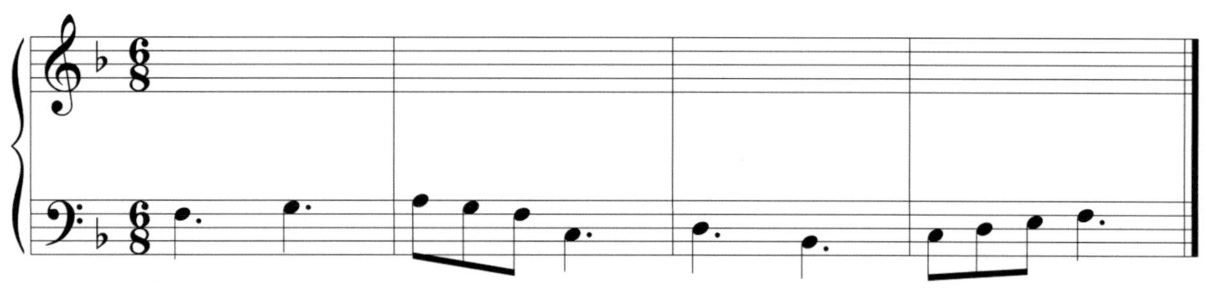

Numerals ____

(d)

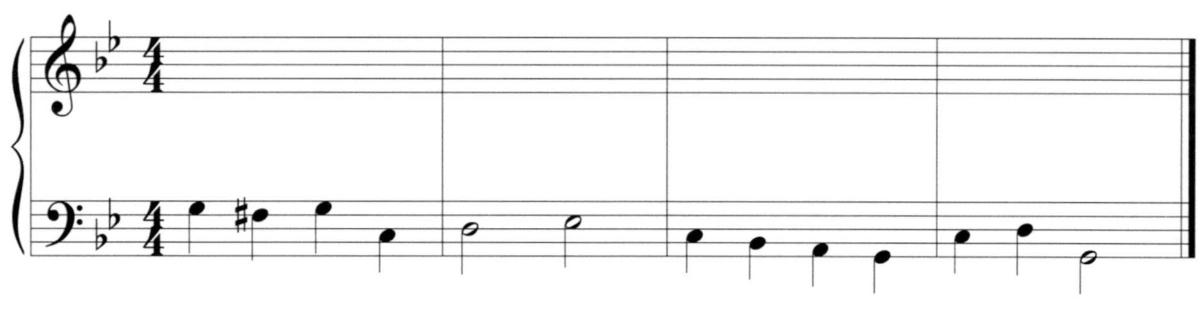

Numerals ____

Exercise 15.2

Sing each soprano line using solfa. Add a bass line to indicate your choice of harmony. Watch out for possible idiomatic opportunities. Include roman numerals.

(a)

Numerals ____

(b)

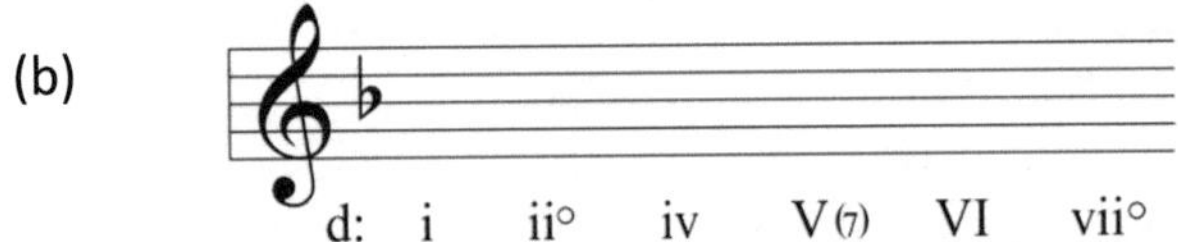

Numerals ____

(c)

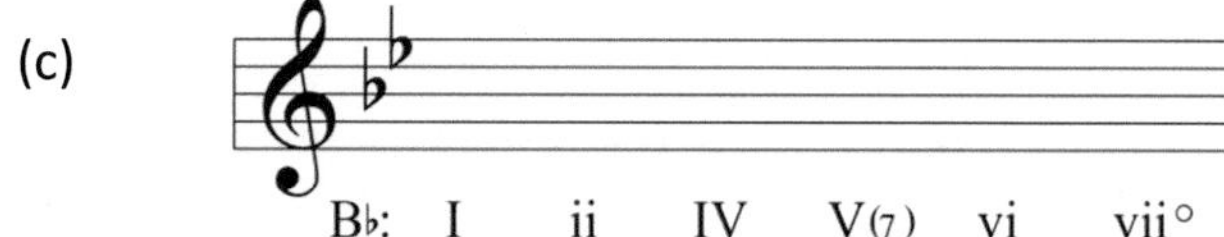

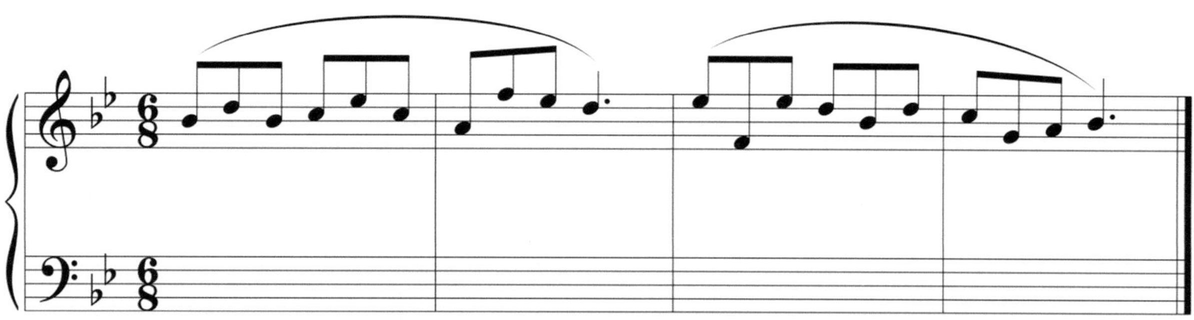

Numerals ____

(d)

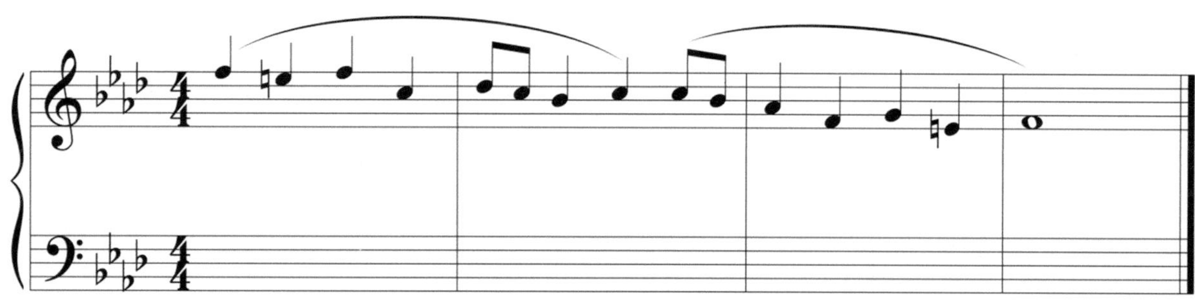

Numerals ____

Exercise 15.3/ 

The task here is to listen to this completed harmonisation and analyse the progressions by writing the roman numerals below the bass stave. Circle any idioms which you spot along the way.

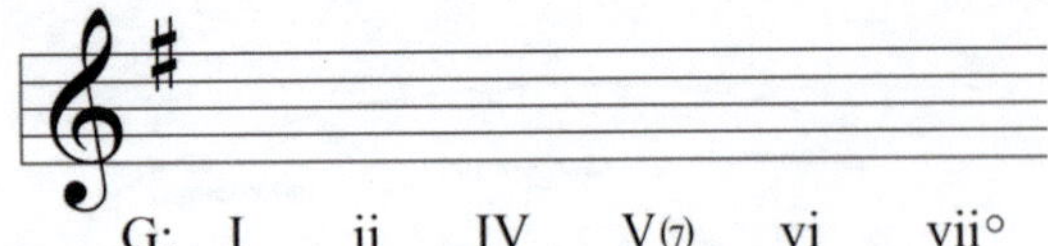

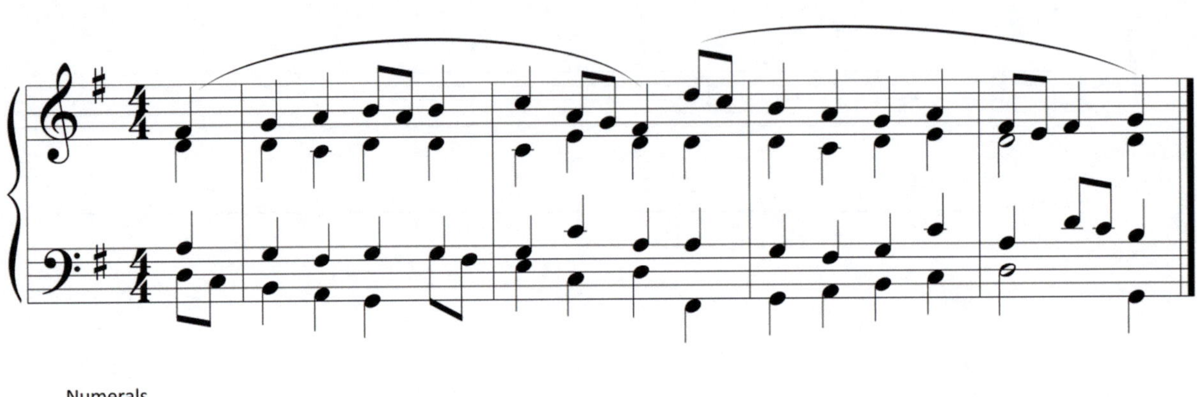

Numerals ____________________

Exercise 15.4

Add alto and tenor parts to the given soprano and bass. Include roman numerals to indicate your harmonic choices.

(a) 

Numerals ____________________

Before completing the final exercise review the following points.

Checklist ✓

- **iib**: in general double the 3rd in both major and minor keys
- **iib** is normally followed by **V**
- **iib – V**: soprano, alto and tenor normally fall in contrary motion to the bass
- **Ib – iib:** use triadic layout for soprano, alto and bass. Watch the tenor doubling.
- **IV – iib** adds interest to a repeated bass note

Exercise 15.5

Add SAT parts to the given bass lines. Begin by carefully crafting the soprano line. Then add alto and tenor parts. Include roman numerals.

(a)

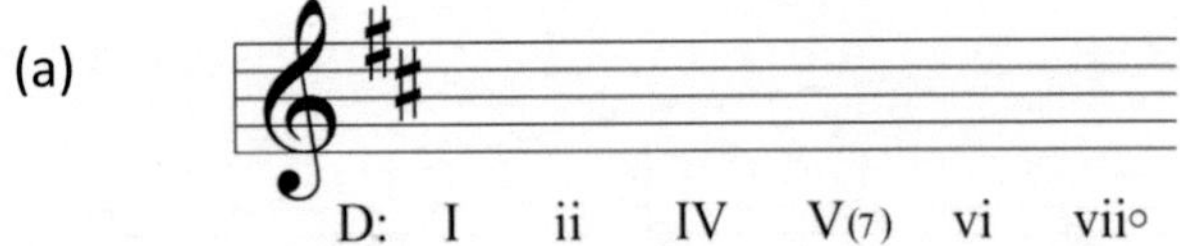

Numerals ____________________

(b)

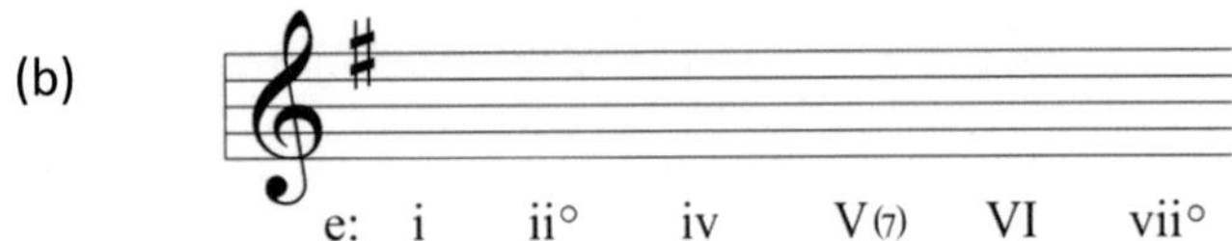

Numerals ____________________

CHAPTER 16

SECOND INVERSIONS

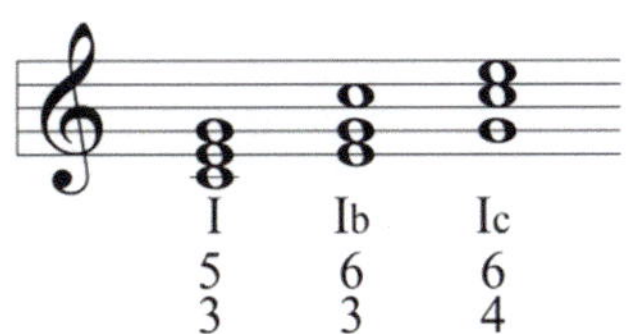

This is a triad in its root, first and second inversion.

Remember, the figured bass calculates the intervals formed from the bottom note to the upper notes of the triad: $^{6}_{4}$ with no abbreviation.

A small **c** is added to the roman numeral to indicate a second inversion.

In general, second inversion chords are somewhat unstable. They are used in a decorative way, and as such are restricted to particular contexts:

- The cadential $^{6}_{4}$
- The passing $^{6}_{4}$
- The auxiliary $^{6}_{4}$

The second inversion chords commonly used are **Ic, IVc** and **Vc**.

Listen to Audio 16.1 to hear the overall effect of the second inversion chords in context

The Cadential $^6_4$

Let us examine the features of the cadential $^6_4$

Its most important function is to decorate chord **V** at a cadence. **Ic** both enhances and enriches the cadential effect.

Perfect Cadence	**V – I**	becomes	**Ic – V – I**
Interrupted Cadence	**V – VI**	becomes	**Ic – V – VI**
Imperfect Cadence	**? – V**	becomes	**? – Ic - V**

The cadential $^6_4$ has a 'leaning effect' and therefore the rhythm is vitally important. The nature of the chord demands accentuation as an appoggiatura chord preceding and resolving onto chord **V**.

At a Perfect Cadence

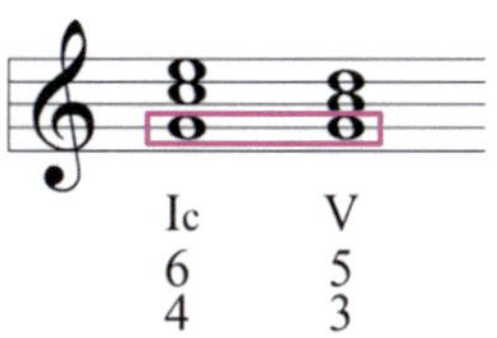

- **Ic** shares the same bass note as **V**, i.e. the 5th of chord **I**. This note must always be doubled.

- Only two voices move, each falling a step ***d – t***, ***m – r*** (***l – si***, ***d – t*** minor key).

- When using figured bass it is necessary to include the $^{5}_{3}$ figures for chord **V** to clarify the resolution of the $^{6}_{4}$ chord.

- In both examples above, **Ic** is placed on a strong beat before resolving to **V** on a weaker beat.

- The doubled bass note can be sustained in two voices (example A) or the bass may drop an octave (example B).

Listen to Audio 16.2 to hear examples A and B.

At an Interrupted Cadence

(A)

(B)

Notice that the movement of **Ic - V** is identical to the previous examples. The only difference is that the final chord changes to **vi**.

Listen to Audio 16.3 to hear the decorated interrupted cadence in both examples.

At an Imperfect Cadence

(A)

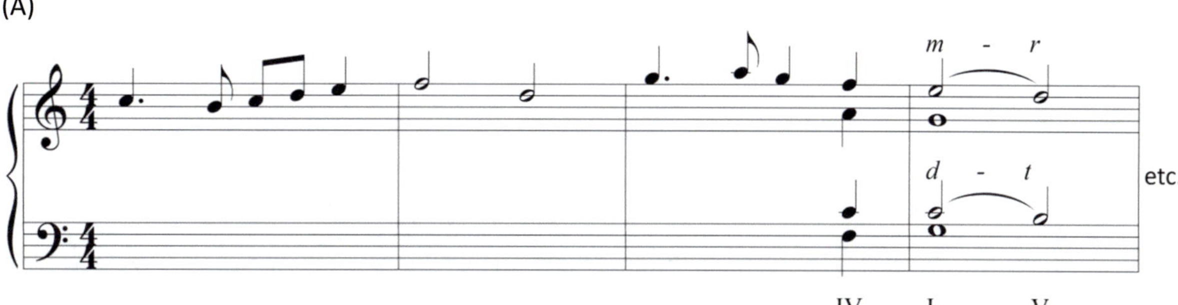

(B)

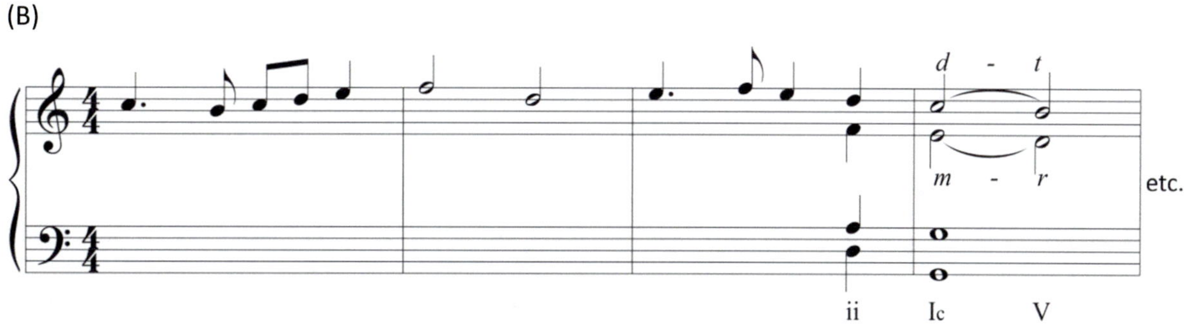

(C)

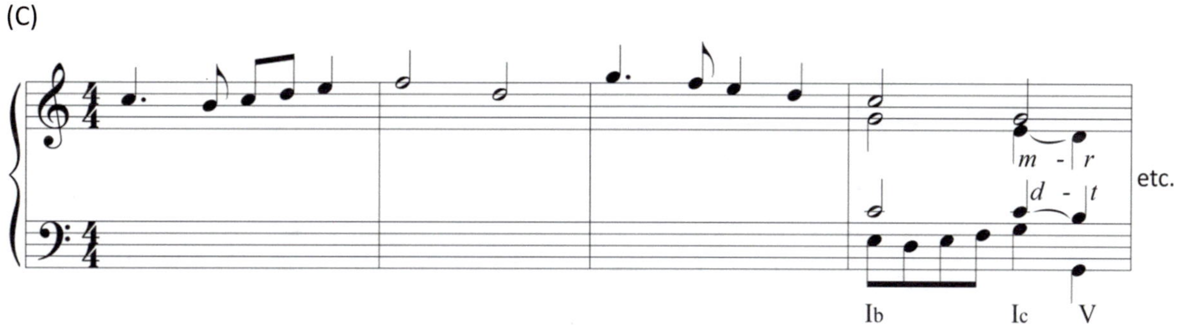

Again, the detail of the movement in **Ic – V** is identical to all the previous examples. The only difference is that chord **V** is the goal of the phrase.

Listen to Audio 16.4 to hear the three examples of the decorated imperfect cadence.

Listen to Audio 16.5 and study the following example in A minor which demonstrates the cadential $\substack{6\\4}$ at three different cadence points. Notice that the detail and layout in the minor key is exactly the same as that in the major.

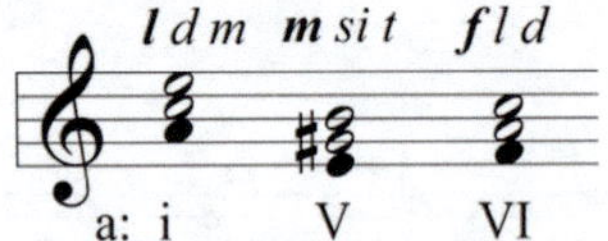

Exercise 16.1

Harmonise **only** the cadence points in the following exercises by adding alto, tenor and bass parts. The sign ⌐ - - - - ¬ indicates where **Ic – V** is appropriate.

(a)

(b)

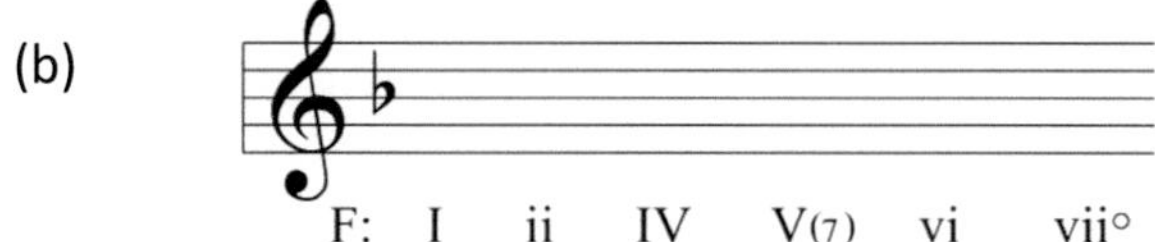

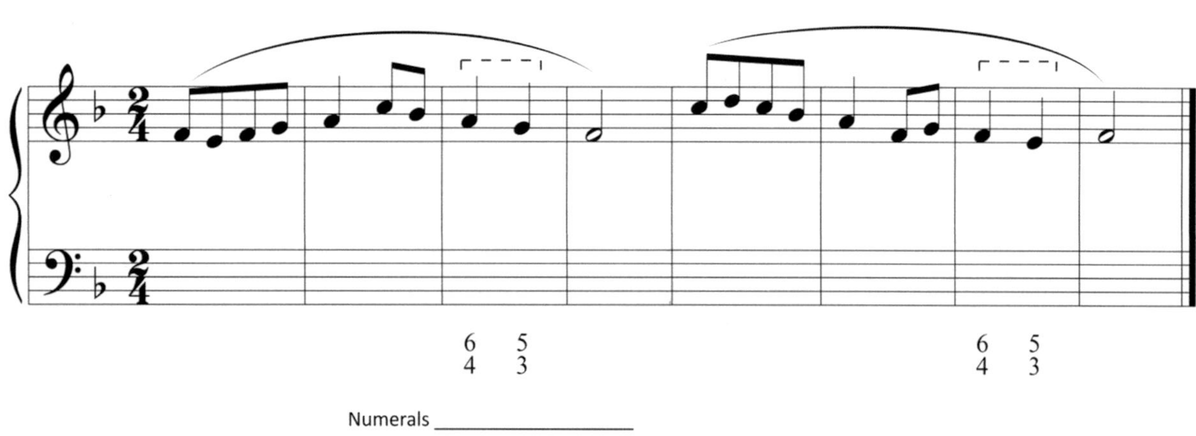

Numerals ____________________ ____________________

(c)

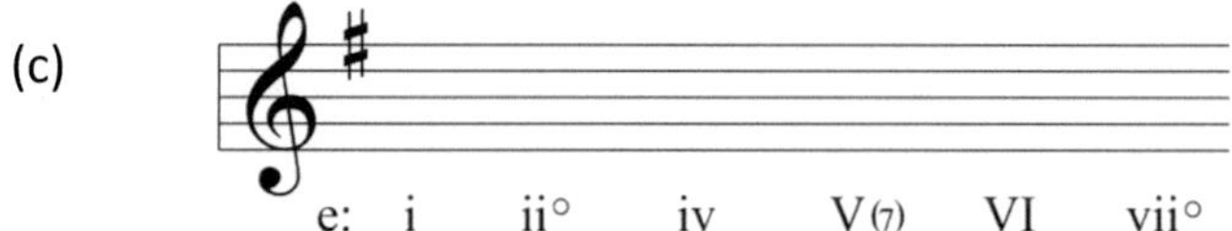

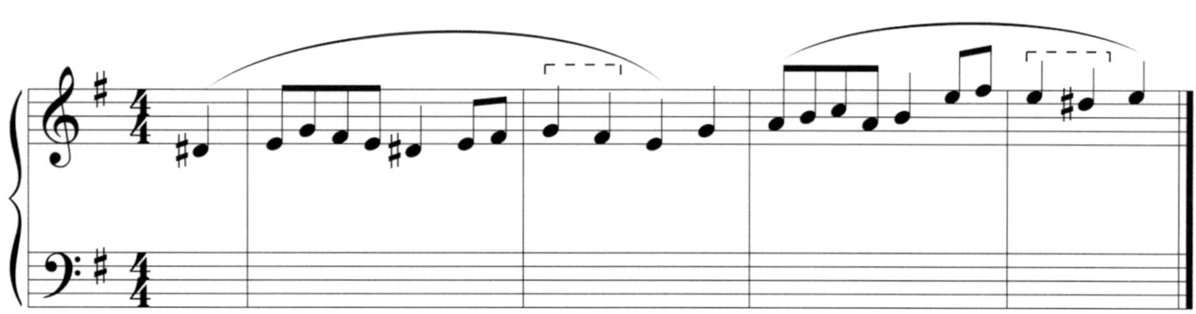

Numerals _____________ _____________

(d)

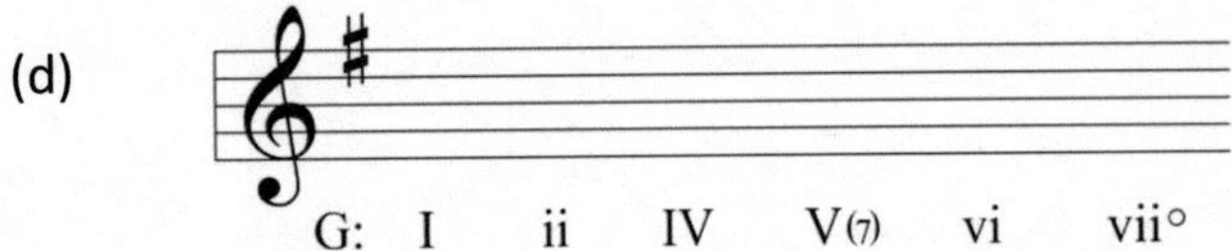

Numerals ____________ ____________

(e)

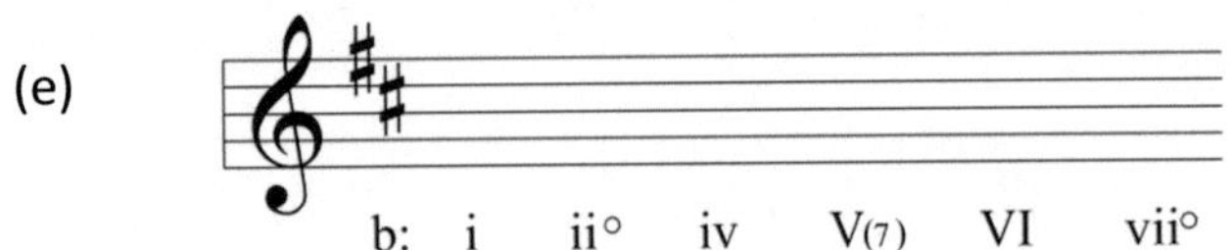

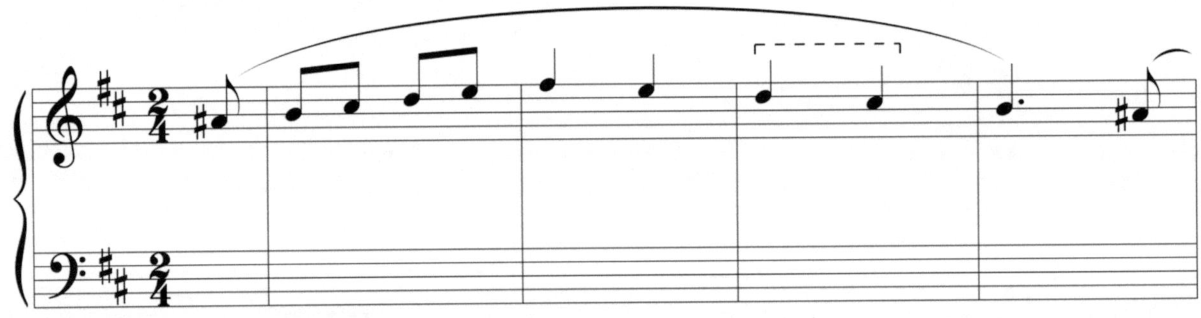

Numerals ____________________________

____

Rhythmic considerations

These are the rhythmic possibilities for **Ic – V** in compound time.
Notice that **Ic** is always in a stronger rhythmic position than **V**.

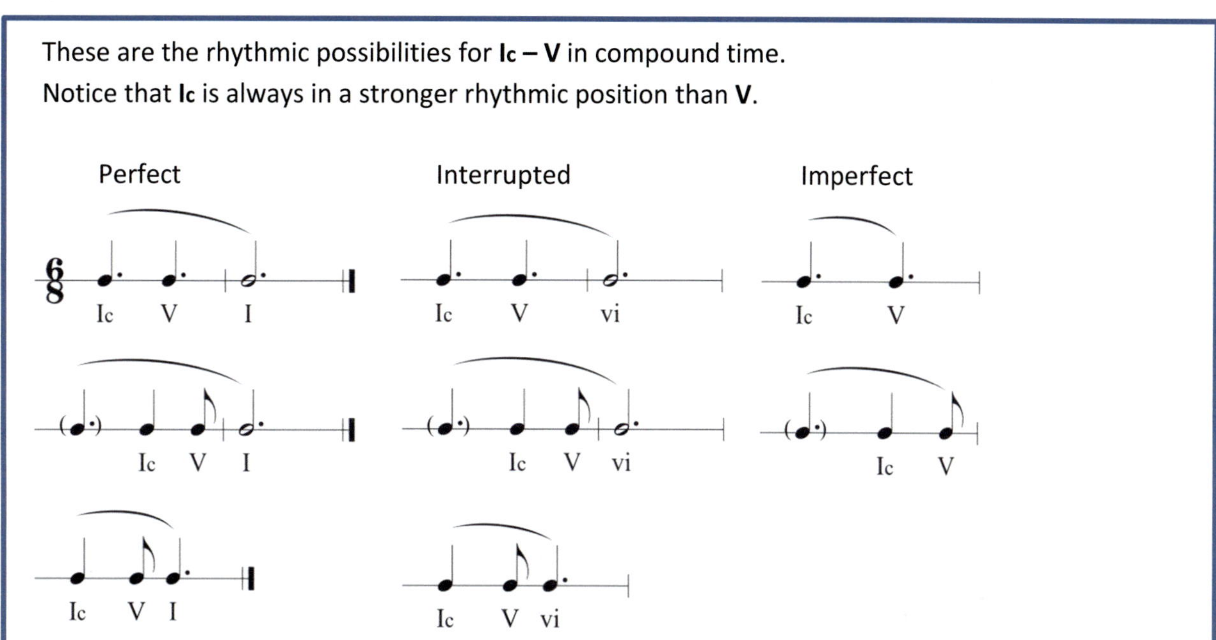

In simple triple time the typical rhythmic profile for **Ic – V** is: Ic V

However, occasionally the following is a possible exception: Ic V I/vi

Some helpful hints in spotting opportunities for **Ic - V** when harmonising a melody:

- Sing the melody adding solfa
- Focus on the cadence points
- At a perfect or interrupted cadence look for the melody moving either ***d – t – d*** (***l – si – l*** minor key) or ***m – r – d*** (***d – t – l*** minor key), taking particular note of the rhythmic layout.
- At an imperfect cadence, look out for the melody moving ***d – t*** (***l – si*** minor key) or ***m – r*** (***d – t*** minor key) in a **strong to weak** rhythm. The use of **Ic – V** can often be overlooked here. It is very effective, so try not to miss it.

Exercise 16.2

Choose chords to harmonise each of the given soprano lines by adding the bass line. Follow the guidelines given.

(a)

Numerals ______________________________

(b)

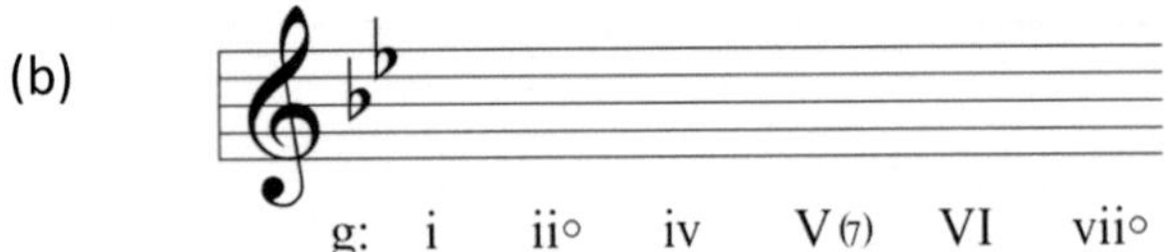

Numerals ______________________________

(c)

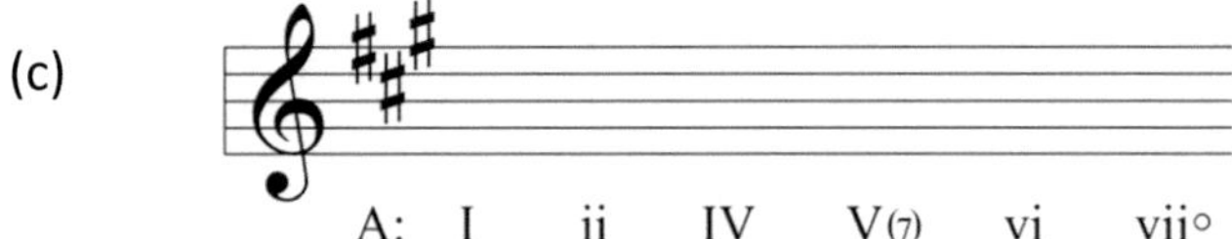

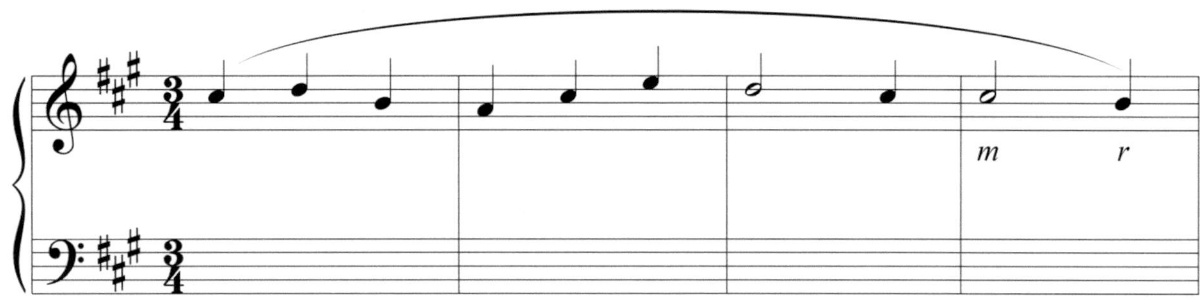

Numerals ___

m r d

___

(d)

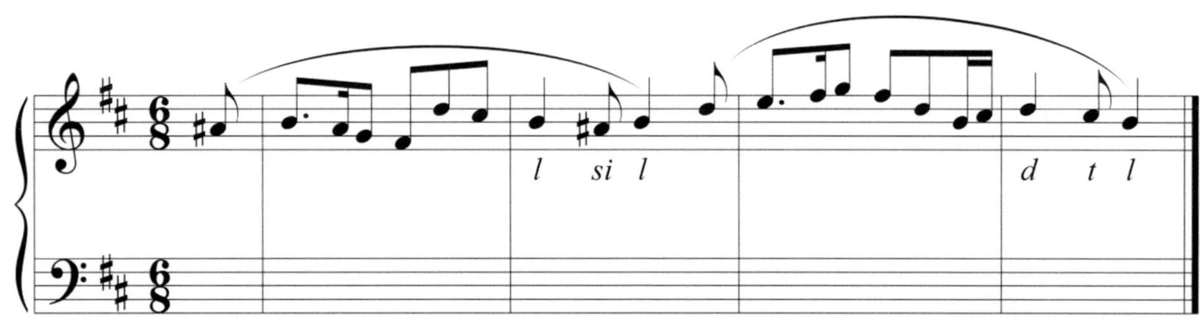

Numerals ___

Cadential $^6_4$ - something extra!

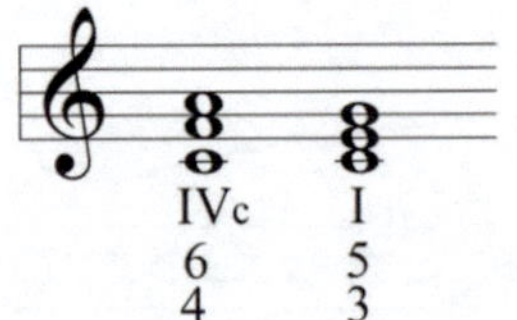

A final, long tonic chord may be enhanced by decorating it with **IVc** which then resolves to chord **I**.

These are some examples in C major.

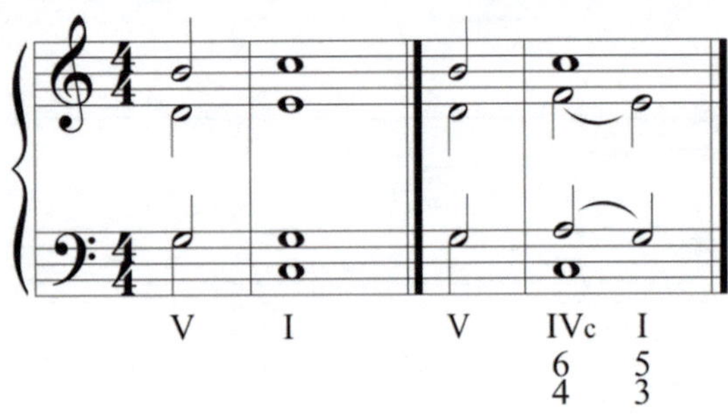

Notice the doubled bass in both chords and the downward stepwise motion as **IVc** resolves to **I**.

In all cases the second inversion chord must be accented.

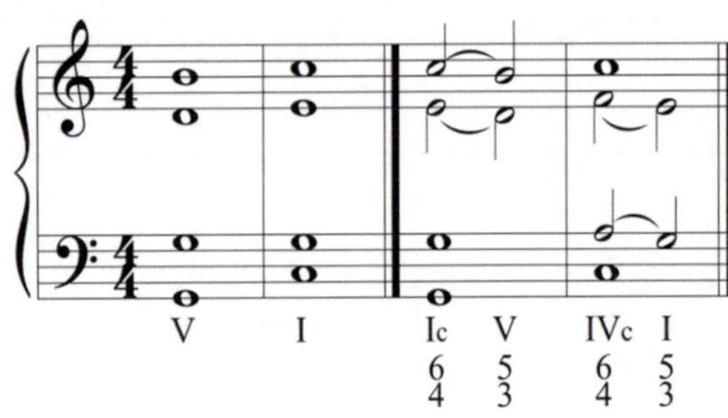

The same procedure is followed for minor keys.

Audio 16.6

Listen to Audio 16.6. By comparing each pair of examples, the effect of the decoration will be clear.

Exercise 16.3

Soprano and bass parts are given in the following exercises. Complete the harmonisation by adding alto and tenor parts. Include roman numerals as required.

(a)

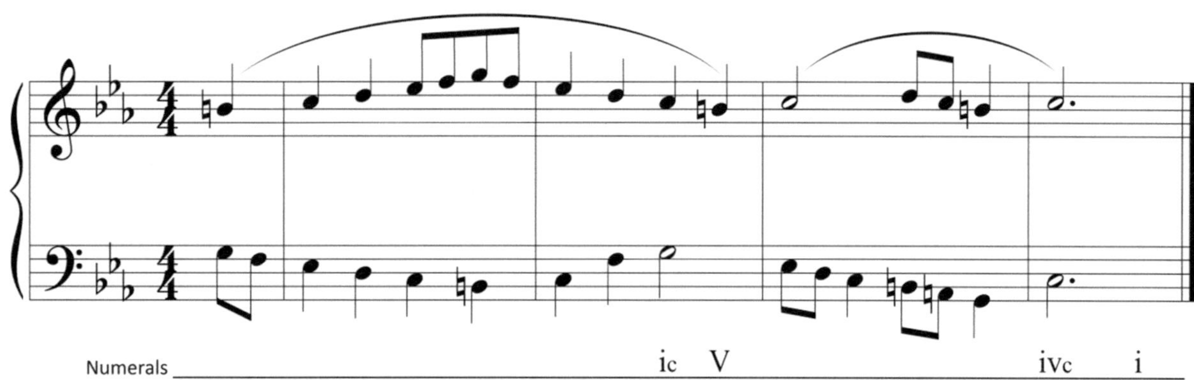

(b)

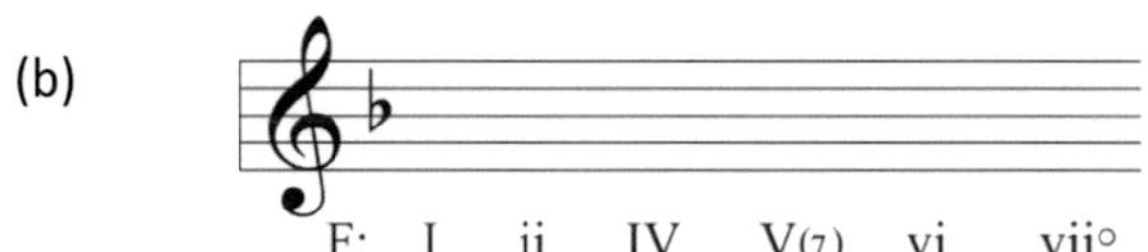

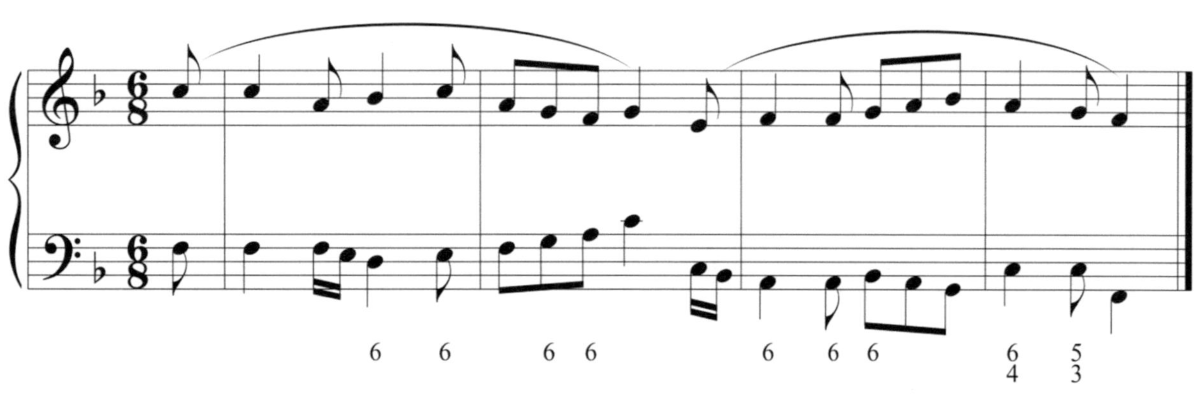

(c)

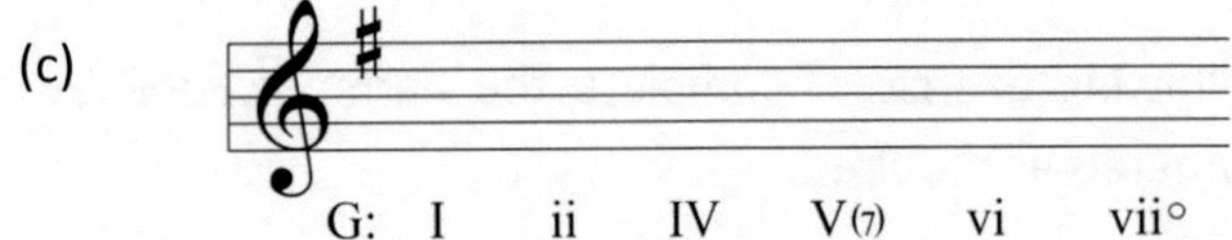

Numerals ____

(d)

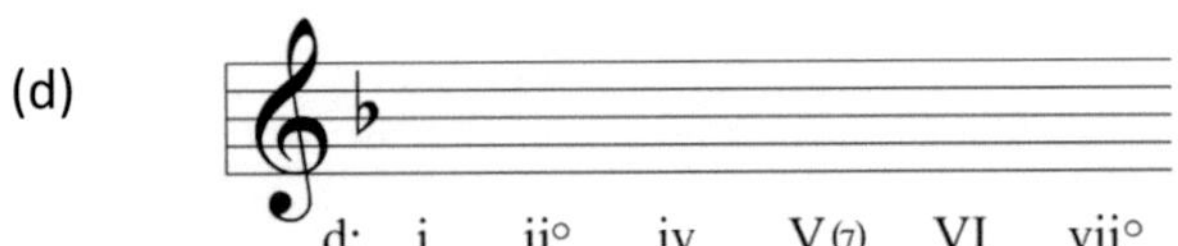

Numerals ____

The Passing $\substack{6\\4}$

This type of second inversion is used in passage work rather than at a cadence. It is normally used in a stepwise bass.

Unlike the cadential $\substack{6\\4}$, the passing $\substack{6\\4}$ is unaccented. The part-writing is extremely smooth. Study the following, noting the doubled 5th in the second inversion chord.

Audio 16.7

Listen to Audio 16.7 to hear the above progressions in the major key.

The next example shows that the part-writing is the same in the minor key.

Audio 16.8

Study and listen carefully to Audio 16.8 in the key of A minor.

Notice that the bass shape of **I – Vc – Ib/ Ib – Vc – I** is identical to that of **I – viib – Ib/ Ib – viib – I**. The **one** pitch difference between the two progressions is highlighted below.

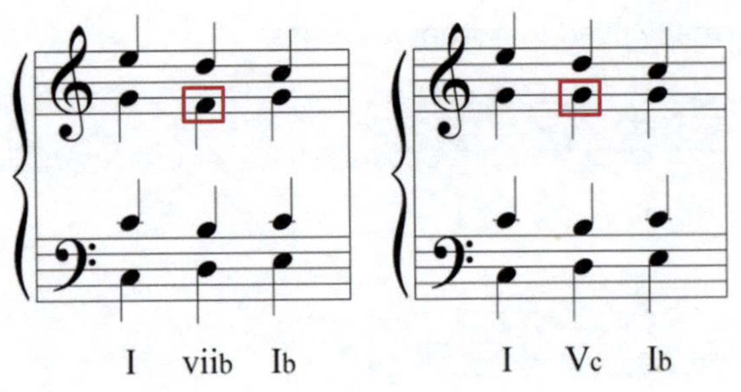

The repeated note is normally sustained (alto part in this example).

I Vc Ib

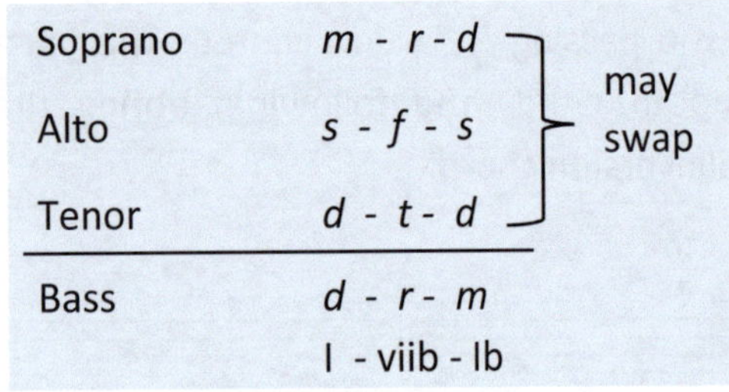

Soprano	*m - r - d*	may swap
Alto	*s - f - s*	
Tenor	*d - t - d*	
Bass	*d - r - m*	
	I - viib - Ib	

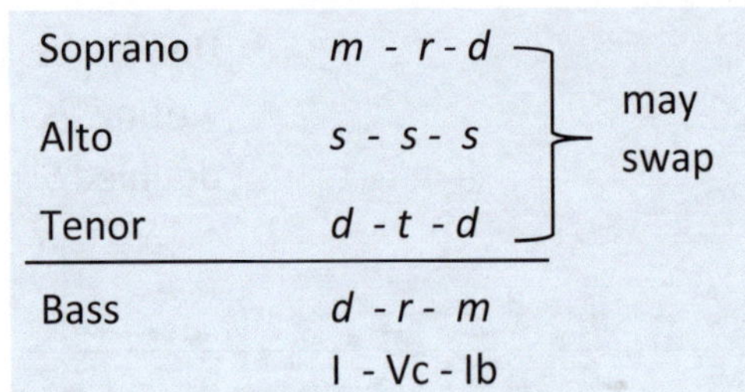

Soprano	*m - r - d*	may swap
Alto	*s - s - s*	
Tenor	*d - t - d*	
Bass	*d - r - m*	
	I - Vc - Ib	

Which to use?

I – viib – Ib is the better of the two progressions as it gives a stronger harmonic outcome, whereas **I – Vc – Ib** is chosen where a gentler effect is appropriate.

When to use?

Only consider **I – Vc – Ib** if **Vc** falls on a weak beat.

The Auxiliary ${}^{6}_{4}$

This type of second inversion is useful as a decoration on long sustained tonic or dominant bass notes in both major and minor keys. It tends to be reserved for passage work and is more commonly unaccented.

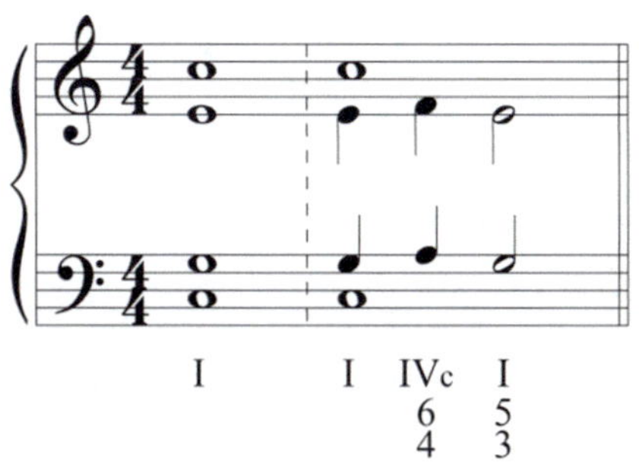

Notice the smooth part-writing, with only two voices moving in the shape of upper auxiliary notes. Note the doubled 5th in the second inversion chord.

Listen to Audio 16.9 and study the minor key example below. Focus on bars 1 and 2 where the harmony uses the auxiliary ${}^{6}_{4}$.

Exercise 16.4

The soprano and bass parts are given. Add alto and tenor parts and include roman numerals.

(a)

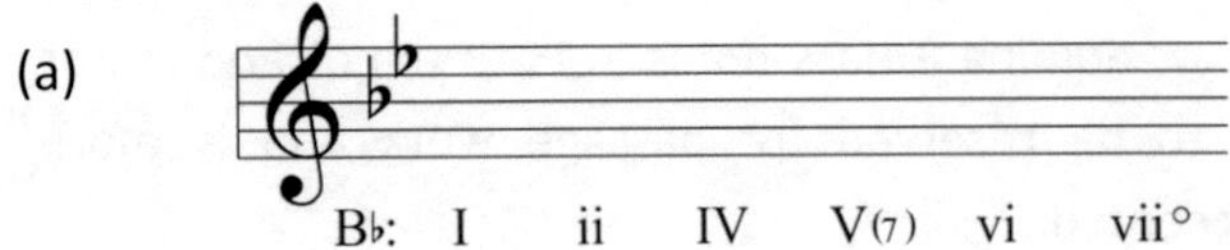

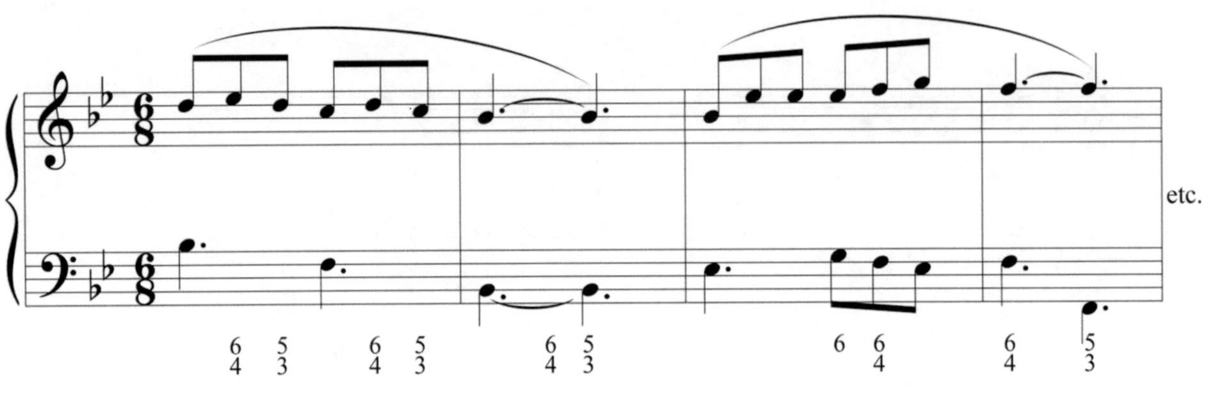

Numerals ______________________________

(b)

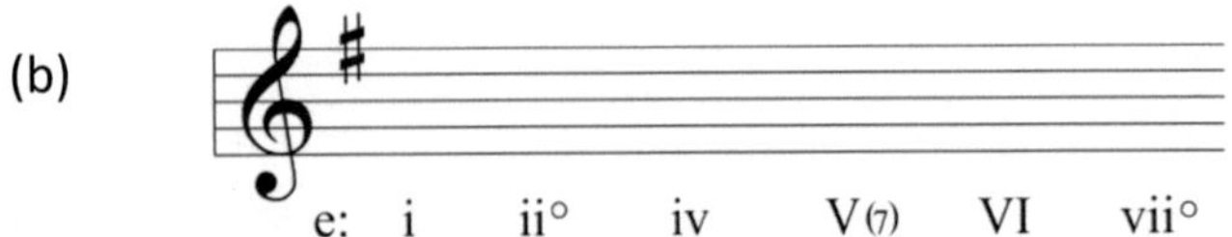

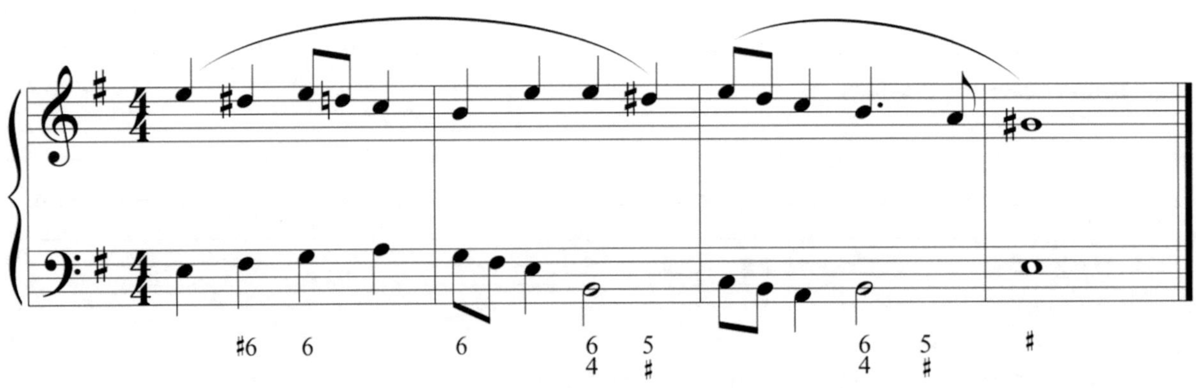

Numerals ______________________________

(c)

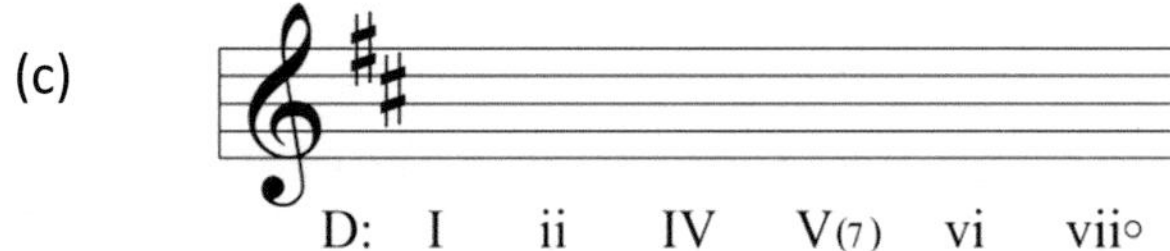

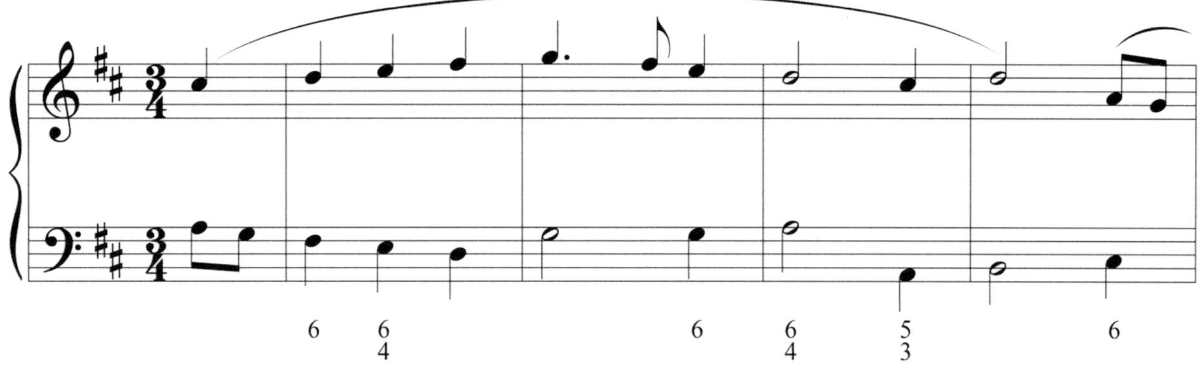

Numerals ____________________

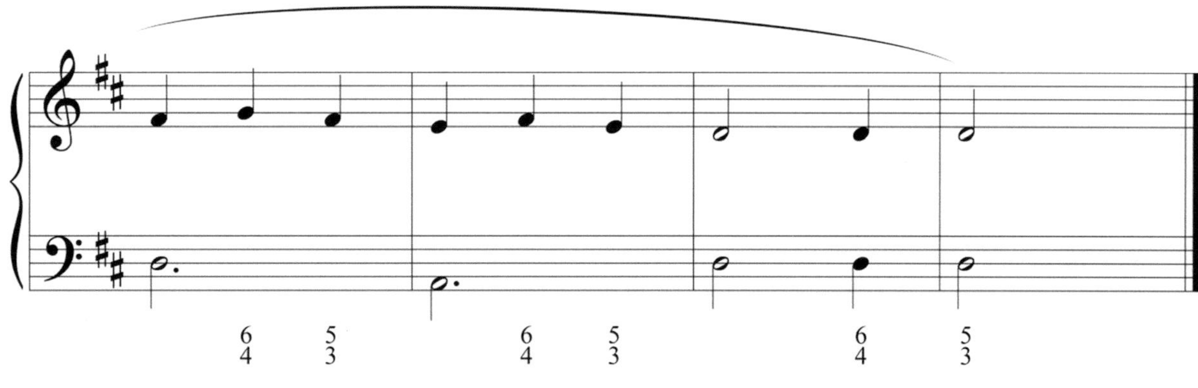

____

(d)

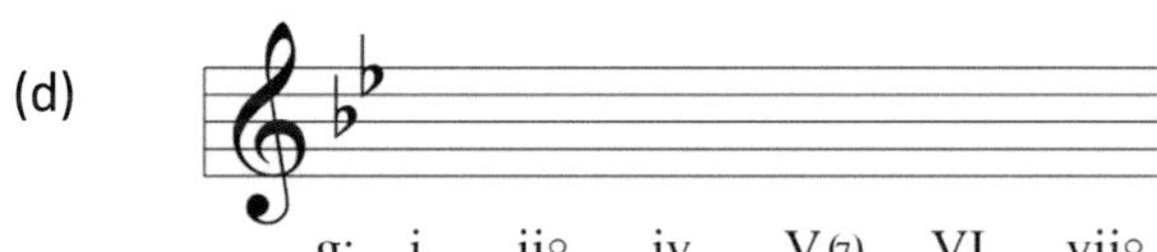

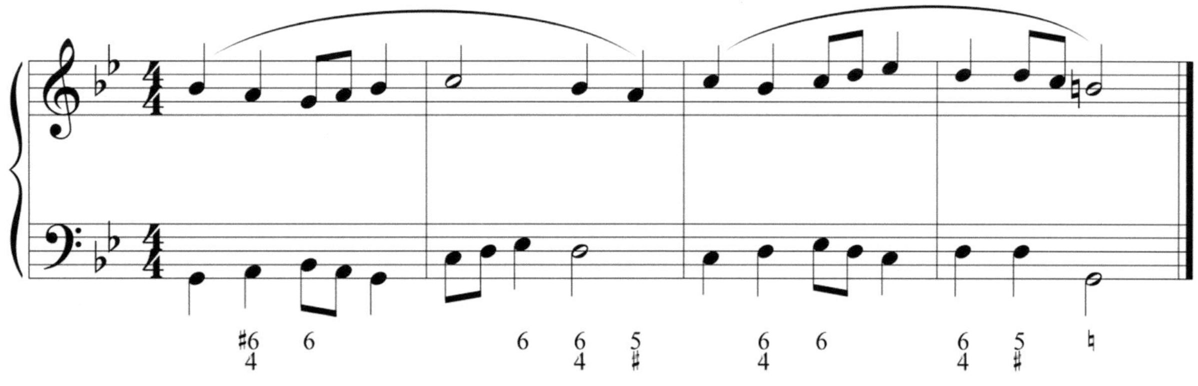

Numerals ____________________

Exercise 16.5

Study the given figured bass and add roman numerals. Complete the soprano melody first. Finally add parts for alto and tenor.

(a)

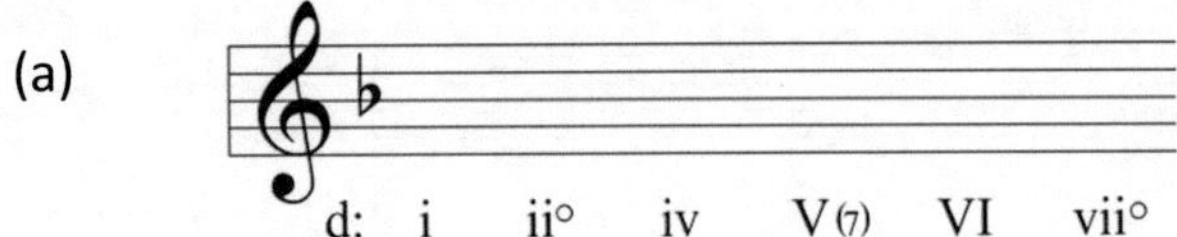

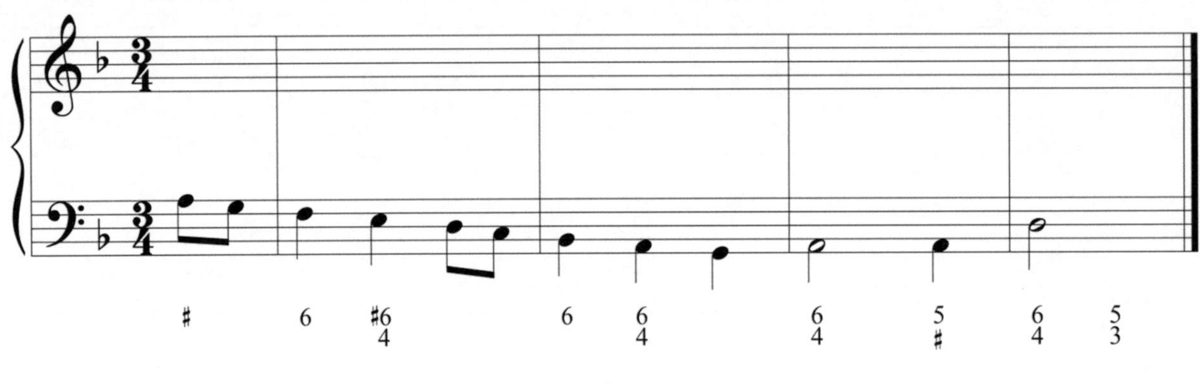

Numerals ___

(b)

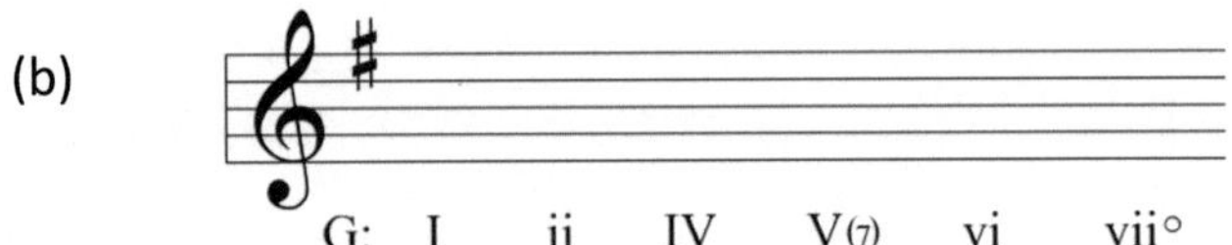

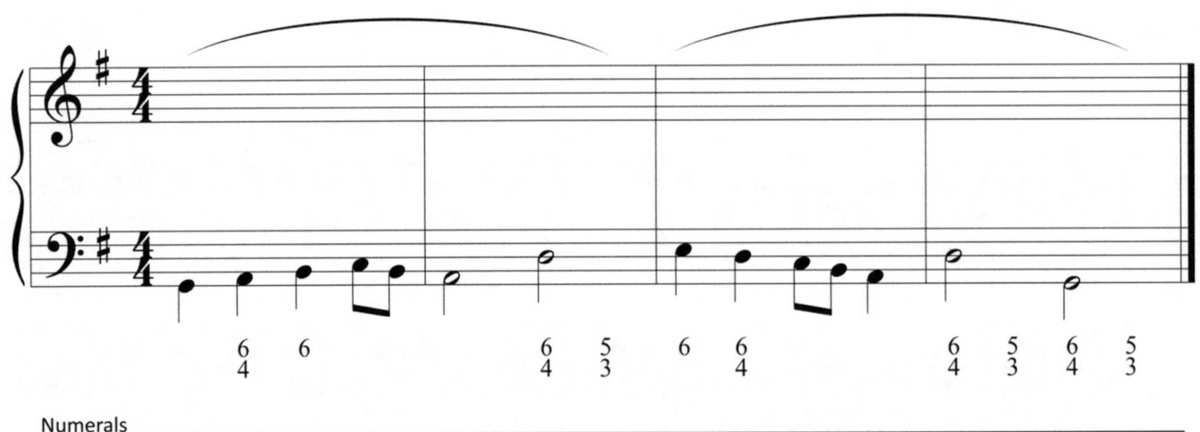

Numerals ___

Exercise 16.6

Sing each given melody adding solfa. Look for opportunities to include appropriate second inversion chords. Complete the bass line, adding roman numerals. Finally fill in alto and tenor parts.

(a)

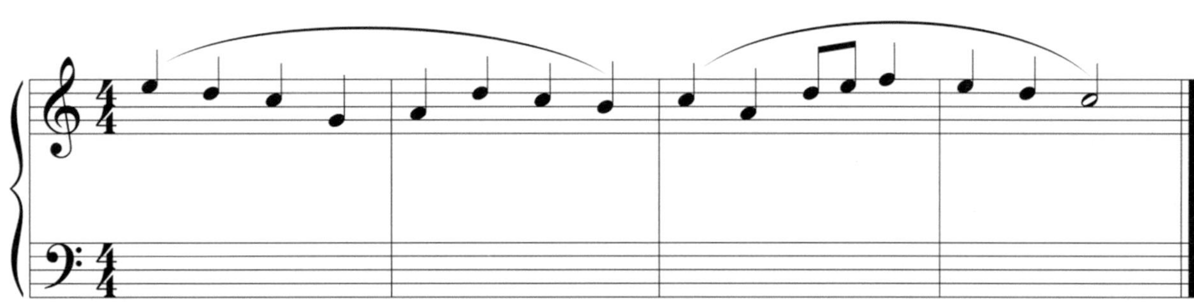

Numerals ____________________

(b)

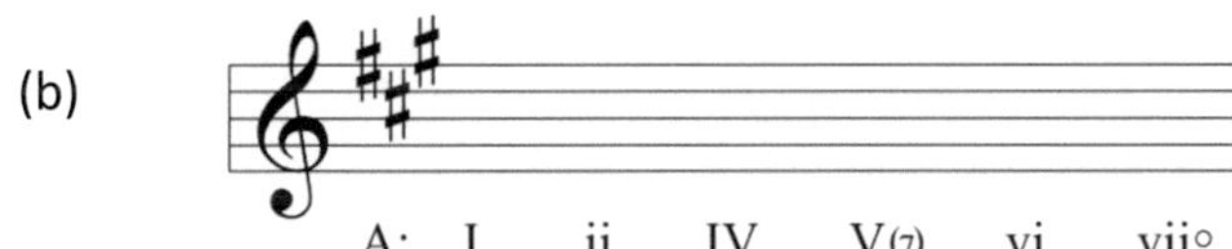

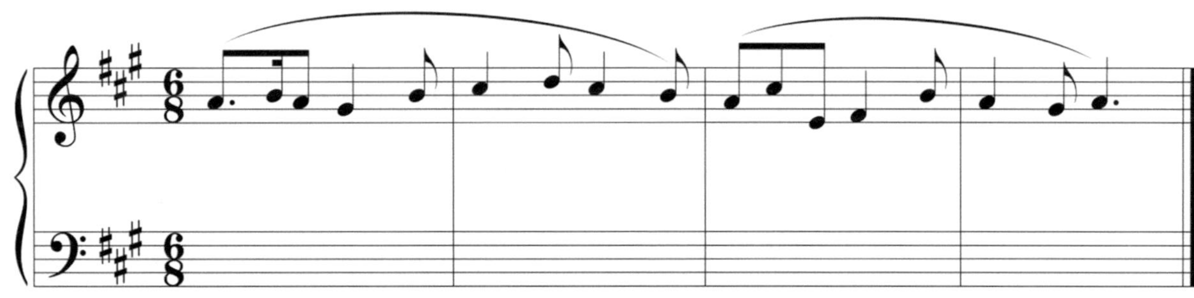

Numerals ____________________

(c)

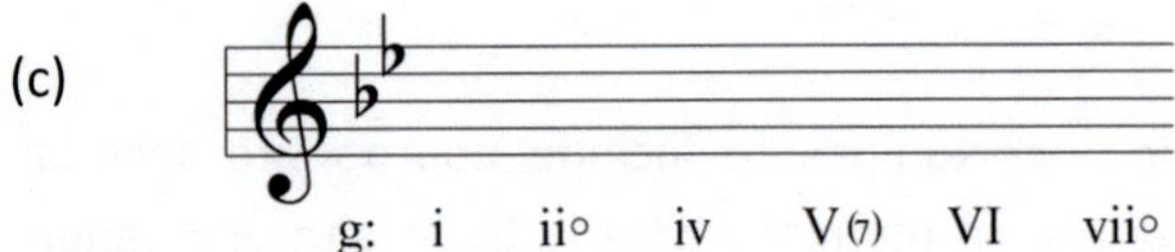

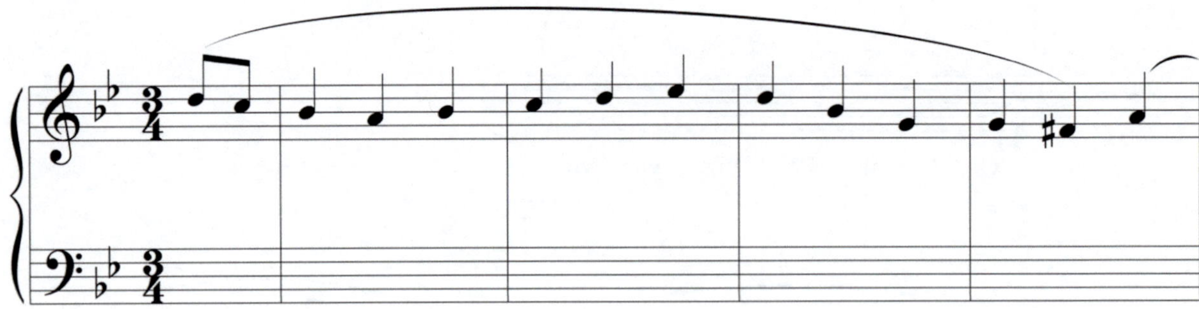

Numerals ___

___

Summary

- The second inversion is labelled **c** and figured $\begin{smallmatrix}6\\4\end{smallmatrix}$
- Three types: cadential, passing and auxiliary
- Context and rhythmic placement are very important
- Part-writing is essentially smooth
- Always double the 5th of the second inversion chord

CHAPTER 17

DOMINANT 7th INVERSIONS: V7c and V7d

This is the dominant 7th chord in all its positions.

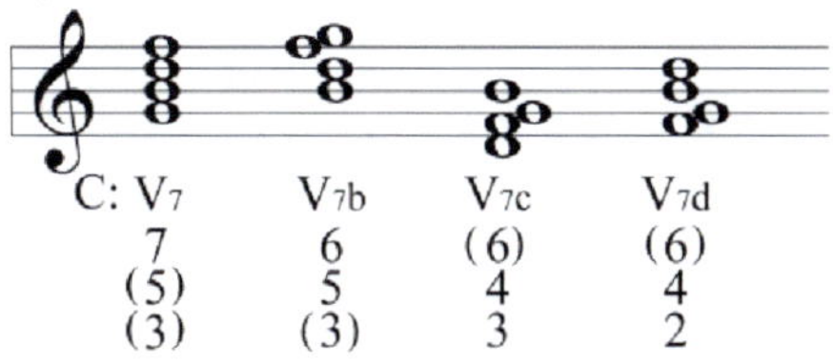

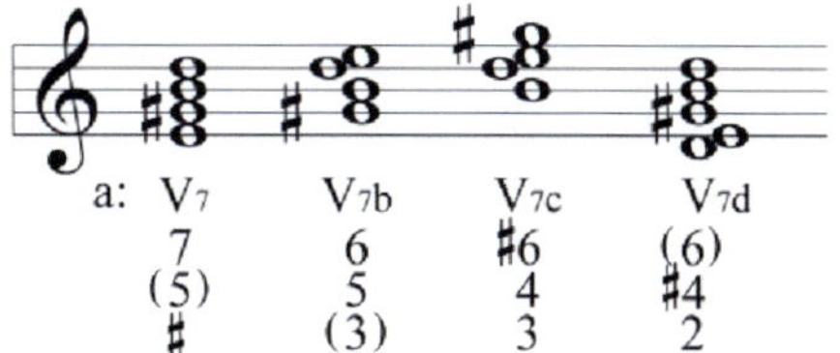

In a figured bass it is usual to omit the figures shown here in brackets.

Remember the necessary resolutions in a dominant 7th chord:

- The leading note rises a step to the tonic (***t – d/ si – l***) →
- The 7th of the chord falls a step (***f – m/ r – d***) →

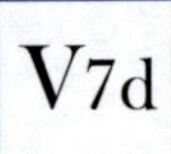

Of the inversions, the **V7d** position is the most striking. **V7d** resolves to **Ib**.

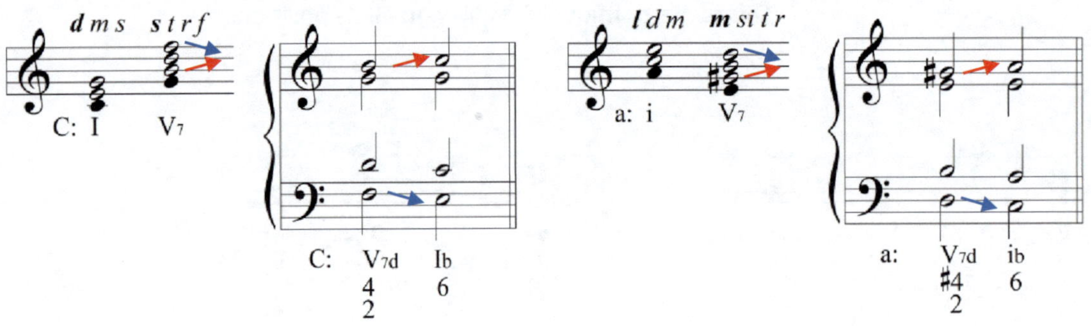

Listen to Audio 17.1 to hear the strong effect of **V7d - Ib**.

The **V7c** position is the least strong of all the inversions.

When **V7c** is followed by chord **I**, both discords resolve as expected.

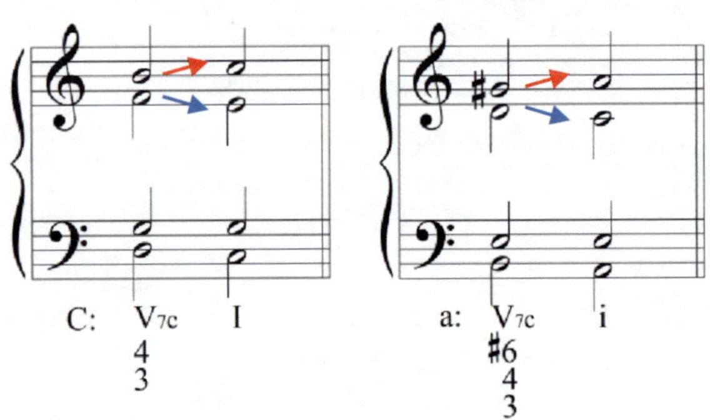

Listen to Audio 17.2 to hear this progression.

V7c can also be used idiomatically when moving between **I** and **Ib**, namely **I – V7c – Ib.** In general you will only encounter this idiom when the following soprano shapes appear: ***m – f – s*** (***d – r – m*** minor key) and ***m – s – d'*** (***d – m – l'*** minor key). As a consequence there is a necessary adjustment to the part-writing as indicated below by the modified arrow ⇛.

V7c – Ib requires special part-writing:

- The leading note rises ***t – d*** (***si – l*** *minor key*) →
- The 7th of **V7c** rises a step ***f – s*** (***r – m*** *minor key*) ⇛

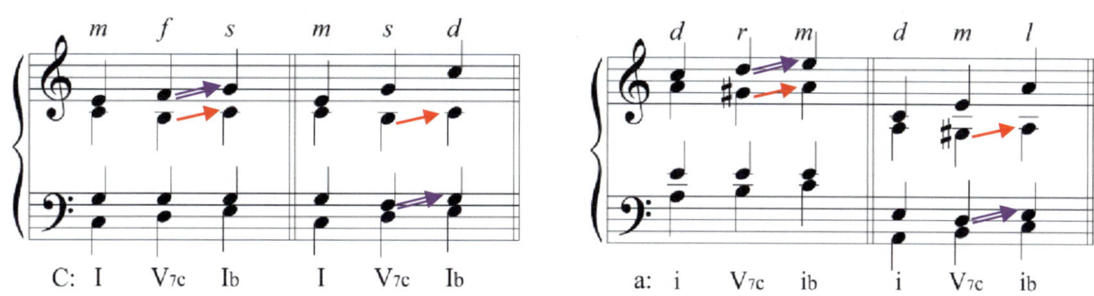

Note the acceptable 5ths (soprano and alto) in both examples; diminished followed by perfect.

Study the following example paying particular attention to the highlighted areas where the dominant 7th chord is used extensively.

Exercise 17.1

(a) Write these progressions in the following major keys. Add SAT and include roman numerals.

Numerals ____

(b) Write these progressions in the following minor keys for SATB. Include figured bass.

figured bass ____

Exercise 17.2

Exercise 17.2 has two Audio examples (Audios 17.4 and 17.5).Listen to each several times. Then analyse the harmonies by writing the roman numerals below each bass line. Finally add the figured bass.

Migrating 7th or transferring the 7th

With so many positions of the dominant 7th available, there is ample opportunity to use the various positions when a long dominant harmony arises. As a result, mobility within the parts is possible, adding interest and avoiding a static, block harmony.

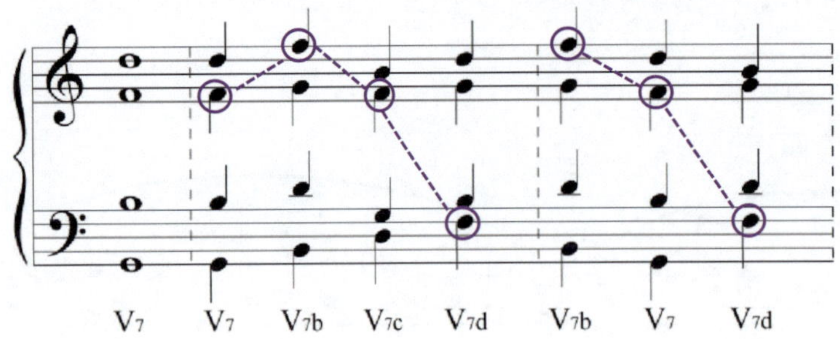

It can be seen from the above examples how the parts interchange freely. Notice that the path of the migrating 7th is highlighted.

Resolution – when and where?

'When' – at the next **change** of harmony

'Where' – from the **last voice** singing the 7th

Be aware that the **V7d** position carries with it a lot of 'punch'. So, if included, it is perhaps best placed last and just prior to the resolution.

Listen to Audio 17.6 to hear the changing positions of the dominant 7th and the final resolution.

Striking Intervals!

In a given soprano or bass, when intervals of a minor 7th ***s – f*** (***m – r*** minor key) or intervals of a diminished 5th ***t – f*** (***si – r*** minor key) are included, don't hasten to look for a change of harmony. Rather, keep within the realm of the dominant 7th chord. Study the bass of bar 2 and the soprano of bar 3 in the example below.

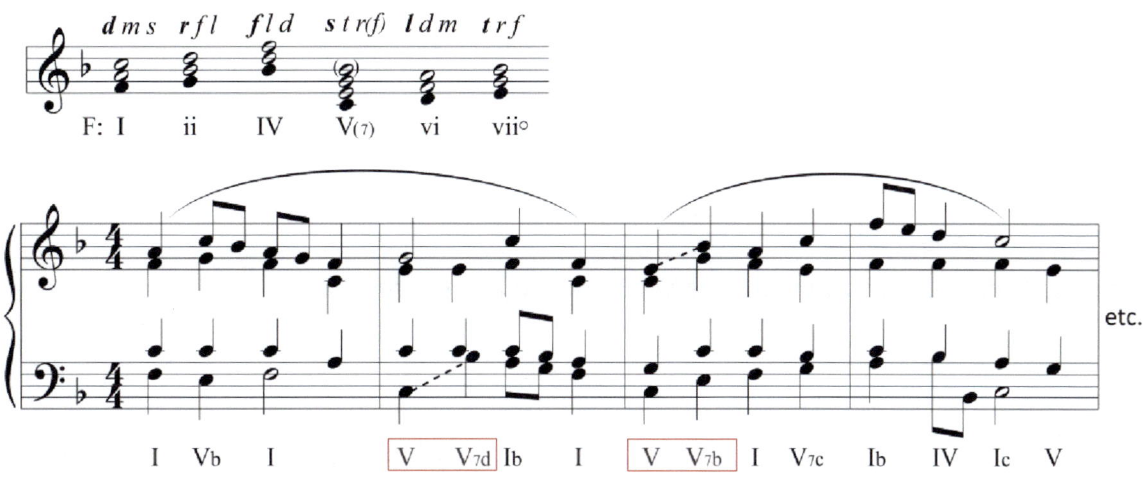

 Audio 17.7

Listen to Audio 17.7 paying particular attention to the highlighted intervals and the chosen dominant 7th harmony.

A special repeated bass

In general, avoid repeating a bass pitch across a bar line. A notable exception is the repeat of the 4th note ***f*** (***r*** minor key), provided the harmonic choice is strong enough. Give the **repeated** note the 'punch' of **V7d**. In other words, place the **V7d** on the **strong** beat.

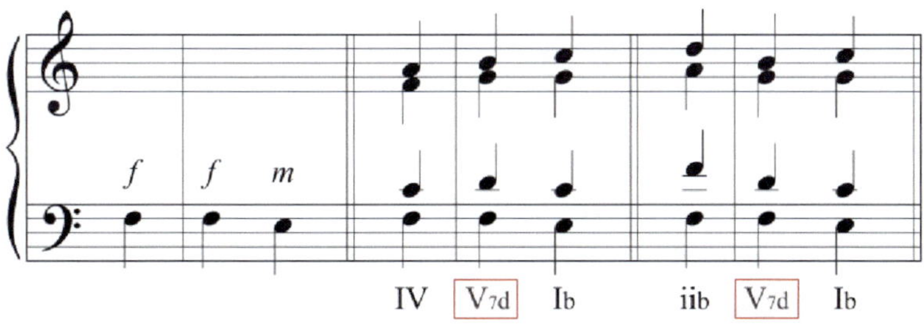

 Audio 17.8

Listen to Audio 17.8 to hear the impact of **V7d** on the repeated bass note.

Another opportunity for V7d!

When a given bass moves ***s – f – m*** (***m – r – d*** minor key), **V – V7d – Ib** provides good harmonic strength and colour.

Audio 17.9

Listen to Audio 17.9 to hear the striking harmonic colour of the above.

Exercise 17.3

Analyse the figured bass adding the roman numerals. Then complete the harmonisation by filling in the alto and tenor parts.

(a)

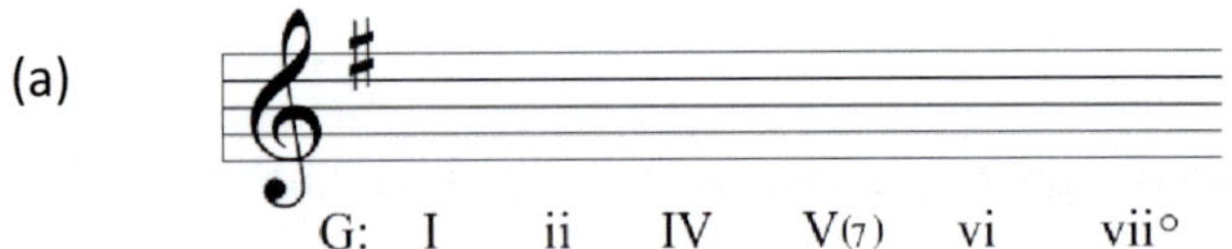

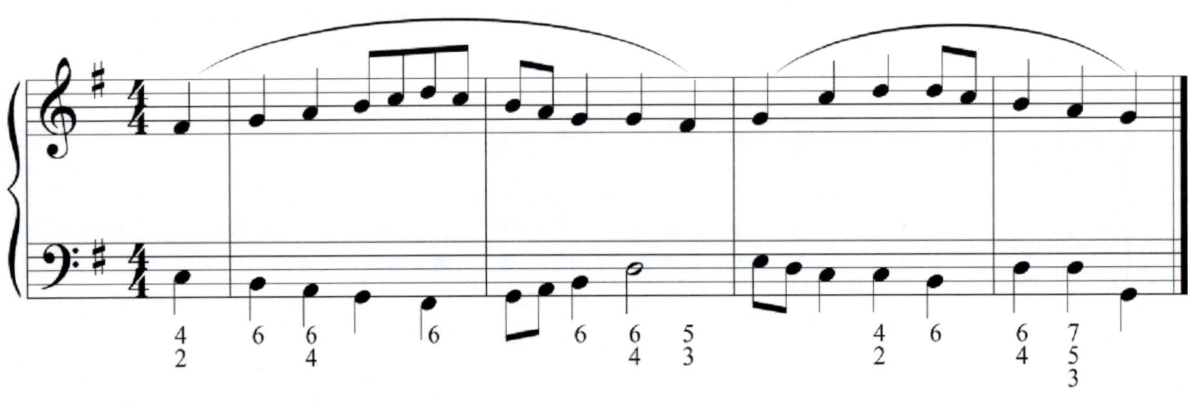

Numerals ________________________________

(b)

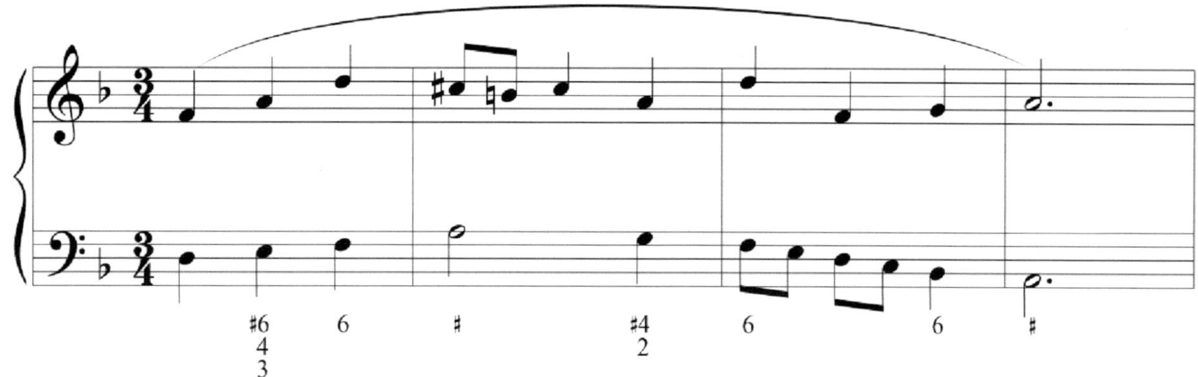

Numerals ______________________________

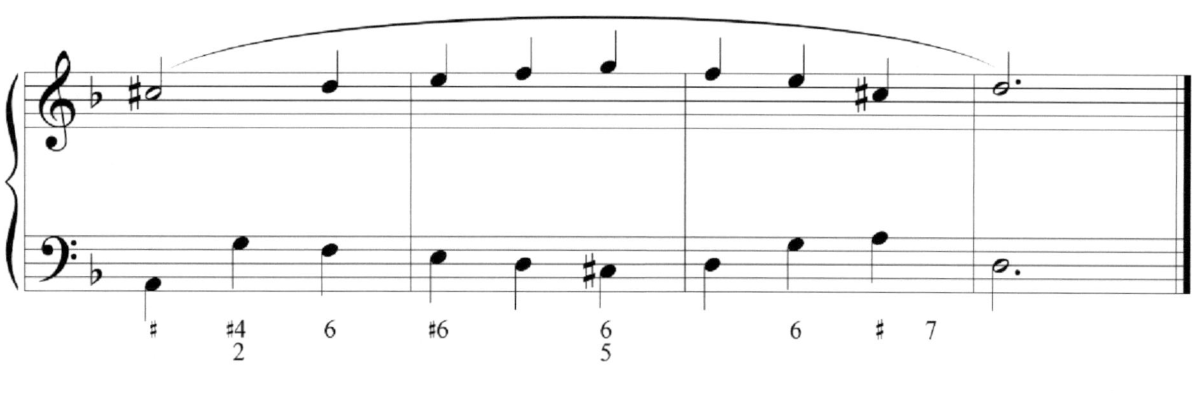

____

(c)

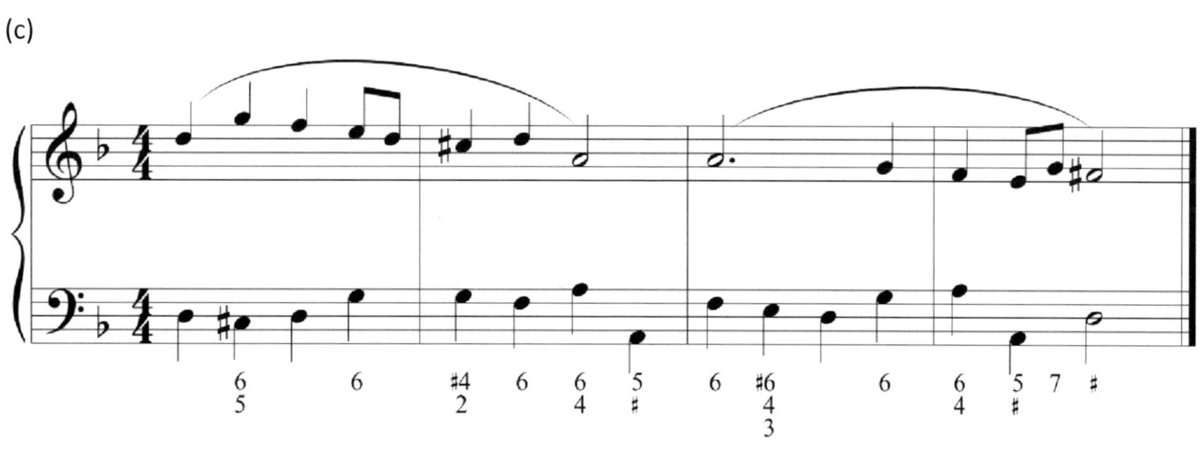

Numerals ______________________________

Exercise 17.4

Add roman numerals as indicated by the figured bass. Then complete the soprano melody, followed by alto and tenor parts.

(a)

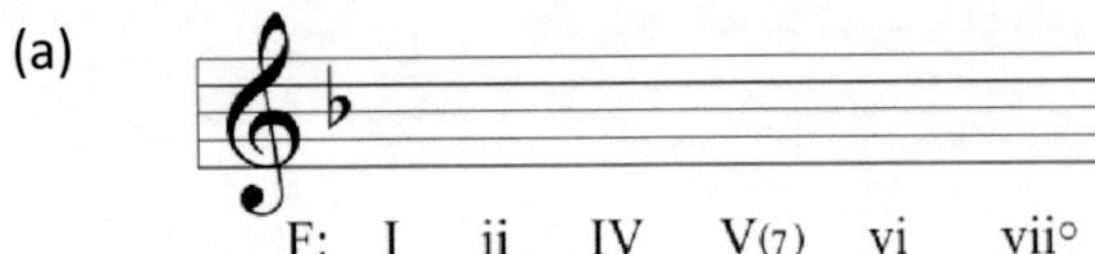

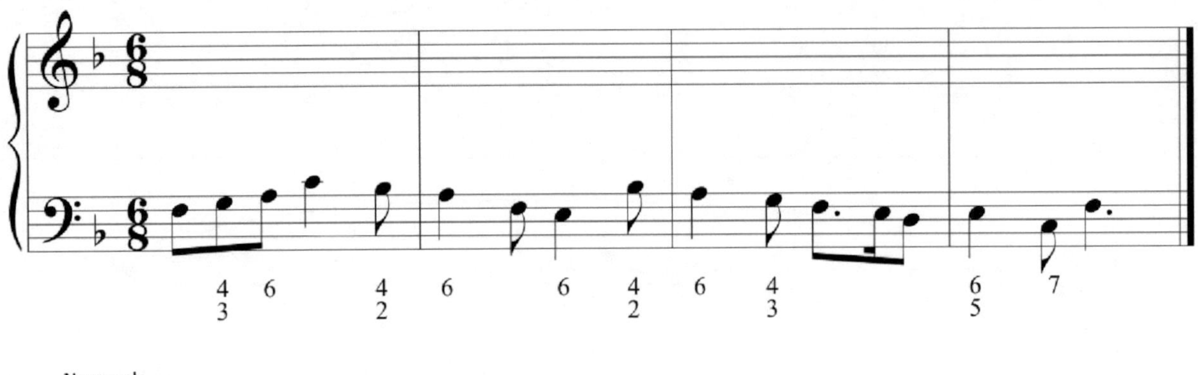

Numerals ______________________________

(b) Sing the given bass lines. Some solfa is included to help you when choosing the chording. Add roman numerals. First complete the soprano melody, followed by parts for alto and tenor.

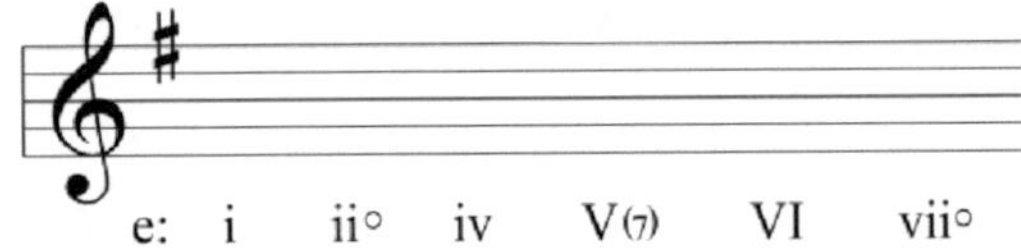

Numerals ______________________________

(c)

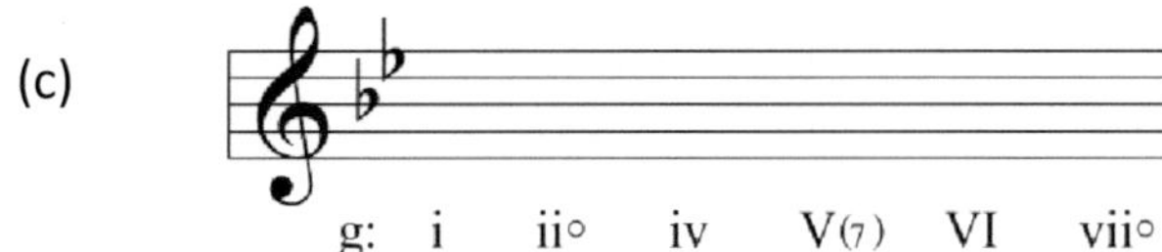

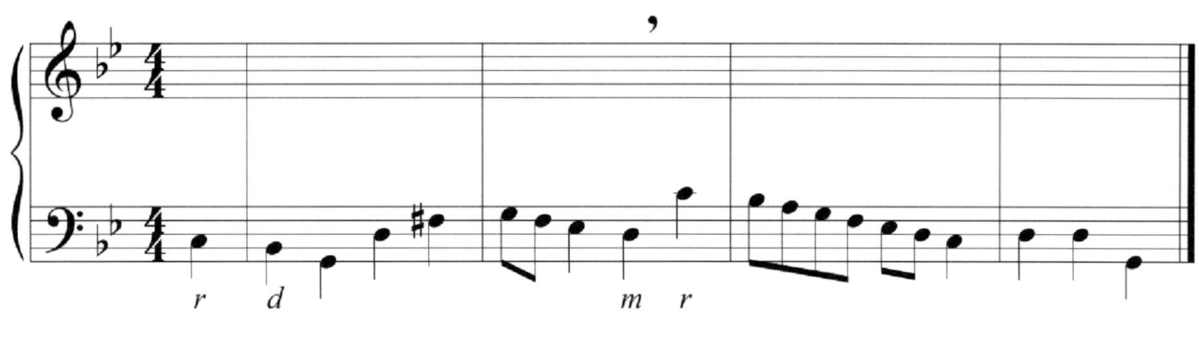

Numerals ____

(d)

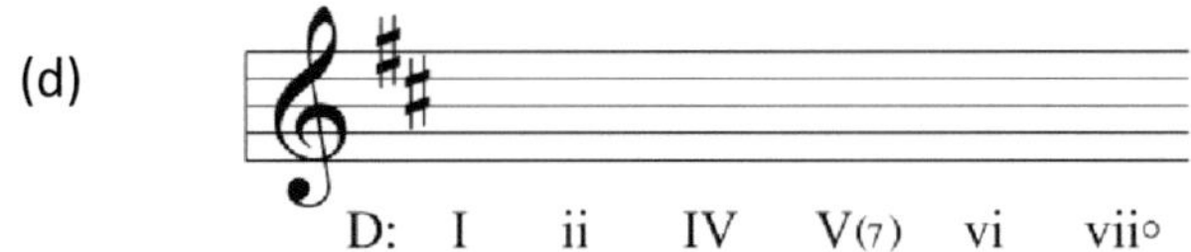

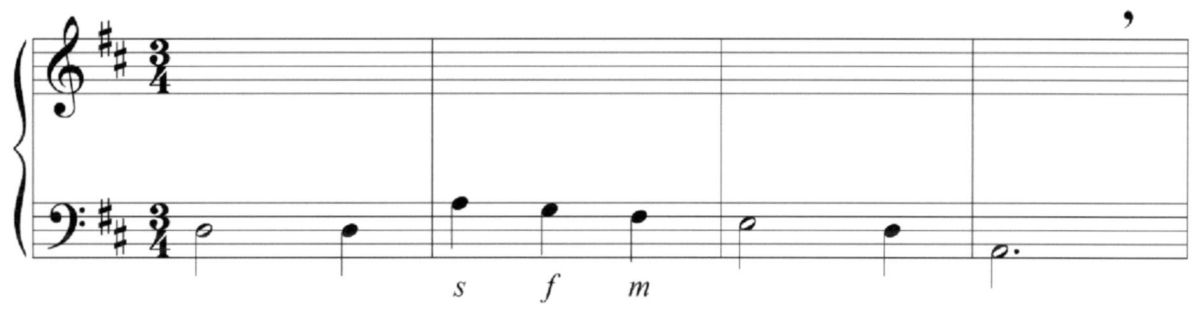

Numerals ____

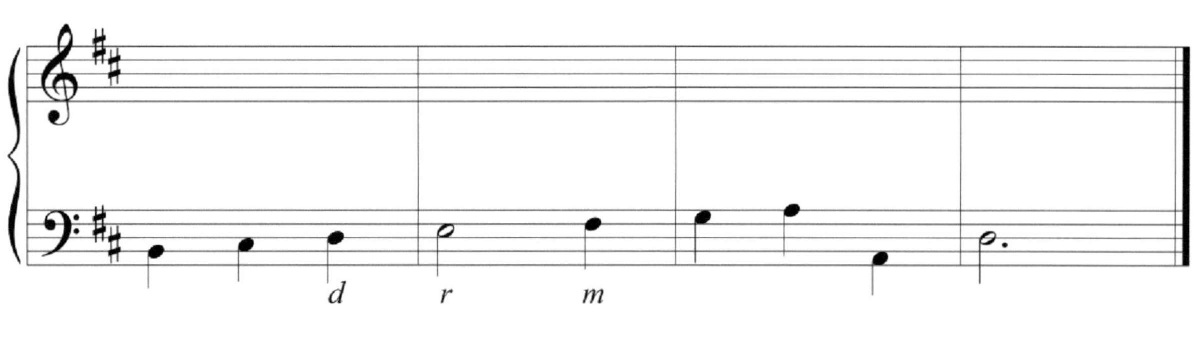

____

Now for some guidance in spotting opportunities for using the dominant 7th and its inversions in the harmonisation of a melody.

- Sing the melody adding solfa
- Decide the cadence points first
- Dominant 7th harmony in some form is always possible where the soprano moves ***f* – *m*** (***r* – *d*** minor key) or ***t* – *d*** (***si* – *l*** minor key).
- Identify any particular idiomatic shapes that suggest the dominant 7th e.g. ***m* – *f* – *s*** or ***m* – *s* – *d'*** (***d* – *r* – *m*** or ***d* – *m* – *l'*** minor key).

Plot in the cadential points.

Bar 2: **Ic – V** is the best choice here to suit the strong to weak ***d* - *t***.

Bar 4: Root position **V** gives a clear cut imperfect cadence. Remember an imperfect cadence normally does not include the 7th.

Bar 7 - 8: Root position perfect cadence to finish.

Complete the bass line.

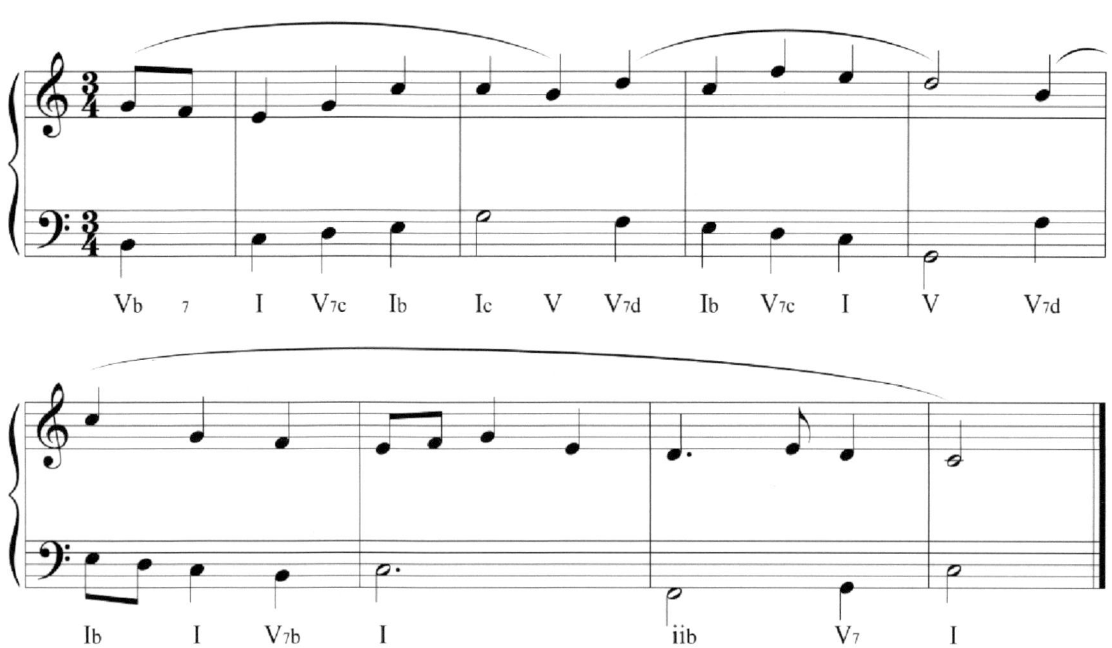

The initial upbeat suggests **V – I** across the bar line but **Vb – I** gives a smoother bass line. The 7th is added on the passing quaver in the melody and resolves appropriately.

Bar 1: ***m – s – d'*** suggests the idiom **I – V7c – Ib**.

Bar 2: Beat 2 ends on ***t*** which does not resolve directly in beat 3. This is a clue to retain the dominant harmony. **V7d** is an effective choice on beat 3, resolving to **Ib** across the bar line.

Bar 3: ***f – m*** suggests the dominant 7th in some form. **V7c – I** is chosen to give a smooth bass shape.

Bar 4 – 5: ***t – d*** again gives an opportunity for the dominant 7th harmony. **V7d – Ib** works effectively.

Bar 5 – 6: ***f – m*** considering the bass shape, **V7b – I** extends the stepwise bass line.

Bar 6: Remains on chord **I,** giving a sense of harmonic space.

Bar 7: **iib** gives a strong lead into the final cadence.

Complete the alto and tenor parts.

The inner voices are added, observing smoothness in the melodic lines. Notice the special treatment of the 7th in the idiom in bar 1 (**I - V7c - Ib**) with the 7th rising a step.

Also noteworthy is the part-writing in the approach to the final cadence **iib – V7**, in bar 7.

- Contrary motion of the upper parts to the bass has always been the recommendation in order to avoid the mistake of consecutive 5ths and octaves.

- However, in this instance, the presence of the 7th in **V7** eliminates the consecutive octaves.

Audio 17.10

Listen to Audio 17.10. You hear the four stages that go towards the building of the completed harmonisation.

Exercise 17.5

Complete for SATB. Build the harmonisation by following the recommended stages in order to arrive at a successful musical solution. Begin by singing the given soprano line.

(a)

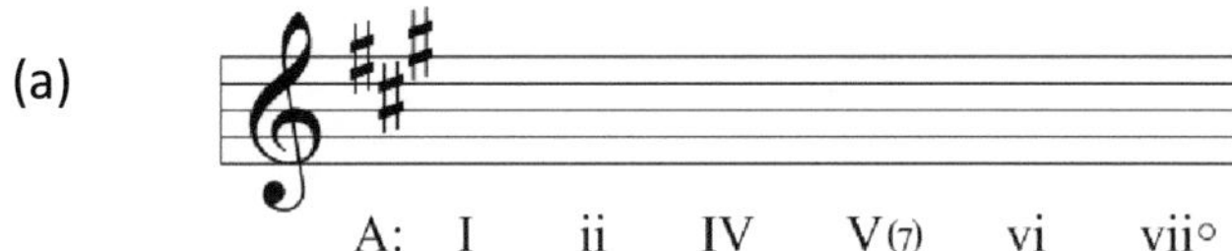

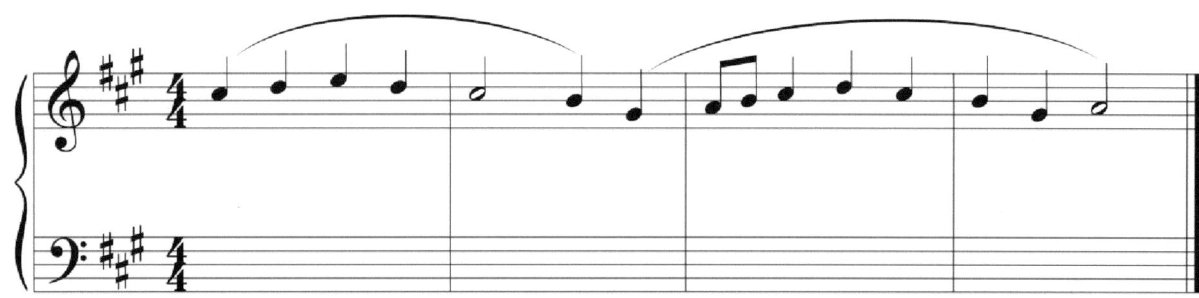

Numerals ______________________________

(b)

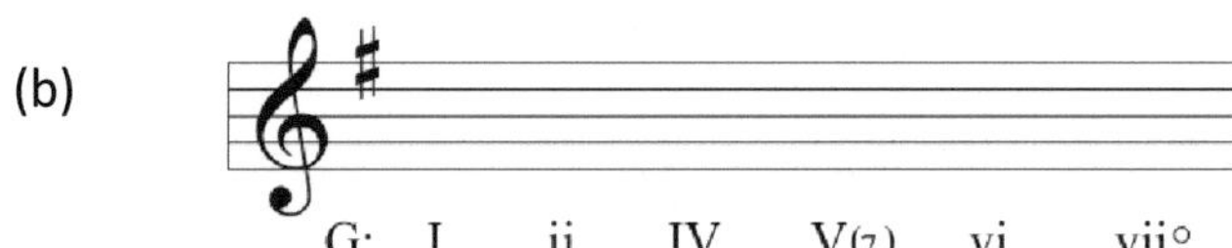

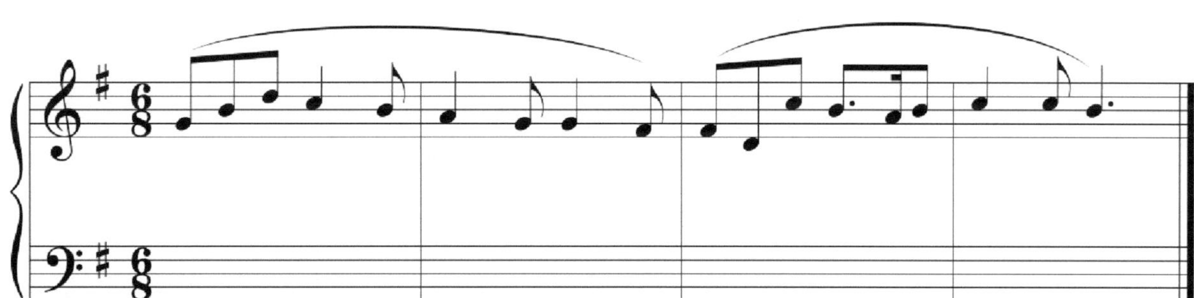

Numerals ______________________________

(c)

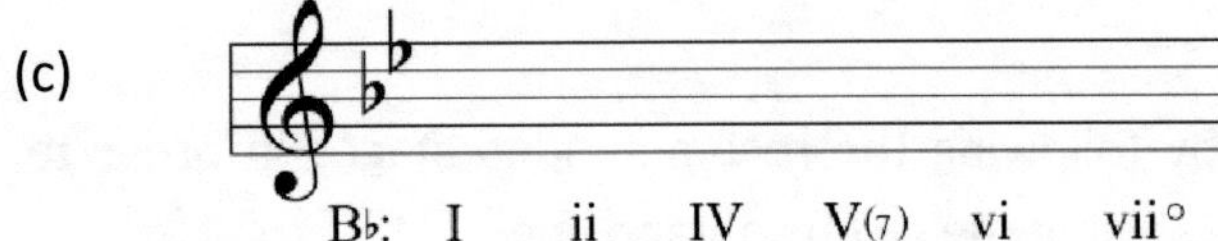

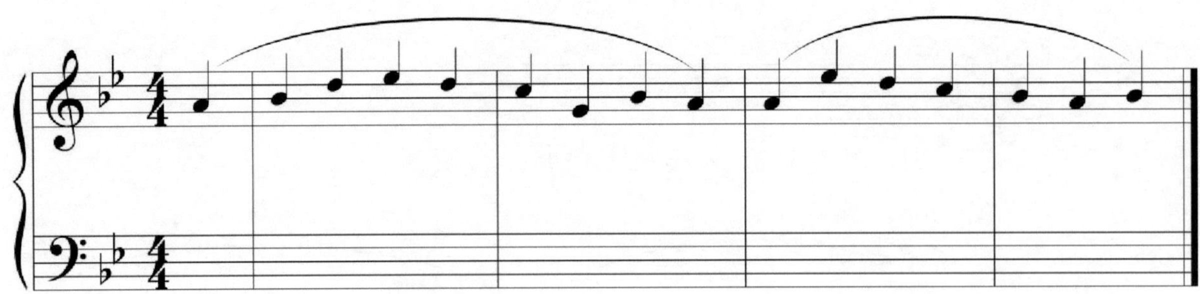

Numerals ____

(d)

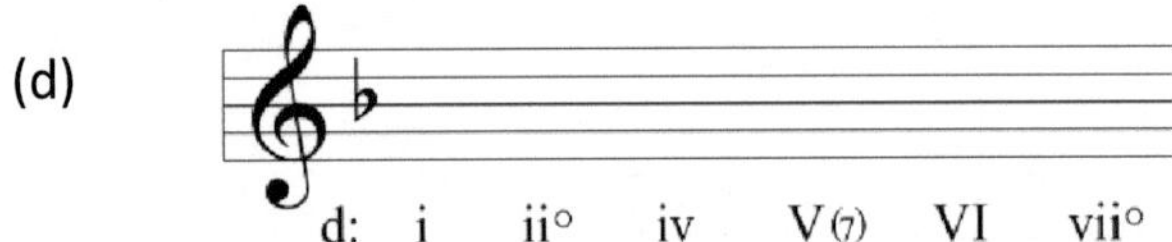

Numerals ____

____

Analysis

In this section you will encounter musical examples from Arne to Brahms. Listen carefully to the extracts before you respond. You may listen as often as you wish.

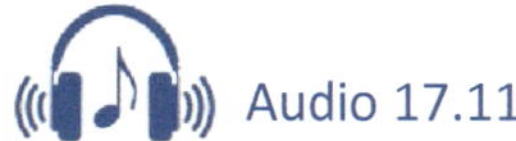

Audio 17.11

This is an extract from the 3rd movement of Mozart's Piano Sonata in F major, K 280. Listen carefully before answering the following questions.

a) Identify using roman numerals the harmony highlighted.
b) Name the cadence at the end of the extract:____________________
c) Identify the circled pitch in bar 5 as either a:
   passing note [ ] or auxiliary note [ ]

This is an extract from the 1st movement of Mozart's Piano Sonata in G major, K 283.

a) Identify using roman numerals the harmony highlighted.
b) Name the type of cadence at the end of the extract:_______________

This extract is from Beethoven's 'Happy and Sad', WoO 54. Listen carefully and answer the questions below.

a) Name the key:______________
b) Identify using roman numerals each of the harmonies highlighted.
c) Name the final cadence:_____________
d) Identify the circled pitches in bar 1 as either:
   Passing notes ☐ or auxiliary notes ☐

The extract below is the opening phrase of Brahms' Waltz in D minor, Op. 39. The harmony changes per bar. Identify using roman numerals, each chord change.

Audio 17.15

Below is an extract from Heller's Study in E major 'Celestial Voices' Op.45, No.9.

a) Identify using roman numerals, the chording in the highlighted areas.
b) Identify the type of cadence ending the extract:________________

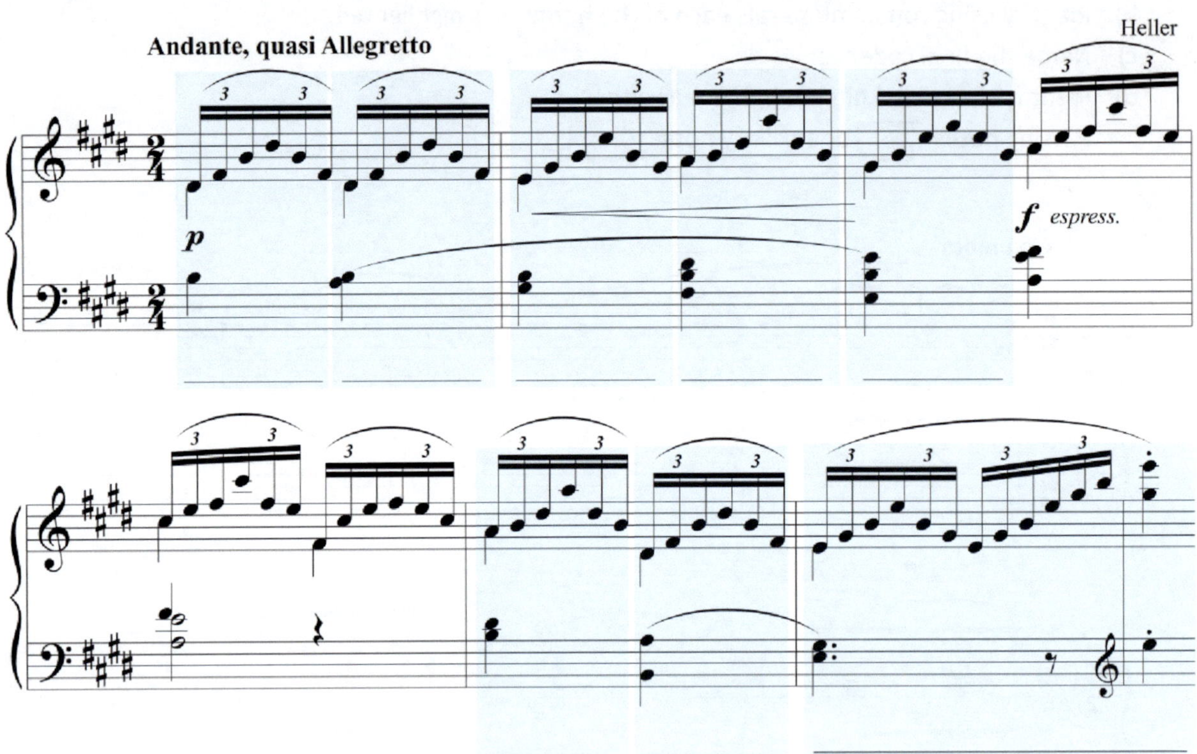

Audio 17.16

This extract is from Sonata No. 6 (2nd mvt. Gig) by Thomas Arne. Listen and answer the following questions.

a) Name the key:__________________
b) Identify using roman numerals, each chord change.
c) Identify the circled notes as passing or auxiliary:
Bar 2, C: ___________ A: ___________ Bar 3, B: ___________ Bar 4, A: ___________

This extract is from the 2nd movement of Mozart's Piano Sonata, K 280. Listen carefully and answer the following questions.

a) Name the key:_________________________
b) There are two harmonic changes per bar. Using roman numerals identify the harmonic activity as highlighted.
c) Name the final cadence:_________________

This extract is from Beethoven's Minuet in G major, WoO 10, No. 2. Listen carefully and answer the following questions.

a) Identify using roman numerals, the harmony in the highlighted areas.
b) Name the type of cadence at the end of the extract:____________

This is an extract from Schubert's Minuet in C sharp minor, D600.

a) Identify using roman numerals, the chords highlighted.
b) Name the cadence at the end of the extract:__________________

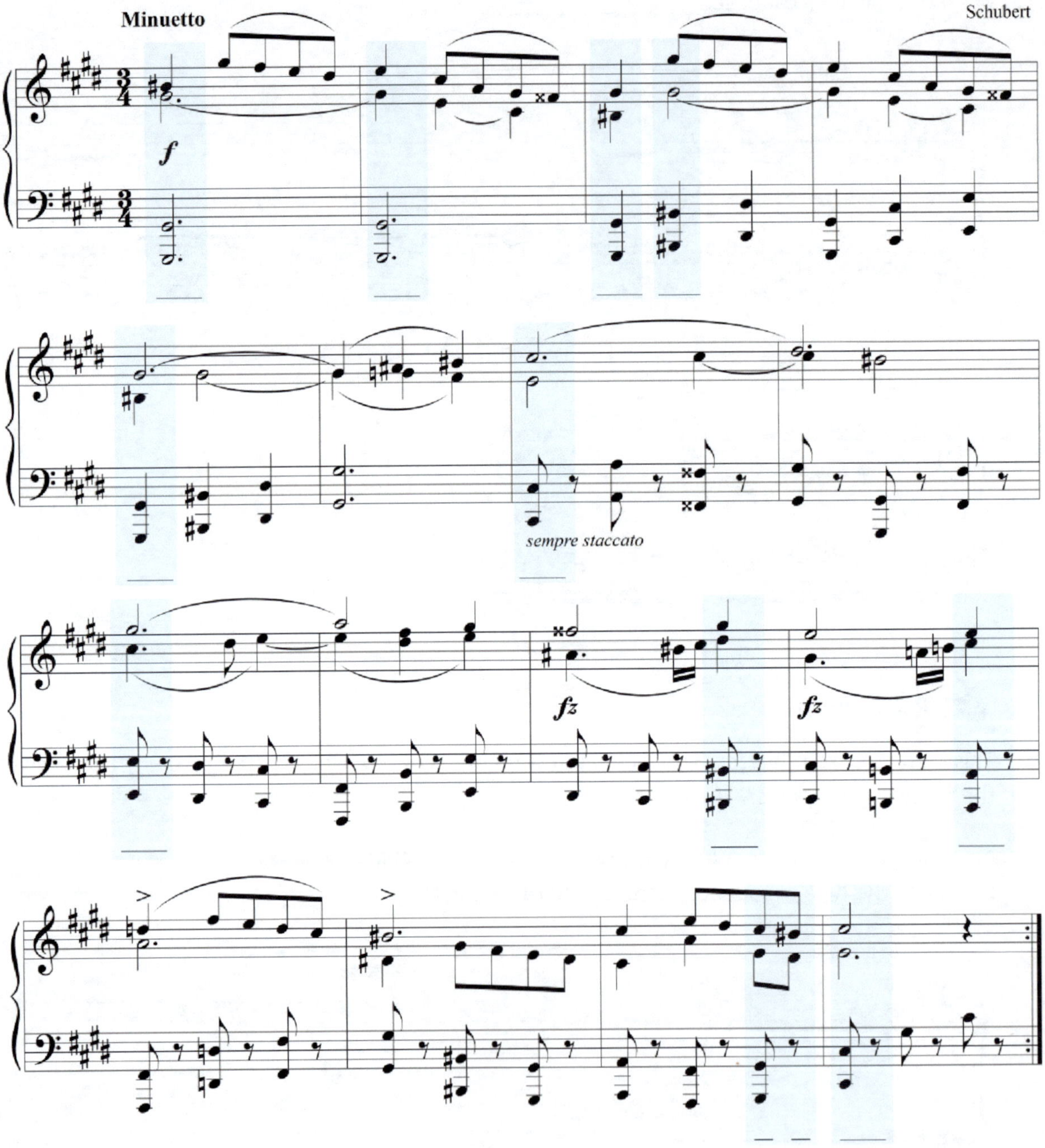

Minuetto

Schubert

sempre staccato

This extract is from Brahms' Waltz in E major, Op. 39. For the most part the harmony changes per bar (bars 1 - 6).

a) Identify the chords using roman numerals.
b) Name the final cadence:______________

This extract is part of the Toccata from Paradisi's Piano Sonata in A major. The harmony changes per quaver in the highlighted area.

a) Identify using roman numerals the harmony used.
b) Name the type of cadence concluding the extract:______________

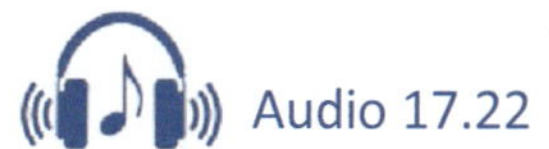 Audio 17.22

This extract is from the 3rd movement of Haydn's String Quartet Op. 2 No. 4.

a) Name the key:______________

b) Identify using roman numerals the chords in the highlighted area.

c) Name the cadence formed across bars 9 – 10:______________________________

d) Comment on the quality of the final chord:______________________________

Haydn

Adagio

This extract is from the 1st movement of Haydn's String Quartet Op. 2, No. 4 in F major.

a) Identify using roman numerals, the harmony in the highlighted areas.

b) Name the cadence that occurs at the end of the extract:________________

c) Identify the circled pitches in bar 12 as either:
passing ☐ or auxiliary ☐

Presto

Haydn

This extract is from the 3rd movement of Haydn's String Quartet Op. 17, No. 1.

a) Name the key:________________
b) The harmony changes per bar in the highlighted area at the beginning of the quartet. Identify using roman numerals, the chords used.
c) Identify the chords in the final bar.
d) Name the cadence formed at the end of the extract:_______________
e) Identify the circled pitches in the first violin part, as either passing or auxiliary notes.
   E: _________________ A: ___________________

This extract is from the Finale of Haydn's String Quartet Op. 2, No. 2.

a) Name the tonic key: _______________

b) Identify using roman numerals, the final three chords.

c) Name the cadence:_____________

APPENDIX 1

Supplementary Exercises

CHAPTER 5
Supplementary Exercises

Ch. 5 – Supp. Ex. 1

Sing each of the given soprano melodies. Choose chords to harmonise by writing in the bass part.

(i)

Numerals ____

(ii)

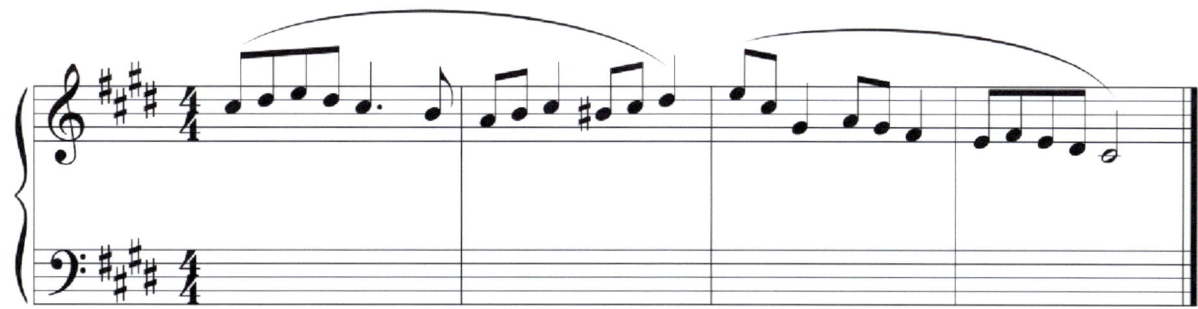

Numerals ____

(iii) 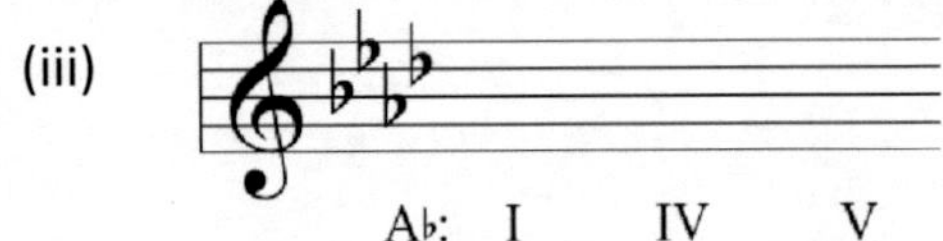

Numerals ____

(iv) 

Numerals ____

(v)

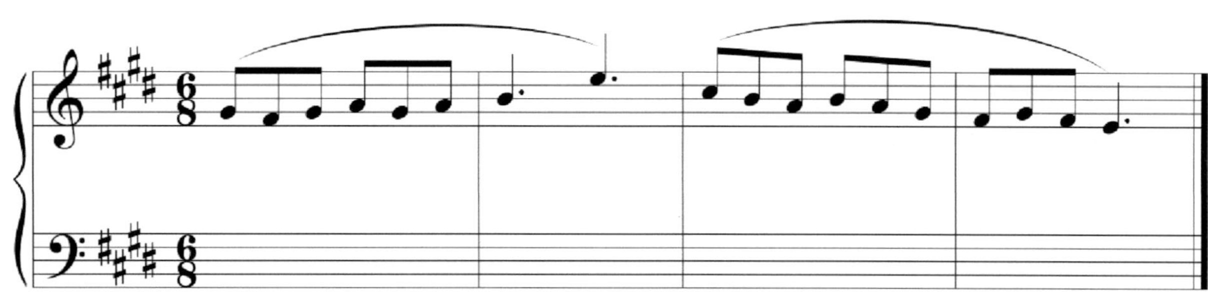

Numerals ____

(vi)

Numerals ____

CHAPTER 7
Supplementary Exercises

Ch. 7 - Supp. Ex. 1

Complete each harmonisation by adding alto and tenor parts. Include **V7** where appropriate. Add roman numerals below the bass.

(i)

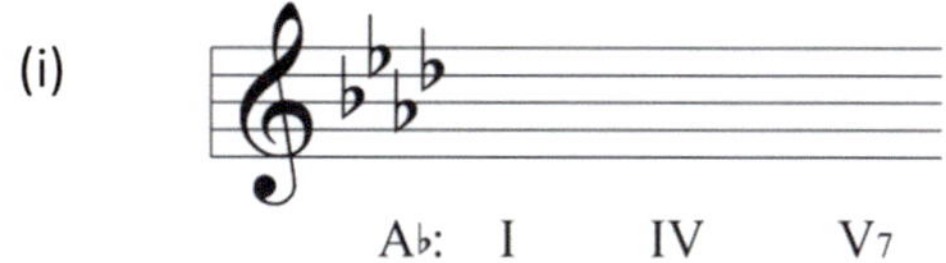

Numerals____

(ii)

Numerals____

Ch. 7 - Supp. Ex. 2

Add roman numerals below the bass, including **V7** where appropriate. Write a melody for soprano.

(i)

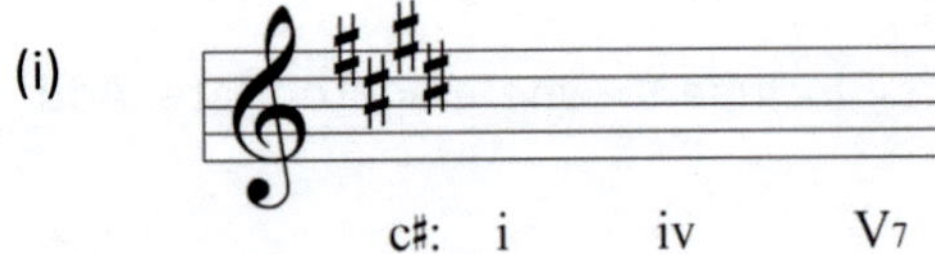

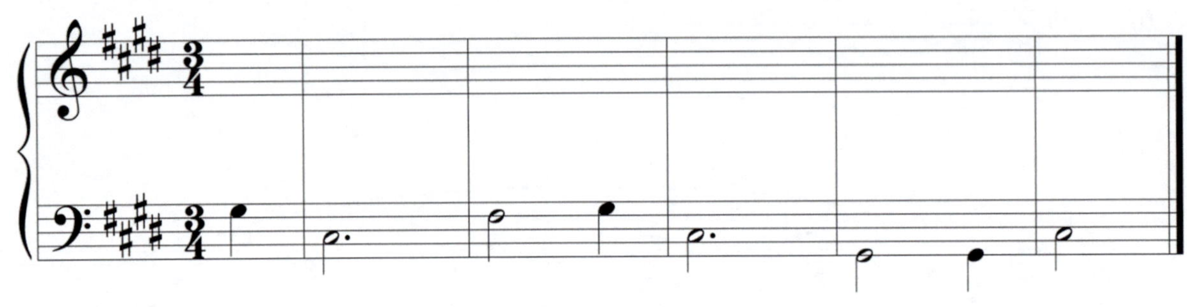

Numerals____

(ii)

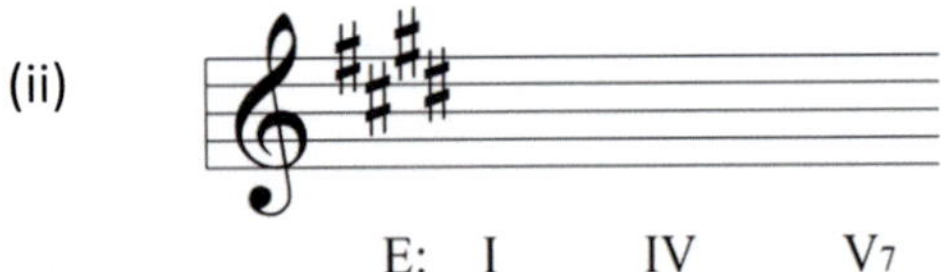

Numerals____

Ch. 7 - Supp. Ex. 3

Add a bass line to harmonise each melody. Don't forget to sing the melody!

(i)

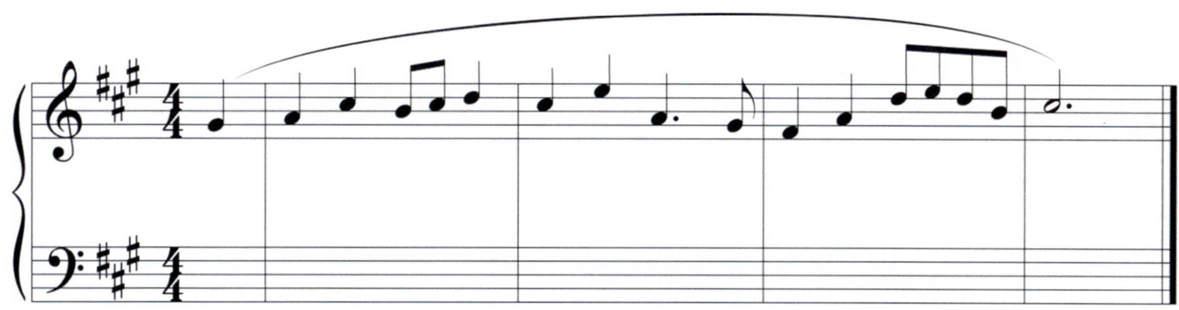

Numerals____

(ii)

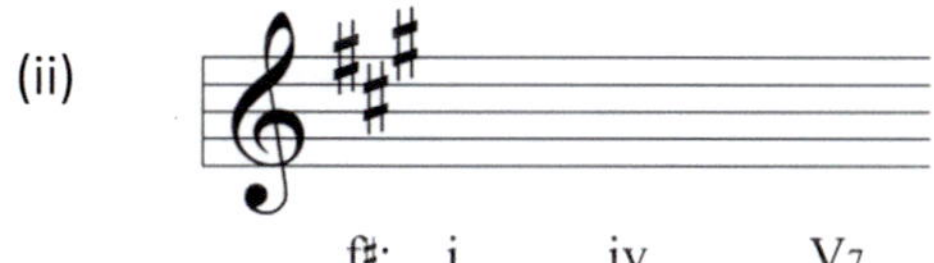

Numerals____

CHAPTER 8
Supplementary Exercises

Ch. 8 – Supp. Ex. 1

Complete the harmonisation by adding alto and tenor parts. Include roman numerals.

(i)

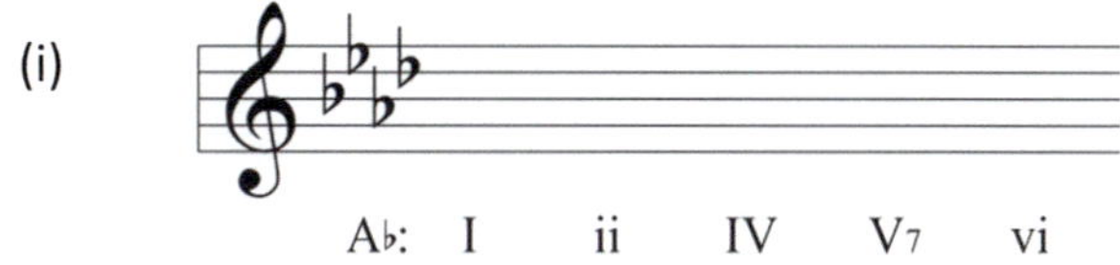

Numerals____

(ii)

Numerals____

Ch. 8 – Supp. Ex. 2

Create a musically shaped soprano line above each of the given bass lines. Add the roman numerals. Always remember to sing as you write.

(i)

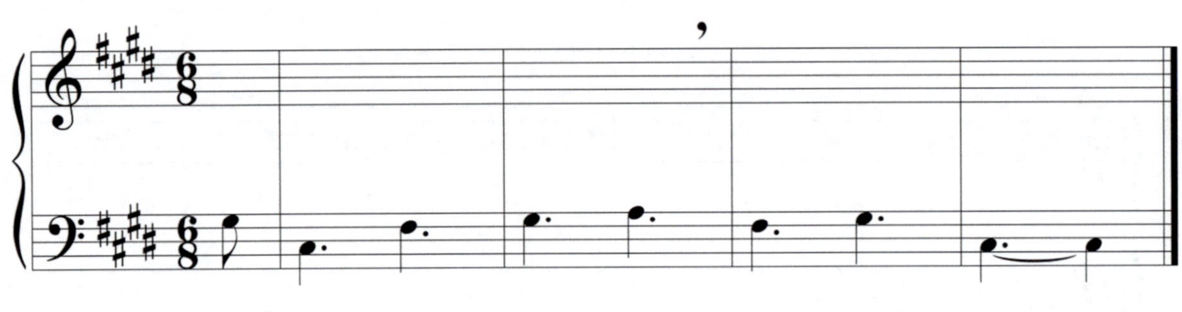

Numerals____

(ii)

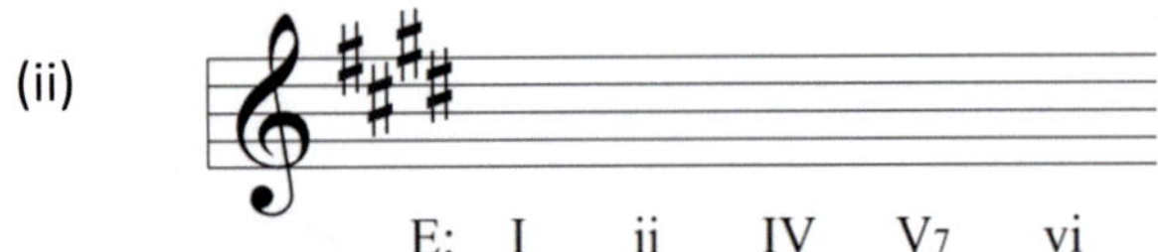

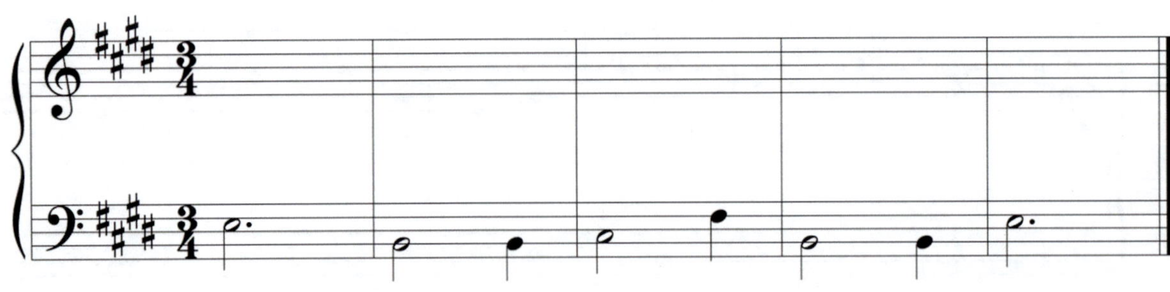

Numerals____

Ch. 8 - Supp. Ex. 3

Sing each of the given melodies. Choose chords to harmonise by writing the bass line. Include roman numerals.

(i)

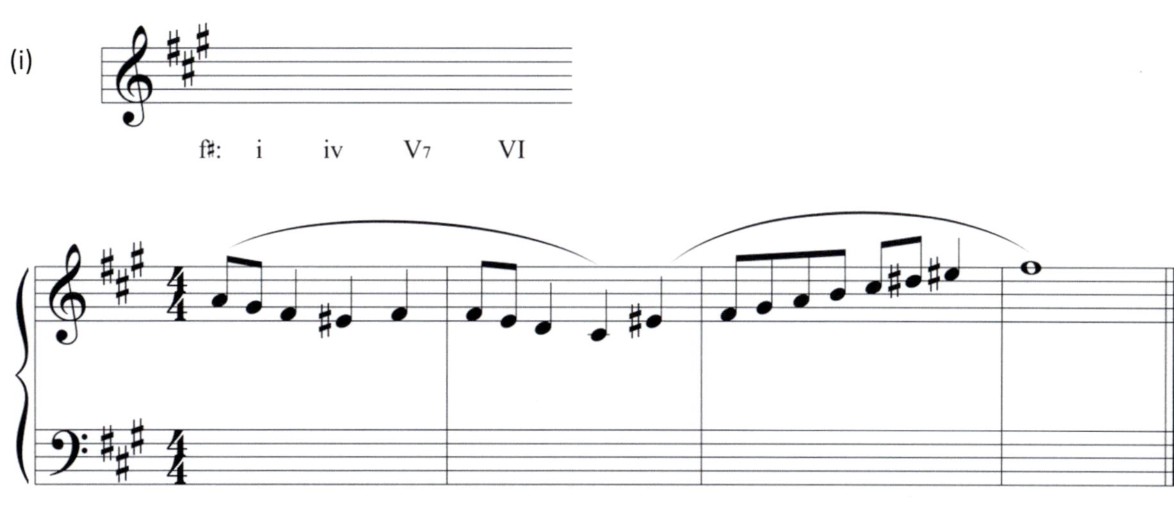

Numerals____

(ii)

Numerals____

CHAPTER 14

Supplementary Exercises

Ch. 14 – Supp. Ex. 1

Harmonise each melody by adding the bass line. Add the solfa and sing the melody. Sketch in possible idiomatic shapings.

(i)

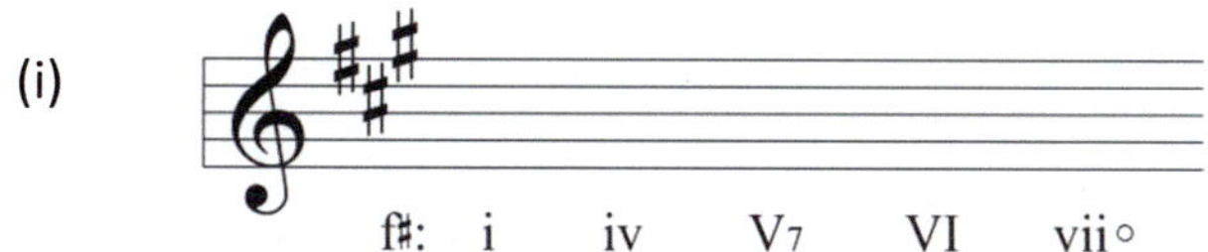

Numerals ____

(ii)

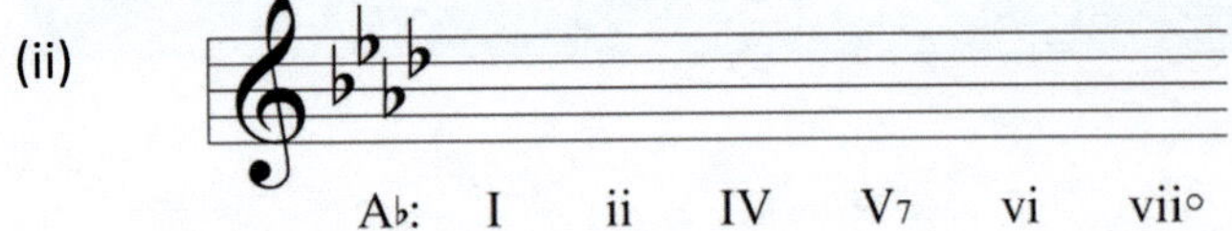

Numerals ___

Ch. 14 - Supp. Ex. 2

Study the given soprano and bass lines. Complete the harmonisation by adding parts for alto and tenor voices.

(i)

(ii)

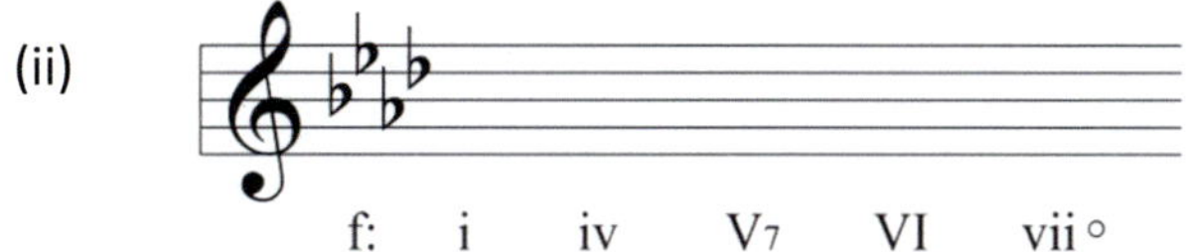

Ch. 14 - Supp. Ex. 3

Carefully study the given bass lines. Choose progressions looking out for idiomatic usage of **viib**. Add a melody for soprano, shaping it as musically as you can.

(i)

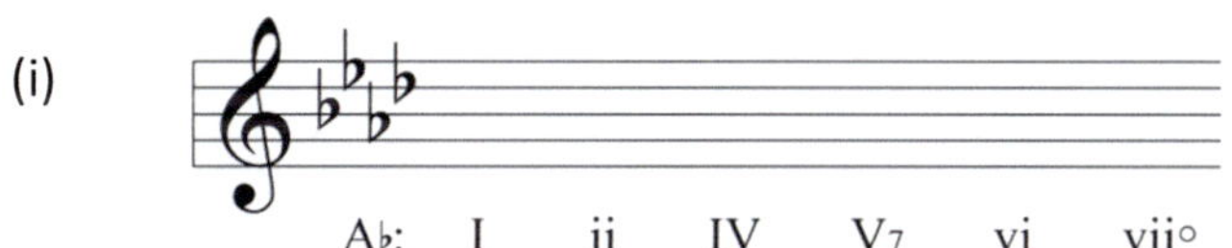

Numerals ____________________

(ii)

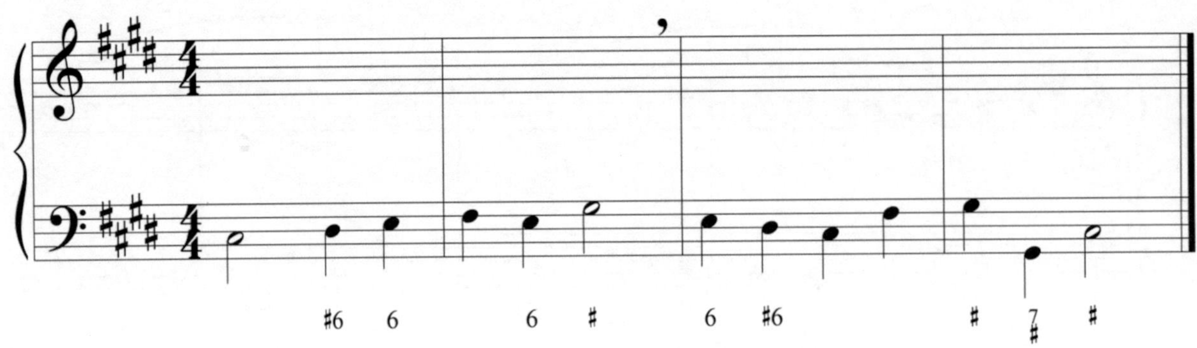

CHAPTER 16
Supplementary Exercises

Ch. 16 – Supp. Ex. 1

Study the given soprano and figured bass lines. Complete the harmonisation by adding parts for alto and tenor voices.

(i)

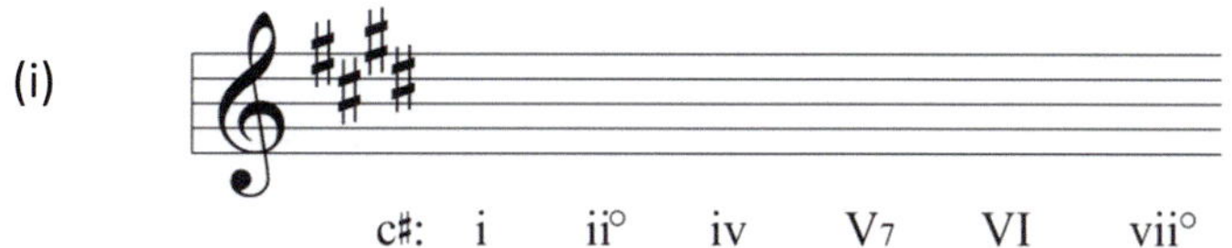

(ii)

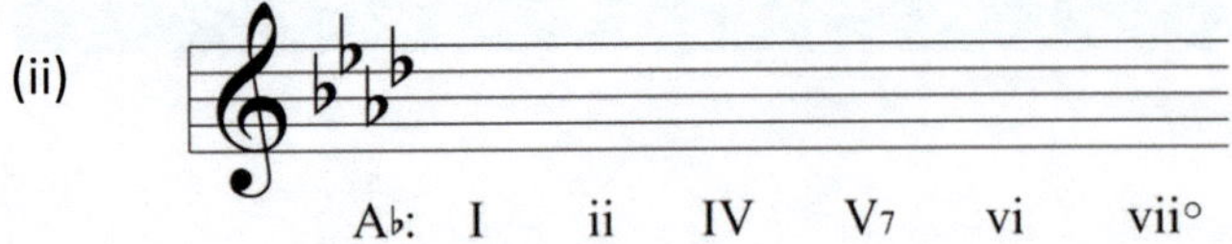

Ch. 16 – Supp. Ex. 2

Study the given figured bass. Complete the soprano melody first. Finally add parts for alto and tenor.

(i)

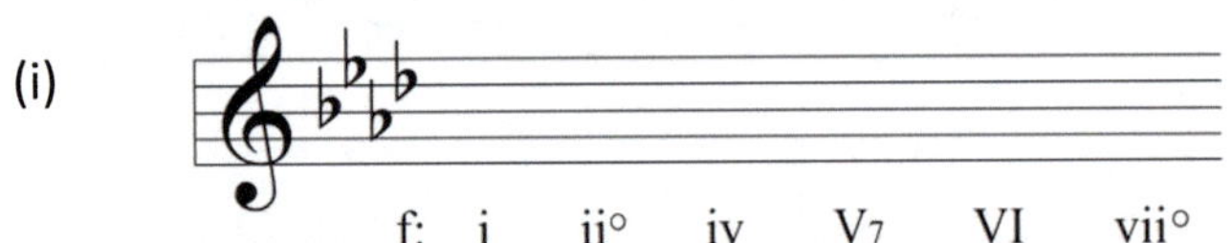

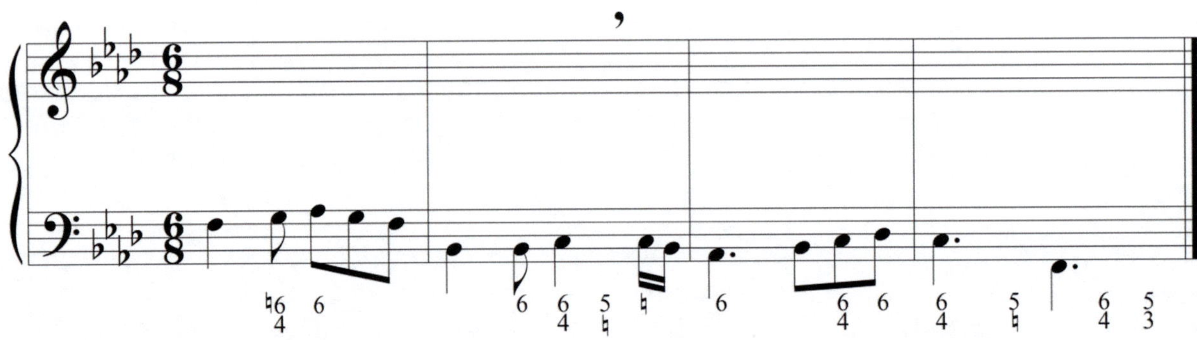

(ii)

Numerals ____

Ch. 16 - Supp. Ex. 3

Sing each given melody adding solfa. Look for opportunities to include appropriate second inversion chords. Complete the bass line, adding roman numerals. Finally fill in alto and tenor parts.

(i)

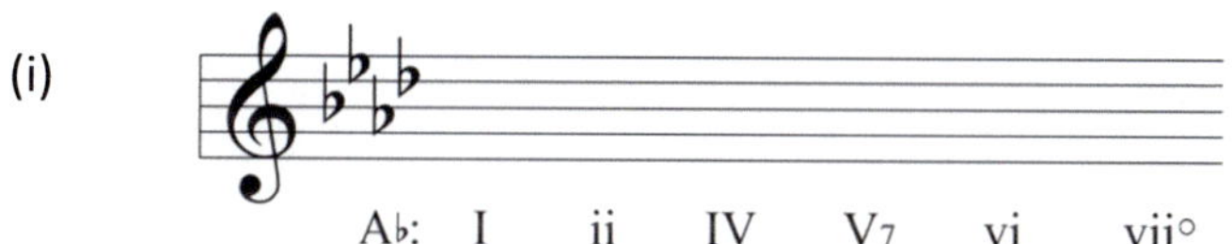

Numerals ____

(ii)

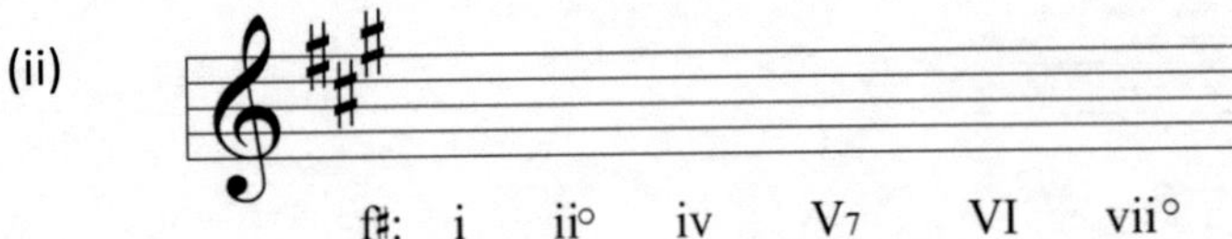

Numerals ____

____

CHAPTER 17
Supplementary Exercises

Ch. 17 – Supp. Ex. 1

Study the soprano and bass parts together with the figures given. Complete the harmonisation by adding the alto and tenor parts.

(i) 

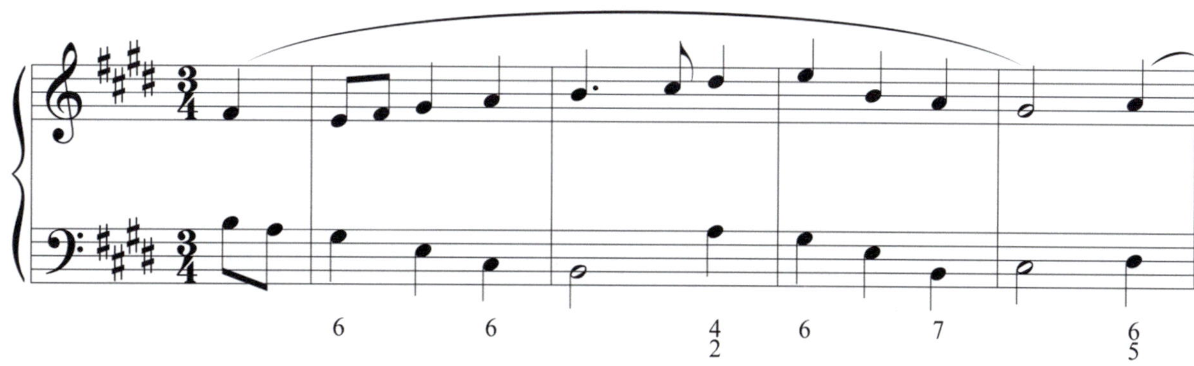

(ii)

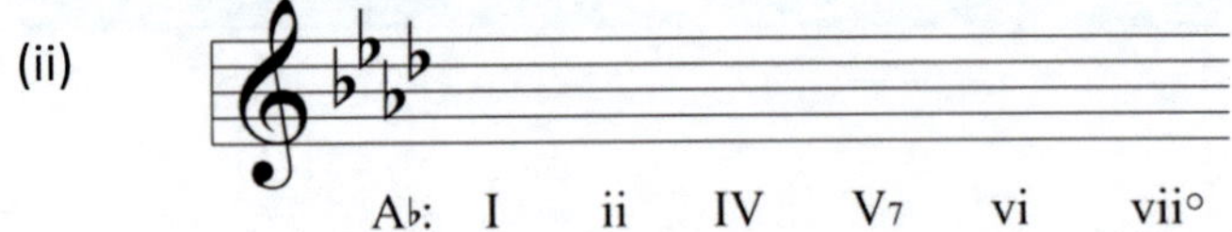

Ch. 17 – Supp. Ex. 2

Add roman numerals as indicated by the figured bass. Then complete the soprano melody, followed by alto and tenor parts.

(i)

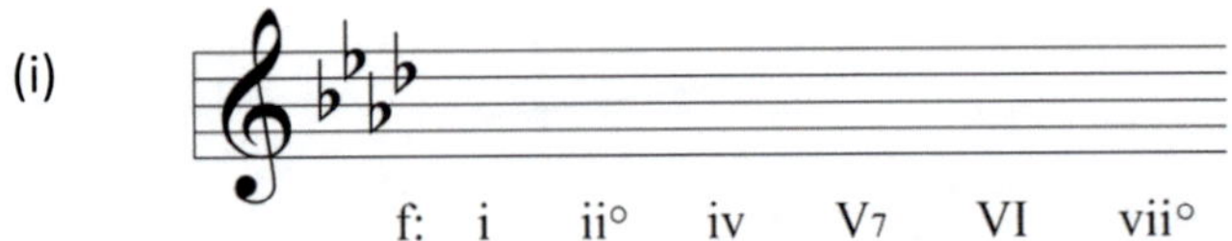

Numerals ____

(ii)

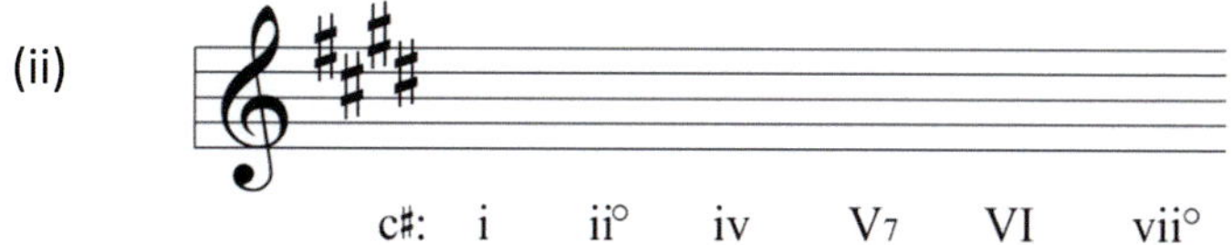

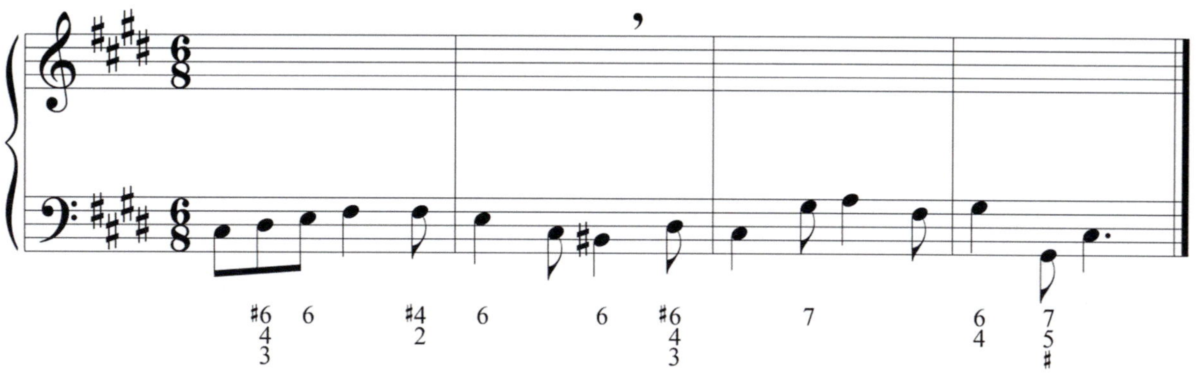

Numerals ______________________________

Ch. 17 – Supp. Ex. 3

Firstly sing each given soprano line, then choose the harmony by adding a bass line. Finally add parts for alto and tenor voices.

(i)

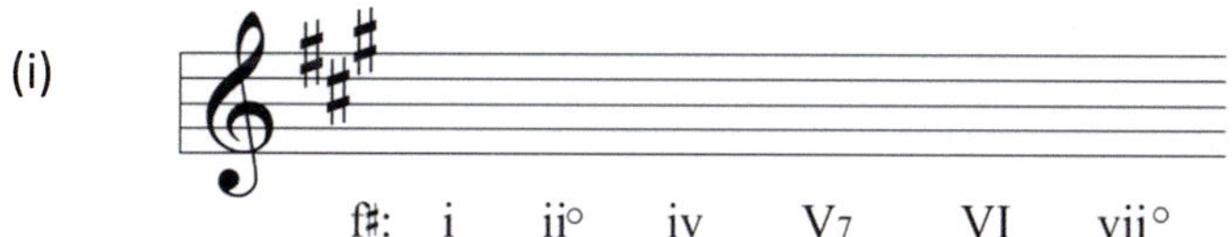

Numerals ______________________________

(ii)

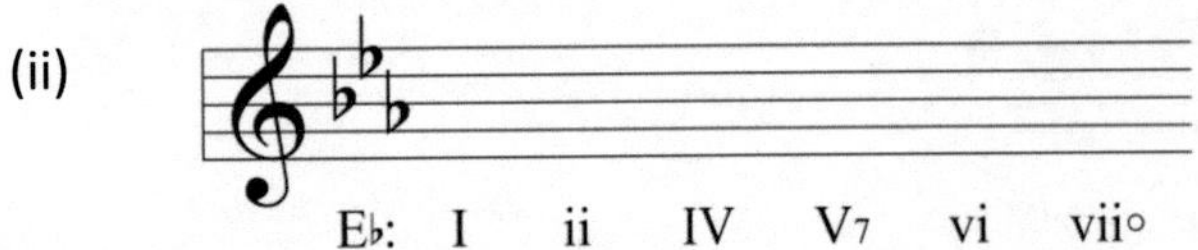

Numerals ____

____

APPENDIX 2

Sample Answers for Supplementary Exercises

SAMPLE ANSWERS

Ch. 5 – Supp. Ex. 1. Sample Answers

(i)

(ii)

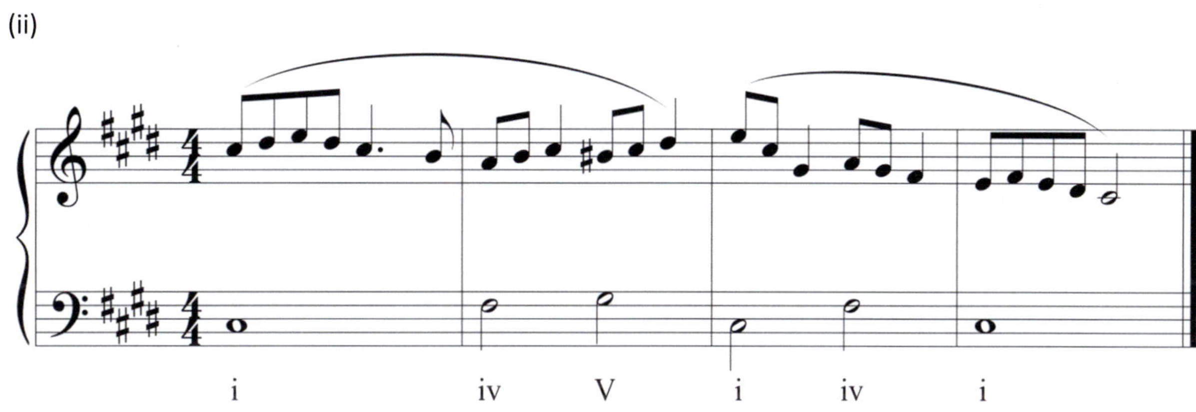

(iii)

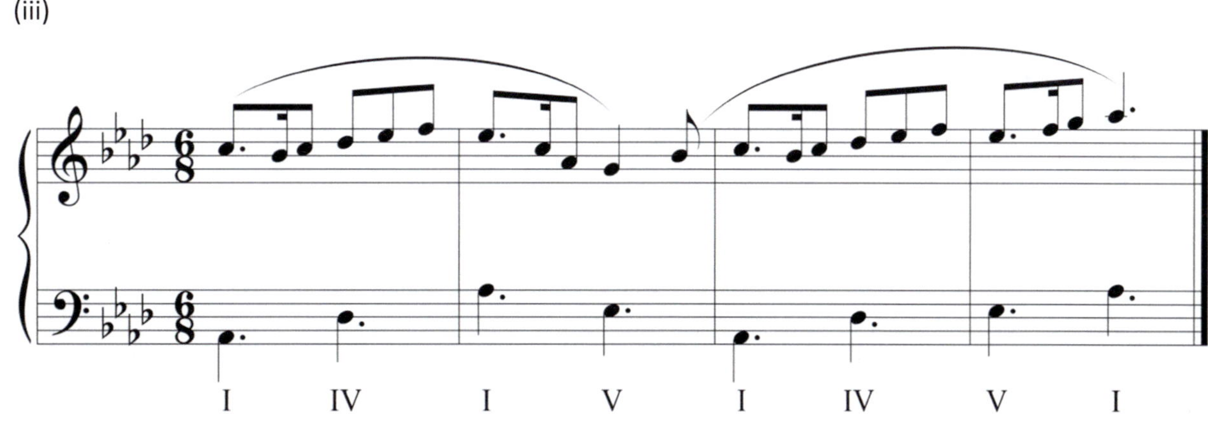

(iv)

(v)

(vi)

Ch. 7 – Supp. Ex. 1. Sample Answers

(i)

(ii)

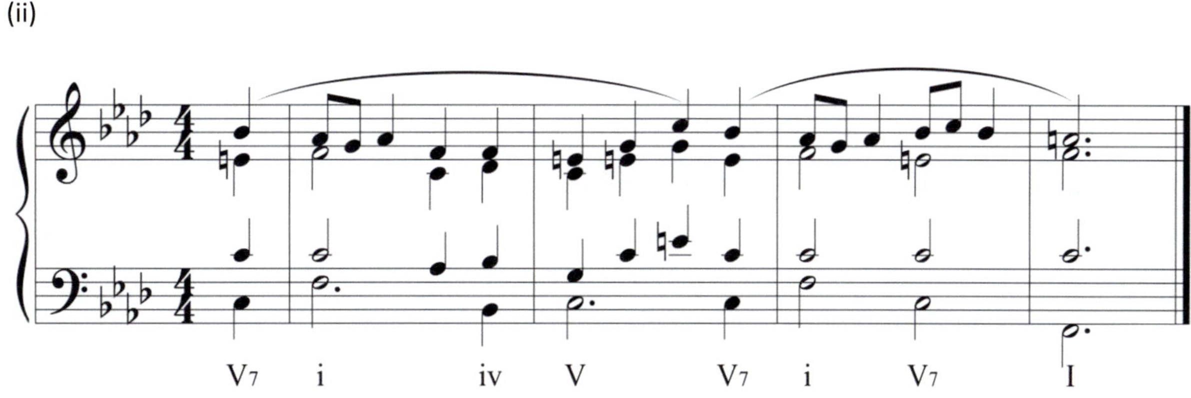

Ch. 7 – Supp. Ex. 2. Sample Answers

(i)

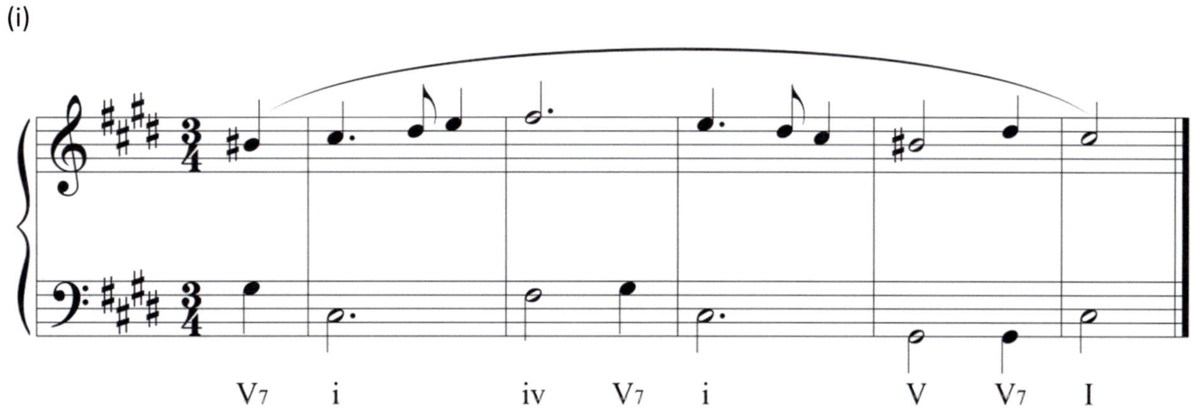

(ii)

Ch. 7 – Supp. Ex. 3. Sample Answers

(i)

(ii)

Ch. 8 – Supp. Ex. 1. Sample Answers

(i)

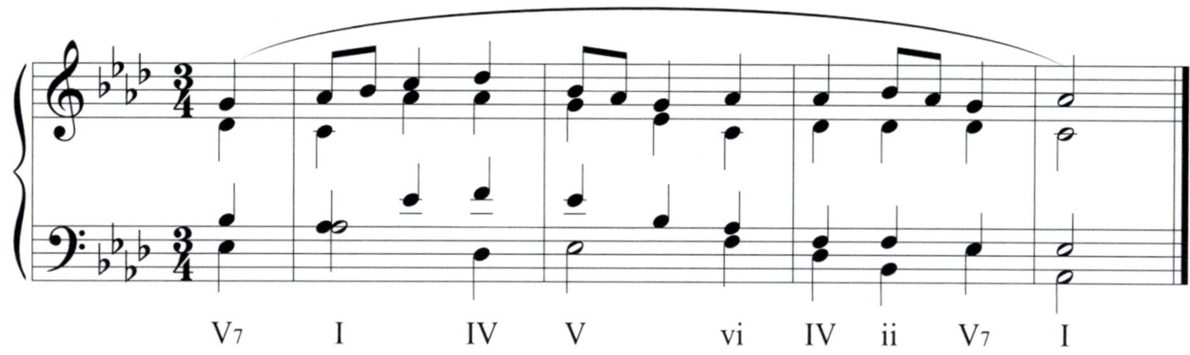

(ii)

Ch. 8 – Supp. Ex. 2. Sample Answers

(i)

(ii)

Ch. 8 – Supp. Ex. 3. Sample Answers

(i)

(ii)

Ch. 14 – Supp. Ex. 1. Sample Answers

(i)

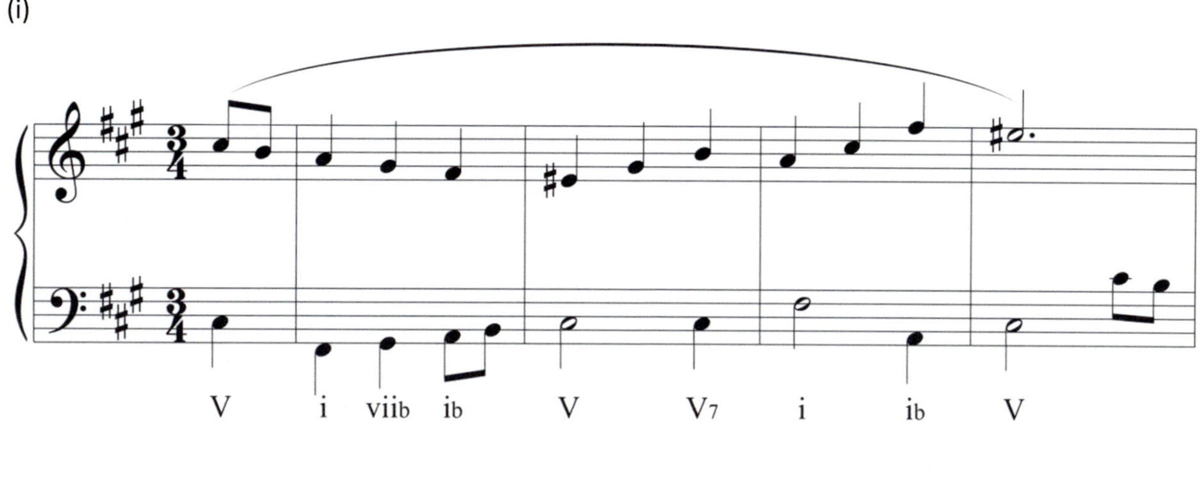

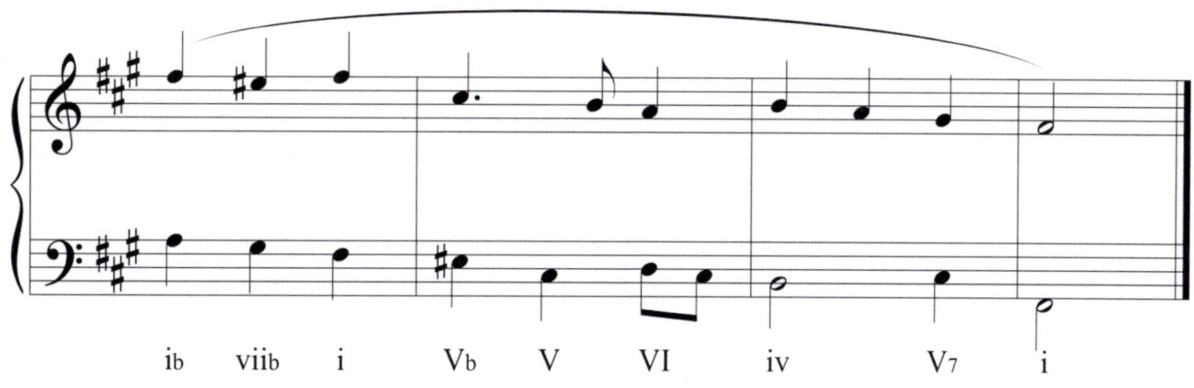

(ii)

Ch. 14 – Supp. Ex. 2. Sample Answers

(i)

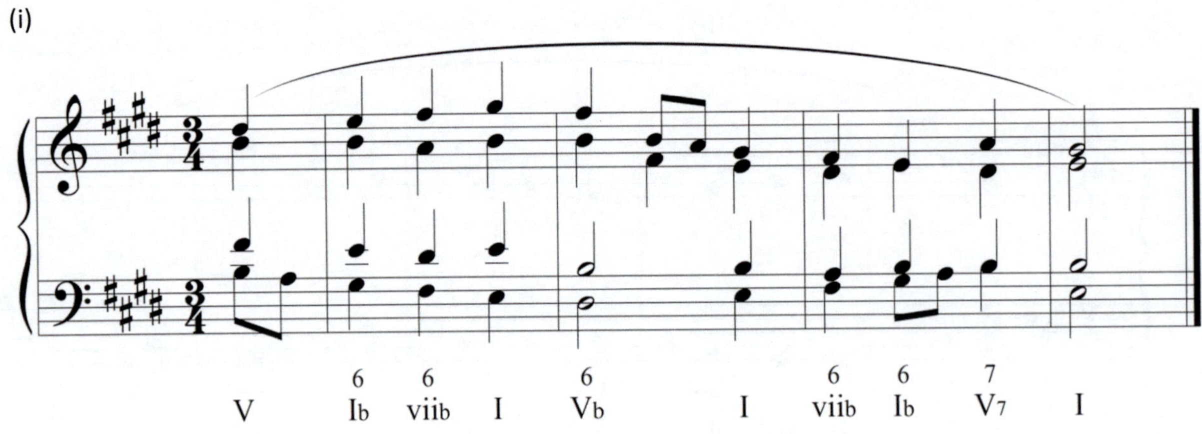

(ii)

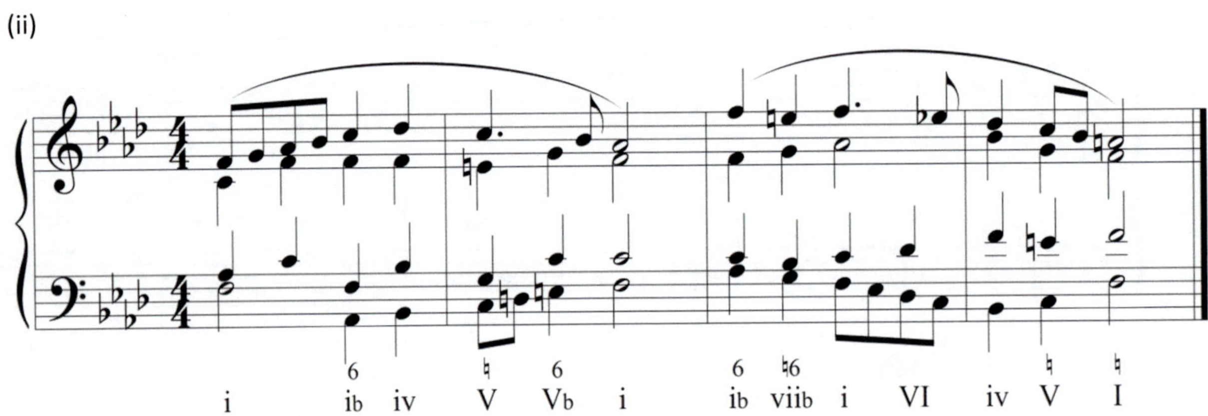

Ch. 14 – Supp. Ex. 3. Sample Answers

(i)

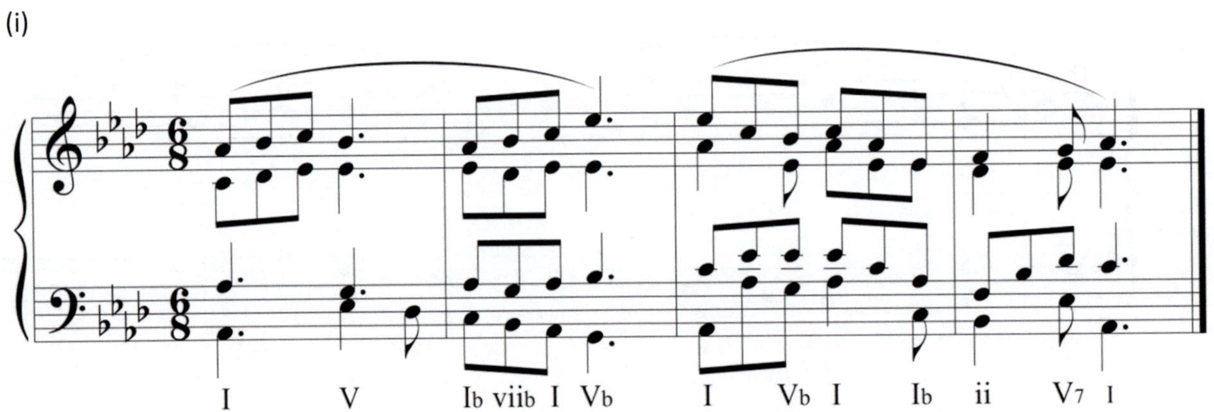

(ii)

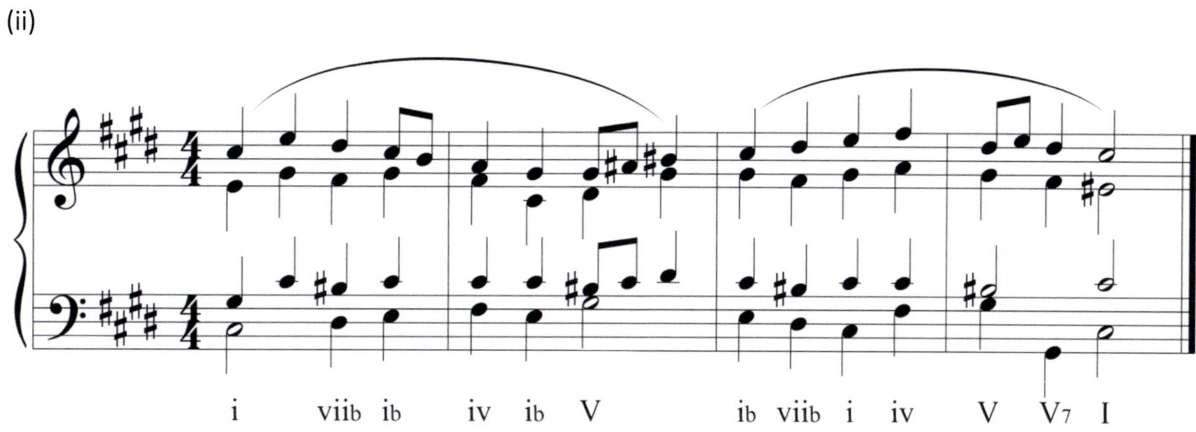

Ch. 16 – Supp. Ex. 1. Sample Answers

(i)

(ii)

Ch. 16 – Supp. Ex. 2. Sample Answers

(i)

(ii)

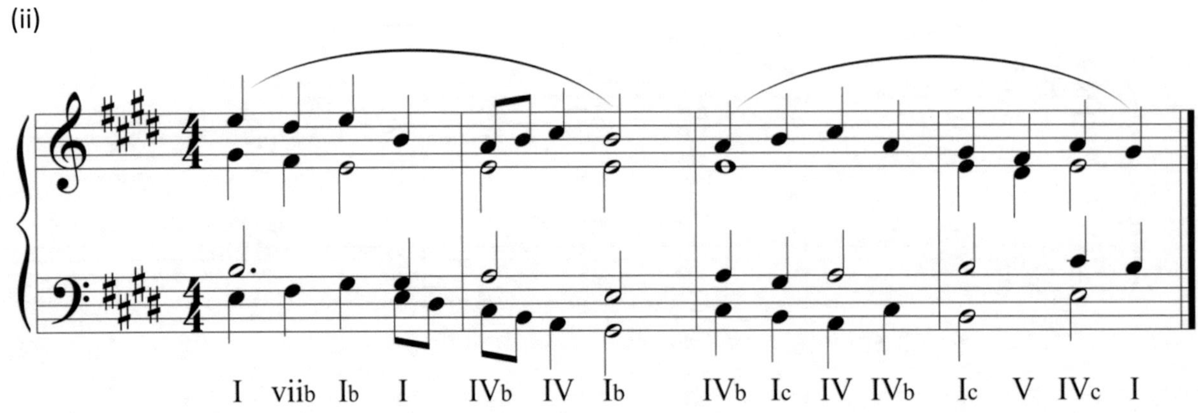

Ch. 16 – Supp. Ex. 3. Sample Answers

(i)

(ii)

Ch. 17 – Supp. Ex. 1. Sample Answers

(i)

(ii)

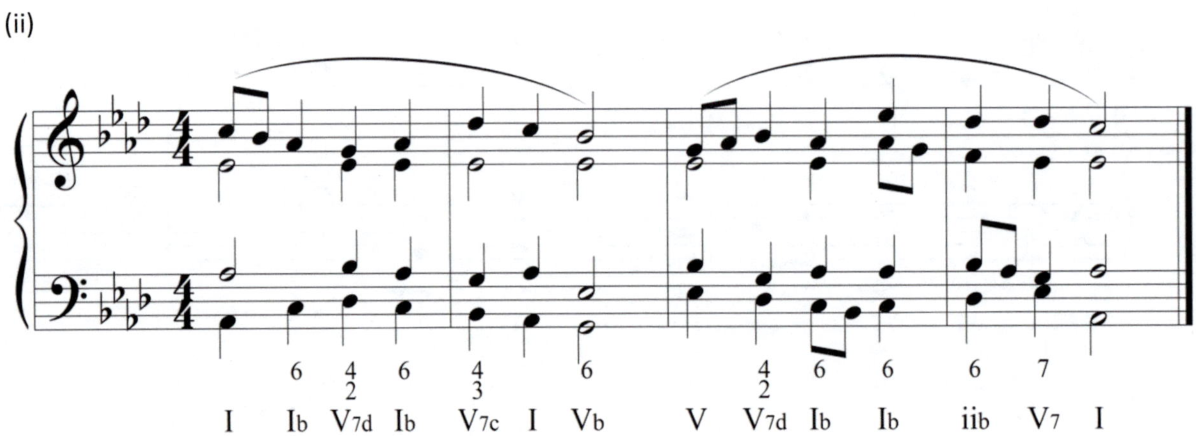

Ch. 17 – Supp. Ex. 2. Sample Answers

(i)

(ii)

Ch. 17 – Supp. Ex. 3. Sample Answers

(i)

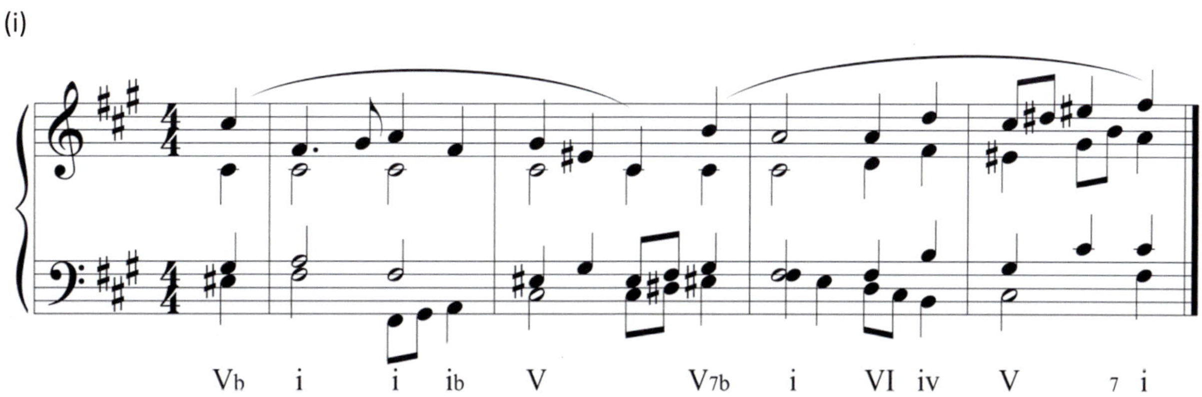

(ii)